Preface

This textbook presents a unique system for observing and recording the development of young children ages two- to six-years-old in an early childhood classroom setting. The text is designed to be used by college students preparing to be teachers in prekindergarten programs, nursery schools, day-care centers, Head Start classes, preschools of all kinds, and kindergarten classrooms. The book can also be used by teachers and assistant teachers in such programs who want to learn more about children in order to make individual curriculum plans to promote development. Staff members who are preparing a Child Development Associate (CDA) Professional Resource File will find this textbook helpful with its suggestions for activities that are developmentally appropriate for young children.

The text focuses on observation of the six major aspects of child development: emotional, social, motor, cognitive, language, and creative. Each of these aspects is further divided into two specific areas: self-identity and emotional development; social play and prosocial behavior; large and small motor development; cognitive development of classification and seriation skills, as well as cognitive development of number, time, space, and memory skills; spoken language and prewriting and prereading skills; art skills and imagination.

These areas of child development are outlined in a *Child Skills Checklist,* which includes specific, observable child behaviors in the sequence in which they occur. Each of 12 chapters discusses one of these areas, giving ideas for classroom activities for children who have not shown the specified behavior. The most recent child development research in each area is presented as background for the Checklist items as they are discussed. Each chapter concludes with a discussion of an actual child observation in the particular area, and an interpretation of the data gathered.

The text may serve college students as a guide for observing and recording the development of young children in their student teaching and course work. The book is especially well suited to be a supplementary text for child development courses. It also can be used by in-service teachers and assistants who are upgrading their skills

v

in observing children, as well as learning to plan for individuals based on developmental needs.

Unique aspects of *Observing Development of the Young Child* include the latest information on the development of human emotions from babyhood through kindergarten, a new look at moral development in young children (called "prosocial behavior"), a discussion of written language and reading as the natural development of "emergent literacy" rather than as something that has to be taught to children, and a section on the development of the imagination as an important aspect of creativity.

Perhaps the most useful features of this textbook are the activities for children that are described after each checklist item. One of these activities, "Read a Book," highlights the latest children's books on each of the topics discussed.

New Features in the Third Edition

The text begins with a new chapter, "Assessment of Development," that includes the latest information on determining young children's development. Guidelines for appropriate assessment of young children established by the National Association for the Education of Young Children are included, as well as a comparison of 10 preschool assessment tools. An expanded discussion of "Observation as Assessment" follows in Chapter 2.

Chapter 12 is a new chapter on prewriting and prereading skills that discusses the latest information on the natural emergence of literacy among preschool youngsters. Emergent writing from scribbles, to mock writing, to invented spelling becomes a part of the revised Child Skills Checklist, as does print awareness. Ideas to promote this recently recognized development include the use of predictable books.

Social play development in Chapter 5, "Social Play," highlights the child's development of skills to gain access to groups, to maintain roles in dramatic play, and to resolve play conflicts. Another current issue features the positive aspects of superhero play.

Use as a Companion Text

This third edition of *Observing Development of the Young Child* is designed to be used as a companion volume with the author's text *Skills for Preschool Teachers* (Merrill/Macmillan, 1992). While *Observing Development of the Young Child* is intended as a child development textbook, the companion volume *Skills for Preschool Teachers* is a teacher development book, focusing on 13 areas of teacher competencies.

Like this textbook, *Skills for Preschool Teachers* is also based on an observational checklist, the Teacher Skills Checklist, which documents teacher competencies in the 13 CDA Functional Areas of safe, healthy, learning environment, physical, cognitive, communication, creative, self, social, guidance, families, program management, and professional.

Together, the two textbooks form a cohesive, whole training program for pre-service teachers, beginning teachers, and in-service teachers preparing for the CDA cre-

Third Edition

Observing Development of the Young Child

Janice J. Beaty

Professor Emerita
Elmira College

Merrill,
an imprint of Prentice Hall

Englewood Cliffs, New Jersey   Columbus, Ohio

Library of Congress Cataloging-in-Publication Data
Beaty, Janice J.
    Observing development of the young child / by Janice J. Beaty. - 3rd ed.
    p.   cm.
    "Designed to be used as a companion volume with the author's text
Skills for preschool teachers (Merrill, 1992)" - Pref.
    Includes bibliographical references and index.
    ISBN 0-02-307741-7
    1. Child development. 2. Education, Preschool. 3. Preschool
teachers--Training of. I. Beaty, Janice J.   Skills for preschool
teachers. II. Title.
LB111.5.B32   1994
155.4--dc20   93-12933
                                                              CIP

Cover art/photo: Scott Spiker/West Stock, Inc.
Editor: Linda A. Sullivan
Production Editor: Julie Anderson Tober
Art Coordinator: Lorraine Woost, Vincent A. Smith
Text Designer: Jill E. Bonar
Cover Designer: Cathleen Norz
Production Buyer: Jeff Smith
Artist: Jane Lopez
Electronic Text Management: Ben Ko, Marilyn Wilson Phelps

This book was set in Souvenir by Macmillan Publishing Company
Photo credits: pp. 41, 210, Ben Chandler/Macmillan Publishing;
p. 82, Anne Vega/Macmillan Publishing; all other photo courtesy
of Janice J. Beaty.

© 1994 by Prentice-Hall, Inc.
A Simon & Schuster Company
Englewood Cliffs, New Jersey 07632

Printed in the United States of America
10 9 8 7 6 5 4 3

ISBN   0-02-307741-7

Prentice-Hall International (UK) Limited, London
Prentice-Hall of Australia Pty. Limited, Sydney
Prentice-Hall Canada Inc., Toronto
Prentice-Hall Hispanoamericana, S.A., Mexico
Prentice-Hall of India Private Limited, New Delhi
Prentice-Hall of Japan, Inc., Tokyo
Simon & Schuster Asia Pte. Ltd., Singapore
Editora Prentice-Hall do Brasil, Ltda., Rio de Janeiro

In memory of my mother and father

About the Author

Janice J. Beaty, Professor Emerita, Elmira College in Elmira, New York, is presently a fulltime writer of early childhood college textbooks and the president of her new early childhood caregiver training company, Bright Visions, Inc., near Pensacola, Florida. Dr. Beaty continues her long career of preparing teachers and caregivers to work with young children in this country and abroad. Her writing includes the children's books: *Nufu and the Turkeyfish*, *Plants in His Pack*, and *Seeker of Seaways*. College textbooks she has written include *Skills for Preschool Teachers*, *Observing Development of the Young Child*, *The Computer as a Paintbrush* (with W. Hugh Tucker), and *Preschool Appropriate Practices*. She is currently engaged in visiting early childhood classrooms in countries such as the former Soviet Union and Poland, and in serving as a delegate to an educational conference in Beijing, China.

dential. Both of these books focus on positive behaviors in children and teachers. The development of children and the training of teachers thus involve "areas of strength and confidence" and "areas needing strengthening" in order to set up individualized training plans.

Acknowledgments

Many thanks to Bonny Helm, Elmira College CDA Field Supervisor who read the original text; to Elmira College undergraduate students in my class "Observing and Recording Child Development" and graduate students in my class "The Young Child: Aspects of Development," for their suggestions and practical applications of the *Checklist*; to Joan Hibbard of Gingerbread House Day Care center and Bonny Helm of the Helm Nursery School for allowing me to photograph their children; to the Gannett Tripp Learning Center and its research librarians at Elmira College; and to the many people in the field who have used the text and offered their constructive criticism for this revised edition. Finally, I would like to thank the reviewers of this text: Cecelia Benelli, Western Illinois University; Toni Campbell, San Jose State University; Sandra DeCosta, West Virginia University; and Barbara Nilsen, Broome Community College (NY).

Janice Beaty

Brief Contents

Contents

8   Small Motor Development   188

9   Cognitive Development: Classification and Seriation   210

10 Cognitive Development: Number, Time, Space, Memory   **238**

11 **Spoken Language**   **268**

12 **Prewriting and Prereading Skills**   **290**

Checklists and Figures

Tables

1 Assessment of Development

T he assessment of preschool children is an issue of great importance and concern to early childhood educators. Programs for young children have always attempted to determine children's needs and to evaluate their accomplishments, sometimes successfully, sometimes not. But it is only recently that the assessing of young children has reached such proportions that *guidelines for assessment* have had to be issued by professional organizations. The National Association for the Education of Young Children (NAEYC) in conjunction with the National Association of Early Childhood Specialists in State Departments of Education published an important set of such guidelines in March 1991, "Guidelines for Appropriate Curriculum Content and Assessment in Programs Serving Children Ages 3 Through 8."

They define assessment as "the process of observing, recording and otherwise documenting the work children do and how they do it, as a basis for a variety of educational decisions that affect the child" (NAEYC, 1991, p. 32). Their purposes for assessing young children include the following:

1. to plan instruction for individuals and groups and for communicating with parents
2. to identify children who may be in need of specialized services or intervention
3. to evaluate how well the program is meeting its goals (NAEYC, 1991, p.32)

This textbook concurs with their definition, purposes, and guidelines, but takes them a step in a somewhat different direction. The focus in this text is on assessing *children's development* through observation. The purpose for such assessment is to plan individual curricular activities for children in order to promote children's further development and their success in the classroom. Observation of young children is one of the primary means for gathering data on the needs and accomplishments of individuals. Observation also can be used to determine the level of children's development.

The text then gives students of child development and teachers of young children ages 3 through 5 a tool for observing and recording this natural development: the *Child Skills Checklist* (see Chapter 2). This recording tool will help observers to determine where each child stands in areas of emotional, social, physical, cognitive, language, and creative development.

The purpose for assessing children's development in this manner is twofold: (a) for students of child development to gain an in-depth understanding of real children and their sequences of growth; and (b) for teachers of young children to become aware of each child's growth, in order to support individual development and to give special help where developmental lags are apparent.

TESTING AS A PRESCHOOL ASSESSMENT PROCEDURE

With the great proliferation of programs for young children springing up in the 1980s and 1990s has come a commensurate need to assess young children to answer questions such as

1. What are their needs?
2. What are their problems?

3. Do they have developmental lags?
4. What program is best for them?
5. How are they doing in the program?
6. In which development areas do they need help?
7. Are they ready to be placed in kindergarten?
8. Are they ready to begin formal reading instruction?
9. Are they gifted children or children with special needs?
10. Do they have potential learning problems?

To answer such questions many educators have turned to the traditional means for finding out: testing. A great many testing instruments and procedures have been developed and validated by researchers in the field. But when applied to young children the results are often mixed. What works with older children does not always seem to work with preschoolers and kindergartners. Test developers sometimes blame the validation procedures used to develop the new tests. Early childhood educators often nod wisely and think to themselves, It's the kids.

Young children have little interest in tests. Why should they? They don't need to prove to anyone what they know or what they can or cannot do. Oh, yes, they can be talked into cooperating with a tester. A teacher can administer a test to a child and occasionally get valid results on a particular day. Next week it may not be the same. Honest researchers have had to admit such things as "the major conclusion of this study is that it is inadvisable to routinely test young children prior to or immediately after their entry into kindergarten" (Wenner, 1988, p. 17). Wenner found that even highly respected and widely used tests predicted little more than a quarter of the actual academic performance of kindergarten children (Wenner, 1988, p. 17).

Nevertheless, assessment procedures routinely include tests of many kinds. Many are reliable and valid instruments. However, for their results to be used with confidence, teachers and testers alike need to be aware of "the young child factor": young children don't test well. Thus assessors need to include other more informal but reliable types of assessment, such as observation of children in the regular classroom, to round out the picture when they are evaluating young children.

Of the wide range of assessment instruments on the market today, Table 1.1 includes 10 commonly used tests that can be administered by teachers themselves (so long as they remember that test results need to be tempered with other assessment procedures). Eight of the tests included are popular developmental screening tools. A screening device is just that; it screens a child for *possible* developmental problems. If problems show up, then further testing by a professional in the area of concern is necessary. Only screening tests administered by the teachers are included here.

What teachers use tests such as these, you may wonder, and for what reasons? There are at least four particular groups of teachers who need to gather developmental data on children for these specific reasons:

1. public school teachers, to screen children for entrance into prekindergarten and kindergarten, and for track placement in kindergarten and first grade

2. special education teachers, to screen children for referral, placement, or special intervention

3. teachers of government-sponsored early intervention programs, as part of the evaluation component of their grants

4. college laboratory school teachers and graduate students, for child development research projects

Tests such as those in Table 1.1 can be helpful in determining that a certain child may need further assessment by a professional or special help of some kind. But, again, it must be stressed that tests alone are not the only answer—and may not even be the best answer. The classroom teacher who needs child assessment data in order to plan activities to support individual needs must first understand what is meant by appropriate assessment.

GUIDELINES FOR APPROPRIATE ASSESSMENT

Because of the flood on the market of assessment instruments for evaluating preschool children, it is essential that teachers involved become knowledgeable about what is *appropriate assessment* of young children and what is not. The guidelines developed by the National Association for the Education of Young Children (NAEYC) should be considered carefully by all early childhood educators, and followed rigorously whenever young children are to be assessed. These guidelines* can be summarized as follows:

1. Assessment is related to program curriculum, goals, and objectives.

2. Assessment results in benefit to the child such as adjustment of the curriculum or individualized instruction.

3. Children's development in all domains (physical, social, emotional, and cognitive) is routinely assessed by teachers through observing and listening to children.

4. Assessment is used to support children's learning and development, to plan for individuals and groups, and to communicate with parents.

5. Assessment involves regular and periodic observation of the child in a wide variety of circumstances that represent the child's behavior over time.

6. Assessment relies on procedures that reflect typical activities of children and avoids approaches that place children in artificial situations.

7. Assessment relies on demonstrated performance during real, not contrived, activities.

8. Assessment utilizes an array of tools and a variety of procedures (e.g., collections of representative work by children, records of systematic observations by teachers,

---

*Adapted from "Guidelines for Appropriate Curriculum Content and Assessment in Programs Serving Children Ages 3 Through 8," by NAEYC, March 1991, *Young Children, 46,* pp. 32–34. Copyright 1991 by NAEYC. Reprinted by permission.

TABLE 1.1
Preschool Assessment Instruments

Title	Publisher, Date	Type	Format
Basic School Skills Inventory—Diagnostic (BSSI—D)	Pro-Ed, 1983	Developmental screening	Observing by teacher; questions and response by child; pictures; cards
Brigance Preschool Screen for 3- and 4-Year-Old Children (Preschool Screen)	Curriculum Associates, Inc., 1985	Developmental screening	Observation form; rating scale; parent and teacher; pupil sheet; building blocks
Developmental Indicators for the Assessment of Learning (DIAL-R)	Childcraft Educational Corp., 1983	Developmental screening	Formal testing; rating scale; child score sheets
Developing Skills Checklist	CTB/McGraw-Hill, 1990	Developmental screening	Screening test; two observation checklists; manipulatives
Early School Assessment (ESA)	CTB/McGraw-Hill, 1990	Readiness/ achievement	Group administered; pictorial multiple choice test in six sessions
Early School Inventory—Developmental (ESI—D)	The Psychological Corp., 1986	Developmental screening/ readiness	80-item observation checklist of child; performance ratings
Early School Inventory— Preliteracy (ESI—P)	The Psychological Corp., 1986	Screening for literacy	Checklist; picture panels; cards; paper and pencil
Early Screening Inventory (ESI)	Teachers College Press, 1988	Developmental screening	Test sheets; paper and pencil; manipulatives
Miller Assessment for Preschools (MAP)	The Psychological Corp., 1988	Developmental screening	Observation forms; test sheets; drawing booklet; manipulatives
School/Home Observation and Referral System (SHORS)	CTB/McGraw-Hill, 1978	Developmental screening	Observational checklists for teacher and parents

NOTE: Based on information from Strand (1989)

Purpose	Teacher Observation	Child Paper and Pencil Tasks	Child Performance Tasks
Measure readiness for kindergarten	Yes	Yes	Yes
Identify and refer at-risk children; for testing, placement, and program planning	Yes	Yes	Yes
Identify potentially gifted and problem children	No	Yes	Yes
Plan individual instruction	Yes	Yes	Yes
Measure readiness for kindergarten and grade 1	No	Yes	Yes
Measure readiness for prekindergarten, kindergarten, and grade 1; teacher planning	Yes	No	No
Measure readiness for reading; teacher planning for individuals	No	Yes	Yes
Identify and refer children with potential learning problems or handicapping conditions	No	Yes	Yes
Identify and refer children at risk for learning problems	Yes	Yes	Yes
Identify and refer children at risk for learning problems	Yes	No	No

records of conversations and interviews with teachers, summaries of children's progress as individuals and in groups).

9. Assessment recognizes individual diversity of learners and allows for differences in styles and rates of learning, as well as their ability in English or their native language.

10. Assessment supports children's development and learning, and does not threaten children's psychological safety or feelings of self-esteem.

11. Assessment supports parents' relationship with their children and does not undermine parents' confidence in their children's or their own ability, or devalue the language and culture of the family.

It is important that teachers become knowledgeable about what is appropriate assessment of young children and what is not.

12. Assessment demonstrates children's overall strengths and progress: what children *can* do, not just their wrong answers or what they cannot do or do not know.

13. Assessment is an essential component of the teacher's role: the teacher is the *primary* assessor.

14. Assessment is a collaborative process involving children and teachers, teachers and parents, school and community; and information from assessment is shared with parents in language they can understand.

15. Assessment encourages children to participate in self-evaluation.

16. Assessment addresses what children can do independently and what they can demonstrate with assistance.

17. Information about each child's growth, development, and learning is systematically collected and recorded at regular intervals, and is used for planning instruction and for communicating with parents.

18. A regular process exists for information sharing between teachers and parents about children's growth and development and performance that provides meaningful descriptive information and not letter or numerical grades.

Important points made by these guidelines include the fact that the classroom teacher is the primary assessor of the children rather than an expert from outside the program. In addition, the assessment should be based on typical activities children engage in and not contrived activities in artificial situations. Assessment should not threaten children, nor should it focus on wrong answers or what children cannot do.

As the 10 assessment instruments in Table 1.1 illustrate, not all of them follow every guideline. They were, of course, developed before the guidelines came out. But several of these instruments include a comprehensive procedure in which the teacher observes children in addition to administering a performance-task-type test. There is a place in early childhood assessment for such screening devices that can identify children with special needs. The NAEYC addresses this type of assessment with a second set of guidelines.

Guidelines for Identifying Children with Special Needs

1. Results of screening tests are *not used alone* to make decisions about school- or special-program-entrance, but as part of a thorough process of diagnosis.

2. Any standardized screening or diagnostic test is valid and reliable in terms of child's background and test's purpose.

3. When a child is formally tested, procedures conform with all regulations contained in P.L. 94-142* (parents informed in advance; test results shared with parents; test scores interpreted in nontechnical language and how results will be used).

4. Screener approaches all interactions with children in positive manner; screener has knowledge of and prior experience with young children.

5. The younger the child, the more critical it is that screening activities involve manipulation of toys and materials rather than pictures and paper/pencil tasks.

---

*Individuals with Disabilities Education Act

6. If results indicate the child has not performed within an average developmental range, the child is seen individually by an experienced diagnostician who is also an expert in child development.

7. If a comprehensive diagnostic process is recommended after screening, this should be delineated and documented for parents in nontechnical language. (NAEYC, 1991, p. 33)

It is obvious that the purpose for the assessment should help to determine the kind of assessment instrument to be used. Planning for individuals in the classroom is quite different from screening children for handicapping conditions or developmental delays. Different procedures and different assessment tools are called for. This means that tests or checklists designed to screen for children with handicapping conditions are not usually appropriate for use as a general assessment of all young children.

PORTFOLIO ASSESSMENT OF PRESCHOOL CHILDREN

In recent years the use of a portfolio as an assessment device for students' accomplishments in kindergarten through grade 12 has grown in popularity. The portfolio is an individual systematic collection of documents that reflects what a student does in a classroom. It is assembled by both teachers and students, and emphasizes both process and product in the documents collected (Tierney, Carter, & Desai, 1991).

Can such a collection be used to assess young children at the prewriting, prereading stage of their development? Teachers of preschool children have long participated in such collections of youngsters' art work and writing scribbles. To make such collections a part of an ongoing assessment of child development, teachers need only take the next step: collect representative documents in a systematic manner (with dates for each one), and expand their collections on each child to include examples from each of the areas of child development. The *Child Skills Checklist* described in Chapter 2 can be a guideline for the kinds of information to be collected about a child's development:

Self-identity	Photos of child engaged in activities; self-accomplishments
Emotional development	Teacher's records of how child handles stress, anger, joy
Social play	Photos of child playing with others
Prosocial behavior	Teacher's records of how child shares, takes turns, helps
Large motor development	Teacher's records and photos of child's motor accomplishments
Small motor development	Teacher's records and photos of child's small motor skills

Cognitive development	Teacher's records, photos, tapes of child singing, counting
Spoken language	Tapes of child speaking
Prewriting & prereading	Writing scribbles; name printing; list of favorite books, recipes, computer games
Art skills	Dated series of easel painting, crayon art, finger painting; photos of clay or play dough creations
Imagination	Photos of child in dramatic play roles, block building; tapes of creative speaking

A completed *Child Skills Checklist* should also be included in such a portfolio in order to preserve this important observational record of evidence and dates of accomplishments for each child. Although portfolios can add valuable information in the assessment of young children, this textbook follows the NAEYC guidelines for appropriate assessment that stress the *observation* of children in natural settings by the children's own teachers. How that can be accomplished effectively is described in the chapters to follow.

REFERENCES

NAEYC. (1991, March). Guidelines for appropriate curriculum content and assessment in programs serving children ages 3 through 8, *Young Children, 46*(3), 21–38.

Strand, Terri. (1989). *Bibliography of tests for early childhood Chapter 1 evaluation.* Washington, DC: Department of Education. (EDRS No. ED 331 581)

Tierney, Robert J., Mark A. Carter, & Laura E. Desai. (1991). *Portfolio assessment in the reading-writing classroom.* Norwood, MA: Christopher-Gordon.

Wenner, George. (1988). *Predictive validity of three preschool developmental assessment instruments for the academic performance of kindergarten students.* State University of New York College at Buffalo. (EDRS No. ED 331 867)

OTHER SOURCES

Kranowitz, Carol Stock. (1992, March). Catching preschoolers before they fall: A developmental screening. *Early Childhood Information Exchange, 84*, 25–29.

Leavitt, Robin Lynn, & Brenda Krause Eheart. (1991, July). Assessment in early childhood programs. *Young Children, 46*(5), 4–9.

Seefeldt, Carolyn. (1990). Assessing young children. In Carolyn Seefeldt (Ed.), *Continuing Issues in Early Childhood Education* (pp. 311-330). New York: Merrill/Macmillan.

Taylor, Ronald L., Paula Willits, & Nancy Lieberman. (1990). Identification of preschool children with mild handicaps: The importance of cooperative effort. *Childhood Education, 67*, 26–31.

LEARNING ACTIVITIES

1. Read "Assessment in Early Childhood Programs" by Leavitt and Eheart in *Young Children*, July 1991, and do a comprehensive assessment of a child in your classroom as described, including daily routines, interest inventory, developmental summary, and typical day.

2. Acquire information from parents about one of the children as suggested in the article, "Assessment in Early Childhood Programs."

3. Look over the "Guidelines for Appropriate Assessment" and decide which of the 18 guidelines your program has been following and how you can improve your assessment process.

4. Look at the "Guidelines for Identifying Children with Special Needs" and decide which of the seven guidelines your program has been following and how you can improve your assessment of special needs children.

5. Obtain one of the preschool assessment instruments in Table 1.1 and learn to use it to assess a child.

2 Observation as Assessment

WHY ASSESS YOUNG CHILDREN'S DEVELOPMENT THROUGH OBSERVATION?

The number of instruments available today for assessing the development of preschool children is almost mind-boggling. Literally hundreds of testing instruments and procedures have come into use in the past 20 years as noted in Chapter 1. They include behavior rating scales, tests of visual perception, performance inventories, developmental profiles, portfolios, language batteries, self-concept screening devices, social competence scales, sociometric tests, personality inventories, pictorial intelligence tests, case studies, developmental screening tests, performance-based interviews, video and audio recording, and many others.

Some of these assessment tools and procedures use the observation of children, some don't. Some need to be administered by professional testers, others do not. Some assessment procedures place children in artificial rather than naturalistic situations. Others ask children to perform contrived activities. Although such tools and tasks may be helpful to researchers and professionals who are evaluating children for developmental problems, they are not appropriate for nonspecialist teachers in ordinary classrooms.

A great deal of assessment and evaluation of children today is focused on What's wrong with the child? and How can we intervene to help him or her? This textbook takes a different point of view. It looks for answers to the question: What's right with the young child? and How can we use his or her strengths to help in the development of the child? The best method we have found to determine these strengths is, as we have noted, to observe the young child in the regular classroom.

Early childhood specialist Carolyn Seefeldt agrees when she declares: "Observing is probably the oldest, most frequently used and most rewarding method of assessing children, their growth, development, and learning" (Seefeldt, 1990, p. 313). She and others have found that this is one of the best ways to look at an individual young child. It might not work so well with an older child, but it is eminently suited to a preschooler because

> Young children, who have a limited repertoire of behaviors that can be assessed, may best be studied through observation. In fact, to assess young children, who are unable to express themselves fully with words, with any method other than direct observation may not be possible. Further, young children reveal themselves through their behaviors. Unlike older children and adults, the young are incapable of hiding their feelings, ideas, or emotions with socially approved behaviors, so observing them often yields accurate information. (Seefeldt, 1990, p. 313)

That young children do not test well needs to be stated over and over, lest we forget. They do not understand the purpose for testing, nor are they particularly interested in an activity that has little meaning for them. Although they will often submit to answering questions or completing tasks for an adult who has established rapport with them, the answers they give and the tasks they complete may have little to do with their real knowledge, abilities, or feelings. Testers who have repeated the same

15

test with the same child *even in the same week*, have obtained such widely differing results as to make their assessment wholly invalid (Kellogg, 1970, p. 191). Thus it is that early childhood educators have turned to child observation in a *natural setting* as the most effective means for assessing the learning, development, and behavior of preschool and kindergarten children. The child behaves in a natural manner in the classroom as the observer watches and records. The most important aspects of child assessment then become:

1. what to look for
2. how to collect and record observational data
3. how to interpret recorded data
4. how to make application of interpretation

WHAT SHOULD CHILD OBSERVERS LOOK FOR?

What observers look for depends on the purpose of the assessment. Teachers who want to find out why a certain child is not getting along with others may spend time observing that child's interpersonal behaviors with peers. Speech correctionists may observe and listen for certain children's spoken language. Psychologists look at the behavior of troubled children to determine what their problems are. Researchers observe particular child behaviors in order to test hypotheses about child development or to formulate new theories.

This text looks at the *sequence* of a child's development. It uses an observation tool, the *Child Skills Checklist,* to help teachers and child caregivers determine where a child stands in various developmental sequences so that they may plan activities to further the child's growth. Many similar textbooks teach observational skills focusing on children's behavior. These techniques are particularly important for researchers and child psychologists. However, this text goes beyond that level to teach the nonspecialist to understand children through observing their developmental sequence in six major areas of child development: emotional, social, physical, cognitive, language, and creative.

All children go through a sequence of development that can be observed. From large to small motor coordination, from simple ideas to complex thinking, from one-word utterances to lengthy sentences, from scribbles to representational drawings—all children everywhere seem to proceed through a step-by-step sequence of development that can be traced by a knowledgeable observer who knows what to look for. This data is then recorded by the observer and later interpreted in order to make appropriate plans for individual children.

The *Child Skills Checklist,* the basis of this text, helps observers to focus on six major areas divided into 12 important topics of child development. Each chapter then expands on the developmental sequences of one of the 12 topics outlined in the *Checklist:*

Emotional

Chapter 3. Self-Identity

Chapter 4. Emotional Development

Social

Chapter 5. Social Play

Chapter 6. Prosocial Behavior

Physical

Chapter 7. Large Motor Development

Chapter 8. Small Motor Development

Cognitive

Chapter 9. Cognitive Development: Classification and Seriation

Chapter 10. Cognitive Development: Number, Time, Space, Memory

Language

Chapter 11. Spoken Language

Chapter 12. Prewriting and Prereading Skills

Creative

Chapter 13. Art Skills

Chapter 14. Imagination

Each chapter treats one of these 12 topics of development, and each topic focuses on eight observable items of child behavior based on recognized developmental sequences. Not every detail of development is included, but instead, eight representative items are examined. This makes the observations inclusive enough to be meaningful, but not so detailed as to be cumbersome. For items the observer does not check as apparent when observing a child, there is a section of ideas following the item that should be useful in planning for individual needs. These ideas are also listed in an index following Chapter 15, "Observing the Whole Child."

Observational assignments at the end of each chapter include not only use of the *Child Skills Checklist*, but also use of other assessment tools such as anecdotal records, running records, specimen records, time sampling, event sampling, and rating scales to record observations.

HOW CAN OBSERVATIONAL DATA BE COLLECTED AND RECORDED?

Systematic observation of children (i.e., observation using a particular system) is different from informal observation, which is really little more than watching. In systematic observation there is a specific purpose for gathering the information about the children, as well as a particular method for collecting and recording it. Systematic observation always implies recording. Not only must observers have a particular reason to look at a child and know what they should be looking for, but they also need a method for recording the information gathered. A number of useful methods have been developed over the years by observers of young children. The following will be included for discussion in this chapter: anecdotal records, running records, specimen records, time sampling, event sampling, and the use of observation tools such as rating scales and checklists.

Methods for Observing and Recording

Anecdotal Records

Anecdotal records are brief narrative accounts describing an incident of a child's behavior that is important to the observer. Anecdotes describe what happened in a factual, objective manner, telling how it happened, when and where it happened, and what was said and done. Sometimes they include reasons for the child's behavior, but *why* is better kept in the commentary part of the record. These accounts are most often written *after* the incident has occurred by someone who witnessed it informally, rather than *while* it was occurring by someone who was formally observing and recording.

Anecdotal records have long been made by teachers, physicians, psychologists, social workers, and even parents who recorded when their babies first walked and talked. Sometimes these are referred to as "baby biographies."

Although anecdotal records are brief, describing only one incident at a time, they are cumulative. A series of them over a period of time can be extremely useful in providing rich details about the person being observed. Other advantages for using anecdotal records include the following:

1. The observer needs no special training in order to record.
2. The observation is open-ended. The recorder writes anything and everything he or she witnesses, and is not restricted to one kind of behavior or one type of recording.
3. The observer can catch an unexpected incident no matter when it occurs, for it will be recorded later.
4. The observer can look for and record the significant behavior and can ignore the rest.

As in all observational methods, there are disadvantages too. Observers need to decide why they are observing, what they want to find out, and which method will be most useful. Some of the disadvantages of the anecdotal record method are as follows:

1. It does not give a complete picture because it records only incidents of interest to the observer.

2. It depends too much on the memory of the observer. Witnesses to events are notoriously poor at recalling details.

3. Incidents may be taken out of context and thus be interpreted incorrectly or used in a biased manner.

4. It is difficult to code or analyze narrative records like this; thus the method may not prove useful in a scientific study.

Such records can be more useful if recorded on a vertically divided page with the anecdote on the left side and a space for comments on the right, or the page can be divided horizontally with the anecdote at the top and commentary at the bottom. An example of the latter format is shown in Figure 2.1.

This anecdote tells what happened in an objective manner. Especially good are the direct quotes. The anecdote could have included more details about the child's

FIGURE 2.1
Anecdotal record of observation

Anecdotal Record

Child's Name ___Stevie___ **Age** ___4___ **Date** ___2/23___

Observer ___Anne___ **Place** ___S. Nursery___ **Time** ___9:00–10:00___

Incident

Stevie went over to the block corner and asked two boys, Ron and Tanner, if he could help them build. They told him it was okay. As they were building he accidentally knocked some blocks down. "I can put it back up," he said, and handed the blocks to Ron. For awhile he watched Ron build and then said, "I found a smokestack, Ron," and handed him a cylinder block. Ron told him where to put it, and Stevie then began getting cylinders off of the shelf and handing them to Ron and Tanner to place. Finally, he started placing his own cylinders around the perimeter of the building. The teacher asked him if he wanted to finger-paint but he replied, "I'm not gonna finger-paint unless Ron finger-paints."

Comment

Stevie is often involved in a lot of dramatic play with several other boys. He especially likes to be near or playing with Ron. He seems to look up to him. Whatever rules Ron sets in the play, Stevie follows. Once engaged in play, he likes to continue, and will usually not let another child, or even the teacher, distract him.

facial expression, tone of voice, and gestures. The reader does not get the feeling of whether Stevie was enjoying himself as a helper, trying to ingratiate himself with another child who was not paying much attention, or whether he was desperately trying to gain the attention of the other boy. Such details are sometimes missing from anecdotes because they have not been written down until the end of the day or even later, and by then are forgotten.

The comments contain several inferences and conclusions based on insufficient evidence. Obviously this observer has spent some time watching Stevie, indicated by her comments, "Stevie is often involved . . ." and "Once engaged in play, he likes to continue and will usually not. . . ." She would need an accumulation of such anecdotes in order to make valid statements of this nature based on evidence. If this were one page in an accumulation of anecdotes about Stevie, the comments would perhaps be more accurate.

The observer states that Stevie "likes to be near or playing with Ron," although there is not sufficient evidence here to make that definite an inference. Perhaps she should have said, "Whatever rules Ron sets in the play, Stevie follows," if Stevie actually placed a cylinder block where directed. However, this was only hinted at and not stated. Particular words are very important in objective recording. Her conclusion about Stevie not letting another child or even the teacher distract him is only partially accurate, because no evidence about another child is recorded.

If you were writing the comment about this particular anecdotal record, what things might you infer from the incident? Can you make any conclusions based on this information alone, or is it too limited? Are there things you might want to look for in the future when observing this boy that you should include in the commentary?

It is also helpful to indicate the purpose for the particular observation. Most observation forms do not provide a space for this, but the usefulness of the observation is enhanced if it is included. In this case the observer was looking for evidence of involvement in social play for this child.

Running Records

Another popular type of observing and recording method is the *running record*. It is a detailed narrative account of behavior recorded in a sequential manner as it happens. The observer writes down everything that occurs over a specified period of time, which may be as short as several minutes or may be intervals recorded from time to time during a full day. The running record is different from the anecdotal record because it includes all behavior and not just selected incidents, and it is written as the behavior occurs instead of later.

As with all factual recording the observer must be careful not to use descriptive words or phrases that are judgmental. For instance, if the observer records the child as "acting grumpy this morning," he needs to avoid this judgment and instead record the actual details that explain what happened such as: "Jonathan would not respond to the teacher's greeting at first, and when he did, he muttered 'good morning,' in a low voice with his head bent down."

The running record has a number of advantages for persons interested in child development:

1. It is a rich, complete, and comprehensive record not limited to particular incidents.
2. It is open-ended, allowing the observer to record everything he or she sees, and not restricting the observations to a particular kind of behavior.
3. It does not require that the observer have special observational skills and therefore is particularly useful to the classroom teacher.

There are also several disadvantages to using this method, once again depending on the purpose for gathering the information:

1. It is very time-consuming, which makes it difficult for the observer to find periods of uninterrupted time.
2. It is difficult to record everything for any length of time without missing important details.
3. It works best when observing an individual, but is very inefficient and difficult when observing a group.
4. Observers must keep themselves apart from the children, which is sometimes difficult if they are the teachers.

Running records are more useful if recorded on a form where the observer can make comments later as shown in Figure 2.2. It is difficult for the observer to record every word of all that is said and every facet of all that occurs when children are busily playing together. The observer in Figure 2.2 has caught the essence. The dialogue is especially well recorded. His inferences and conclusions are carefully kept on the commentary side of the record. Although we cannot make the same conclusion about Katy being more comfortable playing with only one child at a time based on this evidence, the observer had been gathering this evidence for several weeks and perhaps felt he could. Such an explanation should then be included on the record. It also would be helpful to record the time that the various incidents occurred in order to know how much time had elapsed on the gun play, the slide play, and the running back and forth.

Because the running record captures so much important developmental behavior of the preschool child, it has been chosen as the primary recording method to be used with the *Child Skills Checklist* in the assessment of an individual child's development as discussed in this textbook. Its use in combination with the *Checklist* is discussed at the end of the chapter.

Specimen Records

Specimen records, or *specimen descriptions* as they are sometimes called, are similar to running records but more detailed and precise. They are most often used by

FIGURE 2.2

Running record of observation

Running Record

Child's Name <u>Katy</u>   **Age** <u>4</u>   **Date** <u>2/9</u>

Observer <u>Rob</u>   **Place** <u>S. Nursery School</u>   **Time** <u>9:00–10:00</u>

Observation	Comments
Katy is playing by herself with plastic blocks, making guns; she walks into other room; "Lisa, would you play with me? I'm tired of playing by myself." They walk into other room to slide & climbing area.	Clips blocks together to make gun; then copies it to make one for Lisa. Cleverly done. Intricate. Shows creativity. (Does teacher allow guns?)

K: "I am Wonder Woman."
L: "So am I."
K: "No, there is only one Wonder Woman. You are Robin."
L: "Robin needs a Batman because Batman & Robin are friends."

All this takes place under slide & climber. Lisa shoots block gun which Katy has given to her. Katy falls on floor.

L: (to teacher) "We're playing Superfriends and Wonder Woman keeps falling down."
K: Opens eyes, gets up, and says: "Let's get out our Batmobile and go help the world." She runs to other room and back, making noises like a car.
L: "Wonder Woman is died. She fell out of the car." She falls down.
K: "It's only a game, wake up. Lisa, you be Wonder Woman, I'll be ___ ."
L: "Let's play house now."

Katy begins sliding down the slide.

K: "We have a lot of Superfriends to do." She says this while sliding. "Robin is coming after you!" she shouts to Lisa, running from the slide and into the other room. Lisa has gone into the housekeeping area and says to Katy: "Katy, here is your doll's dress." (Lost yesterday). John joins the girls.
L: "I'm Wonder Woman."
K: "I'm Robin."
J: "I'm Batman. Where is the Batmobile?"
K: "It's in here." They run into the other room and Katy points under the slide telling John what the Batmobile can do. Then all run to the other room and back again. Then Katy says: "John we are not playing Superfriends any more."

Comments (right column):

Seems to be the leader here as in other activities I have observed. Lisa is the friend she most often plays with.

Katy switches roles here. She shows good concentration and spends much time on one play episode.

She can distinguish reality from fantasy.

Shows good large motor coordination. Spends much time every day like this running and skipping around room. Seems to know she is good at this & spends a lot of time doing it.

Seems to be more comfortable playing with only one child at a time.

researchers who want a full and complete description of behavior, whereas the running record is used especially by teachers in a more informal way. The observer is definitely not a part of the classroom activities and must keep aloof from the children.

Like running records, specimen records are narrative descriptions of behaviors or events as they happen, but are usually based on predetermined criteria such as the time of day, the person, the setting, and so forth (Irwin & Bushnell, 1980, p. 103). The amount of detail to be recorded depends upon the purpose for the observation. Enough detail should be recorded to give the reader of the observation a sense of how things actually happened. The test of a good specimen record is whether it can be dramatized. Does the description tell how the children moved, what their facial expressions and gestures were, and not only what they said but also how they said it? It is better to record too much detail than not enough. Here is an extract from one:

> Mark's friend Rob was playing in the play grocery store taking empty food boxes off the shelves, so Mark watches him for a moment and begins to take the boxes off the shelves and places them in a toy shopping cart. Two girls proceed over to where Mark is and they knock his boxes over (which were teetering because there were so many in the cart). Mark then opens his eyes wide, grits his teeth, and places his hands on his hips, saying, "You guys, why do you knock it down like that?" Meanwhile the girls appear little affected by his question and walk off. Meanwhile his friend Rob is still taking the boxes off the shelves and Rob says to Mark, "We are stealing stuff." So Mark joins the act, hiding the boxes in the rear by the playhouse. It appears that no one pays any attention to their act of "stealing" so Mark loses interest.

Can you dramatize this specimen record? That is the test of a good recording. This particular recording does not tell us exactly how the girls took action, or what Mark does to show his loss of interest, but otherwise it is rich in detail.

Specimen records are later coded by researchers to elicit findings regarding kinds of behavior, lengths of incidents, interaction patterns, or other information relevant to the purpose of the observation. Advantages and disadvantages of this particular method are the same as for the running record.

Objective Recording of Narrative Data

Objective recording of the narrative data gained from observing young children—a process required with anecdotal, running, and specimen records—is not a simple task. We are used to observing what happens around us and making simultaneous interpretations about it. In objective recording we must separate these two roles, and guard against confusing observations and interpretations. What we record must be the objective facts only, no judgments, inferences, or conclusions. Perhaps if we think of ourselves as witnesses at a trial, we can more easily discern what information is acceptable and what is not.

If we see a child come into the room in the morning, refuse to greet the teacher, walk over to a table and sit down, push away another child who tries to join him, and shake his head in refusal when the teacher suggests an activity, how can we record it? An anecdotal record might read like this:

> Jonathan walked into the room this morning as if he were mad at the world. He would not look up at the teacher or respond to her greeting. He sort of slumped as he walked across the room and plunked himself down in a chair at one of the activity tables. Richie tried to join him but was pushed away. The teacher went over and asked him if he wanted to help mix play dough, but he shook his head no.

This record is rich enough in detail for us to visualize it, but is it factually objective? No. The words "as if he were mad at the world" are a conclusion based on insufficient evidence. The recorder might have described his entrance better—and objectively—like this:

> Jonathan walked into the room this morning with a frowning kind of look on his face. He lowered his head when the teacher greeted him, and did not respond.

This behavior was unusual for Jonathan. Later the teacher found out that he was not "mad at the world," but sad because his pet cat had been killed by a car the night before. We realize then that frowning looks, lowered head, and refusal to speak or participate may be the result of emotions other than anger. It is up to us to sift out our inferences and judgments, then, and make sure we record only the facts.

The following are judgmental phrases and sentences sometimes found in observation records. Should they ever be used? If not, what could you substitute for them?

He was a good boy today.

Marcie was mad at Patty.

shouted angrily

showed his strength

lost her temper

got upset

would never talk like that

Other observer errors include (a) omitting some of the facts, (b) recording things that did not happen, and (c) recording things out of order. Here is the "Jonathan incident" again with some of these errors included. Can you find them?

> Jonathan walks in the classroom this morning. He doesn't look at the teacher but goes straight to a seat at one of the tables. The teacher wants him to help mix play dough but he refuses. Richie comes over to play with him but he pushes him away.

Omitted facts from this observation are the following:

1. has frowning look on face
2. does not respond to teacher's greeting
3. walks across room with shoulders slumped
4. drops himself down into seat at activity table
5. when teacher asks him to help mix play dough, he shakes his head no

A fact that was added to the observation is that Richie comes over "to play with him." A fact recorded out of order is that Richie tries to join him before the teacher asks Jonathan to help mix play dough.

Such errors can creep into an observation almost without the recorder being aware. You need to practice with at least two observers recording the same incident, and then compare results. If you find discrepancies between the records, check carefully that you have adhered to the following *guidelines for objective recording*:

1. Record only the facts.
2. Record *every* detail without omitting anything.
3. Do not interpret as you observe.
4. Do not record anything you do not see.
5. Use words that describe but do not judge or interpret.
6. Record the facts in the order that they occur.

Behavior Tallying Methods for Recording Information

Time Sampling

In the *time sampling*, the observer records the frequency of a behavior's occurrence over time. The behavior must be overt and frequent (at least once every 15 minutes) to be a candidate for sampling (Irwin & Bushnell, 1980, p. 149). For example, talking, hitting, and crying are such behaviors, because they can be clearly seen and counted. Problem solving is not a good candidate for time sampling because this behavior is not always clear to the observer, nor can it be counted easily.

Time sampling thus involves observing specified behavior of an individual or group, and the recording of the presence or absence of this behavior during short time intervals of uniform length. The observer must prepare ahead of time, determining what specific behavior to look for, what the time interval will be, and how to record the presence or absence of the behavior.

For example, in order to help an aggressive child named Jamie change his ways, the teacher wants to know how frequently Jamie's negative behavior occurs. First, Jamie's aggressive behavior must be specifically defined. It includes:

hitting

pushing

kicking

holding another against his or her will

taking another child's toy

These particular behaviors are usually determined by previous formal or informal observations made to discover exactly what the observer needs to look for in her sampling. Jamie, for instance, did not use words aggressively. Another child might have expressed aggression quite differently, and the observer would sample that.

Next the decision is made about what time intervals to use. It may be decided to sample the child's behavior for 5-minute intervals during the first half hour of each morning for a week. The teacher already knows that this seems to be the most difficult time for Jamie.

The teacher then must decide what and how to record on the sheet she has blocked off into time intervals. Often a time sampling observer simply records "1" after the interval if the behavior occurs, and "0" if it does not. This is called *duration recording* and is concerned with the presence or absence of the behavior (Bell & Low, 1977, p. 65).

Check marks or tally marks can also be used if the teacher wants to know how many times the behavior occurred, rather than its presence or absence. This is called *event recording* and is concerned with the frequency of the behavioral event.

Furthermore, the teacher may be more concerned with specific categories of aggression rather than just aggression in general. In that case each of the categories can be given a code:

h = hitting

p = pushing

k = kicking

hd = holding

t = taking

The teacher will be doing event recording of specific categories rather than frequency of occurrence. The observation form can be set up like any of the following examples or in the teacher's own manner, depending on the information desired. The observation for Jamie's first half hour of one morning could look like any one of those in Figure 2.3.

From this observation the teacher might conclude that Jamie's aggressive actions on this morning occurred mainly during the first 15 minutes and involved mostly hitting and pushing of the other children. If this turned out to be the pattern for the rest of the week, the teacher might want to plan an interesting transition activity for Jamie to do by himself as soon as he arrived. Once he had made the transition from

FIGURE 2.3

Event recording of specific categories

	Time Intervals (5 minutes each)					
	1	2	3	4	5	6
Duration Recording (presence or absence)	1	1	1	0	0	0
Event Recording (frequency)	𝍤𝍤	|||			0	0	0
Event Recording (presence or absence)	h,p	h,p,t	h	0	0	0

home to school by getting involved in an activity, he might then be able to interact with the other children nonaggressively. Future observations would help the teacher to determine whether the intervention strategy had been successful.

Time sampling is thus a useful method for observing children for some of the following reasons:

1. It takes less time and effort than narrative recording.
2. It is more objective and controlled because the behavior is specified and limited.
3. It allows an observer to collect data on a number of children or a number of behaviors at once.
4. It provides useful information on intervals and frequencies of behavior.
5. It provides quantitative results useful for statistical analysis.

There are, of course, certain disadvantages as well:

1. It is not an open method and therefore may miss much important behavior.
2. It does not describe the behavior, its causes, or results because it is more concerned with time (when or how frequently the behavior occurs).
3. It does not keep units of behavior intact because its principal concern is the time interval, not the behavior.
4. It takes the behavior out of its context and therefore may be biased.
5. It is limited to observable behaviors that occur frequently.
6. It usually focuses on one type of behavior (in this case a negative behavior), and thus may give a biased view of a child.

Event Sampling

Event sampling is another method in which the observer waits for and then records a specific preselected behavior. Event sampling is used to study the conditions under which particular behaviors occur or their frequency of occurrence. It may be important to learn what triggers a particular kind of behavior—biting, for instance—in order to find ways to control it. Or, the observer may want to find out how many times a certain behavior occurs. Time sampling would be used if time intervals or time of day were the important factor. But if the behavior occurs at odd times or infrequently, then event sampling is more appropriate.

The observer must first define the event or "unit of behavior." Then the setting in which it is likely to occur must be determined. The observer takes the most advantageous position to observe the behavior, waits for it to occur, and records it.

Recording can be done in several ways, depending upon the purpose for the observation. If the observer is studying causes or results for certain behaviors, then the "ABC analysis" is especially useful (Bell & Low, 1977, p. 73). It is a narrative description of the entire event, breaking it down into three parts: A = antecedent event, B = behavior, C = consequent event. Each time the event occurs it is recorded, for example, as in the event sampling for Darrell in Figure 2.4.

If subsequent observations of Darrell show the same sort of sequence as in the event sampling presented, the teacher could interpret this to mean that Darrell does not initiate the kicking, but rather responds to interference with his activities in this inappropriate and harmful manner. Intervention strategies may therefore need to be different with this boy. The teacher may need to help him learn an acceptable way to vent his frustration other than kicking. In addition he may need help in getting along with other children and in feeling accepted in the classroom. Until these issues are resolved, he may have to keep his shoes off in the classroom to prevent injury. This in itself may reduce his kicking, since his own uncovered toes will soon teach him how it hurts to kick.

If *frequency* of occurrence is the main concern, the observer can record with tally marks rather than with narrative description. However, this procedure tends to be more useful for research than for practical classroom applications.

The advantages for using event sampling are:

1. It keeps the event or behavior intact, making analysis easier.
2. It is more objective than some methods because the behavior has been defined ahead of time.
3. It is especially helpful in examining infrequent or rarely occurring behaviors.

There are several disadvantages as well, depending on the purpose for the observation:

1. It takes the event out of context and thus may lose other happenings that are important to the interpretation.

FIGURE 2.4
Event sampling of observation

Event Sampling

Name _____ Darrell _____   **Age** _____ 3 1/2 _____

Center _____ Head Start _____   **Date** _____ 10/5 _____

Observer _____ Sue S. _____   **Time** _____ 9–12:00 _____

Behavior: Kicking: striking out at other children or teacher with right foot, hard enough to make children cry.

Time	Antecedent Event	Behavior	Consequent Event
9:13	Darrell playing alone in block corner; Rob comes in & puts block on Darrell's building	Darrell looks at Rob with frown; stands; pushes at Rob; Rob pushes back; Darrell kicks Rob on leg	Rob cries & runs to teacher
10:05	On playground; Darrell waiting turn in line with others to go on slide; Sally tries to cut in	Darrell kicks Sally hard on leg Darrell kicks teacher	Sally cries; teacher comes & takes Darrell away by arm to talk to him

2. It is a closed method that looks only for specified behavior and ignores other important behavior.

3. It misses the richness of the many details that anecdotes, specimen records, or running records provide.

Tools for Observation

Rating Scales

Rating scales are tools that indicate the degree to which a person possesses a certain trait or behavior. Each behavior is rated on a continuum that goes from the lowest to the highest level (or vice versa) and is marked off at certain points along a scale. The observer must make a judgment about where on the scale the child's behavior lies. As an observation tool, rating scales work best where particular degrees of behavior are well defined or well understood by the observer, and there is a distinct difference between the behavior at the various points on the scale.

These tools are useful in diagnosing a child on a wide range of behaviors all at the same time. The observer watches the child and checks off or circles the point on the scale to indicate the child's current position in regard to behaviors or abilities. Such scales are simple to make: simply state the behavior, draw a line, then mark off a number of points or intervals along the line. Five intervals are often used so that there is a middle (neutral position) and two intervals on either side of it.

Graphic Scales

Figure 2.5 is an example of a rating scale for only one behavior, although many similar behaviors could be listed on this same scale. Such scales are called *graphic scales* and can be drawn either horizontally, as shown here, or vertically. Many traits can be listed on the same sheet. Graphic scales may be easier to construct than to use, however. The observer must know children well, be able to interpret their behavior, and be able to make an objective judgment within a limited period of time.

Numerical Scales

Other rating scales may be *numerical* in form, that is, they are scored by the number of the behavior that is circled. As an example, two items, "attention span" and "curiosity," are shown in the sample scale in Figure 2.6, but altogether there are a total of 12 items on this scale.

Raters observe children for as long as it takes to circle a number for each item, or they can observe on a daily basis and then average their scores. The numbers on the scale in Figure 2.6 are also represented by words:

1 = Definitely needs help
2 = Could use help
3 = Adequate
4 = Strength

Semantic Differential

A third type of rating scale sometimes used with children is the *semantic differential,* sometimes called the Osgood scale because it was developed by Charles Osgood (Irwin & Bushnell, 1980, p. 209). It uses a 7-point scale with adjectives of opposite meanings (bipolar) at either end. Figure 2.7 presents two traits as an example. Obviously a number of traits should be included to develop a comprehensive profile of a child.

FIGURE 2.5
Graphic scale for a single behavior

Graphic Scale

Shares toys: _____

      Always   Often   Sometimes   Seldom   Never

FIGURE 2.6
Numerical scale for observation

Numerical Scale

Attention Span

1. Rarely finishes task, moves rapidly from one to another.
2. Usually needs encouragement to stay with task until complete.
3. Can usually remain with task appropriate to age level until it is finished.
4. Can stay with a chosen activity for very long periods, even returning next day.

Curiosity

1. Shows little or no interest in anything new.
2. Can be intrigued by really exciting things but often uninterested.
3. Actively explores any new things in the room.
4. Interested in new ideas, words, and relationships as well as things.

NOTE: From Hodgden, 1974, p. 119

Forced Choice

A fourth type of rating scale, shown in Figure 2.8, is the *forced choice* scale where observers must choose one out of the several ranges of behavior listed for each trait (Hodgden, 1974, p. 67).

Rating Scale Observer Errors

A different kind of observer error can affect the use of rating scales. Contrary to other types of observation, the use of this tool calls for observers to make an on-the-spot judgment. It is extremely difficult for such observers to be totally unbiased and objective. They may be influenced by other things they already know about a child or the child's family, or by outside influences completely unrelated to the situation they are observing. For example, one observer persistently gave lower ratings to an overweight child. When asked about it later, the observer admitted a prejudice against overweight children because he had been one himself.

FIGURE 2.7
Semantic differential scale for observation

Semantic Differential Scale

Happy └──────┴──────┴──────┴──────┴──────┴──────┘ Sad

Friendly └──────┴──────┴──────┴──────┴──────┴──────┘ Hostile

FIGURE 2.8
Forced choice scale for observation

Forced Choice Scale

Ball Catching:

Fearful	Usually misses	Often misses	No accommodation	Uses body	Hands only
_____	_____	_____	_____	_____	_____

NOTE: From Hodgden, 1974, p. 67

    To guard against these tendencies, observers should rate all of the different children they are observing on the same trait before going on to another trait. To check objectivity, a second rater can observe the same child and compare results with the first.

    Rating scales may be used on their own, implemented with other observation methods as a part of the procedure, or filled in later after the observation is completed from data gathered through specimen records or running records. As with the other methods, there are several advantages to using rating scales:

1. They are easy to design and less time-consuming to use.
2. They provide a convenient method to observe a large number of traits at one time, or more than one child at a time.
3. They make it possible to measure difficult-to-quantify traits such as shyness for example.
4. They can be used by nonspecialist observers.
5. They are easier to score and quantify than most other methods.

    The disadvantages also need to be considered before the observer decides to use a rating scale:

1. Rating scales utilize a closed method. They examine specified traits and may overlook other important behavior.
2. They feature the negative as well as the positive side of each trait.
3. Clearly differentiating between each point on the scale is sometimes difficult, both for the designer and the observer.
4. It is difficult to eliminate observer bias when judgments must be made quickly on so many different traits.

Checklists

Checklists are lists of specific traits or behaviors arranged in a logical order. Observers must indicate the presence or absence of the behaviors either as they observe or later when they reflect upon their observation. Checklists are especially useful for types of behaviors or traits that can easily and clearly be specified. We tend to see what we look for; thus a checklist can prove to be a valuable tool for focusing our attention when many different items need to be observed. A survey or inventory of a situation can be done more efficiently, for instance, with a checklist than with almost any other observation tool. If an observer needs to know whether a child displays the specified behavior or not, a checklist is the instrument of choice to use.

Both checklists and rating scales often include large numbers of traits or behaviors. The difference in the two is not necessarily in their appearance but in their use. An observer using a checklist merely checks off the presence of the trait (a blank denotes absence). The observer using a rating scale must make a judgment about the degree to which the trait is present.

Checklists can be used in a number of ways, depending on the purpose for the observation. A different checklist, for instance, can be used for each child in the class if the results are to be used for individual planning. On the other hand, all of the children's names can be included on the same checklist along with the checklist items if it is the observer's purpose to make a general survey of the class.

The items on a checklist can simply be checked off, or the date or time when they first appear can be entered to make a more complete record. A different checklist can be used for each observation, or a single checklist can serve in a cumulative manner for the same child all year if dates are recorded for each item. A single checklist can be used by one observer or by several observers who will add to the cumulative data over a period of time.

Finally, information gained from anecdotal, specimen, and running records can be transferred to checklists for ease in their interpretation. It is much simpler to scan a list of checked behaviors than to read through long paragraphs of wordy description when attempting to interpret observational evidence. Obviously checklists need to be prepared carefully. The items listed should be specified very clearly in objective, nonjudgmental terms. The items should be easily understood by the users; thus, it makes sense to put items through a pretest before actual use in an observation tool. All checklist items should be positive in nature, unlike rating scale items in which a range of behavior from positive to negative exists.

Checklist items that an observer does not witness are left blank, indicating absence of the particular behavior. If the observer does not have the opportunity to observe certain behaviors, these items should not be left blank, but indicated by some symbol (e.g., N, meaning no opportunity to observe). Some suggestions for developing checklist items include the following:

1. Items should be short, descriptive, and understandable.

2. They should be parallel in construction (i.e., word order and verb tense the same for each).

3. They should be objective and nonjudgmental (e.g., not "jumps high" but "jumps over a 1-foot object").

4. They should be positive in nature.

5. They should not be repeated elsewhere in the checklist.

6. They should be representative of children's behavior, but not include *every* behavior.

Overall, the format of the checklist should allow the observer to scan the items at a glance. The *Child Skills Checklist* that follows is an example of an observation tool that looks at 12 important areas of child development, breaking down each area into 8 observable items. Each item is brief, represents an important aspect of development, is parallel in construction (beginning with a verb), and is positive in nature. The eight items are listed in a sequence of known child development. Together they form the profile of a whole child as he or she works and plays in the environment of an early childhood classroom.

Advantages for using checklists of this nature include:

1. They are easy, quick, and efficient to use.

2. They can be used with ease by a nonspecialist observer.

3. They can be used in the presence of the child or later from remembered behaviors.

4. Several observers can gather the same information to check for reliability.

5. They help to focus observation on many behaviors at one time.

6. They are especially useful for curriculum planning for individuals.

There are also disadvantages for using checklists. The observer must weigh advantages and disadvantages against each other, always keeping in mind the particular purpose for observing. Checklist disadvantages include the following:

1. They are closed in nature, looking at particular behaviors and not everything that occurs; thus they may miss behaviors of importance.

2. They are limited to presence or absence of behavior.

3. They lack information about quality of behavior (how), duration (how long), and a description.

Choosing the Method for Observing and Recording

Table 2.1 compares the seven methods for observing and recording young children discussed in this chapter. Each has advantages and disadvantages that an observer needs to consider before choosing a particular method. The final choice is often based on the purpose for the observation.

A checklist was chosen as the basis for this book because of the unique ability of a checklist to give an observer a good overview of child development. It is a teaching tool as well as an observational tool. The *Child Skills Checklist* at the end of this chapter will thus assist the observer not only in gathering information on specific children, but also in learning the sequences of child growth in the areas of emotional, social, physical, cognitive, language, and creative development.

Using the *Child Skills Checklist*

The *Child Skills Checklist,* around which this book is written, is as much a learning device for the observer as it is a planning tool for helping the child. With sequences of child development as its focus, it presents the areas of emotional, social, physical, cognitive, language, and creative development by dividing each of these areas into two major categories, and then subdividing each category into eight representative items of development.

Emotional development, for example, is divided into "self-identity" and "emotional development," with a chapter devoted to each of these topics. The observer learns from the chapters some representative behaviors in the sequence of emotional development that can be seen in the early childhood classroom.

Using One *Checklist* Section at a Time

As a learning device for the observer, the *Checklist* is best used one section at a time. To understand the sequence of emotional development as it appears in the early childhood classroom, for instance, the observer should first plan to use the "Self-Identity" section of the *Checklist* in observing a child *for enough time to see if all eight items are present.* This means coming into the classroom early enough to see how the child enters the room, what she does when her parent leaves, and how she becomes involved in the classroom activities. It also means coming early to the classroom *more than once* in order to observe how the child behaves on different days, and to record this information. The observer should not only check off the items as they appear, but also record evidence for each item.

The observer should then read Chapter 3, "Self-Identity," paying special attention to the items that were not checked, to gain insight into why the child did not perform certain items. The "Helpful Ideas" section after each item in the chapter gives suggestions that may assist the observer/teacher in planning for the child.

Making a Running Record and Transferring Data to the *Checklist*

To use the *Checklist* most effectively, many observers prefer to make a running record of the child they are observing as the action occurs. Afterward they transfer the data they have gathered by marking items on the *Checklist* that they observed the child performing, and by recording evidence for their check mark in the space provided. In this way observers combine the best of both methods of observation: the open-ended and rich description advantages of the running record with the focus on a particular sequence of behaviors of a developmental checklist.

Here is a running record made for 3-year-old Sheila on October 22:

Sheila's mother brings her into classroom. Sheila holds tightly to her hand. She begins to cry. Mother says, "Now, Sheila, you like it here. Be a good girl. See you later." Mother leaves. Sheila stands at the entrance to the room crying. Tch. comes over and S. immediately grabs her hand. Tch. takes S. over to girls in doll corner and says something to her. S. shakes her head. When tch. leaves S. begins following tch. around. Tch. sits S. down at small table with large box of crayons in middle & blank sheet of paper in front of two chairs. S. finally takes crayon & starts coloring. Beth comes over and sits down at S.'s table. She takes crayon out of box & starts coloring on her paper. Neither girl talks at first. Finally Beth asks S. "May I borrow your orange?" S. says "No" & covers crayon with hand. Beth grabs her hand, takes crayon with other hand & pops it into her mouth! S. says,

TABLE 2.1
Methods for observing and recording

Method	Purpose
Anecdotal Record: A narrative of descriptive paragraphs, recorded *after behavior occurs*	To detail specific behavior for child's record; for case conferences; to plan for individuals
Running Record: A narrative written in sequence over a specified time, recorded *while behavior is occurring*	To discover cause and effects of behavior; for case conferences; to plan for individuals
Specimen Record: A detailed narrative written in sequence over a specified time, recorded *while behavior is occurring*	To discover cause and effects of behavior; for child development research
Time Sampling: Tallies or symbols showing the presence or absence of specified behavior during short time periods, recorded *while behavior is occurring*	For behavior modification baseline data; for child development research
Event Sampling: A brief narrative of conditions preceding and following specified behavior, recorded *while behavior is occurring*	For behavior modification input; for child development research
Rating Scale: A scale of traits or behaviors with check marks, recorded *before, during, and after behavior occurs*	To judge degree to which child behaves or possesses certain traits; to diagnose behavior or traits; to plan for individuals
Checklist: A list of behaviors with check marks, recorded *before, during, and after behavior occurs*	To determine presence or absence of specified behaviors; to plan for individuals; to give observer an overview of child's development or progress

"That's not fair!" and calls teacher. When tch. comes S. says, "She ate my orange crayon so I can't finish my pumpkin!" Teacher says to Beth, "People shouldn't eat crayons," but tch. is distracted by other children & leaves area. Then S. gets up & goes to book corner & takes book. She carries book around room, looking carefully at what is going on, but not joining in. She whispers to Brian: "Becky painted yesterday & she's going to paint again today. See!" & points to easel. Brian does not respond & she whines to teacher,"I wanna paint! I wanna paint!" Tch. tells her she can paint when Becky is finished.

Advantages	Disadvantages
Open-ended; rich in details; no special observer training	Depends on observer's memory; behavior taken out of context; difficult to code or analyze for research
Open-ended; comprehensive; no special observer training	Time-consuming; difficult to use for more than one child at a time; time-consuming to code and analyze for research
Open-ended; comprehensive and complete; rich in details	Time-consuming to record; time-consuming to code or analyze for research; difficult to observe more than one child at a time
Objective and controlled; not time-consuming; efficient for observing more than one child at a time; provides quantitative data for research	Closed; limited to observable behaviors that occur frequently; no description of behavior; takes behavior out of context
Objective; helpful for in-depth diagnosis of infrequent behavior	Closed; takes event out of context; limited to specified behaviors
Not time-consuming; easy to design; efficient for observing more than one child at a time for many traits; useful for several observers watching same child	Closed; subjective; limited to specified traits or behaviors
Efficient for observing more than one child at a time for many behaviors; useful for an individual over a period of time; a good survey or inventory tool; useful for several observers at once; no special training needed	Closed; limited to specified behaviors; no information on quality of behavior

Rather than making observer comments as shown in the running record in Figure 2.2, the observer fills out the "Self-Identity" section of the *Checklist* as shown in Figure 2.9.

As the observer reads the chapter on self-identity, she should pay special attention to the items that she did not check. She will learn from her reading that a 3-year-old

FIGURE 2.9
Self-identity observations for Sheila

Child Skills Checklist

Name _Sheila — Age 3_ Observer _Connie R._

Program _Head Start_ Dates _10-22_

Directions:
Put a ✔ for items you see the child perform regularly. Put *N* for items where there is no opportunity to observe. Leave all other items blank.

Item	Evidence	Date
1. Self-Identity		
___ Separates from parents without difficulty	Sheila clings to mother & cries	10/22
___ Does not cling to classroom staff excessively	She grabs teacher's hand & follows teacher.	10/22
✔ Makes eye contact with adults	She makes eye contact with teacher	10/22
___ Makes activity choices without teacher's help	Teacher places Sheila at crayon table	10/22
___ Seeks other children to play with	No. She does not.	10/22
N Plays roles confidently in dramatic play		
✔ Stands up for own rights	Calls out to teacher: "She ate my orange crayon".	10/22
___ Displays enthusiasm about doing things for self	Watches, but does not get involved.	10/22

FIGURE 2.10

Emotional development evidence for Sheila

2. Emotional Development		
✓ Shows interest/attention in classroom activities	*Goes around room trying out everything*	*10/22*

like Sheila may still not be secure enough in herself to let go of her mother easily when she first comes to the preschool. The observer should not be all that concerned when Sheila transfers her clinging to the teacher, for the observer learns that 3-year-olds often exhibit such behavior at the beginning of school. The section "Helpful Ideas" after each item in Chapter 3 gives suggestions that may assist this child to make the transition from home to school more easily. Because Sheila has been in school for a month and still has difficulty making this transition, she may need special help.

Using the Entire *Checklist*

Once observers are familiar with each of the *Checklist* areas and items, they can use the entire *Checklist* for one child to gain a complete overview. Again, many observers prefer to make a running record of the child they are observing, and then afterward transfer the data they have gathered by checking off items on the *Checklist* and filling in their evidence.

From the running record previously made about Sheila, the observer can continue to complete the *Child Skills Checklist* under the 11 other areas, checking off items and filling in "Evidence." Obviously a number of other observations need to be made of Sheila at various times during the day—arrival, free choice, snack, outdoor play, lunch, nap, and departure—in order to get a comprehensive picture of the child.

From the running record previously made, the observer can check off items and fill in evidence for Sheila under "Emotional Development" such as in Figure 2.10. Under "Social Play" items such as those in Figure 2.11 can be checked. Additional items that can be checked based on this running record include those shown in Figure 2.12. Other observations on Sheila can be made, recorded, and dated on the same *Checklist* until a comprehensive picture of her emerges.

FIGURE 2.11

Social play evidence for Sheila

3. Social Play		
✓ Plays by self with own toys/materials	*Uses crayons on own*	*10/22*
✓ Plays parallel to others with similar toys/materials	*Colors on own but next to Beth*	*10/22*

FIGURE 2.12
Additional developmental evidence for Sheila

6. Small Motor Development ✓ Uses drawing/writing tools with control	Draws pumpkin with crayon	10/22
9. Spoken Language ✓ Speaks in expanded sentences	"She ate my orange crayon so I can't finish my pumpkin".	10/22
11. Art Skills ✓ Makes pictorial drawings	Draws a pumpkin	10/22

INTERPRETATION OF DATA

Once you have observed a child and recorded data about her in a running record and on the *Child Skills Checklist*, the next step is to interpret the information. It is a fascinating process, learning to know and understand a child. Objective observing and recording like this helps make possible a deeper understanding than a lifetime of merely being around children can do. We need to step back from children and look at them impartially and objectively. Only then do we truly see who they are and what they are. Only then do we begin to understand how we can help them to reach their highest potential.

Interpreting the information you have acquired from your observations takes knowledge and skill. You need to know a great deal about child development both from reading and studying about children and from actual experience with them. Then you can begin to make valid inferences and conclusions about children based on your observations.

This textbook is organized to help you gain such knowledge. Using the *Child Skills Checklist* will focus your attention on important child behaviors in each area of child development. Reading the chapters that feature these areas will help you to acquire knowledge of the particular area. Interpreting the data you acquire will then be more meaningful to you and helpful to the child as you apply it in your individual planning.

Inferences

The first step in interpreting the data you have gathered is to read it through carefully, both the running record and especially the *Checklist*, to see if you can make any inferences about the child. An inference is a statement considered to be true, tentatively at least, because it is founded upon objective information believed to be true. In other words, it is a possible explanation derived from the behavior you have witnessed. In order to make an inference, you must actually have seen and recorded objectively the behavior upon which you are basing the inference.

Objective observing and recording of a youngster's behavior makes possible a deeper understanding of children than does a lifetime of merely being around children.

Looking back at the running record made for Sheila, we might consider making the following inferences:

Incident	Faulty Inference	Valid Inference
Sheila would not let Beth borrow her orange crayon.	Sheila does not know how to share.	Sheila was not finished using her orange crayon.
Sheila whispers to Brian that Becky painted yesterday and she's going to paint again today.	Sheila likes to tattle on other children.	Sheila is alert to what Becky did with paint yesterday and today.

After reading carefully the first incident in the running record involving Sheila (which states that she says no when Beth asks to borrow her orange crayon, and then covers the crayon with her hand), we need to ask ourselves what we can infer, if anything, from this. Do the words tell us that Sheila does not know how to share?

They do not seem to indicate this. Then the inference "Sheila does not know how to share" is probably not a valid one. We just do not have enough information to make this particular inference. We may want to observe Sheila further to see if she is able to share materials with others before we can infer that she does not know how to share. Does the running record tell us that Sheila was not finished using the orange crayon? Yes. The words say, "She ate my orange crayon so I can't finish my pumpkin." Thus we can infer that Sheila was not finished using the crayon.

The second incident, in which Sheila whispers to Brian that Becky painted yesterday and she's going to paint again today, should be approached in the same way. What, if anything, can we infer from this incident? Does it mean that Sheila likes to tattle on other children? We do not have any indication that this is true, thus such an inference is faulty. We can infer that Sheila is alert to what Becky did with paint yesterday and now today. That is about all. We may want to infer that Sheila is using such an approach to gain access to an activity she likes, or that Sheila whispers about others in order to get attention, or that Sheila just likes to stir up things in the classroom in this manner—but we truly do not have such information about Sheila, and thus cannot make any of these three latter inferences.

Try making your own inferences from an anecdotal or running record you have made after observing a child. One thing you will learn from such an exercise is the importance of recording with rich detail. You need to learn this skill through practice. There is always something more you can add to a running record: facial expressions, gestures, reactions of other children. They may be the keys to the inferences you are trying to elicit about a child.

The principal stumbling block in making valid inferences based on recorded observational data is that we try to read more into the data than is actually there. We are used to making judgments continuously about people and situations in our lives. Often they are faulty judgments based on insufficient information or misinterpreted information. Do not allow yourself to be misled like this when you have the written data before you on child observations. Look at the data and ask yourself the question: Is there evidence to support my inference? If there is, then you can make it.

Conclusions

The final step in your interpretation of recorded data about children is to make whatever conclusions you can. A conclusion in this case is a reasoned judgment based on *accumulated observational evidence and interpreted inferences.* As with inferences, you cannot make such a judgment unless you can show sufficient evidence. Read through your observational data. Based on what you have recorded, what is possible to conclude about the child? In Sheila's case, very little can be concluded from the one running record. We cannot really conclude that she is always so alert to other children and activities in the classroom unless future observations show this same behavior. It may be that she is only concerned with painting. To make valid conclusions an observer needs a great deal of recorded information about a child.

Observing, recording, and interpreting in this careful, objective manner should help you to sort out what children are really like. You may be surprised by what you discover.

PLANNING FOR CHILDREN BASED ON OBSERVATIONS

The ultimate reason for observing and recording is not just to learn what children are like, but to help them grow and develop. That is why they have come to your class-room. You can assist them in this goal if your observations have helped you identify their strengths and their areas that need strengthening.

After observing Sheila for only one morning and transferring her observational data from a running record to the *Child Skills Checklist*, you can begin to get a pic-ture of her strengths and her areas needing strengthening. From this picture as shown on the *Checklist*, you can begin to make plans for Sheila that will help to build on her strengths and speak to her needs—always accentuating the positive.

Learning Prescription

Creating a "learning prescription" for Sheila is the next step in the process of plan-ning for an individual child based on interpreted observational data. To create such a prescription you should look over the *Child Skills Checklist* to find at least three *areas of strength*. Although her *Checklist* is far from complete, it is still possible to come up with real strengths for Sheila: for example, she stands up for her own rights, she also speaks in expanded sentences, and she really seems to enjoy art.

Then we look for *areas needing strengthening*. We do not call these *weaknesses*, a negative term. Words are important, and we should use them carefully. If we talk in terms of negatives, we will think in terms of negatives regarding Sheila and our other children. If we think in terms of areas needing strengthening, we should be able to plan a positive program for Sheila that will help her to continue in her development and improve in areas that need improvement. Put yourself in the same position. Wouldn't you prefer to be involved in a training program that would help you to improve in your areas needing strengthening rather than a program to overcome your weaknesses?

Finally, the learning prescription needs to include specific ideas for helping the child to improve in her areas needing strengthening by *drawing on her strengths*. Specific ideas for activities can come from your own experience or from the ideas listed in the various chapters after every *Checklist* item and called "If You Have Not Checked This Item: Some Helpful Ideas." An initial learning prescription for Sheila might read something like the example in Figure 2.13. Then see page 53 for a repro-ducible copy of a *Learning Prescription* form.

The teachers in Sheila's class will want to continue their observing and recording to evaluate how these activities help Sheila and the other children as well as what other individual plans are needed.

The chapters to follow in this text can serve as guidelines for you in evaluating children's strengths and needs, and then in planning for activities to help individuals or small groups of children with similar needs. The ideas listed under "If You Have Not Checked This Item: Some Helpful Ideas" should prove useful not only for assisting children in areas of their needs, but also in providing the stimulus for your own ideas for activities. Chapter 15, "Observing the Whole Child," brings together the 12 separate *Checklist* areas and applies them to a single child. Observers learn how to use the *Checklist* in a classroom situation, how to interpret the results, and finally, how to convert check marks into an individual learning prescription. Once you have learned where one child stands developmentally, then you can make similar plans for each of the children in your own program.

FIGURE 2.13
Learning prescription for Sheila

Learning Prescription

Name ___Sheila___   Age ___3___   Date ___10/22___

Areas of Strength and Confidence

1. _Stands up for her own rights_
2. _Speaks in expanded sentences_
3. _Enjoys art & displays art skills_

Areas Needing Strengthening

1. _To separate from mother more easily_
2. _To rely less on adults in classroom_
3. _To play with other children_

Activities to Help

1. _Transition activity when S. arrives: S & Becky could clean the rabbit cage & feed the rabbit._
2. _S. could record her voice & then show Becky how_
3. _S. and Becky could paint large box for class "spaceship" and others could join in_

Child Skills Checklist

Name _____ **Observer** _____

Program _____ **Dates** _____

Directions:

Put a ✔ for items you see the child perform regularly. Put *N* for items where there is no opportunity to observe. Leave all other items blank.

Item	Evidence	Date
1. Self-Identity		
_____ Separates from parents without difficulty		
_____ Does not cling to classroom staff excessively		
_____ Makes eye contact with adults		
_____ Makes activity choices without teacher's help		
_____ Seeks other children to play with		
_____ Plays roles confidently in dramatic play		
_____ Stands up for own rights		
_____ Displays enthusiasm about doing things for self		
2. Emotional Development		
_____ Allows self to be comforted during stressful time		
_____ Eats, sleeps, toilets without fuss away from home		

Item	Evidence	Date
_____ Handles sudden changes/ startling situations with control		
_____ Can express anger in words rather than actions		
_____ Allows aggressive behavior to be redirected		
_____ Does not withdraw from others excessively		
_____ Shows interest/attention in classroom activities		
_____ Smiles, seems happy much of the time		
3. Social Play _____ Is unoccupied during free play (or follows teacher)		
_____ Spends time watching others play		
_____ Plays by self with own toys/ materials		
_____ Plays parallel to others with similar toys/materials		
_____ Initiates activity/play with others		
_____ Gains access to ongoing play in positive manner		
_____ Maintains role in ongoing play in positive manner		
_____ Resolves play conflicts in positive manner		

Item	Evidence	Date
4. Prosocial Behavior		
_____ Shows concern for someone in distress		
_____ Shows delight for someone experiencing pleasure		
_____ Shares something with another		
_____ Gives something of his/her own to another		
_____ Takes turns without a fuss		
_____ Complies with requests without a fuss		
_____ Helps another to do a task		
_____ Helps (cares for) another in need		
5. Large Motor Development		
_____ Walks down steps alternating feet		
_____ Runs with control over speed and direction		
_____ Jumps over obstacle, landing on two feet		
_____ Hops forward on one foot		
_____ Climbs up and down climbing equipment with ease		
_____ Moves legs/feet in rhythm to beat		

Item	Evidence	Date
_____ Claps hands in rhythm to beat		
_____ Beats drum alternating hands in rhythm to beat		
6. Small Motor Development _____ Shows hand preference (which is _____)		
_____ Turns with hand easily (knobs, lids, eggbeaters)		
_____ Pours liquid into glass without spilling		
_____ Unfastens/fastens zippers, buttons, Velcro tabs		
_____ Picks up and inserts objects with ease		
_____ Uses drawing/writing tools with control		
_____ Uses scissors with control		
_____ Pounds in nails with control		
7. Cognitive Development: Classification and Seriation _____ Recognizes basic geometric shapes		
_____ Recognizes colors		
_____ Recognizes differences in size		

Item	Evidence	Date
_____ Sorts objects by appearance		
_____ Recognizes differences in musical tones		
_____ Reproduces musical tones with voice		
_____ Arranges events in sequence from first to last		
_____ Arranges objects in series according to a rule		
8. Cognitive Development: Number, Time, Space, Memory _____ Counts to 20 by rote		
_____ Counts objects to 20		
_____ Knows the daily schedule in sequence		
_____ Knows what happened yesterday		
_____ Can build a block enclosure		
_____ Can locate an object behind or beside something		
_____ Recalls words to song, chant		
_____ Can recollect and act on directions of a singing game		

Item	Evidence	Date
9. Spoken Language _____ Speaks confidently in the classroom		
_____ Speaks clearly enough for adults to understand		
_____ Speaks in expanded sentences		
_____ Takes part in conversations with other children		
_____ Asks questions with proper word order		
_____ Makes "No" responses with proper word order		
_____ Uses past tense verbs correctly		
_____ Plays with rhyming words		
10. Prewriting and Prereading Skills _____ Pretends to write by scribbling horizontally		
_____ Includes features of real letters in scribbling		
_____ Writes real alphabet letters		
_____ Writes words with invented spelling		
_____ Retells stories from books with increasing accuracy		

Item	Evidence	Date
_____ Shows awareness that print in books tells story		
_____ Attempts to match telling of story with print in book		
_____ Wants to know what particular print says		
11. Art Skills		
_____ Makes random marks or covers paper with color		
_____ Scribbles on paper		
_____ Forms basic shapes		
_____ Makes mandalas		
_____ Makes suns		
_____ Draws human as a circle with arms and legs attached		
_____ Draws animals, trees, flowers		
_____ Makes pictorial drawings		
12. Imagination		
_____ Pretends by replaying familiar routines		
_____ Needs particular props to do pretend play		

Item	Evidence	Date
_____ Assigns roles or takes assigned roles		
_____ May switch roles without warning		
_____ Uses language for creating and sustaining plot		
_____ Uses exciting, danger-packed themes		
_____ Takes on characteristics and actions related to role		
_____ Uses elaborate and creative themes, ideas, details		

Learning Prescription

Name _____ Age _____ Date _____

Areas of Strength and Confidence

1. _____

2. _____

3. _____

Areas Needing Strengthening

1. _____

2. _____

3. _____

Activities to Help

1. _____

   _____

2. _____

   _____

3. _____

   _____

REFERENCES

Bell, Donald, & Roberta M. Low. (1977). *Observing and recording children's behavior.* Richland, WA: Performance Associates.

Hodgden, Laurel (Ed.). (1974). *School before six: A diagnostic approach.* St. Louis: CEM-REL.

Irwin, D. Michelle, & M. Margaret Bushnell. (1980). *Observational strategies for child study.* New York: Holt, Rinehart, & Winston.

Kellogg, Rhoda. (1970). *Analyzing children's art.* Palo Alto, CA: National Press Books.

Seefeldt, Carolyn. (1990). Assessing young children. In Carolyn Seefeldt (Ed.), *Continuing issues in early childhood education.* New York: Merrill/Macmillan.

OTHER SOURCES

Bentzen, Warren R. (1991). *Seeing young children: A guide to observing and recording behavior.* Albany, NY: Delmar.

Boehm, Ann E., & Richard A. Weinberg. (1987). *The classroom observer: Developing observation skills in early childhood settings.* New York: Teachers College Press.

Cartwright, Carol A., & G. Phillip Cartwright. (1984). *Developing observational skills.* New York: McGraw-Hill.

Cohen, Dorothy H., & Virginia Stern. (1983). *Observing and recording the behavior of young children.* New York: Teachers College Press.

O'Sullivan, Barbara. (1989). Observing and recording behavior. *Day Care and Early Education, 17*(2), 19–21.

LEARNING ACTIVITIES

1. Have two different observers use the *Child Skills Checklist* to observe the same child at the same time period for three days. Compare results. How similar were the observations? In what areas were there differences? In what ways can you improve future observing and recording?

2. Make an anecdotal record of a child after you have observed the child for an hour. At the same time have another observer make an on-the-spot running record. Compare the two. Which showed more detail? Which was more accurate? Which would be more helpful to you in understanding or planning for the child? Why?

3. Have two different observers make a running record of the same child for 30 minutes. Compare the results. Which, if any, of the problems mentioned for running records turned up? How can you overcome these problems in the future?

4. Make an anecdotal record for a child after you have observed the child for an hour. What inferences can you make about this child? What specific evidence is each inference based on? Can you make any conclusions? Why or why not?

5. Construct a graphic rating scale on five social behaviors of children and use it to observe children in your class. Discuss your results. Did you have any problems making judgments? How can you use the information gained?

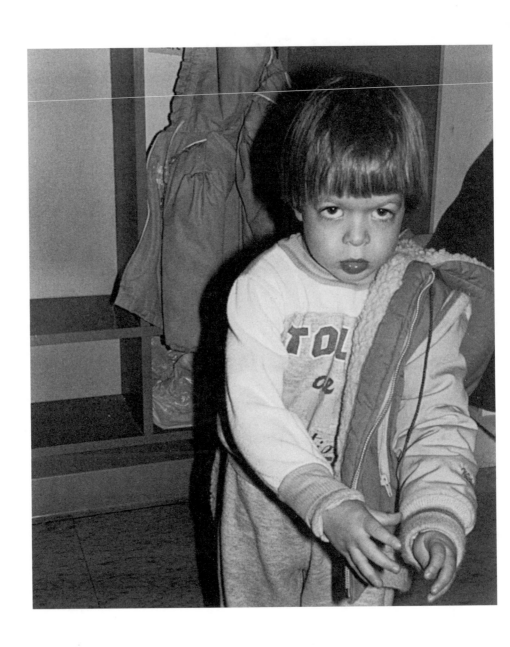

3

Self-Identity

Self-Identity Checklist

❑ Separates from parents without difficulty

❑ Does not cling to classroom staff excessively

❑ Makes eye contact with adults

❑ Makes activity choices without teacher's help

❑ Seeks other children to play with

❑ Plays roles confidently in dramatic play

❑ Stands up for own rights

❑ Displays enthusiasm about doing things for self

From the moment of birth, the young human being is engaged in the dynamic process of becoming himself or herself. The child continually develops into a whole person with a temperament, personality, and value system—with a physical, cognitive, language, social, emotional, and creative makeup that is uniquely his or her own. It is a totally engrossing process that will take a lifetime to complete, but its early stages are perhaps its most crucial, for they set the pattern for all that is to follow.

This chapter will discuss some of the developmental sequences that are observable in children 3 to 5 years of age as they strive to develop in the setting of the child development center or classroom. Although children carry their own unique package of genetic traits and home influences, the caregivers they meet and the care they receive at the center will nevertheless have a strong bearing on their future development.

Each item of the *Child Skills Checklist* will be discussed separately in this and the chapters to follow. Each *Checklist* item is positive in nature and should be checked if the observer sees the child performing in the manner described. Suggestions for helping and supporting the child's development in the unchecked items will follow the discussion of the item.

❑ SEPARATES FROM PARENTS WITHOUT DIFFICULTY

Initial Attachment

Most studies of young children agree that a key ingredient to their successful development is a strong initial attachment to a primary caregiver, usually the mother. Without such an attachment babies may seriously lag in their development and in some cases even die. It seems a great paradox, then, to suggest that for successful development to continue, the young human must learn at the same time to separate from the parent. But such is the case. This separation should occur first in the home—not only with the child, but also with the parents, who must encourage the infant to become independent of them and who must also let go of the infant.

Many current attachment/separation studies are based on the work of John Bowlby (1969, 1973) and Mary Ainsworth (1974) who talk about children's attachment to their parents as a condition of trust in their parents' reliability. Attachment occurs during the first year or two as a result of many interactions between infants and parents. The first separation of the child from the mother is of course the physical one that occurs at birth. Some psychologists believe that much of life thereafter is the striving of the developing being to achieve that perfect state of oneness once again with another human (Kaplan, 1978, p. 43).

But in the first few months of life the baby hardly recognizes herself as a separate being apart from her mother or primary caregiver. When she cries her mother feeds or changes her. When she gurgles or coos her mother holds her close or smiles. Little by little as visual memory develops—and "person permanence" occurs—the infant comes to recognize this primary caregiver as being different from everyone else. The child then strives to be near the caregiver or to bring this person close as often as possible. Person permanence means that the infant has developed the ability to hold the memory of the person in her mind when the person is out of sight (Damon, 1983, p. 34).

It is necessary, therefore, that this primary caregiver be a consistent one. The formation of a strong attachment becomes complicated if the infant has too many primary caregivers. If the mother works during the day, for example, she should make arrangements to turn over the secondary caregiving responsibilities to one consistent person while she is away. She can still function as a primary caregiver when she returns from work, if this is the role she has chosen. If she has turned over the role of primary caregiver to the father or to another person from the beginning, then this should be the consistent person whom the infant can turn to at the end of the day. The baby who has developed person permanence will welcome this person happily when he or she returns.

This is the beginning of the strong initial attachment that is necessary on the part of both infant and caregiver in order for later separation to occur successfully. Such an attachment leads to a sense of security and trust on the part of the infant. The lack of such an attachment often interferes with the child building trust in future relationships. In fact, the failure to thrive in infancy is frequently the result of the breakdown of this initial attachment relationship (Seagull & Kallen, 1978, p. 8).

Both the primary caregiver and the infant play a part in the building of this initial attachment. The adult must respond promptly and in an appropriate manner to the infant's cries—time after time after time. For example, the adult should feed the infant and not spank him when he cries out of hunger. Some adults don't. On the other hand, the infant should also respond appropriately to the caregiver's actions. For example, he needs to stop crying when the adult cares for his needs, or to show delight when the adult plays with him or cuddles him. Some babies don't.

It is difficult for the initial attachment to be a strong one when the actions of one or the other or both are not satisfactory over a period of time. It takes most of the infant's first year to develop a relationship with the caregiver (Damon, 1983, p. 29). But without such an attachment, it is difficult for the infant to develop trust in anyone else, and it becomes doubly difficult for the infant or developing child to separate from the caregiver. After all, if she cannot trust the primary caregiver, how can she risk trusting anyone? This attachment between the infant and primary caregiver, in fact, serves as a model for future human relationships.

Initial Separation

The initial separation of the infant from his mother or primary caregiver begins when he first recognizes he is separate from that person. This develops within the first 6 months of life as the baby recognizes that there is a difference between himself and the caregiver—and later, between himself and others. At this time, his first memories—visual in nature—are occurring. Some psychologists call this the "psychological birth" of the baby (Kaplan, 1978, p. 121). It is the first glimmering of self-identity.

Toward the end of the first year as the infant learns to move about by creeping and finally by her first unsteady steps, an interesting pattern of interaction with the caregiver often emerges. The youngster uses the caregiver as a base from which to explore her environment. She moves out a bit and comes back, moves further and returns, moves out again, and this time may only look back, making the eye contact that will give her the reassurance to continue her exploration. Child-care providers may also notice this same pattern of touching or eye contact between child and parent during the initial school entrance period (Gottschall, 1989, p. 14).

During the last half of the child's first year, or sometimes before, *separation anxiety* also emerges; that is, the infant sets up a strong protest of crying or clinging if the caregiver attempts to leave. This pattern of distress is also exhibited when a stranger appears, making it obvious that the baby recognizes the difference between the caregiver and others.

Thus self-identity develops as the toddler ventures out and scurries back, clings and pushes away, holds on and lets go. But the stronger the initial attachment, the more secure the developing child should feel each time he or she lets go.

The young human also learns who he is by the way other people respond to him (how others seem to be affected by whatever he does). Hopefully, this response is mainly positive, so that by the time he enters nursery school, day care, or Head Start, he already will be feeling good about himself. Table 3.1 summarizes the child's attachment/separation milestones.

School Separation

No matter how good the young child feels about herself, the initial school separation from a parent is often difficult. At 3 years old the sense of self is still a bit shaky. Although the child has an identity at home and can hold on to an image of the caregiver even when the caregiver is not present, at school she is in a strange environment as well. To complicate matters, the parent/caregiver may also be experiencing separation anxiety, and the child often senses this.

TABLE 3.1
Attachment/separation milestones

Attachment

Preattachment
Birth through first 8–12 weeks
> Responds to people but cannot distinguish one from the other; does not recognize self as separate from primary caregiver

Person permanence
First months
> Learns to distinguish primary caregiver from others

Attachment to caregiver
First months to second or third year
> Seeks proximity to caregiver; shows separation anxiety when caregiver leaves; shows stranger anxiety when stranger appears—most common at 7 months

Partnership
Second or third year on
> Comes to understand caregiver's point of view and adjusts own behavior accordingly

Separation

Physical separation from mother
Birth

Psychological birth
First six months
> Recognizes self as separate from mother

Exploration of physical environment
Last months of first year to second, third years
> Explores first by creeping, then walking; uses caregiver as base to explore and return

Strengthening of self-identity
Second or third year on
> Gains stronger recognition of self-identity, as child and parent let go of one another for more frequent and longer periods of time

NOTE: This table includes information from Damon (1983).

Each child handles the situation in his or her own way. One child may be used to the home of a loving baby-sitter, and he will take this new "playroom" in stride. Another may cling to her mother and scream whenever the mother attempts to leave. The child used to playing with others may quickly join a group in the block corner. A shyer child may need the teacher's urging to join in. One fussing, crying child may stop as soon as his mother leaves. Another may withdraw into herself and sit in a corner sucking her thumb.

You as a classroom worker hope that the children will become adjusted to this separation within a few days or a week or so. Most of them will. One or two may not. How can you help them develop a strong enough sense of self that they also feel free to let go of their primary caregiver?

If You Have Not Checked This Item: Some Helpful Ideas

One or more of the children in your center may have unchecked Self-Identity Checklist items. Because you are aware that each item represents a step in the developmental sequence of young children, you may be able to lend children support at the outset by arranging your schedule or setting up your classroom ahead of time to address their problems. Here are some ideas that may help preschoolers separate from their parents with less difficulty.

■ Make Early Initial Contact with Parent/Caregiver and Child

If the child and the parent have met you ahead of time, they may feel less reluctant to separate on the day that school begins. For the child, it is better if this meeting takes place close to the time of school opening rather than the spring before. Memories of a brief visit several months before school begins have little meaning for the young child. An immediate follow-up is more effective. If you visit the child's home you might take a camera with you to record the occasion for later use in the classroom to help the child make an easier transition from home to school.

■ Try Staggered Enrollment

Rather than having all of the children in your class begin school on the same day at the same time, you might consider starting half of them on the first day, and half the second—or half in the morning and the rest in the afternoon of the same day. This strategy will allow staff members to devote more time to the individual children and their parents. In addition, the first day may not be so overwhelming for the children if only half of the class is present at once.

■ Create a Simple Initial Environment

The more complex the classroom environment, the more overwhelming it is for certain children. You might plan to have the classroom arranged with fewer activity areas for the first weeks and less material on the shelves. As the children settle in and become more secure, you can add activities and materials as needed.

■ Use Transition Materials

Children can make the transition from home to school—can separate more easily from their parents—if there are familiar materials available to help bridge the gap. Water is one such material. A water table or basin with an eggbeater, funnel, and squeeze bottles may take a child's mind off his parent long enough to get him happily involved in the center. Toy trucks and dolls often have the same effect. Have a special set of little toys you can allow children to take home with them at the end of the day and return again in the morning to make the transition less difficult.

■ Utilize Parent/Caregiver Visits

Allow the parents to stay as long as necessary on the first days, or come in for visits from time to time. The shy child may use her parent as a base for exploration in the classroom, venturing away from the parent and returning just as she did as a toddler at home. If the separation is a difficult one, have the caregiver return early to pick up the youngster. Little by little the children should be able to stay longer without their parents.

■ Read a Book

Children like to hear stories about other children who have the same feelings as they do. Try reading a book about separation to children having difficulty in this area. Talk about the story and ask the child or children how they feel. *Who's Going to Take Care of Me?* by Michelle Magorian (New York: Harper & Row, 1990), for example, is a simply told but effective tale about little Eric and bigger sister Karin who go to day care together until Karin becomes old enough for school. Eric is worried about who will take care of him in day care now that his sister has gone to school, but learns in the end that he is the one who "knows the ropes" in the day-care center and can even care for the new little boy who sits by himself.

■ Show and Foster Acceptance of the Child

Up until now the child's self-identity has evolved from the reactions of his family to him. Now that he is in your classroom, you and your co-workers and the other children will be adding details to the child's interior picture of himself. These details need to be positive, happy ones. You need to support this process first of all by accepting the child and his family unconditionally. Show your acceptance both verbally and nonverbally. Smile at him frequently. Greet him personally every day. Demonstrate that you enjoy being near him and having him near you. You are the behavior model for the other children as well. If they see that you accept a child no matter what, they will be more likely to do the same.

❏ DOES NOT CLING TO CLASSROOM STAFF EXCESSIVELY

The next developmental step for the children in your classroom is to build up enough confidence to become involved on their own with the other children and the activities available. Those with a strong sense of self may have no difficulty. Others may not be ready during the first days or weeks. A few may not be ready even then.

Psychologists use the term *significant others* in referring to the particular people who have the most important influence on our lives (Seagull & Kallen, 1978, p. 13).

For the young child this usually means her immediate family. Once she enters your classroom, however, you and your co-workers will also become significant others. This means that your reactions toward the child will have an effect on what she thinks about herself. This may reinforce the view of self learned at home, or it may modify that view. If the responses to her are generally positive, then her feelings about herself as a good person are strengthened. The opposite of course is also true.

The development of a self-identity is thus a subtle but lengthy process. No one knows for sure how long it takes—probably much of a person's life. The early childhood years are the most crucial because they set the course. That is why it is so important for the young self in its most sensitive formative period to receive positive responses from the adults around it.

Many children develop a similar kind of attachment to one or more of the adults in the early childhood classroom as they did to their primary caregiver at home. The child needs a consistent caregiver in the classroom as well, in order to develop trust in this new environment. It is important, therefore, that the staff of an early childhood center be present consistently throughout the year—not merely dropping in and dropping out.

If the teacher must leave, she should try to have the replacement teacher visit the classroom several times before she departs so that the children may get to know the replacement. The transition will thus be more gradual and hopefully more acceptable to the children. Otherwise, for certain children, changing teachers will be nearly as traumatic as changing primary caregivers.

The child who looks to the teacher as a caregiver may cling to the classroom adult. He or she may not have the necessary trust in the world, or may not have developed a strong enough sense of self yet to let go in a strange new environment. Three-year-olds especially may relate much more comfortably to adults than to other children. After all, much of their life thus far may have been spent in a one-to-one relationship with an adult. A classroom of 15 to 20 children may be totally overwhelming. How can you help such a child?

If You Have Not Checked This Item: Some Helpful Ideas

■ Display Acceptance

You must accept the child's clinging behavior, knowing that it is a normal step in the developmental sequence. But you also need to know ways to encourage and support this child when he is ready to move out. If he feels that you accept his presence near you and will not force him to do something he is not ready to do, then he is much more likely to move out on his own. Forcing a clinging child away from you before he is ready to go may only make him cling more tightly.

■ Have the Child Follow the Adult's Lead

The child who clings to or "shadows" an adult may follow the adult's lead as well. You could lead her to a table and sit down with her to make a puzzle. If she becomes involved with it on her own you might try moving on to another group of children.

Or you could try playing a role in the dramatic play area and invite the child to accompany you on some pretend errand or to help you accomplish some pretend task. If the child accepts your efforts to involve her, you can freely leave the activity. If she does not, she may not be ready yet to move out on her own.

■ Observe the Child

You may be able to tell when the time is right for a child to become involved on his own with the other children and activities by your observations of him. Does he spend a great deal of time observing the others? Is this looking behavior done from the "protection" of your side or does he stand in a "safe" spot and watch? If his eyes seem to be more engaged in following the activities of the others rather than keeping track of you, it may be time to help him become involved with them.

■ Ask the Child to Help an Adult or Another Child

The clinging child will sometimes allow herself to become involved in classroom activities as the adult's helper. Ask her to help you get out the paints or the puzzles, to dress a doll in the housekeeping area, to feed the guinea pig, to deliver a message next door. Little by little she may venture away from you and then return just as she did with her primary caregiver at home. Or you might ask a second child to join you as a helper. The two of them could then do the same tasks, at which point you could try leaving them on their own.

■ Follow Up on the Child's Interest

One of the most successful techniques for involving the clinging child in classroom activities is to discover what interests him. Your conversations with him may give you a clue. If he is nonverbal, your observations of the things that attract his attention may suggest an activity he could pursue by himself and then later with another child when he feels enough at ease. You might leaf through a magazine with him and ask him to point to the pictures of the things he likes. He or you could cut these out and he might paste them in a scrapbook to get him started. Or you could use the information you gain about his interests to involve him more directly with similar classroom activities.

If none of these ideas work, you should continue to be patient about her clinging. Do not push. When she feels secure enough in the classroom she will venture out on her own. The child who never feels secure enough is probably still not mature enough to handle a classroom situation. If she still continues to cling after several weeks in your program, you may want to discuss with the parent the possibility of keeping her at home for another year or placing her in a home-type program with fewer children.

❏ MAKES EYE CONTACT WITH ADULTS

Nonverbal cues are among the most important signals people send out about their feelings. Facial expressions, head position, muscle tension, and body carriage all reveal a person's state of mind regarding himself and those around him. All of us read these expressions subconsciously. Our subconscious minds process this intake and help our conscious minds to make decisions about the people we interact with. We feel that they are friendly, hostile, frightened, or unsure as a result of this constant subconscious processing of visual stimuli.

As teachers of young children we need to read such nonverbal cues consciously as well, because of the important information they can give us about young children. In addition we need to be aware of how important such information is to young children. Because they are not fully verbal at three and four, young children depend heavily on nonverbal cues from us to make determinations about the people and situations they encounter.

We can say polite words to children and their parents, but if our face is tense and our eyes give out signals of distaste, the child picks up and responds to these. That is why we say children instinctively know which adults to trust. Children read nonverbal signals exceptionally well, partly because children are nonverbal themselves and partly because they are more visually oriented than most adults.

Eye signals are the most important. Eyes give messages of affection, love, happiness, contentment, and humor. They show pain, frustration, anger, fright, and despair. The way the eyes are partly or wholly open, the position of the eyebrows, the size of the pupils, the number of blinks, the length of a stare—all are indicative of the feelings of a person. Words may not always tell the truth, but eyes do.

Earlier studies assumed that the size of the pupils of the eye remained constant if the level of light remained the same. Research subsequently has disproved this notion. What research discovered instead was that the pupils increase in size in the presence of pleasant things and become noticeably smaller if people and situations are disagreeable. Eyes also respond to more than visual cues. Laboratory tests have shown that eye pupils change size in response to voices. Loud, harsh, or scolding voices may cause them to shrink. The size of eye pupils is in fact a reliable indicator of a person's feelings (Thompson, 1973, p.90).

Eye contact between people is important. Your first encounter with someone's eyes reveals much about that person's feelings concerning himself. Subsequent contact often reveals a great deal of how that person feels about you. The first actual eye contact itself is a recognition that you exist in a person's world and he exists in yours. If he feels uncomfortable about himself or you, he often shifts his gaze. Hopefully, you will not need to do the same.

Preschool children are at an egocentric stage in their development when they enter your classroom. They see things mostly from their own points of view. If you asked one to hide so that you would not be able to see her, she might very well cover her own eyes. From her self-centered point of view she believes that you cannot see her because she cannot see you. Children who are initially tense or frightened or uneasy in your presence may use this same subterfuge by refusing to make eye contact. If they do not look at you, surely you will not be able to see them; or if they do not look at you, maybe you won't really be there.

Certain cultures and ethnic groups also condition their children not to look adults directly in the eye because they feel it is disrespectful. You need to decide whether your children avoid eye contact because of cultural conditioning or because they are truly uncomfortable with themselves or you. Eventually you will need to have eye contact with all of your children in order for them to recognize the freedom and openness of this new environment—to understand that they are worthy human beings in your sight.

When eye contact finally occurs it often diffuses tense situations. If you can succeed in getting the shy or frightened child to make eye contact with you, you may be able to dispel his fears without saying a word. He will see in your eyes the friendliness, sense of humor, and enjoyment he can expect from your presence. But you need to know that your eyes won't fake it. You must truly project to this young developing child that you like him already, no matter what—because you really do.

Research shows that the more a person likes someone, the more he or she looks at him (Thompson, 1973, p. 91). This applies to teachers as well as their children. It is therefore important that you do not pick favorites or reject any of your children, because their sensitivity to nonverbal cues will soon tell them if you have. You will be looking more frequently at the children you like than at the children you do not like.

If you can succeed in getting a shy or fearful child to make eye contact with you, you may be able to dispel his fears without saying a word.

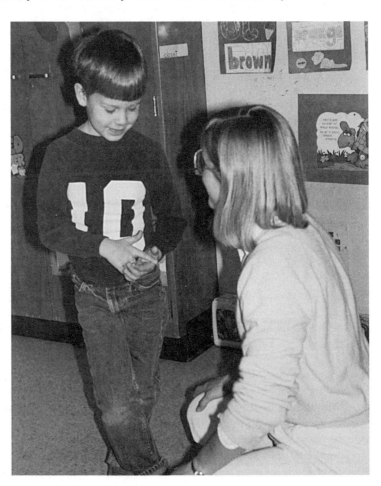

As a professional you cannot afford to pick favorites or dislike a child. Of course it is human to like one person more than another. But in your position as a child-care worker this is not permissible. You must make a concerted effort to correct your feelings if you find yourself responding like this.

If You Have Not Checked This Item: Some Helpful Ideas

■ Acceptance

Many of the same ideas used to help the child who was not checked for the first two items also apply here. This child either is not sure of himself or has not developed basic trust in the people and world around him. Or he may have a disability of some sort. Autistic children seem to avoid eye contact. Some mentally retarded children have difficulty making eye contact with people outside their family.

To help any child develop a self-identity strong enough to make eye contact with strange adults, you, as the strange adult, must show you accept the child unconditionally. Use both verbal and nonverbal cues. Tell her how nice it is to have her in your center. Use her name frequently. Exclaim with delight when she accomplishes something, no matter how insignificant.

■ Make Eye Contact Yourself

You are the model for behavior in your classroom. If you feel it is important for your children to behave in a certain way, then you need to do the same yourself. Make eye contact with the shy child at all times. When she finally has the confidence to return the look, she needs to see you smiling at her.

■ Read a Book

Read to the shy or insecure child a book such as *I Am Eyes—Ni Macho* by Leila Ward (New York: Scholastic, 1987). It is an illustrated story of what an African child sees during the day. You could then ask your child what he or she sees.

■ Have Patience

Do not force the issue. You must remember that the child's avoidance of eye contact is not a negative action but a clue to you that he is still not confident enough in your presence to return the look. You need to do all in your power to help him develop that confidence, but sometimes the best thing to do is nothing. Have patience. Forcing will not help. You must have the confidence to know that his refusal to meet your eyes is nothing personal. When he finally feels at ease within himself and within your center, he will return your look.

All children at one time or another avoid looking at a caregiver. They may be embarrassed or ashamed or feeling foolish about something they have done. But when they finally confront it, if they can see by the look in your eyes that you still accept them, then they will be able to return your look with confidence as they continue on their own unique path of development.

❏ MAKES ACTIVITY CHOICES WITHOUT TEACHER'S HELP

One of the next observable indicators of a child's feelings about herself in your classroom is her willingness to make a choice on her own about the activity she wants to engage in. Once she feels confident enough to leave your side, she needs to explore the new environment and try out the various materials and activities on her own. Many children have a strong enough sense of self to go immediately to the activity areas as soon as they enter the room. Others use the adult who accompanies them as a base for their explorations, going into an area and coming back to the person much as they did during their initial separation from their primary caregiver when they were infants. Some also use the teacher as this base.

Research seems to imply that having a secure base of attachment facilitates exploratory behavior on the part of 2-year-olds in center-based day care (Fein & Schwartz, 1982, p. 88). Children 3, 4, and 5 years old also do better when they have this strong attachment. These attachment findings seems to indicate that, just as within the family, the child who is secure in his relationship with a caregiver will also be secure on his own. Thus, as previously mentioned, it is important to help a child build this relationship initially. It is also important to observe which children are able to become involved with activities independently and which are not quite ready, possibly because the sense of self-identity in these children is not yet strong enough.

Your goal for children who do not participate independently in activities will be to help these children develop a sense of security with you and within the center. Once they develop this feeling of security, they may take the next step toward self-identity—becoming involved in center activities on their own.

You may need to help the clinging child get started, as mentioned previously, but then you should withdraw. Children need to have every opportunity to express their self-identities on their own. They need to explore the center environment. They need to learn to make their own choices.

It is very tempting for teachers to help children make decisions—and the children will listen. They will even ask for help. They are used to having adults tell them what to do. You must resist the temptation to do so. Invite them to look for themselves and then support them in their exploration. You may argue that it is so much simpler to make up their minds for them. But if you do, the children will have lost the opportunity to take the next step in their development as a person. Give them this chance.

If You Have Not Checked This Item: Some Helpful Ideas

■ Provide an Explorable Environment

For younger children your environment needs to be simple, with fewer activity areas and a small number of items within each. This applies especially to 2- and 3-year-olds. Some environments are just too complex for these children to be comfortable. Too many things are going on, and the children respond by refusing to explore or get involved. For this age group you need to simplify your physical environment—at least at the beginning of the year. Later the children will be ready for additional activities.

On the other hand, 4- and 5-year-olds need the stimulation of complexity, novelty, and variation. This age group tends to be less fearful of new things and more venturesome. For them a more complex physical environment may encourage rather than discourage exploration.

■ Give Children Time

Once children feel secure with you and your center they should be able to make activity choices on their own if you will give them enough time. Let them wander around at first during the free choice period. Don't force them into an activity before they are ready to participate. Some children need more time than others. Others need to try out many things before they can settle on one.

■ Act as a Base for Children's Explorations

Sit or stand in an area of the room where children can see you—near but not in any one activity area. Those who still need the security of an adult attachment can make eye contact, receive your smiles of support, and even come over for a moment or so before you encourage them to go off on their own again. The child who is still clinging can explore with his eyes. When he feels secure enough he will join the others, knowing you are nearby.

■ Read a Book

Hearing a book read about a nursery school classroom and all of the interesting activities it provides may motivate the insecure child to look around her own classroom and be more willing to make activity choices on her own. *Gwenda Turner's Playbook* (New York: Viking Kestrel/Penguin Books, 1985) is a beautifully illustrated picture book of nursery school children engaged in all sorts of fascinating play activities.

❏ SEEKS OTHER CHILDREN TO PLAY WITH

Although this particular item seems to relate more to the child's social rather than emotional development, it actually indicates both. Seeking other children to play with is a part of the progression of the developing self as well as a step in the sequence of socialization.

As the preschool child moves away from the parent to stay by himself in the early childhood classroom, and then as he moves away from the teacher to make activity choices on his own, his next step in the development of his self-identity should involve joining the other children in play. Yet he often does not join the others—at least not right away. Depending on his previous experience with peers—or lack of it—he may prefer to play on his own at first. In other words, other children do not replace a child's primary and secondary caregivers as objects of attachment. When children finally do seek other children to play with, it is indeed an indication of the development of a stronger self-identity.

Children seem to recognize that other children, like themselves, are dependent on adult caregivers. From their self-centered perspectives, in fact, children may see peers as competitors for the attention of the caregivers as well as for the use of materials and activities.

Through socialization they will be finding ways to get along with other children, as well as to share and take turns with materials—and even people—in your center. Through development of their self-identity children will eventually be seeking contact with others like themselves.

Even as infants and toddlers, children recognize one another and may engage in social behavior. But this contact is not at the same level, type, or intensity as their interactions with adults. The striving for attachment of infants and toddlers does not involve another child. Although an infant may look at, imitate, and even vocalize with peers, these interactions are few and far between and are not sustained for long periods. With adults, on the other hand, and especially with their mothers, infants' interactions involve touching, holding, and hugging during more instances, for longer periods, and at a more intense emotional level than anything they do with peers. The most frequent initial contact between two infants, in fact, takes place around toys rather than between one another (Damon, 1983, p. 59).

By the time the young child has entered your class he or she in most instances has had a number of contacts with peers. Again the interactions are not the same as with adults. Children look to the adult as their base of attachment. They look to their peers as a reflection of themselves. Those children with a strong sense of self will have less difficulty interacting with the other children in your center from the outset. They are indicating by this behavior how far along they are in the development of their self-identities.

Those who need help developing this sense of security within themselves may not seek other children to play with at first. As with the other areas of self-identity, you may need to help the children progress. Don't expect success to occur overnight in this particular area. Some children need many days or even weeks to make contact with peers. By looking at and treating each child in your center as an individual you will begin to elicit clues about each that can help you support his or her development in this crucial area. As before, you will need to use acceptance and patience whenever a child is slow to move ahead.

If You Have Not Checked This Item: Some Helpful Ideas

■ Find a Friend

For many young children who are used to dealing with a limited number of people at a time, a roomful of lively peers is overwhelming. You may need to help find a friend for the shy child who may be able to relate on a one-to-one basis with one other child before she can cope with a group. Choose someone who gets along with others and ask the two to do an errand for you—perhaps mix paints or play dough, wash the doll clothes, or get out the cots for nap time. Or you might ask the "friend" to show the shy child how to use the saw or how to record her voice on the tape recorder. Make the activities as personal as possible to attract the shy child's interest and get her to focus on the activity or material instead of on her unsure feelings about herself. Once she successfully relates to one other child, she may begin to seek others to play with on her own.

■ Read a Book

Will I Have a Friend? by Miriam Cohen (New York: Collier Books, 1971) is a children's picture book classic about Jim, who worries about finding a friend at nursery school on the first day. Read it to a small group that includes the shy child, and ask the children about their own feelings when they first came to your class. It may relieve the shy child to realize that other children share her feelings and that they, like Jim, will also be able to find a friend.

■ Use Small Groups

Young children are better able to relate to peers when in small groups. You can arrange the physical environment of your classroom so that each of the activity areas accommodates only a certain number of children (say, no more than four). Methods to accomplish this include placing four chairs around a table; using masking tape on the floor to divide the block corner into four building areas; providing only four aprons for water play, two saws or hammers for woodworking, three pillows in the book area, and so forth. When you read to the children, read to two, three or four rather than the total group.

■ Use a Material or Activity for Two or Three Together

This idea is more often used in European programs to teach children to share, but you might also design or designate a certain material or activity in your classroom as for use only by two or three children together. The use of a saw, for instance, can be set up for three—two to hold the wood and one to saw. You might attach one of your wagons to a trike so that one child must pedal while one rides. Your job chart of daily chores (which children choose or are assigned to) could require that pairs or teams work together to do the jobs. Can you think of other team enterprises?

❏ PLAYS ROLES CONFIDENTLY IN DRAMATIC PLAY

Once the young child has begun playing with others in your center you need to be cognizant of another indicator of his developing self-identity. Is he able to take on and play a role in the pretend situations that abound in early childhood programs? Can he pretend to be father or brother or baby in the housekeeping corner? Is he a nurse or doctor or famous skater in the dress-up area? Can he be a race car driver, helicopter pilot, or crane operator on the playground? When a child can play a pretend role with confidence in your center, then he is presenting observable proof that his self-identity has taken on an even more mature aspect.

In order to play a pretend role, children need to be able to see things from a different point of view from their own. Their perspective, in other words, cannot be egocentric. We mentioned how young children cover their eyes and think you cannot see them because they cannot see you. That view is, of course, totally egocentric. At some point in time, however, 3- and 4-year-olds seem to be able to step out of themselves and pretend quite realistically to be someone else.

It is not clear whether this ability is stronger or appears sooner in some children because of opportunity, encouragement, and practice at home, or whether certain children are instinctively or temperamentally more imaginative. But no matter what causes the behavior, it indicates to the observer of children that here is a child who has reached a milestone in his or her development of self-identity.

A child's ability to play a role other than her own says a number of things to the observer, including the following:

1. The child can distinguish reality from fantasy (i.e., she knows she is pretending).
2. The child is able to symbolize things (i.e., represent a real person or event in a make-believe manner).
3. The child can see things from another person's perspective.
4. The child has a strong enough sense of self to step out of herself and be someone else.

Until all four of these statements are true for the young child, she is really unable to play make-believe roles.

Once a child can perform this behavior, then she is able to explore in a wholly new way. She can try out roles. She can see what it's like to be the mother, the older sister, the baby. She can dominate the situation. She can make her father or brother do what she wants them to. This ability is a heady discovery. Of course, in a group situation she is often dominated or at least controlled to some extent by the others, and must remain in an assigned or assumed role. If she plays the role "wrong" then she will be reprimanded by those often strict conformists, her peers.

Adults in the early childhood classroom may wonder aloud: "Is this what we want our children to do? Isn't it wrong to encourage fantasizing like this?" Not at all, say child development specialists. This is a natural progression in the young child's development. This fantasizing is the way young children explore concepts about people and events in the world around them. Although adults look askance at the Walter Mitty–type who seems to live in a world of make-believe, it is not only natural but imperative that our children have the opportunity to use their imaginations playfully in exploring their own world. (See Chapter 14, "Imagination.")

Besides, this playful use of the imagination is the next step developmentally for the young child in his creation of a strong self-identity. He started as a new human being so attached to his mother that he thought she was a part of him. Then he made the separation in which he not only recognized he was separate, but also realized he could move out from her. Next he developed confidence enough to come to a new environment and allow other adults to be his caregivers. From these adults he moved out to explore his new environment and interact with his peers. Now he has developed a strong enough sense of himself that he can try out being someone else.

A great deal of power surrounds gaining control over people and situations, even imaginary ones. Until now the young child has been virtually powerless in a world controlled by adults. But when she plays a role in dramatic play, she is able to take a stand, be what she wants to be, and make things come out the way she wants them. Her self-identity is thus strengthened as she expands her horizons, gains control over ideas and feelings, and receives immediate feedback from the other players as to how her role affects them.

Also, in playing such pretend roles, the player gets to find out more about himself. The other children's reactions to his role and his own reactions to it help him realize his capabilities and understand his limits. He can explore gender roles more fully— what it's like to be male or female.

Children in our society are treated differently from the moment of birth, it seems, depending on their gender. In dramatic play the young pretender can try out being the mother, father, sister, or brother in the family. Because children often play these familiar family roles in a very stereotypical, exaggerated manner—their own interpretation of the way real family members act—the players soon learn which roles are considered the "best" and how the others feel about mothers and fathers, boys and girls.

For a child who did not participate in dramatic play upon first entering your program, now doing so signifies a major step. It means she not only has a strong enough sense of self to try being someone else, but she also now has this unparalleled opportunity to practice her budding interpersonal and communication skills, thus strengthening her self-identity in a manner that was impossible before. Again a paradox exists. Once she is able to be someone else, she becomes more of herself.

If You Have Not Checked This Item: Some Helpful Ideas

■ Provide Dramatic Play Materials

Set up at least one area of your classroom for dramatic play. This section can be a family area with child-size table, chairs, refrigerator, stove, and sink; a bedroom area with doll beds, dresser and mirror, and chest of drawers; a store with shelves of empty food containers and a toy cash register; or any other such setting. If you take your class on a field trip, you should consider setting up a similar pretend area in your room (for them to try out the roles they saw enacted on the trip)—a doctor's office, a clinic, a laundromat, a barber or beauty shop.

In addition to life-size settings and props, you need miniature toys to encourage role-playing as well. Little cars, trucks, people, animals, boats, and planes can be placed strategically in the block corner, at the water table, and with the table blocks. A box full of dramatic play props can be taken out on the playground. Pictures of people in a variety of roles —from family members to community helpers—can be hung at children's eye level around the room to encourage the exploration of roles. Ask the children what kinds of roles they would like to try out and have them help you assemble the props. Books such as *Be What You Want to Be* by Phyllis and Noel Fiarotta (1977) are full of ideas for making your own props from discarded material.

■ Allow Time to Pretend

Because the best dramatic play is spontaneous—even though you may have provided the props—you need to set aside a particular time during the day for free choice activities to occur. Often these activities are scheduled at the beginning of the day, but they can take place any time. Allow enough time for children to become involved in their roles. The amount may vary from day to day depending upon the children's interests and yours, but free choice activities should be scheduled to occur at the same time every day so that the children can depend upon a set period for pretending and playing roles.

■ Play a Role Yourself

Sometimes the only way to help the nonparticipant to become involved is to play a role yourself. Obviously, if a child is not ready emotionally, your efforts may be wasted. But some children who are ready to play a role may not know how to get started. In that case you might pretend to be a mother and invite the child to go on a pretend errand with you, ending up in the dramatic play area where the other children are often delighted to see the teacher playing as they are. If the child accepts your lead and becomes involved with the others, you can gradually withdraw.

■ Be an Observer of Pretend Play

It will help you immensely in your understanding of children if you take time out to observe and record the various children's engagement in pretend play. Station yourself unobtrusively in an area of the room where a particular child is playing and jot down as many details as possible in a running record. Do this for several days if possible. Some of the things to look for can include

1. theme of the play
2. role the child is playing
3. who else is playing and what their roles are
4. type of interaction with other children
5. dialogue
6. length of time the child sustains the role

What can you conclude about the child from your observations? Have you learned anything that can help you plan your program differently so that other children will become more easily involved in dramatic play? Could you add props or suggestions to help the children sustain their play? Chapter 14, "Imagination," provides additional suggestions.

❏ STANDS UP FOR OWN RIGHTS

In order for preschool children to stand up for their rights within the classroom, they need to have developed a strong enough self-identity to believe in themselves as individuals with a point of view worth other people's consideration. Thus far in their development of a self-identity they have been able to make the separation from their parents, not cling to the adult caregiver, make eye contact with classroom adults, choose activities on their own, seek other children to play with, and try out roles confidently in dramatic play because they could see things from another person's point of view. Now the children are progressing further by developing their own points of view worthy of other children's consideration.

What are some of the classroom rights such a self-confident child might insist on? One is the right of possession. If a child is playing with a piece of equipment, he should be able to continue using it unless some previous turn-taking rule is in effect. Many childhood squabbles take place over objects, often because of children's egocentric perspectives. A child feels he should have a toy because he wants it. The fact that another child is playing with it does not count in his mind. The development of mutual respect is difficult among 3- and 4-year-olds, because so many of them lack the ability to understand the other's perspective (Berndt, 1982, p. 255). The child who feels his right is worth defending will often refuse to give in.

A child's choice of participation is another personal right often established in early childhood classrooms. If a child opts to join or not join a particular activity, you and the other children need to honor that choice. Use enticements rather than force if you feel the child should be involved when he or she chooses not to be.

Completing independent projects their own way is a right that self-confident children will defend. If a child is painting, modeling clay, constructing a building, or dressing a doll on her own, she should be able to do it as she sees fit so long as she is not interfering with others. In like manner, others should not be allowed to interfere with her. The child with a strong self-identity will continue in her own fashion, disregarding or rejecting the attempts of others to impose their will.

Protecting property is another right that self-confident children will insist on. Toys or games they have brought from home are often the focus of conflict. You need to provide a private space like a cubby for each child to store his possessions. Block buildings are also important to the children who have built them. The child who insists on saving his building may want help in making a sign informing others: Please Leave Jeffrey's Building Standing.

Children may stand up for their own rights in a number of ways. They may physically prevent another child from doing something or making them do something. They may verbalize their position with the child. They may tell the teacher. Some of their actions may not even be acceptable in a classroom full of children. Use of power or aggression is of course not appropriate. You need to help such children find more acceptable means for making their point.

As you observe your children on this particular item, look to see which ones do not allow another child to urge or force unwanted changes on them and which ones do not back down or give up a toy or a turn. At the same time, take note of children who always give up or give in to the demands of another. They also need your support in the strengthening of their self-confidence.

If You Have Not Checked This Item: Some Helpful Ideas

■ Model Behavior

You need to model the behavior you want your children to follow. Stand firmly on decisions you have made. Let your children know why. If you are wishy-washy or inconsistent in your treatment of them, they may have trouble standing firmly themselves.

■ Allow Children Choices

One way to help children learn that their rights can count is to give them a chance to make choices that are important to them. Let them choose a favorite activity to participate in or a toy to take home.

■ Stand Up for the Child

When it is clear to you that a child's rights have been infringed upon by another child, you should take a stand yourself, supporting the child and at the same time letting the others know why—for example, why Karen can finish her painting now and Bobby can't.

❑ DISPLAYS ENTHUSIASM ABOUT DOING THINGS FOR SELF

The lifelong quest to develop an identity is, in the final analysis, a struggle for autonomy. If young children are successful in this quest, then they will be able and willing to behave independently in many ways. Louise J. Kaplan (1978) describes the importance of the struggle:

> In the first three years of life every human being undergoes yet a second birth, in which he is born as a psychological being possessing selfhood and separate identity. The quality of self an infant achieves in those crucial three years will profoundly affect all of his subsequent existence. (p. 15)

Your observations in the area of self-identity will have helped you determine which children in your class are well on the road to developing strong self-identities and which ones are not. The most successful children will be those who can and want to do things for themselves. They will have achieved enough self-assurance about their own abilities to be able to try and eventually succeed in doing things on their own. Achieving this competence will then allow them a measure of independence from the adults around them.

What are some of the activities you may observe such children perform independently in your classroom? Here is a partial list:

Dressing and undressing	Painting with brush
Tying or fastening shoes	Mixing paints
Using own cubby	Getting out toys
Toileting	Putting toys away
Washing hands and face	Returning blocks to shelves
Brushing teeth	Dressing dolls
Setting table for eating	Handling hammer, saw
Pouring drink	Cutting with scissors
Dishing out food	Cutting with knife
Handling eating implements	Mixing dough
Eating	Using climbing equipment
Cleaning up after eating	Making puzzles

The adeptness level of 3- and 4-year-old children in these various activities depends on their own sense of self, the practice they have had at home or elsewhere, and the encouragement or discouragement the adults around them have offered. This author has noticed that children from low-income families are often more adept at accomplishing many of the self-help skills than children from middle- and upper-income families. We might infer that children in low-income families have had to do many self-help activities on their own and thus have become skilled sooner than their middle- and upper-income counterparts.

In like manner, children who have always had things done for them by the adults around them often give up the struggle for autonomy. You and your co-workers need to beware of the temptation to "help" the little children in your care more than necessary. Children can do many more things for themselves than we realize. You need to allow time for children to learn to zip jackets and pour their own drinks. Otherwise you are denying them an unparalleled opportunity to develop their own independence.

The way adults behave toward children during these formative years can indeed make a difference in children's feelings about themselves and thus in the way they behave. Research regarding gender stereotyping has found that mothers and fathers treat their young daughters differently from their sons when it comes to independent behavior. Parents often allow and encourage boys to behave independently earlier than girls in such areas as using scissors without adult supervision, crossing the street alone, playing away from home, and riding the bus. When girls ask for help they often get it, but boys more often receive a negative response. Boys are encouraged to manipulate objects and explore their environments, whereas girls are more often discouraged. Thus it *seems* that parents value independence in boys more than in girls (Brooks-Gunn & Matthews, 1979, pp. 145–146).

This type of discriminating behavior may of course result in girls feeling less capable than boys and therefore attempting fewer things on their own. Or this behavior may cause girls—and therefore women—to become dependent on men and less willing to risk using their own capabilities.

You and your co-workers need to take special care that stereotypical attitudes about the roles of men and women do not color your behavior toward the boys and girls in your center. As in all areas of development, your goal should be to help each child become all he or she is capable of being. When all the children show enthusiasm about doing things independently, then you know they are well on their way to developing a strong sense of self-identity.

If You Have Not Checked This Item: Some Helpful Ideas

■ Assess Your Center for "Independent" Possibilities

What can children do on their own in your center? It gives them great satisfaction to accomplish difficult tasks. Walk around your physical area and make a list of things that children can do. Some items that can go on your daily job chart for individuals or teams to choose can include

Feeding the rabbit	Taking own attendance
Cleaning the aquarium	Getting out playground toys
Watering the plants	Sweeping the floor
Scraping carrots for snack	Sponging off the tables
Delivering mail to the office	Getting out cots for naptime

■ Encourage Performance of Self-Help Skills

Teach children how to tie their shoes when their small motor coordination allows them this capability. Or have another child help them get started with buttons or zippers or Velcro tabs. Allow enough time for even the slowest child to perform this task on his or her own.

■ Help Children Get Started

Sometimes the first step is all a child needs to start her on her way to independence. Sit next to the child who tells you she can't make the puzzle and put in a piece yourself. Then ask her to look for the next one. Stay with her until she completes the puzzle if need be. Then ask her to try it again on her own. Give her positive verbal support all the way, but refrain from helping this time.

■ Read a Book

There are many picture books about individual children doing things on their own. Read one such as *I Can Do It By Myself* by Lessie Jones Little and Eloise Greenfield (New York: Crowell, 1978) to a small group of children. The story is about Donny who has to overcome a number of problems in order to buy his mother a plant for her birthday—all by himself.

■ Be Enthusiastic

Enthusiasm always scores very high on lists of the characteristics of successful teachers. You as a behavior model in your classroom need always to be enthusiastic and positive about everything you do. If children see you acting on your own with vigor, they will be encouraged to do likewise.

OBSERVING, RECORDING, AND INTERPRETING SELF-IDENTITY

Self-identity was chosen as the first topic on the *Child Skills Checklist* because this is the first area of child development that you as a teacher should be concerned with when you meet new children in your center for the first time. In order to determine how children feel about themselves in their new environment and which children may need help in making the transition from home to school, you may want to observe and record the behaviors of all of the children in your class at one time.

To do this, list the names of the children down the left side of one sheet of paper and the checklist items along the top. Draw lines horizontally and vertically to section off the names and items. Now you can mark the items you have seen each child performing under "Self-Identity." When you find a number of blank spaces for a particular child, you may want to observe this child more closely, using the entire *Checklist*.

You will then be able to design a learning prescription for the particular child, as was done for Sheila in Chapter 2 (Figure 2.9). The *Checklist* results will tell you which areas of strength and confidence the child displays, as well as which areas needing strengthening should be addressed. Then you can begin planning for the individual by listing several activities to help the child based on his or her strengths. Such activities can come from your own repertoire or from those suggested in the chapter.

Be sure that observation of such children is an ongoing process in your center. Do a follow-up of children who seem to need special help. Has your learning prescription been helpful? Did the activities you planned really help this child? Share your observations with your classroom team and with the child's parents. Ask them to make similar observations. Include their ideas in your individual plan for each child.

REFERENCES

Ainsworth, M. D. S., S. M. Bell, & D. J. Stayton. (1974). Infant-mother attachment and social development: "Socialization" as a product of reciprocal responsiveness to signals. In M. M. Richards (Ed.), *The integration of a child into a social world.* London: Cambridge University Press.

Berndt, Thomas J. (1982). Fairness and friendship. In Kenneth W. Rubin & Hildy S. Ross (Eds.), *Peer relationships and social skills in childhood* (pp. 253–278). New York: Springer-Verlag.

Bowlby, John. (1969). *Attachment and loss: Vol. 1. Attachment.* New York: Basic Books.

Bowlby, John. (1973). *Attachment and loss: Vol. 2. Separation anxiety and anger.* New York: Basic Books.

Brooks-Gunn, Jeanne, & Wendy Schempp Matthews. (1979). *He and she: How children develop their sex-role identity.* Englewood Cliffs, NJ: Prentice-Hall.

Damon, William. (1983). *Social and personality development: Infancy through adolescence.* New York: Norton.

Fein, Greta, & Pamela M. Schwartz. (1982). Development theories in early education. In Bernard Spodek (Ed.), *Handbook of research in early childhood education* (pp. 82–104). New York: Free Press.

Fiarotta, Phyllis, & Noel Fiarotta. (1977). *Be what you want to be.* New York: Workman.

Gottschall, Sue. (1989). Understanding and accepting separation feelings. *Young Children,* 44(6), 11–16.

Kaplan, Louise J. (1978). *Oneness and separateness: From infant to individual.* New York: Simon & Schuster.

Seagull, Elizabeth A. W., & David J. Kallen. (1978). Normal social and emotional development of the preschool-age child. In Norbert B. Enzer with Kennith W. Goin (Eds.), *Social and emotional development: The preschooler (pp. 3–46).* New York: Walker.

Thompson, James J. (1973). *Beyond words: Nonverbal communication in the Classroom.* New York: Citation Press.

OTHER SOURCES

Balaban, Nancy. (1985). *Starting school: From separation to independence, a guide for early childhood teachers.* New York: Teachers College Press.

Balaban, Nancy. (1987). *Learning to say goodbye: Starting school and other early childhood separations.* New York: New American Library.

Beaty, Janice J. (1992). *Skills for preschool teachers.* New York: Merrill/Macmillan.

Briggs, Dorothy Corkille. (1970). *Your child's self-esteem.* Garden City, NY: Doubleday.

Solomon, Judith, & Carol George. (1990). *Conflict and attachment: The experience of disorganized/controlling children.* Paper presented at the International Conference on Infant Studies, Montreal. (ERIC Document Reproduction Service No. ED 319 496, pp. 1–15)

LEARNING ACTIVITIES

1. Observe all of the children in your classroom each morning of the first week of school, using the items in the Self-Identity Checklist as a screening device (as mentioned under the last topic in this chapter, "Observing, Recording, and Interpreting Self-Identity"). Note which children can separate without difficulty from their parents and which children cannot. Make a written learning prescription for a particular child to help him or her overcome this initial anxiety. Discuss the plan with your supervisor and then implement it. Discuss the results.

2. Choose a child who seems to have difficulty getting involved with other children or activities. Make a running record of everything the child does or says during three different

arrival periods. Transfer this information to the *Child Skills Checklist* under "Self-Identity." How do you interpret the evidence you have collected? Can you make any conclusions yet about this child?

3. Meet with one or more parents of children in your classroom. Discuss how children develop their self-identities, and give the parents ideas that can be used at home to help strengthen their child's self-concept. Ask them for suggestions about how they would like you to work with their child.

4. Observe a child playing a role in dramatic play for three days. Keep a running record of everything the child does or says. Pay special attention to the things to look for discussed in this chapter under the heading, "Plays Roles Confidently in Dramatic Play." Can you make any conclusions about the child's self-identity based on these observations?

5. Choose a child for whom you have checked "Displays enthusiasm in regard to doing things for self." Observe this child during the first half hour of class for three days. Which of the other items can you check for this child based on your observations? What is your evidence for each check mark? What conclusions can you make about this child based on these observations?

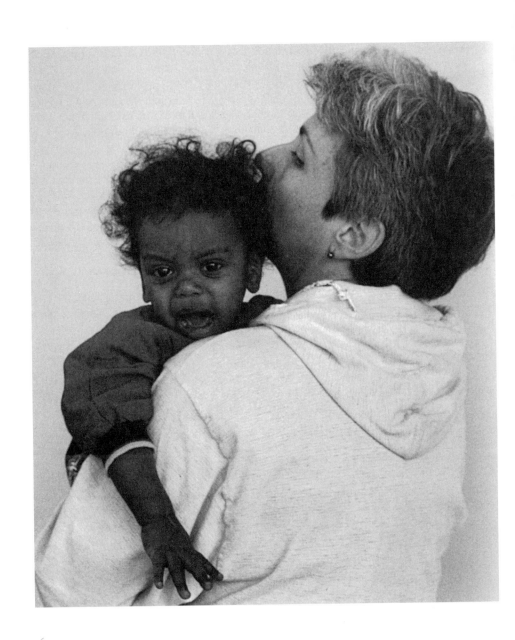

4 Emotional Development

Emotional Development Checklist

❑ Allows self to be comforted during stressful time
❑ Eats, sleeps, toilets without fuss away from home
❑ Handles sudden changes/startling situations with control
❑ Can express anger in words rather than actions
❑ Allows aggressive behavior to be redirected
❑ Does not withdraw from others excessively
❑ Shows interest/attention in classroom activities
❑ Smiles, seems happy much of the time

The emotional development of the preschool child is somehow different from other developmental aspects. True, emotional growth happens simultaneously with physical, social, cognitive, language, and creative development and is interdependent upon them. But it seems as if the youngsters do not stay developed, or, rather, that they must repeat the same sequences of emotional development over and over until they get it right—throughout life.

In some respects this observation is true. Emotional development does have a physical and cognitive basis for its expression, but once the basic human abilities are in place, emotions are much more situational in their appearance.

If we agree that emotions are certain particular reactions to specific stimuli, then we note that these reactions may not change much in a developmental sense over a person's lifetime. Many of us get red in the face when we are angry and cry when we are sad, both as infants and as adults. In other words, it is the situation—the stimulus—rather than our development that seems to govern our emotional responses.

Actually, emotional development is even more complex. Whereas physical and cognitive development seem to be based on *nature* and *nurture* and their interaction—that is, the genetic traits children inherit plus the environment in which they are raised—emotions have three internally interacting dimensions:

1. the conscious feeling or emotional experience
2. the process in the brain and nervous system
3. the observable expressive patterns or reactions (Izard, 1977, p. 4)

Obviously, the brain and nervous system, because they are physical, can exhibit inherited traits. But can emotions themselves be inherited and then develop through maturation and surroundings just like the ability to think? Many psychologists have trouble accepting the idea that emotions are at all biological and based on maturity. However, scientists have to admit that certain emotional responses—separation anxiety, for instance—occur at about the same time and for the same reasons in infants and toddlers around the world. Similarly, other types of emotions seem to trigger universal *fight* or *flight* responses in adults.

Psychologists studying universal responses talk in terms of the functions of emotions (how they help the human species to adapt and survive). These scientists note that certain emotions that trigger necessary survival responses in infants have outlived their usefulness when they occur in older children and adults. The acute distress felt by the infant and expressed in tears or screams when mother leaves the home, for example, has outlived its usefulness if it is a daily occurrence for a 4-year-old when mother leaves him at the child-care center. Although such basic emotions seem to serve in helping to preserve the self or the species, the higher emotions serve social purposes, and their appropriate responses must be learned.

Thus we should focus on the response—not the emotion itself—when we speak of emotional development in preschool children. And what most concerns us is not the development, but the control of the response. In the areas of physical and mental development we want the young child to grow, mature, and extend his abilities to the utmost. With emotional development we want the child to learn to make appropriate emotional responses, and especially to control negative responses. An emotionally disturbed child is, after all, often one who is out of control.

This chapter, then, looks at observable emotional responses of young children in eight different areas, each followed by suggestions for improving the child's behavior if the particular item is not demonstrated. Each of the checklist items refers to a particular emotion. It should be noted, however, that the order in which the items are listed is not a developmental sequence, because sequence as such does not seem to be an important factor in emotional development.

Many psychologists recognize either 8 or 10 basic emotions and their combinations. These are sometimes listed as interest-excitement, enjoyment-joy, surprise-startle, distress-anguish, anger-rage, disgust-revulsion, contempt-scorn, fear-terror, shame/shyness-humiliation, guilt-remorse (Izard, 1977, p. 46). The emotional responses of preschool children seem to be involved principally with the following seven emotions (plus one response):

1. distress
2. fear
3. surprise
4. anger
5. aggression (a response)
6. shyness
7. interest
8. joy

In order to help children develop emotionally, the preschool teacher should be concerned with promoting positive emotions and helping the children to control negative emotions. Although techniques to accomplish this control may vary depending upon the emotion and the situation, the following four strategies can be used to control negative emotions:

1. Remove or reduce the cause of the emotion.
2. Diffuse the child's negative reaction by allowing him to "let it out" through crying, talking, or transferring his feelings into nondestructive actions.
3. Offer support, comfort, and ideas for self-control.
4. Model controlled behavior yourself.

Your goal for the children should be the same as in the other aspects of their development—for them to gain self-control. In order to help children acquire this control, you first need to find out where they stand in their present development. Do they exhibit crying, whining, or complaining much of the time? Do they ever smile? Do they show anger or aggression toward others? The *Child Skills Checklist* lists eight representative items of emotional behavior of children 3 through 5 years of age in early childhood programs. Observe the children in your class to determine which ones have accomplished the emotional self-control described in the checklist. Children who have not exhibited these checklist behaviors may benefit from the ideas and suggestions discussed in the remainder of the chapter.

❏ ALLOWS SELF TO BE COMFORTED DURING STRESSFUL TIME

Distress

Children who do not allow themselves to be comforted during stressful times are often exhibiting the emotion known as distress. At its lower extreme, distress may result from physical discomfort due to pain, extremes of temperature, or noise; at its upper level, distress may take the form of anguish, grief, or depression due to the loss of a loved one. A basic cause of distress throughout life is physical or psychological separation, especially from a loved one. Children who perceive themselves as having been abandoned by an adult, even when this is not true, experience the same emotions as children who actually have been abandoned.

Children express distress by crying, whining, or showing a sad face. Sometimes they cling to an adult caregiver. Distressed children may feel uncomfortable, disappointed, lonely, sad, or rejected.

Distress is not the most severe negative emotion found in children, therefore adults do not always take it seriously. They should. Distress is an indication that all is not well with a child. Failure to reduce the distress or its causes over a period of time tends to break down the child's trust in adults. Furthermore, she may learn to become unsympathetic to others who are distressed because that is the way she has been treated.

Every human being endures the initial distress of the birth experience, which is not only a physical discomfort but also a separation ordeal in the extreme. As such, birth is greeted with lusty crying by the distressed infant. Psychologists feel that distress, whenever it occurs, thus serves as a warning to others that something is wrong with this person and something should be done about it. Because it is concerned with separation, distress also seems to serve as a device to keep one's group (e.g., family, clan) together (Izard, 1977, p. 293).

What are the principal causes of distress in the child-care center? For many youngsters the separation from their primary caregiver is the most stressful. Discomfort or pain from a physical cause, rejection by peers, dissatisfaction with a performance, and lack of a skill are other causes of distress. A stressful situation in the family, such as the birth of a new baby, a death, a hospitalization, a move, or a divorce, may also be carried over into classroom behavior by the child who is disturbed by it.

The Teacher's Role

How can you help? Your principal role in the children's emotional development should be to help them master their feelings. You should not be the controlling device yourself, but instead you should help them find a way to control their feelings from within. Adults are often tempted to take control of an emotional situation. Young children, in fact, look to you to solve the emotional problems that so often are overwhelming. *You do children a disservice if you comply.* Your role should be that of a facilitator, not a controller. Otherwise, without you, the children will be no better off the next time the emotional situation occurs. As with all other aspects of development, your overall goal for children should be the development of their emotional independence, in other words, emotional self-control.

Although the particular situation may determine your response, distress most often requires that you first of all give comfort to the child. She is upset and uncomfortable; she may be whining or crying. You can show your concern through comforting words and actions such as holding or hugging.

Requiring a child to stop crying right away is not usually the way to approach helping him master his emotions. Venting through tears is after all a catharsis. He may feel that you are not sympathetic to his plight if you insist he stop crying. He may in fact stop on his own when he hears your comforting words or feels your touch. Recent studies have found that crying is not only of therapeutic value psychologically, but also physically. Chemical toxins that build up during stress are released in tears. Even blood pressure, pulse rate, and body temperature seem to be lowered by crying (Frey & Langseth, 1985). As psychologist Aletha Solter points out:

> Crying is not the hurt, but the process of becoming unhurt. . . .A child who has been allowed to cry as long as needed will feel happier and more secure at school, in the long run, than a child who has been repeatedly distracted from her feelings. (Solter, 1992, p. 66)

Once the child can verbalize, she can begin to take charge of her emotions. She may be able to tell you what happened or how she feels. This is the first step toward self-mastery of emotions. She might even be able to tell you what would make her feel better.

If the situation is too overwhelming for a child to stop crying or to verbalize his feelings, your best strategy may be to redirect his attention *when the time seems right*. This means after he has stopped crying. If he was injured on one leg, perhaps you can get him to show you the other leg. How does it look? How does he think it feels? Maybe together you can do something to make the injured leg feel like the uninjured one. Distress, then, can often be relieved when you

1. give comfort
2. allow child to cry
3. redirect attention
4. help the child to verbalize

As for mastering distress so that it will not happen again, this is probably not possible and certainly not appropriate. Distress may be relieved and perhaps controlled, but not completely mastered. Nor should we want it to be. Distress is a necessary symptom signaling that all is not well with the individual. In your child-care program, you should hope to help relieve—not prevent—distress in a child. If you are successful, then a distraught child will allow herself to be comforted or redirected. But if her sense of self is not strong enough or if the distress is too overwhelming, she may not even allow this. What can you do to help such a child?

If You Have Not Checked This Item: Some Helpful Ideas

■ Hold and Rock

It's a good idea to have an adult-size rocking chair in your center. Sometimes the best help for a distraught child is to hold and rock him.

■ Have the Child Hold a Huggable Toy

A child is often comforted by holding something soft. That is why toddlers carry "security blankets." Your center should have cuddly stuffed animals or similar toys available, not only for play but also for stressful situations. The child who does not allow you to comfort her may help herself by holding such a toy. Be sure the toy is washable so it can be cleaned for use by other children.

■ Use a Material with Soothing Properties

Water play and finger painting are activities with soothing qualities. Distressed children can take out their frustrations by moving paint around a surface with their hands or by swishing water, thus transferring their negative energy in a harmless fashion.

■ Have the Child Talk to a Puppet

Again, verbalizing negative feelings is one of the best ways for defusing and controlling them. You could designate one of the puppets in your room as a "feelings" puppet and keep it in a special place for the times when children are feeling sad or upset.

They can talk to the puppet about how they feel and ask the puppet how it feels. Model the use of this puppet yourself when upsetting occasions arise so that the children can follow your lead.

■ Read a Book

Sometimes distraught children will allow you to read a favorite book to them. Or you could keep particular books for them to look at on their own during troubling times. The following books are especially suitable for stressful situations.

Feelings

Sometimes I Like to Cry by Elizabeth and Henry Stanton (Chicago: Whitman, 1978) is about Joey, a little boy who smiles and laughs at his cat, frog, and brother, but sometimes cries when he cuts a finger, is not invited to a party, or experiences the death of his hamster.

My Dad Takes Care of Me by Patricia Quilan (Toronto: Annick Press, 1987) tells the story of Paul and his dad, who is out of work and staying home to take care of Paul. Emotions are expressed, including the father's crying, but the loving, accepting atmosphere makes it an upbeat story.

Separation

Sarah loses her doll, Abigail, in the shopping mall and Mama loses Sarah in *Don't Worry, I'll Find You* by Anna Grossnickle Hines (New York: Dutton, 1986). But the lost ones stay put as directed and are finally found.

In *My Mom Travels a Lot* by Caroline Feller Bauer (New York: Warne, 1981), the little girl narrator lists all the good things and bad things about her mom's traveling, the best being: "She always comes back!"

In *Friday Night Is Papa Night* by Ruth A. Sonneborn (New York: Puffin Books, 1970), Pedro, a little Hispanic boy, waits with apprehension for his businessman father to come home on the weekend, which he finally does.

In the large, colorfully illustrated *At the Crossroads* by Rachel Isadora (New York: Greenwillow Books, 1991), South African black boys wait all night at the crossroads for their fathers to come back from 10 months of working in the mines.

Moving

In *Maggie Doesn't Want to Move* by Elizabeth Lee O'Donnel (New York: Macmillan, 1987), little Simon complains to his mother, giving all the reasons why his baby sister, Maggie, doesn't want to move. But when the family arrives at their new location Simon (and Maggie) finally accepts the move.

Moving Gives Me a Stomach Ache by Heather McKend (Windsor, Ontario: Black Moss Press, 1980) reveals how a boy must pack his toys to move and tries to joke about it because he feels bad. Older children (5- and 6-year-olds) might understand the humor better.

The Leaving Morning by Angela Johnson and David Soman (1992) is a wonderfully illustrated story about an inner-city African-American boy and his sister who are saying good-bye to their friends in their apartment building and neighborhood on the morning they move.

Death

The Tenth Good Thing About Barney by Judith Viorst (New York: Atheneum, 1971) is about a sad little boy whose cat, Barney, dies. The boy's mother tries to comfort him by having him think of 10 good things to say about Barney when they bury him in the backyard.

My Grandson Lew by Charlotte Zolotow (New York: Harper & Row, 1974) is a touching story about 6-year-old Lewis who misses his deceased grandfather. Lewis finally shares memories of his grandfather with his mother.

Nana Upstairs & Nana Downstairs by Tomie de Paola (New York: Putnam, 1973) is the story of Tommy, who makes visits to his grandmother and great-grandmother in the same house where one lives one floor above the other. When the great-grandmother dies, Tommy's mother comforts him by telling him that his great-grandmother will come back in his memory whenever he thinks about her.

❑ EATS, SLEEPS, TOILETS WITHOUT FUSS AWAY FROM HOME

Fear (Anxiety)

Children who have difficulty eating, falling asleep, or using the toilet in your center generally behave this way because of tension. This tension is most often produced by anxiety, which is one of the most common expressions of fear.

Fear first appears as an emotion in the second half of the first year of infancy, according to many psychologists. Somewhere between 5 and 9 months of age, babies begin to recognize an unfamiliar face and are afraid of it. Before that point, their physical and cognitive development have not progressed to where they can distinguish between friend and stranger. After that recognition occurs, infants see unfamiliar faces as a possible threat—until they learn differently.

Thus, the emotion fear is caused by the presence of something threatening or the absence of safety and security (Izard, 1977, p. 356). Fear may result when the possibility of potential harm appears, when a strange person, object, or situation is confronted, and when specific fright-producing elements—heights, the dark, thunderstorms, particular animals such as dogs and snakes—are present. When humans are afraid they feel anxious and alarmed. They may tremble, cower, hide, run away, cling to someone, or cry, depending on their degree of fright. They often seek protection.

Fear is in some ways age related. Young children are generally not afraid of heights, the dark, or animals much before their second year. It is as though they really don't know enough to be frightened before then. As they grow older, children add new fears to their repertoire and drop some of the old ones. Fear, like distress, seems to serve as a warning signal for the human species: Reduce the threat or seek protection. When this warning feeling persists but is no longer useful to the young human, you as a child-care worker need to intervene.

We know of course that extreme fear can be paralyzing, but we need to realize that even lesser fears like anxiety produce tension of some sort: a tightening up of the body and the mind. Anxiety "is the most constricting of all the emotions" (Izard, 1977, p. 365). The anxious person has trouble relaxing and feeling at ease in tense situations and in unfamiliar settings that somehow pose a threat.

For young children used to the security of home, the early childhood classroom can be such a tense setting at first, no matter how relaxing and nonthreatening you have made it. Some children may view the setting as a threat for three reasons: (a) The setting is unfamiliar, (b) they lack initial trust in the setting and the people there, and (c) their parents or caregivers have left them.

Most children display some anxiety when they first experience an early childhood classroom. It is a natural reaction to being left in a strange place. But if they have a strong enough sense of self and sense of trust in the world and the people around them, the children should soon come to feel perfectly at ease in your center. For children who do not achieve this sense of ease, you may need to provide special attention in order to help them overcome their anxiety.

The routine functions of eating, sleeping, and toileting and how they are carried out can often provide the careful observer with clues concerning who is at ease in the classroom and who is not. Because these routines are of such a personal nature and so closely connected with the home and the primary caregiver, eating, sleeping, and toileting are deeply significant to the child. From her earliest memories she is used to having her mother feed her or help her to feed herself. She expects her mother to tuck her in and kiss her goodnight. She is at ease in using the toilet—a rather formidable piece of equipment for a young child—in her own home, because she has learned it will not flush her away.

Suddenly the child is thrust into a new and unfamiliar environment where these very personal processes are to be directed by strangers. Even the most secure and experienced young explorer may have moments of anxiety in the beginning. Anxiety produces tension in which muscles actually tighten up, whether or not the tense person is aware of it. Unless the tense child is able to relax, he or she may certainly experience difficulty in eating, falling asleep, or using the toilet.

The anxious child in your classroom may not have difficulty with all three of these acts. One or the other may be more meaningful in his life at home and thus cause more problems for him away from home. His difficulty may also have causes other than anxiety. A health problem, for instance, could also cause a disruption in his normal functioning. However, if a child exhibits persistent difficulty in eating, sleeping, or toileting at any time while he is in your care, the cause may be anxiety and the child may need your help to overcome the negative effects of this emotion.

Eating

Eating is the act most closely connected with the child's mother. From babyhood when he nursed at his mother's breast or was held close to her while being bottle-fed, the child not only received life-sustaining nourishment but also comfort and love. It is not surprising then, that he makes a connection between food and comfort. Later as he is weaned from breast or bottle and learns to take solid food, he may perceive this either as a happy experience or a battle of wills. By the time he enters your center the child has had at least 3 years of experience with the emotional nature of eating. You hope this has been positive. But no matter what, you need to make sure eating is a positive experience for the child in your program.

Once you are aware of the emotional nature of eating and how a child's anxiety can interfere with his eating habits, you will be better prepared to deal with children who refuse to eat. Be sure at the outset that your meals take place in an atmosphere of friendliness and relaxation. Are meals served family style in your classroom around small group tables? School cafeterias are too large, noisy, impersonal, and rushed for children this young. If you have been assigned to a cafeteria, talk with the supervisor in order to explain the needs of young children; ask whether the food could be carried to your room instead.

Do you eat at the table with the children? It is important in family style eating that a member of the staff sit at each table to converse informally with the children, answering their questions about the food and assisting them in their own pouring and serving. Help the children take a little of everything. If their portions are too large, they may not even want to begin. Involving them with their own dishing out and passing of the food, however, is a physical step that psychologically connects them to eating.

What about rules concerning food? Mealtime should be pleasant and relaxing. Too many rules about portions, second helpings, and dessert may create tension even in relaxed children. Is withholding of dessert used as a punishment for children who have misbehaved? No matter how food is used in the homes of your children, it should never be used in a punitive manner in your center. All of the food served, including dessert, should be nutritious, appealing, and available to all of the children all of the time.

Are you a good eating model yourself? Practice what you preach is a cliché worth repeating when it comes to eating. Your children should see that you take a reasonable-sized portion of each food, eat all your food, talk about how good it tastes, ask politely for seconds if this is appropriate, refrain from nagging, and make positive comments about the children who have cleaned up their plates.

If You Have Not Checked This Item: Some Helpful Ideas

■ Refrain from Pressure

Do not use force or pressure to get a reluctant child to eat. Force probably will not work anyway, but more importantly, it will certainly not reduce the anxiety and tension that may be the cause of a refusal to eat in the first place. All attempts to resolve the problem should be positive in nature, aimed at removing or reducing the cause of the negative emotion and helping the child to gain inner control over her reactions. Sometimes patience alone is the only solution. When the child feels at ease in your program, she will eat.

■ **Talk with Parents**

Ask parents what they expect of their child and what they hope he will gain from your program. Talk about food habits and how the child eats at home. But be aware that the basic problem may not be food but anxiety and how the child reacts to it. Is the child under pressure at home? How does he react to pressure? How can you and the parents relieve him of this pressure?

■ **Read a Book**

Perhaps a lighthearted approach will work to encourage eating. If you think the reluctant eater can deal with food in a playful manner, you might try reading together one of the following books:

Gregory, the Terrible Eater by Mitchell Sharmat (New York: Scholastic, 1980) is the story of little goat Gregory who will not eat the goat food his mother serves (tin cans, rugs, bottle caps). He only wants fruits, vegetables, and eggs—"Good stuff like that." When junk food gets too much for him, he and his family finally reach a compromise.

Bread and Jam for Frances by Russell Hoban (New York: Scholastic, 1964) is the classic story of little girl badger Frances who only wants to eat bread and jam—until she finds out that is all her family will serve her.

Sleeping

If the children spend all day in your center, then you must provide them with a nap period in the afternoon. For some children this is a welcome relief from the exuberant activites of the morning. They welcome the chance to rest and will promptly fall asleep. For others, naptime is a time of tossing and turning, whispering and squirming, disturbing other children and the teacher. Some may be children who have outgrown naptime. Others may be so wound up they need to relax before they can fall asleep. A few may be the anxious children we have been discussing, who cannot fall asleep because of tension.

First of all, you need to prepare all of your children for naptime. They can help to get out the cots or mats. They can choose their own area of the room to sleep in. They need to know that when the lights are turned out or the curtains pulled, it is time to close their eyes. You might try playing dreamy music at a low volume on the record player. Or you could read a story in a monotone or whispery voice. You might read a sleep story such as Margaret Wise Brown's *Goodnight Moon* (New York: Scholastic, 1947) or Robert Kraus's *Good Night Richard Rabbit* (New York: Windmill Books, 1972) or Russell Hoban's *Bedtime for Frances* (New York: Harper & Row, 1960). For some children, rubbing their backs helps them let go and fall asleep. If you rub backs for some, however, be sure to do it for all who want it. Children like you to trace their names on their backs with your finger. What if some children still do not fall asleep?

If You Have Not Checked This Item: Some Helpful Ideas

■ **Naptime Toys**

If after 10 or 15 minutes, certain children show no signs of falling asleep, you may decide to allow them to play quietly on their cots with some sort of "naptime toy," perhaps a tiny car or doll from a basket you pass around to the nonsleepers. Because they do not move from their sleeping quarters, the nonsleepers still have the chance to fall asleep if they want. On the other hand, some teachers prefer to have a different area where nonsleepers can go to play quietly.

■ **Reduce Tension**

If some children are still too anxious and tense to allow themselves to fall asleep, you may need to try a variety of methods for reducing tension. Can these children take a teddy bear to bed? Ask them how they can help themselves get sleepy. Will rocking help? What do they do at home? In the end, your acceptance of them as worthy human beings should eventually help them to relax and take a nap if their bodies have the need for it.

Toileting

Children's bathroom habits are as different from one another as their eating habits. Children will probably learn the most about what is expected of them in your center from their peers. But you also need to be aware of what the children expect or need. Do you have a single classroom bathroom or a public type bathroom with several stalls? Are the children used to being in a bathroom with other children? Can they handle their clothing, clean themselves, and wash their hands alone?

You may need to talk to newcomers in the beginning about what they can expect and ask them what they are used to. You may need to go in the bathroom with them in the beginning to help them and get them used to the equipment.

If parents tell you their children are not using the center facilities or if the children begin to have accidents in the classroom, you will want to talk with them about it as gently as possible. Because toilet training—unfortunately—is controlled in some homes through the negative method of shaming, you need to be careful that your concern will not make the child feel ashamed.

Is the child too shy to use the bathroom with other children? You may need to accede to his feelings at first until he is used to your center and his peers.

If You Have Not Checked This Item: Some Helpful Ideas

■ **Use Rewards**

This behavior modification idea of giving a reward is always controversial, but for some children it works. An external reward can become an internal behavior if the child plays her part. Try keeping a private chart on which you put a check or smiley face each time the child uses the toilet. Once a child is in the habit or has overcome her anxiety about using your facilities, the use of the chart should fade away.

■ Display Acceptance

Use every strategy you know to show the child you accept him. Nonverbal cues such as smiles or hugs and friendly words, special activities, and jobs or errands make a child feel accepted. Help him to be accepted by the other children as well. Once anxiety about your center and its inhabitants is lessened, a new child should not be so tense about using the bathroom facilities.

■ Read a Book

An especially good book about using the toilet is *Toilet Tales* by Andrea Wayne von Konigslow (Toronto: Annick Press, 1985). This hilariously illustrated story tells why big boys and girls can use the toilet and why animals like elephants, lions, snakes, and beavers cannot. When your children are finished laughing, all the tension about toilets should be gone!

❏ HANDLES SUDDEN CHANGES/STARTLING SITUATIONS WITH CONTROL

Surprise (Startle)

Surprise is different from the other emotions in that it lasts only for a moment, although its results may continue for some time with young children. A sudden or unexpected external event causes a reaction of surprise, or startle. The event could be a loud noise such as an explosion or clap of thunder at one extreme, or the unexpected appearance of a person at the other extreme. A startled person's mind goes blank for an instant and his muscles contract quickly. He may even jump if the incident is surprising enough. Depending upon the situation, the person may be shocked, bewildered, confused, or embarrassed because of his reaction. Or he could be delighted.

Although a startle reflex appears in babies a few hours after birth, this reflex does not seem to be the same as the emotion of surprise, which occurs in infants between the fifth and seventh month. By that time enough cognitive development has occurred to enable the infant to form expectations (Izard, 1977, p. 283).

Because everything is new for the child, there will be many startling events in her young life. If most of her surprises are pleasant ones, she will come to view surprises positively. If the opposite is true, then surprises may cause the child to cry or exhibit defensive behavior.

Many mothers help to prepare their children for surprises, perhaps unintentionally, by playing low-key surprise games such as peekaboo with their children. The surprise is always a pleasant one, of course: the revealing of mother's hidden face. But if children are scolded or ridiculed too severely at home when they cry or make a fuss over unexpected happenings, they may become fearful of anything different, whether or not it is sudden.

Research shows that most adults view surprise as pleasant. Their experience has taught them this. Young children, on the other hand, do not necessarily show the same response. Perhaps because their experience is limited, or because the occurrence of sudden happenings leaves them overwhelmed, they tend not to greet unexpected things as adults do. Most young children, for instance, do not react happily to surprise birthday parties. Young children are, in fact, more likely to cry or withdraw. It may take some time for the shock to wear off and for them to become their pleasant selves again. Sensitive adults will not impose such startling events on children. Children enjoy the pleasant anticipation of parties, rather than startling surprise.

What about the children in your center? How do they respond to the unexpected? They need to be prepared for it in their lives, and they need to be able to control their responses. Like the other emotions, surprise/startle cannot be eliminated, nor should it be. It serves the useful function of preparing an individual to deal with an unexpected event. But if a child's reaction is one of such alarm as to immobilize her, then you need to help her deal with it in a better way.

What are some startling events you might anticipate? Most centers have fire alarms that they may or may not be able to control. Ask your building supervisor if your children can have a chance to practice a fire drill with the alarm until they are able to do it with ease. Practicing with simulated emergency situations is one of the best ways to learn to deal with real emergencies.

In addition to practice, your children can learn to handle sudden changes or surprising events by acting the way you do. You need to be calm and collected yourself, modeling the behavior you would like your children to emulate.

Some children go to pieces when they are startled. They may be the ones who have not developed a strong enough sense of self or a sense of trust about the people around them. These children may cry, or cling, or withdraw long after the event is past. How can you help them?

If You Have Not Checked This Item: Some Helpful Ideas

■ Read a Book

Children may be helped to overcome their negative responses if they hear how others like themselves deal with surprises. Books about startling situations should be read not only to a group of children, but also to individuals who have exhibited a poor emotional response to a surprise. Books with this theme include the following:

Peek-A-Boo! by Janet and Allen Ahlberg (New York: Viking Press, 1981) is about a baby in his crib, his high chair, his stroller, and so on. Although this story seems to be directed to infants, it is much too complex for any babe-in-arms. A preschooler, however, should enjoy shouting Peek-a-boo! and looking through the dollar-size hole in every other page to guess what complicated things the other members of the family are doing.

Maybe a Monster by Martha Alexander (New York: Dial Press, 1968) is a small-format book in which a little boy narrator builds a trap and a cage to catch a monster and becomes afraid as he thinks about it. The building and the suspense take up all but the ending of the book, when the little boy is surprised to catch—a rabbit.

Jim Meets the Thing by Miriam Cohen (New York: Greenwillow Books, 1981) can be reassuring to many young children who are startled and frightened by the things they see on television. In this story young Jim seems to be the only one in his class who is scared by the monster movie on TV the night before. But when playing superheroes on the playground at lunchtime, only Jim stays calm when a praying mantis suddenly lands on Danny.

Drummer Hoff by Barbara and Ed Emberly (Englewood Cliffs, NJ: Prentice-Hall, 1967) may help to diffuse the fear of children frightened by loud noises. A cumulative folktale-like story, this book tells about colorful playing-card soldiers who put an old cannon together piece by piece and then fire it off at the end.

Although some teachers have indicated that certain quiet children are frightened even by book experiences, you might ask the children themselves if hearing a book like *Drummer Hoff* will help them to get over their fear of loud noises. Let the children be the ones to say the "ka-a-a-a-boooom!" at the end.

Storm in the Night by Mary Stolz (New York: Harper & Row, 1988) tells, with illuminating words and illustrations, how a little African-American boy, Thomas, his grandfather, and his cat Ringo deal with a frightening thunderstorm that puts out their lights.

❏ CAN EXPRESS ANGER IN WORDS RATHER THAN ACTIONS

Anger

Anger is the negative emotion of most concern not only in the child-care center, but also in society at large, perhaps because anger has the potential for such destruction. We are very much concerned that people learn to control their anger. Therefore we begin teaching what to do—or rather what not to do—very early. We are often not very successful. There is, however, a positive approach to controlling anger that can diffuse the anger so that children do not turn it against others or themselves.

First, we need to look at the emotion itself to understand what it is, what causes it, and what purpose it serves. Anger is the emotion or feeling that results when we are physically or psychologically restrained from doing something, frustrated in our attempts, interrupted, personally insulted, or forced to do something against our will. We feel hurt, disappointed, irritated. We frown, our face gets hot, our blood "boils," our muscles tense, our teeth clench, our eyes stare. At anger's highest level we feel rage that threatens to erupt in an explosive manner. At the other extreme we feel hostility, a cold type of anger.

With anger comes a sense of physical power and a greater self-assurance than with any other negative emotion (Izard, 1977, p. 331). The body, in fact, rallies its resources in readiness to strike out against the cause of the anger. In primitive humans anger mobilized the body's energy quickly and was important for survival. In modern humans the anger still appears but its primary purpose has all but vanished.

Here we are, then, ready to turn this rush of physical energy against the "enemy." What should we do with it? This energy must be released or somehow diffused, otherwise we will turn it against ourselves. Repressed anger has been implicated as one of the causes of skin diseases, ulcers, migraines, hypertension, and certain psychological disorders (Izard, 1977, p. 351).

Most parents teach their children from the start not to display anger. When they allow angry feelings to begin to show on their faces, children sense their parents' displeasure. Many children soon learn to conceal or disguise their expression of anger. Others let anger out in acts of aggression. Neither response is satisfactory, yet many of us carry these responses throughout life.

Instead, we need a positive approach that teaches children from the start what they should do (expression) rather than what they must not do (repression). Anger definitely calls for some sort of release, but children and adults need to "let off steam" harmlessly.

One of the most satisfactory methods used by many preschool teachers coaches children to verbalize their feelings. Verbalizing involves not yelling or name-calling, but expressing in words how the child feels about whatever is causing the anger. This approach has at least two advantages: It gives children an acceptable release for their strong feelings and it puts the children in control. They—not adults—deal with the situation. And solving the problem on their own strengthens the children's sense of self.

Strong feelings such as anger overwhelm and thus frighten young children. A method for learning control from the inside and not being controlled from the outside will help children in the future when adults are not around. The anger emotion calls for action. But if children learn to speak out rather than strike out, they will not have to suffer the guilt or remorse afterward for an unacceptable act.

Expressing anger in words is not easy in the beginning. It does not come naturally for young children whose communication skills are still limited. It is even more difficult for the child caught up in the throes of an overwhelming emotion who finds it simpler to strike out physically or shout or cry. Yet 3-, 4-, and 5-year-olds can learn the response of telling how they feel in words.

How do you teach them? First of all, you have to model this behavior yourself. When you become angry tell the individual or the group how you feel and why you feel this way: "I feel very upset to see you dropping the tape recorder on the floor like that! If you break it no one can enjoy the music any more," or "Paul and Gregory, I am so angry to see you ganging up on Leslie again! Two against one is not fair!"

You must also convey to your children that their actions—not them as individuals—make you angry. You must show you still respect and like the children no matter how angry they get or how upset you feel over their actions. Show the children both verbally and nonverbally that you still accept them as good people.

You also must intervene every time the children display temper, and you must help them repeatedly to express their feelings in words: "Shirley, tell Rachel how you feel when she takes your book." "Von, don't hit Tony. Tell him how you feel."

Make *eye* contact with the children. Help them to make *eye* contact with one another in order to help diffuse their anger. "Von, look Tony in the *eyes* and tell him."

Teaching children to express anger in words is a time-consuming process, but so is all learning. If you believe children must gain inner control over their anger, and if you understand they must have some acceptable way to vent their feelings, then you will find it worthwhile to put in the time and effort necessary to divert anger's destructive energy into words. You will know you have been successful when the children begin telling one another, "Don't hit him Bobby, tell him!"

If You Have Not Checked This Item: Some Helpful Ideas

■ Talk About Feelings

Establish a "feelings" corner in your room with pictures of people looking sad and angry and glad. Ask the children to tell you what they feel when they look like that. Provide a "feelings" hand puppet that the children can hold and talk to about the feelings they have.

■ Read a Book

Read a book about feelings to a child or small group at any time of the day (not only when tempers are short).

I Was So Mad by Norma Simon (Chicago: Whitman, 1974) lets many different children tell about what makes them mad, how they feel, and what they do about their feelings. They talk about being teased, picked on, and blamed; not being able to do something; having an activity interrupted or ruined; and being forced to do something they did not want to do. The story ends with the words and music to the song one father sings: "There Was a Man and He Was Mad." Your children can learn the song.

The Temper Tantrum Book by Edna Mitchell Preston (New York: Puffin Books, 1976) is about a lion, a tiger, an elephant, and other animals who get upset enough to have a temper tantrum until they can diffuse their anger by expressing in words why they feel furious.

❏ ALLOWS AGGRESSIVE BEHAVIOR TO BE REDIRECTED

Aggression

Aggression is not an emotion but rather the expression of one. It is the action commonly taken by an individual as a result of anger or frustration. Hostile actions or angry words are intended to harm or defeat or embarrass the person who caused the anger. Aggressive behavior in the classroom most commonly takes the form of hitting, throwing things, name-calling, spitting, biting, kicking, pushing or pulling, physically forcing someone to do something, restraining someone, destroying property, and forcefully taking someone else's possessions or turn.

Young children who have not learned to control their negative emotions often resort to this aggressive behavior. Children who have been neglected or treated harshly sometimes use aggression to strike out at the world around them. Children who have had to fend for themselves among older peers without much adult guidance may have learned aggressiveness as a survival strategy. Other children with highly permissive parents may have learned certain aggressive acts to get their own way—hitting and name-calling, for instance.

Research tells us that boys are more aggressive than girls. Since Helen Dawe's early observational study of the quarrels of preschool children in 1934, all findings everywhere have shown boys to be more aggressive (Brooks-Gunn & Matthews, 1979, p. 130). We can blame boys' aggression on genetics—physical development and hormones—but we also need to look at society's expectations for boys and girls. Society expects boys to be more aggressive than girls; thus boys are *allowed* to be more aggressive. If aggressiveness were considered a feminine trait, then no doubt the findings would quickly change.

Is all aggressiveness among children bad? Not according to researcher Wendy Matthews, who found in 1972 that among preschoolers in Paris the most popular child in play groups was also the most aggressive both physically and verbally, whether or not the child was a boy or girl. Aggressive children were the leaders, using forceful behavior to keep their followers in line (Brooks-Gunn & Matthews, 1979, p. 131). This type of forceful behavior, however, is not the same as aggression due to anger and frustration.

How, then, can you as a preschool teacher help children control their unwanted aggressive behavior? Putting negative feelings into words of course helps achieve inner control. But if their actions are already aggressive, then the children need to be redirected into a less destructive activity.

Children who strike out aggressively could be redirected to hit a ball of clay, hit a nail with a hammer, punch a pillow, kick a ball, hit a tetherball, throw a beanbag at a target, or use rhythm band instruments. Activities that will calm down overwrought children include finger painting, water play, working with play dough, mixing dough, and listening to music or a story.

If You Have Not Checked This Item: Some Helpful Ideas

■ Hold the Child on Your Lap

Sometimes you must physically restrain a child from hurting someone else. Because you are bigger, you can hold the child so she cannot hit or kick, until she calms down enough to control herself. Hold the child on your lap and restrain her from using her arms. If she also kicks, you may need to remove her shoes. This child is totally out of control and needs your help to restore herself to normalcy. Do not lose control yourself. Children are afraid of their own overwhelming emotions. They need you to remain calm and to prevent them from doing damage. If you are in a rocking chair, rock back and forth, humming a tuneless song over and over. Finally, ask the child if she feels calm enough for you to let her get up. If she can't tell you, she is not ready yet.

▪ Read a Book

At a later time, some children who use aggression to solve problems may want to listen to a book about others who do the same.

The Grouchy Lady Bug by Eric Carle (New York: Crowell, 1977) is a time/counting book about a ladybug who challenges one after another of the animals all around the world to a fight. When each agrees, the ladybug flies off, telling them they are not big enough. Finally the whale, without even knowing it, slaps some sense into the grouchy ladybug.

No Fighting, No Biting! by Else Holmelund Minarik (New York: Harper & Row, 1958) is a classic book containing four different stories about two little children and their older cousin, Joan, who will not let the younger cousins sit with her while they continue to fight and pinch. The other stories focus on two little alligators who also fight and bite.

❑ DOES NOT WITHDRAW FROM OTHERS EXCESSIVELY

Shyness (Shame)

As you observe the children in your classroom at the beginning of the year, you may note that certain ones seem to stay by themselves. They may stand apart or sit apart. If you try to get them involved, they may lower or avert their eyes, turn their heads, or even suck their thumbs. They seem to want to shrink into invisibility if only they could. They seem, in fact, to be exhibiting all of the indications of painful shyness.

Shyness is one of the least studied of the negative emotions. Yet nearly all humans experience shyness at one time or another. Early childhood is a common time for such an occurrence. Shyness results from a heightened degree of self-awareness in which the individual feels exposed, helpless, incompetent, and somehow shameful about it all.

As with so many of our feelings about ourselves, shyness seems to come from a combination of inherited traits plus first-year experiences (Izard, 1977, p. 405). The earliest "shame" feelings that infants experience occur when they first recognize the face of a stranger around the age of 5 months to 7 months. Previously they have been fascinated with the human face. It has been a stimulus for excitement and joy. They want contact with it. They want some kind of interaction.

Then something occurs within the cognitive development of infants that allows them to discriminate one face from another. And suddenly, when a stranger appears, they realize they are not looking at a familiar, friendly countenance. They no longer respond joyfully, but, instead, seem to realize their mistake and thus suffer their first embarrassment. They may cry, become red in the face, or try to get away.

If children have a series of negative experiences with strangers at this time, then they may learn that they are subject to this sort of shame whenever they meet a stranger (Izard, 1977, p. 395). Highly sensitive children seem to exhibit such embarrassment whether or not their experiences have been negative.

Something else is also happening within children at this time. They are becoming aware of themselves as separate beings. This awareness has to happen before embarrassment—and therefore shyness—can occur. The shyness (shame) emotion is, after all, the feeling of exposure of self, of extreme self-consciousness, in which a person feels that all eyes are on him and he is uncomfortably out of place. According to research, these feelings occur most frequently in large groups, in new situations, and with strangers (Izard, 1977, p. 399).

Is it any wonder then that certain children exhibit this emotion in your classroom, especially at the beginning of the year? These children may be the sensitive ones, or the ones whose parents have used shaming as a method of discipline. Or they may be children who have not yet developed a strong enough sense of self to be comfortable among strangers. Shyness can be emotionally crippling to a child. It can prevent her from enjoying the best of herself and of others in your center. You need to find a way, using the utmost tact and sensitivity yourself, to help the shy child.

Children have no need to feel ashamed. They often do so because they are not able to live up to their expectations of themselves. They look around at other people and see themselves as a shameful example of what they would like to be. To help them change this inaccurate perception, you need to let them know how good they really are. Tell them verbally, show them nonverbally, and involve them actively in important duties and projects. You need to engage these children in activites where they will find out for themselves how worthy they are. But never at any time should you use shaming or ridicule as a method of discipline or scolding (e.g., never say anything like, Look what you did to the paints! How could you be so clumsy!).

The shyness/shame emotion does have a use in human development. Shame is the emotion—and a very powerful one—that keeps us from acting shamefully among others so that we do not invite ridicule. Rules for behavior (such as polite manners) are one result of this emotion. People who lack a sense of shame may commit such shameful acts as incest or child abuse. On the other hand, people who are overcome with an irrational sense of shame may also be emotionally crippled by it.

Some young children have this irrational feeling of shyness/shame. Because shame results from a real or perceived put-down of the self, and not just from an act the self has performed, there is real danger in allowing the child to feel that he is not good. If you do nothing to help the child correct this negative perception of himself, he may come to believe it. He may express his belief by withdrawing from others excessively. Thus you must make a concerted effort to correct the situation.

If You Have Not Checked This Item: Some Helpful Ideas

■ Focus on the Child's Strengths

Because the shyness emotion expresses the feeling that a child has not accepted herself, you can best help a shy child by finding ways for her to feel good about herself. Is she wearing a brightly colored dress? Maybe she could cut out pictures from a magazine of other dresses the same pretty color as hers. Or have her look at her pretty hand (she may be too sensitive to look at her face in a mirror at first). Could she trace around her fingers and then color the hand and cut it out? Perhaps she will allow you to display it on the classroom wall.

■ Do Not Dwell on Shyness

Reading books about shy children may not be a good idea. Shy children are already painfully aware of how they feel. To point out this shyness by reading a book about it may only make it worse.

■ Pair with Another Child

If one other child accepts him, the shy child may find it easier to accept himself and become involved with the others. You may need to take the initiative in this case, asking another child to work with the shy child on a puzzle or go on an errand for you together.

■ Talk with Parents

Does the child exhibit this same behavior at home? Maybe not. Many children act completely differently at home than at school. This may mean that it is in your classroom where the child feels self-conscious and thus exhibits shyness. In that case continue your activities to show acceptance and to help her accept herself. But if the parents admit that the child behaves the same at home, you may want to discuss tactfully with them the methods of discipline they are using. If shaming or ridiculing are involved, perhaps the parents could learn another way. You might consider having a meeting for all parents where a speaker or film discusses the discipline issue.

❑ SHOWS INTEREST/ATTENTION IN CLASSROOM ACTIVITIES

Interest (Excitement)

Interest is the most frequent and pervasive positive emotion that human beings possess. Children show interest by directing their eyes toward an object or person that catches their attention and then exploring it with their eyes and, if possible, their other senses. Interested people are alert, active, self-confident, and curious. Interest is the motivator for much of children's learning, as well as for their development of creativity and intelligence. Thus it is crucial for growing children to have their interest stimulated by the interesting people, objects, and ideas in their environment.

Psychologists believe that change or novelty is the basis for the interest emotion. The novelty of an object first attracts the person's attention. Once he is aroused and curious, he should be motivated to find out more about the object, thus increasing his knowledge, skill, and understanding. Interest, in other words, is the impulse to know, which then sustains our attention in the things we are curious about. Excitement is the most intense form of interest.

For an infant to perceive an object, she must first pay attention to it over a period of time. It is the emotion of interest that keeps her attention. Without this emotion she may become passive, dull, and apathetic, with little initiative or movement. The final result may be developmental lags or even retardation.

The interest emotion appears very early in an infant's life. Interest is evident in the attention she shows to the human face: eyes riveted to her mother's face and turning to follow it. Objects such as rattles, bottles, mobiles, her own fingers and toes are fascinating fields for exploration with her eyes and then her mouth. Later she shifts from external exploration to manipulation. What will objects do when you kick them, throw them, drop them?

When he throws his cereal dish on the floor, the child is not being naughty, only normal. He finds out about his world this way. Acts like this against physical objects obviously teach the child many additional things about the feelings of the people around him. If the family is strict or harsh or punitive about his actions, then such exploration motivated by interest will be inhibited. If the child is punished too many times he may cease exploring altogether, which poses dire consequences for his future development. On the other hand, encouragement to explore, play with things, and be curious will stretch his mind, his senses, and his physical skills.

Poverty frequently interferes with the development of strong interests because the variety of objects or activities available in the child's environment is often limited. In cases where the parents must also spend much of their energy struggling to survive, they may have little or no time to interact with their youngsters. The parents may, in fact, actively discourage them from exploratory endeavors. If, in addition, negative emotions dominate the atmosphere, interest quickly fades away.

Thus it is important for you to know which children in your classroom have retained their native curiosity and which have not. The interest and attention individual children pay to classroom activities may give you a clue. But you need to remember that interest is stimulated by novelty and change, so a truer test might be to set up a new activity area and observe which children notice it, who plays in it, and for how long. Because interests by now are very much individualized and personalized, what interests one child will not necessarily cause a flicker of attention in another. For this reason you must provide a wide range of activities and materials for your group. And remember to add something new once in awhile.

The basic interest emotion also affects attention span. Children must first be attracted to an activity through interest that is activated by change or novelty. If they find it interesting, they are likely to pay more attention to it, that is, to give their attention longer to the activity. Although we know that age and maturity have a great deal to do with how long a child's interest can be held (i.e., the older, the longer), we can also increase the attention span by providing highly attractive materials and activities. Because children must attend (i.e., pay attention) in order to learn, the length of attention span is crucial in every learning situation. Teachers thus need to know what kinds of things are attractive to 3-, 4-, and 5-year-olds.

If You Have Not Checked This Item: Some Helpful Ideas

■ Focus on the Self

Although children's interests are widely varied, all humans, and especially egocentric youngsters, have a basic interest in themselves. Think of something new and different about the child who shows little interest in center activities. Make it some kind of question, problem, or challenge that is intriguing and fun. Then turn the child loose with it. For instance, have a Slappy Shoe Contest. The child who shows little interest can start. Have her make some kind of paper crown or design that she can tape to the top of her shoes. At some time during the day have her slap out a rhythm with one of her shoes, which you tape record. Play the tape. Let other children try to copy it. Let her choose who will be the Mr. or Ms. Slappy Shoe tomorrow.

This activity may sound strange, but it is not, when you remember how much children love shoes. Can you think of other things about them—their clothing, their hair, their favorite foods or songs or pets—that can be turned into a similar activity? Start with the children who seem to show little interest and go from there.

■ Arouse Curiosity

Children love mysteries. Invite a mystery guest (an adult dressed in a costume and mask) to visit the classroom. Let children guess who it is. Or bring a big stuffed animal in a bag and let the children guess what it is. Give them hints about what it eats, the noises it makes. Maybe the slow-to-respond child would like to think of a name for it.

■ Read a Book

Read a book about a mystery. Steven Kellogg has written several small-sized picture books involving mysteries that the children should enjoy.

The Mystery of the Magic Green Ball by Steven Kellogg (New York: Dial Press, 1978) is the story of Timmy, who loses his big green ball in the woods, and the Mystery Gypsy Fortune Teller, who finds it but won't give it back until Timmy uses some magic himself.

The Mystery of the Flying Orange Pumpkin by Steven Kellogg (New York: Dial Press, 1980) is a startling but hilarious escapade about a pumpkin the children grow in a garden that comes to be owned by a Scrooge-type character. When he refuses to let the children have their pumpkin for Halloween, three "ghosts" make it rise out of the field and fly away, and then involve him in a party to get it back.

The Mystery of the Missing Red Mitten by Steven Kellogg (New York: Dial Press, 1974) is another small-sized book about a little girl who loses her mitten in the snow and after a long search finds it as the heart of the snowman she has built.

The Vanishing Pumpkin by Tony Johnston (New York: Putnam, 1983) is a full-sized book about a 700-year-old woman and an 800-year-old man whose Halloween pumpkin has been snitched, and who must confront a ghoul, a rapscallion, a varmint, and a wizard before finding it—just the thing to tickle the fancy of a bored-acting child. Can he make up his own mystery afterward and tell it to a tape recorder?

■ Start with Something Simple That the Children Like

Do the children like apples? How many things can you do with an apple? The book *Apple Pigs* by Ruth Orbach (New York: Philomel Books, 1976) might get them started when they hear the zany story in rhyme about the family members that were so overwhelmed with apples that they invited an entire zoo to help consume them. Directions are given for making "apple pigs."

❏ SMILES, SEEMS HAPPY MUCH OF THE TIME

Joy (Enjoyment)

Joy, the most positive of the emotions, is also the most elusive. Seek it and you may not find it. Try to experience it directly and it may elude you. But live a normal life and it will appear spontaneously. Joy does not occur so much on its own as it does as a by-product of something else: a pleasant experience, a happy thought, a good friendship. In other words, this emotion is indicative of feeling good about oneself, others, and life in general. The absence of joy tells us that a child is not feeling good about these things. We need to observe the children carefully to see where they

The capacity for joy is inherited, but its development depends on responses of teachers and caregivers to joy in the child.

stand in regard to this important indicator of inner feelings, and we need to take positive action if this emotion is missing.

Joy is the feeling of happiness that may precede or follow a pleasant experience: sensory pleasure such as a hug, a kiss, or a back rub; psychological pleasure such as the remembrance of good times; and the anticipation of seeing a loved one or of having fun with friends. People express joy with smiles, laughter, the lighting up of eyes, increased heartbeat, an inner feeling of confidence, a sense of well-being, a glow. The emotion itself is fleeting, but the good feeling it creates may color a person's actions and responses for many hours.

As with the other emotions, the capacity for joy is inherited and is different for each individual (Izard, 1977, p. 239). Its development, however, depends greatly on how the mother or primary caregiver responds to joy in the infant. A person cannot teach another person to be happy, but she can influence the occurrence of happiness by creating a pleasant environment in the first place, and then responding positively when joy occurs.

Babies may smile during the first days of life. At first they smile in revery or dreams, then during waking hours when a pleasant, high-pitched voice talks to them, and, finally, by the fifth week at the sight of a friendly face coming close (Izard, 1977, p. 239). The first smile, in fact, is almost a spontaneous reflex coming 2 to 12 hours after birth. The elicited smile that comes as a result of a voice occurs soon afterward within the first week. By the second or third month, infants are smiling spontaneously without seeing or hearing anyone—that is, if they have been responded to pleasantly by their caregivers. But the human face remains the single most effective stimulus to smiling (Izard, 1977, p. 248).

Laughter has its own developmental sequence. It first occurs between 5 and 9 weeks, usually in response to patty-cake-type games or tickling. Scientists believe the motor development of the child has some relationship to development of laughter. But both laughter and smiling can be stimulated by the same expressions of joy on the part of another.

Situations that discourage or prevent the emotion of joy from occurring include poor physical health, conditions of fatigue or boredom, harsh treatment or neglect, conditions of poverty that limit a child's possibilities, and the lack of joy on the part of caregivers.

Recognition of a familiar person, object, or situation helps stimulate or encourage the expression of joy. Whereas change and novelty seem to stimulate the emotion of interest, familiarity and being comfortable with things set the stage for joy. Keep this in mind in your child-care center. A little change is challenging. Too much change is overwhelming for young children. They need a stable schedule of daily events they can depend on and a physical arrangement of materials that does not change too drastically overnight. Then they can look forward with joy to coming to the center every day.

If You Have Not Checked This Item: Some Helpful Ideas

■ Talk with Parents

Children who express no joy probably are not very happy. You will need to converse with the joyless child's parents in a sensitive manner, trying to elicit how the child reacts at home, whether there are any particular problems or pressures presently affecting him, and what his basic personality is like. Is the child fundamentally happy? What are his favorite things: foods, colors, toys, activities? What makes him laugh? Perhaps you can use some of these favorites as a focus for an activity to make him feel good.

■ Read a Funny Book

You cannot teach children to be happy, but you can help them experience joy and therefore stimulate them to want more of it. Maybe a humorous book will tickle their funny bones enough to open their lives to joy.

Helen Lester's books fit this category. In *A Porcupine Named Fluffy* (Boston: Houghton Mifflin, 1986), Mr. and Mrs. Porcupine try out a series of nonsensical names like Needleroozer on their new baby before naming him Fluffy. But poor Fluffy stumbles through life being comically unfluffy until he finally meets a rhinoceros named Hippo, and the laughter that ensues makes everything all right. *Tacky the Penguin* (Boston: Houghton Mifflin, 1988), on the other hand, has a name that fits but manners that decidedly don't. Readers will hold their sides laughing at Tacky's odd-bird antics that disturb his perfect brothers but scare off the hunters.

Mert the Blurt by Robert Kraus (New York: Windmill Books, 1980) appeals to the humor of the youngest listeners with its blurting words and hilarious illustrations as Mert blurts out all of the family secrets.

■ Be a Joyful Person

Children and others feel joy when they meet a person who thinks they are delightful and wants to be around them. Make yourself that kind of person.

Table 4.1, "Childhood Emotions in the Classroom," helps you see at a glance the causes and results of these common feelings. Such awareness can assist you in helping children develop more positive responses in emotional situations.

OBSERVING, RECORDING, AND INTERPRETING EMOTIONAL DEVELOPMENT

In order to understand and interpret the emotional growth of individual children, it is helpful to fill out the emotional development section of the *Child Skills Checklist* for specific children. Using data gathered during observations, her teacher filled out this section of the *Checklist* for Sheila, the child discussed in Chapter 2, as shown in Figure 4.1.

Sheila shows confidence in her use of language, as well as in her eating, sleeping, and toileting away from home without a fuss. This seems to indicate she is at ease in the classroom setting. However, she does not seem to be all that comfortable with the other children: She does not play with them yet, and she runs to the teacher whenever anything upsetting happens. The other important indicator is the fact that she does not smile or seem happy. Perhaps Sheila does not display happiness because she is ill at ease with the other children.

TABLE 4.1
Childhood emotions in the classroom

Emotion	Common Cause	Possible Results
Distress	Separation from loved one; abandonment	Crying; whining; clinging
Fear (anxiety)	Presence of threat; absence of safety	Tightening of muscles; refusal to eat, fall asleep, go to toilet
Surprise (startle)	Loud noise; unexpected appearance or event	Crying; withdrawing; clinging
Anger	Physical or psychological restraint; interruption; insult	Red face; loud words or screaming; physical aggression
*Aggression	Anger; frustration	Hitting; throwing; biting; kicking; pushing
Shyness (shame)	Heightened self-consciousness; exposure	Red face; crying; withdrawal
Interest (excitement)	Change; novelty	Looking at something; exploration with senses; wide eyes
Joy (enjoyment)	A pleasant experience; happy thoughts; friendship	Smiling; laughing; lighting up of eyes; talking happily

*NOTE: Not a true emotion

This observation was made at the beginning of the school year before all of the children were used to each other and to the center. Some of the activities listed under "If You Have Not Checked This Item: Some Helpful Ideas" may help Sheila to feel more comfortable with the others. The fact that Sheila goes around the room trying out everything is a sign that she will eventually want to get involved in everything. Perhaps Sheila can do an art activity with another child. Her teacher may want to pair Sheila with a child who is already at ease and will thus help Sheila feel more at home in the center.

FIGURE 4.1

Emotional development observations for Sheila

Child Skills Checklist

Name _Sheila — Age 3_   **Observer** _Connie R._

Program _Head Start_   **Dates** _10-22_

Directions:

Put a ✔ for items you see the child perform regularly. Put *N* for items where there is no opportunity to observe. Leave all other items blank.

Item	Evidence	Date
2. Emotional Development		
✔ Allows self to be comforted during stressful time	Lets teacher calm her down when Beth takes her crayon	10/22
✔ Eats, sleeps, toilets without fuss away from home	Always does these things with ease on own	10/22
____ Handles sudden changes/ startling situations with control	Cries or runs to teacher when upsetting things happen	10/22
✔ Can express anger in words rather than actions	When Beth takes crayon she says to her: "That's not fair!"	10/22
✔ Allows aggressive behavior to be redirected	Allows teacher to involve her in other activities	10/22
____ Does not withdraw from others excessively	Does not play with other children	10/22
✔ Shows interest/attention in classroom activities	Goes around room trying out everything	10/22
____ Smiles, seems happy much of the time	Rarely smiles; does not give evidence of being happy	10/22

REFERENCES

Brooks-Gunn, Jeanne, & Wendy Schempp Matthews. (1979). *He & she: How children develop their sex-role identity.* Englewood Cliffs, NJ: Prentice-Hall.

Frey, W. H., & Langseth, M. (1985). *Crying: The mystery of tears.* Minneapolis: Winston Press.

Izard, Carroll E. (1977). *Human emotions.* New York: Plenum Press.

Solter, Aletha. (1992). Understanding tears and tantrums. *Young Children, 47*(4), 64–68.

OTHER SOURCES

Beaty, Janice J. (1992). *Skills for preschool teachers.* New York: Merrill/Macmillan.

Bullock, Janis. (1988). Understanding and altering aggression. *Day Care and Early Education, 15*(3), 24–27.

Candland, Douglas K., Joseph P. Fell, Ernest Keen, Alan I. Lesher, Robert Plutchin, & Roger M. Tarpy. (1977). *Emotion.* Monterey, CA: Brooks/Cole.

Cherry, Clare. (1983). *Please don't sit on the kids: Alternatives to punitive discipline.* Belmont, CA: Pitman Learning.

Enzner, Norbert B. (Ed.) with Kennith W. Goin. (1978). *Social and emotional development: The preschooler.* New York: Walker.

Kersey, Katharine. (1986). *Helping your child handle stress.* Washington, DC: Acropolis Books.

Kvols-Riedler, Bill, & Kathy Kvols-Riedler. (1979). *Redirecting children's misbehavior: A guide for cooperation between children & adults.* Boulder, CO: R.D.I.C. Publications.

Marion, Marian. (1991). *Guidance of young children (3rd ed.).* New York: Merrill/Macmillan.

Zimbardo, Philip G., & Shirley L. Radl. (1981). *The shy child.* New York: Doubleday.

LEARNING ACTIVITIES

1. Observe the children in your classroom for a week in the eight areas of emotional control. Which children exhibit behavior that seems to show emotional control? Which ones have not yet learned inner control? How can you help them? Write out and discuss a plan with your supervisor.

2. Choose a child who has trouble allowing his or her aggressive behavior to be redirected. Observe the child for three mornings, making a time sampling of the behavior. Use a behavior modification idea as discussed in Chapter 2 to see if you can reduce the number of times this negative behavior occurs. What are the results of your follow-up observation?

3. Choose a child who has trouble either eating, sleeping, or toileting in your center. Observe the child, making a running record of behavior on three different days. What other indications of tension do you find? What suggestions do you have for alleviating the tension?

4. Work with one of the children in your classroom who has difficulty expressing his or her anger in words. What actions can you take to help the child? Observe and record the results.

5. Choose a child for whom you have checked "Smiles, seems happy much of the time." Observe this child on three different days. Which of the other items can you check based on your observations? What is your evidence for each check mark? What conclusions can you make about this child based on these observations? Do you need any additional evidence in order for you to make conclusions?

5

Social Play

Social Play Checklist

- ❏ Is unoccupied during free play (or follows teacher)
- ❏ Spends time watching others play
- ❏ Plays by self with own toys/materials
- ❏ Plays parallel to others with similar toys/materials
- ❏ Initiates activity/play with others
- ❏ Gains access to ongoing play in positive manner
- ❏ Maintains role in ongoing play in positive manner
- ❏ Resolves play conflicts in positive manner

The social development of preschool children is revealed in how they get along with peers. Often, we think of social actions as manners and politeness, but in the study of young children, social actions refer to how children learn to get along with their peers. Getting along for this age group rarely involves manners and usually is not very polite. Young children, in fact, frequently struggle to develop social skills.

They start out completely self-centered, which seems to stem from a survival mechanism in infancy. Chapter 3 discussed how infants do not even recognize themselves as different from their primary caregiver in the beginning. Then, little by little, the infants begin to discover their own self-identities. By the time they arrive in your classroom, the children have begun to know themselves as individuals but mainly in relation to their adult caregivers.

If the children already have developed strong self-identities, they should do well away from home. They will be able to let go of their primary caregiver more easily and will be more willing to try new things and to experience new people. Reviews of current research support this point of view: "The quality of the child's attachment relationship with his mother in infancy has been found to predict the child's social acceptance in preschool," according to the studies examined by Kemple (1991, p. 51). In addition, if the children have siblings at home, they will have learned to respond and react to children as well.

Peers in the early childhood classroom, however, pose a different problem for the young child. Many, if not most, 3- and 4-year-olds simply have not developed the social skills for making friends or getting along with others. The focus of these children is on themselves. Everything has been done for them up to this time. Even if a new baby has replaced them as the youngest in the family, they still struggle to be first in the eyes of their parents.

This egocentric point of view does not serve them well in the world at large because sooner or later they must learn to deal with others and be treated as part of a group. They may have been enrolled in your program to learn precisely this. The purpose of many preschools, especially nursery schools, is to help young children develop basic social skills.

What do these preschoolers need to learn? If socialization is not concerned with politeness and manners, then what social actions are involved in the early childhood classroom? Some important aspects include:

1. learning to make contact and play with other children
2. learning to interact with peers, to give and take
3. learning to get along with peers, to interact in harmony
4. learning to see things from another child's point of view
5. learning to take turns, to wait for a turn
6. learning to share with others
7. learning to show respect for others' rights
8. learning to resolve interpersonal conflicts

Preschoolers' success in developing these skills, either on their own or with your help, may make the difference in how they get along for much of the rest of their lives.

This chapter is particularly concerned with the young child's ability to make contact, interact, and get along with peers. In order to determine where each of your children stands in the development of these skills, you need to be aware of behaviors that will indicate his or her level of development. Because children engage in play—often together—and because play is an observable activity in the preschool classroom, we will focus on observing social play in this chapter.

EARLY RESEARCH

Many early childhood specialists have been interested in determining how children develop the skills to get along with one another. Social play has been the focus of such research since Mildred Parten first looked at social participation among preschool children in the late 1920s and published her findings in 1932. She found that social participation among preschoolers could be categorized, and that the categories correlated closely with age and maturity.

Parten identified six behavior categories that have since served as a basis in several different fields of study for determining the level of children's social skills. Her categories are:

1. *Unoccupied behavior*   The child does not participate in the play around him. He stays in one spot, follows the teacher or wanders around.
2. *Onlooker behavior*   The child spends much time watching what other children are doing and may even talk to them, but he does not join or interact with them physically.

3. *Solitary independent play*   The child engages in play activities, but he plays on his own and not with others or with their toys.

4. *Parallel activity*   The child plays independently but he plays next to other children and often uses their toys or materials.

5. *Associative play*   The child plays with other children using the same materials and even talking with them, but he acts on his own and does not subordinate his interests to those of the group.

6. *Cooperative play*   The child plays in a group that has organized itself to do a particular thing, and whose members have taken on different roles. (Parten, 1932, pp. 248–251)

Since 1932 a great many other researchers have used Parten's categories and find them still "observable." Researchers like to use Parten's play categories when observing children at play because these behaviors really can be seen in the play interactions of young children. Yet since Parten's day, a great deal of new information about the social development of young children has surfaced. Today we acknowledge that these early play categories are indeed a valuable beginning point for gathering observational data about a young child's social development, but we also need to incorporate other up-to-date information. Thus, the *Child Skills Checklist* uses the first four of Parten's play categories under "Social Play," but then uses four categories relating to children's play behavior in initiating play, gaining access to ongoing play, maintaining a play role, and resolving play conflicts.

SOCIAL PLAY DEVELOPMENT

The development of social play is very much age related, and it can thus be observed by the preschool child-care worker in a particular sequence as children progress from solitary play through parallel play to group play. Age-related development thus signifies that the child's social skill level depends upon her cognitive, language, and emotional maturity. It also assumes that the older a child is, the more experience she has probably had with social contacts.

Observers have noted that infants first begin to imitate one another in play toward the end of their first year. Early in their second year they already are engaging in peer play whenever they have the opportunity (Smith, 1982, p. 132). Often 2-year-olds begin peer play by playing alongside another toddler in a parallel manner. If they do interact with an age-mate, it is only with one. Two-year-olds do not seem to be able to handle more than one playmate at a time; a threesome does not last long for children of this age.

Three-year-olds, as they become more mature and experienced, are able to play with more than one other child at the same time. As they become less egocentric and more able to understand another child's point of view, 3-year-olds have more success with social play. Using more mature language, listening to their play partners, and adjusting their behavior to the situation all support such play.

Access Rituals

The trick for many children in your center will be to gain access to play that is already in progress. Sociologists call these maneuvers *access rituals*. Children new to the group may try different strategies to get involved: (a) The youngest children may use nonverbal appeals such as smiles or gestures of interest as they stand nearby and watch, hoping a player will take note and invite or allow them in; (b) other children may walk around and watch, or stand and watch, waiting for an opportunity to insert themselves; (c) they may engage in similar play parallel to the original players, hoping to join the original players if their own parallel play is accepted; (d) they may intrude in a disruptive manner, claiming that the space or the toys are their own; and (e) the oldest preschoolers often use words, asking "Can I play?" or "What are you doing?" to gain access.

The most successful strategy for a child to gain access to ongoing play seems to be to engage in parallel play. The least successful strategy is to be disruptive (Smith, 1982, p. 130). Researchers have noted that parallel play among preschoolers decreases as group play increases. Still, parallel play seems to be the principal mode of social play for 3- and 4-year-olds in most centers.

THE TEACHER'S ROLE

Many children learn how to interrelate and play with peers in an early childhood program without the teacher's assistance. There are others, however, who need your help. Newcomers, shy children, immature children, and others often have difficulty on their own. If yours is a multi-age classroom, it is often the youngest children who have difficulty gaining access to group play, sustaining their role in the play, and resolving conflict when it appears. These children very definitely need your help.

Yours is a special role in helping children develop the social skills related to peer acceptance. It involves several steps:

1. Set up the physical arrangement of the classroom to accommodate small group activities.
2. Observe and record the social skills of the children in order to determine (a) who is unoccupied, (b) who watches, (c) who plays alone, (d) who plays parallel to others, (e) who initiates play activities, (f) who gains access to play, (g) who can maintain his or her play role, and (h) who can resolve conflict.
3. Help children initiate contacts with other children.
4. Help children gain access to ongoing play.
5. Help children maintain their play roles.
6. Help children learn to resolve conflicts with others.

How the teacher carries out this important role in children's social skills development is discussed under each of the checklist items to follow. All eight of the checklist items of unoccupied, onlooker, solitary, parallel, and group play are, of course, descriptive rather than judgmental. We are interested in observing individual children on each item to try to discover the child's level of social skills. We must be careful not to judge a child negatively if we do not check a certain item. The items themselves are not negative or positive. They merely describe behavior. What we infer from the check marks or lack of them will be more meaningful if we also look at the recorded evidence on which the check marks or blanks are based. It is just as important to record descriptive evidence on *items not checked* as on those items you have checked.

❏ IS UNOCCUPIED DURING FREE PLAY (OR FOLLOWS TEACHER)

By using the *Child Skills Checklist* to determine the social play level for the children in your classroom, you can identify those children who have not yet become involved in play with others. These may be some of the children described in Chapter 3 who have had difficulty letting go of mother or their primary caregiver, especially at the beginning of the year. The shyness of children and the newness of the environment may also cause some children to hold back at first.

If the youngsters have not had experience with other children their age, a large group of peers can be overwhelming. This lack of experience with other children may put them at a loss as to how to gain access to group play. Three-year-olds, especially, have usually had more experience with adult caregivers than with other children their age, and may not know how to behave in a peer group.

Their level of cognitive development also governs their ability to play with others. Immature children may simply not know what to do or how to begin. In addition, their immature language skills may prevent them from making contacts through speaking.

Parten describes *unoccupied behavior* in her study as follows:

> The child apparently is not playing, but occupies himself with watching anything that happens to be of momentary interest. When there is nothing exciting taking place, he plays with his own body, gets on and off chairs, just stands around, follows the teacher, or sits in one spot glancing around the room. (Parten, 1932, p. 249)

If You Have Not Checked This Item: Some Helpful Ideas

■ Help but Do Not Pressure the Child

First you may need to help—but not pressure—the child into becoming engaged with an activity on her own, and later to become involved with another child. You might try sitting at the table-for-two with the child and helping her to get started with a puzzle, a pegboard, or some other table game. Once the child is involved, you should unobtrusively extract yourself and let her complete the game on her own. Put another puzzle or game on the table beside the first so that the child can continue her activity or a partner can join her.

■ Have a "Following Child" Do a Chore

If the unoccupied child follows you around, have him help you with something: mix paints for the easel, get out papers and scissors for an art project, find animal books from the bookshelves, sort the pieces in a table game. If he accepts such a chore, perhaps he will then sit down at a table to complete it. If not, ask the child what else he would like to do to help.

■ Arrange Parts of the Room for Two Children

Set up a few small tables, especially at the beginning of the year, for two children to participate in a parallel activity: two puzzles, two table games, two sheets of paper and boxes of crayons, two individual chalkboards and colored chalk, two books to look at, two easels next to one another. This may be all it takes for the unoccupied child to become involved as soon as she feels comfortable. Playing with one other child is not so overwhelming as a whole group. Furthermore, since children imitate one another, the immature child can actually learn how to play in this new environment by copying her tablemate.

❏ SPENDS TIME WATCHING OTHERS PLAY

Onlooking behavior is often the next level of behavior. Some children who are new to a program begin by watching. They may walk around the room to see what is going on, but not join in. Parten describes the *onlooker* in these words:

> The child spends most of his time watching the other children play. He often talks to the children whom he is observing, asks questions, or gives suggestions, but does not overtly enter into the play himself. This type differs from the unoccupied in that the onlooker is definitely observing particular groups of children rather than anything that happens to be exciting. The child stands or sits within speaking distance of the group so that he can see and hear everything that takes place. (Parten, 1932, p. 249)

Onlooking behavior is often the first step toward group participation. Some children take longer than others to become involved with group play. They need to know what is going on around them, who is doing what, and how they can enter this play. If the children seem engaged in watching a group at play, it may be best to leave them alone at first. They may join the others once they are at ease in the center. On the other hand, some children do not seem to know what to do or say in order to get others to play with them or to allow them to join in.

If You Have Not Checked This Item: Some Helpful Ideas

■ Suggest an Initiating Activity

New children need to establish connections with other children in the classroom. They can do this by initiating a conversation with another child. If the onlooking child has not done so, you can suggest that she go over to another child and tell him what she would like to do. "Tell Paul you like to play with blocks. Say to him, 'Let's build a house with the blocks.'"

■ Suggest Parallel Play

If, after some onlooking time has elapsed, the child still has not joined in with the others, you may want to suggest that she build a building next to Paul's, or play with clay at Richard's table, or drive her toy car through Sandra's tunnel after she asks her permission. As mentioned previously, parallel play like this is one of the most successful strategies for a child to gain access to ongoing play.

❏ PLAYS BY SELF WITH OWN TOYS/MATERIALS

Many young children, when they first enter a preschool program, start out playing by themselves. This may occur because of the strangeness of the situation or their lack of self-confidence with unfamiliar children. Solitary play also occurs because children are attracted by the toys and materials and want to try them out by themselves. Some solitary play may occur because certain programs encourage it or because children have an independent project they want to accomplish. You will need to observe and record the child's actual activity during solitary play, as well as the youngster's overall involvement or lack of it with other children.

The following is Parten's description of *solitary independent play*:

> The child plays alone and independently with toys that are different from those used by the children within speaking distance and makes no effort to get close to other children. He pursues his own activity without reference to what others are doing. (Parten, 1932, p. 250)

For some children solitary play is truly a beginning level of social play that precedes their becoming involved in playing with others. If your children do not play at all with others or only play parallel to them, then you might consider solitary play as a beginning level of play for such youngsters.

More recent research, however, by Sara Smilansky in the 1960s and Kenneth H. Rubin in the 1970s and 1980s has looked at children's play in terms of their cognitive development in addition to their social skills. They are saying that levels of play are determined not only by whether children play by themselves or with others, but also by what children do during play (Rubin, 1977; Smilansky, 1968).

To determine whether your solitary players are, indeed, at a beginning level of social play, you should note in your observational data what they are doing. If children are manipulating toys and materials or trying them out to see how they work, then they are at a beginning level of play. In block play, for instance, beginners often pick up a block, put it down, pound with it, or put it in a container and then dump it out. More mature players stack blocks into towers, line them up into roads, or build buildings with them.

Research has also revealed that children from low-income families spend more time doing this sort of manipulative play than middle-income children (Rubin, 1977, pp. 16–24). Can we infer that such children are less socially and cognitively mature than their middle-class peers? Or should we wonder whether their solitary play has to do with the fact that they may have fewer play materials in their homes and thus must spend more time in a solitary manner in your program, manipulating these materials to find out how they work? Whatever the case, we need to provide a wide range of learning materials to encourage children to become involved on their own, as well as with others.

If you observe children constructing or creating something by themselves, this may indicate something altogether different from a beginner who is manipulating materials alone. If they are purposefully using materials toward some end, for instance, making a building, a painting, or a play dough creation, they may be exhibiting higher level creativity skills. This higher level of skill development may have made it possible for such children to get satisfaction out of making something on their own. Instead of discouraging these children from solitary constructive play, you should provide them with many opportunities for expressing this creativity. Such children will join in group play again when the time is right for them.

Particular programs, such as Montessori's, have an approach that features one-person problem-solving materials. Such programs have a great deal more solitary play going on and a lesser amount of group play than other programs. Thus it is important that you take note of a program's goals and curriculum during your observations as well as how the child uses the available materials.

If You Have Not Checked This Item: Some Helpful Ideas

If children are not engaged in solitary play or any other kind of play during the free choice period, you can help them in the following ways.

■ Give the Child a Familiar Material

Many children are familiar with dough at home but have not had an opportunity to play with it. Have the nonplaying child help you mix a bowl of play dough. Then give him some implements such as a small rolling pin and cookie cutters, and let him play.

■ Read a Book

Read a book about a nursery school such as *My Nursery School* by Harlow Rockwell (New York: Puffin Books, 1976), a simple story with a full-page illustration about each activity in the school and a one-line sentence underneath. Then ask the child which of these activities he would like to try. If he can't decide, put out a puzzle for him.

❑ PLAYS PARALLEL TO OTHERS WITH SIMILAR TOYS/MATERIALS

Parallel play is a fascinating phenomenon. If you are unfamiliar with this type of play, you have to see it to believe it. Parallel play often involves two children who seem to be playing together. As you get close enough to witness what is going on, you find that each child is actually playing a different game from a different point of view. If language is involved, the two children seem to be talking to themselves rather than each other. As Parten describes *parallel play*,

> The child plays independently, but the activity he chooses naturally brings him among other children. He plays with toys that are like those which the children around him are using, but he plays with the toy as he sees fit, and does not try to influence or modify the activity of the children near him. He plays beside rather than with the other children. There is no attempt to control the coming or going of children in the group. (Parten, 1932, p. 250)

All kinds of parallel play go on in the preschool setting. More seems to occur with younger than with older children. Parallel play, as previously mentioned, seems to enable younger children to learn to play cooperatively with others in an early childhood center. This statement makes a great deal of sense when you consider that your center consists of a large group of highly egocentric children who are strangers for the most part. They come together in a physical setting full of toys and activities just for them. How are they to deal with such a setting?

They begin by trying out things on their own. Then they play side by side using the same materials but playing a different game. Finally the children begin to cooperate, to interchange ideas, and to come together to play as a group with self-assigned roles and tasks. Once children have learned to play cooperatively, they may abandon parallel play altogether. Thus, a blank on a child's checklist for "Plays parallel to others with similar toys/materials" and a check mark for "Initiates activity/play with others" probably mean that the child has progressed in his or her development of social play beyond the parallel play stage.

If You Have Not Checked This Item: Some Helpful Ideas

■ Try Finger Painting for Two

Set up a small table where two can sit side by side, and put out finger paints to be shared. Invite one of your reluctant participants and one other child to paint. Do not force the reluctant child. Perhaps you could first involve him in a solitary manner and then ask him if another child could work next to him. If he agrees, he will be working not only parallel to the other child, but with the child, because the paints have to be shared.

■ Set Up Tape Recording for Two

It is important to have two cassette tape recorders in your program. They are invaluable because they provide an opportunity for two children to play individually with the same materials in a parallel manner. Tape recording is personal and fun. Even the shy child can talk as softly as she wants as long as she holds the mike up close. She can say anything about herself she wants: her name, the names of her brothers or sisters or pets, her favorite foods, or where she lives. Then comes the fun of listening to what she has spoken. Two children can record at the same table if they each talk into their own microphones. They may eventually want to talk into each other's mikes.

❏ INITIATES ACTIVITY/PLAY WITH OTHERS

As children begin to play with others or show indications that they would like to play with others, there are four social skills they will need to develop in order to play successfully:

1. initiate activities with peers
2. gain access to ongoing play
3. maintain their role in play
4. resolve conflicts during play

As children begin to play with others, they need to develop social skills such as initiating activities with peers.

The first of these skills, initiating activities with peers, focuses on getting together with unfamiliar peers in order to play. The child might try initiating an activity by establishing some kind of common ground with another child. For instance, he could start a conversation with another child, mentioning what he likes or what he is going to do. "Let's play with blocks. I'm gonna build a garage for my car," Rodney could say to Eric. Because children often imitate one another, this may be all it takes for Eric to join Rodney in his play. Even if Eric replies, "I don't wanna," he may be so intrigued with Rodney's building that he'll join him anyway. After all, children like to be invited to join in with someone else.

Another way to establish a common ground with an unfamiliar peer is to explore similarities with that child. For instance, a child could approach another child who has a similar T-shirt or sneakers or who is playing with a toy similar to hers at home. This may be the opening for these two children to play together. As LeBlanc notes, "Children who are able to find something to do with others are more likely to establish contact with peers and to successfully maintain that contact" (LeBlanc, 1989, p. 29).

Some children, however, are not as successful as others in initiating play. Perhaps they are shy or have been rejected by peers previously, or their language skills are not mature enough for them to know what to say. Then it is up to you to help them learn these initiating skills. This is the facilitator's role that you as a teacher of young children must take. Rather than stand in front of the total group and "teach" in the traditional manner, early childhood teachers need to spend their time (a) setting up classroom activities to accommodate small groups, (b) observing individuals to assess their skills and development, and then (c) working with individuals, based on their observed strengths and areas needing strengthening, to help them grow and learn.

If You Have Not Checked This Item: Some Helpful Ideas

■ Coach the Child in What to Say

First talk with the child to find out what he would like to do or who he would like to play with. Then give him an idea of what to say: "Tell Eric your idea about building a garage for your car. Invite him to join you. Why don't you say, 'Eric, let's play with blocks. I'm going to build a garage for my car.' Go try it and see if he'll join you."

■ Model the Initiating Behavior

If the child seems to be unable to make any contact with someone he would like to play with, you can model the initiating behavior yourself. "C'mon, Rodney, you take that car and I'll take this car. We're going to build a garage for our cars. Let's see if we can get someone to help us. Let's ask Eric. Hi, Eric. We're going to build a garage for our cars with the blocks. Want to help us?"

You should be successful because children enjoy playing with the teacher and like to be chosen by the teacher to do things. However, if Eric refuses, then approach another child with the same request. This helps Rodney learn what to do should he be refused. You can extract yourself unobtrusively from this play once the children are engaged.

■ Give the Child a Toy That Can Involve Another Child

Puppets are excellent playthings that can involve more than one child. If your shy player gets involved in playing with a hand puppet you have provided, have him introduce another child to the play who will use another puppet from your supply. You may need to wear the other puppet yourself at first to get him started. Then see if he can entice another child to join in.

Try the same thing another day with a stuffed animal or miniature vehicle. Once the child is involved with the toy, ask him to ask another child to play. This puts the original child in charge of an activity he has already begun, and seems to make it easier for him to initiate a contact with an unfamiliar peer.

❑ GAINS ACCESS TO ONGOING PLAY IN POSITIVE MANNER

Next, children need to find a way to enter ongoing play. Some have no difficulty. Others may need your help. As mentioned previously, disruptive actions are the least successful. In her survey of research on preschool children's peer acceptance, Kristen Kemple found that "researchers have recognized for a long time that generally positive behaviors, such as cooperation, are associated with being accepted by peers, and generally antisocial behaviors, such as aggression, are associated with being rejected" (Kemple, 1991, p. 49).

Children who successfully enter ongoing play seem to have adopted such positive strategies as (a) observing the group to see what is going on, (b) adopting the group's frame of reference, (c) contributing something relevant to the play, and, especially, (d) asking again if they are denied access (LeBlanc, 1989, p. 30).

Communication skills seem to play an important role in children's gaining acceptance in group play. They need to talk with the players, understand what their replies are, and then respond again, replying to their concerns.

If the group is pretending to take their babies to the doctor's, for example, a successful strategy Colleen might use for gaining entrance is to get a doll from the housekeeping area and bring it along with the others, saying, "My baby needs to be examined, too." In this case, she has adopted the group's frame of reference (doctor play) as well as contributing something relevant to the play (bringing her baby to be examined). But just as important, she uses words and does not crash unannounced into the play. Instead, she gets a doll, brings it along with the others, and then communicates clearly: "My baby needs to be examined, too."

Had she merely asked, "Can I play?" it would be easy for the group to reject her. Had she taken one of the other children's dolls or tried to take over the role of the doctor, she would probably have been rejected. Children who have difficulty seeing things from another person's point of view may not understand what is required of them to join ongoing play. Then it is up to you to help.

Jennifer, a shy little girl in nursery school, had trouble gaining access to much of the group play because she tended to be so unassertive. She would watch the others play, but whenever she shyly asked, "Can I play?" she was usually refused. Then she went off by herself. She should not have given up so easily. Over half of the requests made to join preschool play groups are denied, one researcher discovered (Corsaro, 1981). But because group play in preschool is so fluid and brief, there are many opportunities for outside children to join in during a typical day. Just because a child is denied access once does not mean she will be denied if she tries again.

Many children like Jennifer do not try again. Then it is up to the teacher to coach them on their next step, or to model a more successful strategy that they might try. If nothing seems to work for Jennifer, and the group itself will just not accept her, then the teacher may want to spend some time coaching the group on how to admit an outsider.

If You Have Not Checked This Item: Some Helpful Ideas

■ Use Puppets with the Child and/or the Group

Bring out two hand puppets and introduce them with names such as Ollie Outsider and Purely Personal to Jennifer. Tell her that Ollie wants to play with Purely, but Purely won't let her. Ask Jennifer what she thinks that Ollie can do to get Purely to let her play. Whatever Jennifer suggests, you can try out with the puppets. Let the Ollie puppet succeed if Jennifer's suggestions seem appropriate. Give your own suggestions if none of Jennifer's seem to work.

Use this same sort of puppet play to coach a group that will not let an outsider join. First ask the children how they think that Ollie feels when Purely won't let her play. Then ask the group why they think that Purely won't let Ollie join in. Finally, ask the group what Ollie can do and what Purely can do so that everyone can play together. Then act out with the puppets the suggestions given by the group.

■ Provide a Time for Everyone to Join a Group

It is much easier for children to join a play group at the outset. Once the group has started, the outsider usually encounters resistance entering an established group. Therefore, it is important for the preschool teacher to provide a time and an opportunity for everyone to become involved in playing with someone else (Hatch & Johnson, 1991, p. 32). This can be at the beginning of the free choice period. Perhaps a brief total group time can acquaint the children with the activities available. Then they can be encouraged to choose an activity and choose the child or children they want to play with in this activity.

Be careful that you do not choose the activity for the child and force him into it. Gaining access to a group must be learned by the child on his own. If a certain child holds back and does not join with any others, then you can make a suggestion. You can urge the child to choose an activity or a partner. But do not pressure. He may not be ready yet.

■ Read a Book

Read to the outsider child or to the insider group a book such as *I'll Be the Horse If You'll Play with Me* by Martha Alexander (New York: Dial Press, 1975). Then talk about the topic of how someone feels when someone else won't let her play, and how someone can join in play in your classroom. This book addresses the problem of little sister Bonnie who wants to play with big brother Oliver but always gets the worst of the situation.

❑ MAINTAINS ROLE IN ONGOING PLAY IN POSITIVE MANNER

Developing the skill to enter ongoing play is not the end of social skill development for the preschool child, but only the beginning. He must also be able to continue playing with the others. If the play situation is a pretend one, then the child needs to get along with others in the role he has chosen or been assigned. If he is building a block structure with another child, then he needs to be able to cooperate with his play partner in order to complete the building. This give-and-take among preschool youngsters is not always smooth. In order to maintain their role in ongoing play children need to be able to

1. carry on a conversation
2. maintain eye contact when speaking
3. listen to and watch other speakers
4. adjust own conversation content in order to be understood (Smith, 1982, pp. 135–136)

If the play is a group dramatic play situation, then children must also be able to pretend, take a role, take turns, and show respect for others' roles—and all within a playful framework. Quite a complex agenda for 3-, 4-, and 5-year-olds. No wonder not all children are successful at it.

Yet being successful at group dramatic play helps young children to practice and learn the social skills necessary *to be successful in life*. That is why group dramatic play in the preschool classroom is one of the most important activities. Some of the social skills children can learn through group dramatic play include

1. adjusting their actions to the requirements of their role and the group
2. being tolerant of others and their needs
3. not always expecting to have their own way
4. making appropriate responses to others
5. helping others and receiving help from them

Most centers provide a place for group dramatic play, that is, spontaneous role play in an imaginary situation made up by the children during free play. Rubin found that these situations mainly involve the topics of house, store, doctor, firefighter, and vehicle play (Rubin, 1977, p. 21).

A clear sequence of pretend play in young children has emerged over the past 20 years of research. By age 2, children can pretend and often play with imaginary objects. The more complex group dramatic play mentioned here cannot happen until children can articulate verbally, which occurs between 2 and 4 years of age. Such play gradually becomes more and more complex with 5-year-olds in kindergarten until about age 6, when the frequency of group dramatic play begins to decline. By age 7, games with rules are more prominent, and group dramatic play seems to disappear altogether (Smilansky, 1968, pp. 10–11).

Thus, the early childhood classroom needs to take advantage of this recognized sequence of children's activities, and to provide the materials, equipment, space, and time to allow and encourage children to engage in group pretend play—the practice field for the social skills of life itself! Chapter 14 discusses the development of the children's imagination and the themes they choose when making up the roles and situations for group dramatic play. Here we are concerned with the young child's personal interactions with peers in order to continue his or her play with them. Engaging in group pretend play like this helps to transform a preschool child from an egocentric being who is the center of all attention into a socialized human being who recognizes the existence of others' points of view, and can respond appropriately.

If You Have Not Checked This Item: Some Helpful Ideas

■ Turn Field Trips into Pretend Play with Appropriate Props

You will be taking your children on field trips to stores, farms, fire stations, hospitals, laundromats, parks, zoos, pet shops, and construction sites. Upon your return you will want to provide a variety of ways for children to represent and talk about this experience.

An excellent activity is to provide props for them to play the roles seen at the field trip site. Many teachers, after each field trip, make up a prop box filled with paraphernalia to be used in pretending the different roles. A trip to the post office, for instance, could produce a prop box with stamps (canceled postage stamps or stickers of some sort), a stamp pad and stamper, envelopes, a mail bag (tote bag), a mail carrier's hat, and a picture book about a mail carrier. They label each box on the outside with a picture and words the children soon recognize. Then the children are free to take such boxes from the shelf and play with the equipment during free choice period. If children have shown interest in the field trip, they are more likely to become involved with pretend play afterward.

Phyllis and Noel Fiarotta's *Be What You Want to Be* gives dozens of suggestions for making your own props out of discarded materials.

■ Change Your Dramatic Play Area from Time to Time

Everyone is stimulated by change. If you have had housekeeping equipment in your dramatic play period for a number of weeks, try converting the area to something else: perhaps a store or a beauty/barber shop. Talk with the children and have them help to stock it with empty or discarded items from home.

■ Put New Accessory Items in the Block Area

Group pretend play takes place in areas other than the dramatic play corner. Children also can do their follow-up pretending after a field trip in the block corner. Mount pictures of the field trip site at eye level on the wall to give children seated on the floor ideas for creating new kinds of buildings. Add appropriate accessories to the shelves within the block area as well. If you have been to a construction site, put out little trucks, figures of people, string (for ropes and wires), plastic tubing, even stones if you want to be very realistic. Accessories can also be put at the sand or water table, although pretending in these areas is more often solitary or parallel than group play.

■ Help the Shy Child Get Involved

You may need to take a role yourself in order to help the shy child get involved in the playing. She may not have the access skills to enter an engaged group. You both can pretend to be visitors going to the store, doctor's office, or home. Let her carry something to give to the other players: pretend money, a ticket, or a box of something to exchange. Once she is involved in the play you can leave.

❏ RESOLVES PLAY CONFLICTS IN POSITIVE MANNER

Not only does group play teach children the social skills of gaining access and maintaining a role in the playing, but more importantly, it gives young children the opportunity to learn to get along together. This is not always easy. Conflicts of all kinds occur with high frequency in an early childhood classroom. Children need to learn how to resolve such disagreements in a positive manner. During group play major conflicts often focus on

1. roles
2. direction of play
3. turns
4. toys

Pretend roles are important to the children who assume them. In spontaneous dramatic play certain children often insist on being mother, or father, or doctor. If several children want the same role, a conflict often results. This does not necessarily mean a physical fight, but usually an argument and sometimes tears. If the children involved cannot resolve the conflict quickly, play is disrupted and sometimes disbanded.

Conflict also occurs over play themes in dramatic play (Let's play doctor. No, let's play superheroes.), and over the direction of the action, which is generally made up on the spot. Egocentric young players often want their own way and frequently disagree over who will do what, how they will do it, and what's going to happen next.

"It's my turn!" or "It's my toy!" are other comments frequently heard during group play in early childhood classrooms or playgrounds. Youngsters 3, 4, and 5 years old are still for the most part focused on themselves and their desires. It is most annoying for them to find that someone else got there first, or has what they want, or won't listen to them.

Often such children turn to the teacher to resolve these conflicts. You need to be aware, however, that the youngsters themselves have the capability to resolve social play conflicts on their own. That, in fact, should be your goal for the children: to help them resolve play conflicts by themselves in a positive manner. How do you do it? To begin with, your observation of individual children will tell you which youngsters are able to resolve conflicts on their own and which ones are not.

Rather than focusing on the negative behaviors during such conflicts, spend some time observing how certain children are able to settle their disputes positively. We can learn a great deal from children if we are willing to try. Consider the following running record that looks at 4-year-old Alex:

Alex, Calvin, and Dominic are on top of the indoor climber pretending to be astronauts in outer space. Alex is the captain of the space shuttle. All three boys make zooming noises and motions. Alex pretends to steer. Two other boys climb up the ladder to try to join the group but are ignored and finally leave.
Alex: "Duck! There's a meteor!"
Calvin: "It's my turn to be captain, Alex."
Alex ignores Calvin and continues steering.
Dominic: "No, it's my turn. I never get a turn."
Alex: "We're being bombarded by meteors! You need to duck!" (He ducks his head.)
Calvin: "I'm captain now."
Alex ignores Calvin and continues steering.
Dominic: (to Calvin) "You can't be captain. Alex is still captain."
Alex: "You can be copilot. They always have copilots."
Calvin begins pretending to steer.
Alex: "Bang! We've been hit by a meteor! Abandon ship!" (He slides down slide to floor and runs across room; other boys follow.)

This exciting adventure in outer space is typical of the vigorous dramatic play preferred by 4-year-olds. It should also be exciting to an observer to see a 4-year-old like Alex handle a role conflict with such composure and success. Alex is often the leader in such play, and from the way he uses ideas and words, it seems obvious that he is an experienced player. Children who play together a great deal learn by trial and error what works in resolving conflicts and what doesn't work. They also find out what works with particular children and what doesn't work.

Looking at the strategies that Alex uses, the first one is *ignoring*. Alex ignores the boys who try to join his ongoing space shuttle play. They finally go away, so he certainly notes that this kind of ignoring is a successful way to keep out certain unwanted players. Then another potential conflict emerges: Calvin wants a turn to be captain. At first Alex ignores this request as well. Then Dominic joins in and also wants to be captain. Now Alex tries another strategy: *distracting*. He tells them that they are being bombarded by meteors and wants them all to duck. A strategy like this may sometimes work. In fact, here it seems to work with Dominic, who gives up his own demand to be captain, and *cooperates* with Alex. But it does not work with Calvin because he has not given up his demand. So Alex tries another strategy: *negotiating*. He offers Calvin another role: copilot. Calvin accepts and the play continues. This does not mean that either boy knows exactly what a copilot is. But it must sound satisfactory to Calvin because he *compromises* his demand to be captain, accepts the new role as copilot, and plays the role the same as Alex plays the captain's role.

Alex may very well have known that he had to do something to satisfy Calvin, or perhaps Calvin would have gotten up and left or continued his complaints and disrupted the play. Obviously Alex wanted the play to continue and wanted to keep his own role as captain and leader. He was successful in *negotiating a compromise*.

Did all of this actually happen in so short a dramatic play incident, you may wonder? Yes, it did. Observe a child involved in group play for yourself and record everything that happens. Then step back and interpret what you have seen. Obviously the children do not talk or think in terms of strategies. These are adult interpretations. Young children do not conceptualize in this manner. They just do it. Trial and error has taught certain alert youngsters what works for them and what doesn't when conflict arises. Children who are successful in resolving play conflicts in a positive manner often use strategies such as

1. ignoring
2. distracting
3. reasoning
4. negotiating
5. cooperating
6. compromising

If You Have Not Checked This Item: Some Helpful Ideas

If your observations turn up children who do not seem to know how to resolve play conflicts like this, then you may want to consider some of the following solutions.

▪ Have the Child Observe and Discuss Play with You

Have a child who often tries to resolve play conflicts by hitting or shouting observe a group play situation with you and then discuss it. If the child had sat next to you as you observed and recorded the Alex-Calvin-Dominic play incident, you might say to him:

> *Alex is captain of the space shuttle, isn't he? But Calvin wants to be captain, and so does Dominic. What does Calvin do? Yes, he tells Alex that he wants to be captain. Does Alex let him? No, he doesn't pay attention to him. So then what does Calvin do? Does he yell at Alex? No. Does he hit Alex? No. He tells him again that he wants to be captain. Does Alex let him? He lets him be a copilot. Is that like being captain? What would you do if you were on the space shuttle with Alex, Calvin, and Dominic? Do you think your ideas would work?*

If the play situation you observe with the child contains some aggressive behavior, ask the child what was the result of the behavior. Most children will not continue to play with peers who act aggressively. Often they won't allow such peers in their play groups in the first place.

▪ Use Puppets

For a child who gets into arguments frequently with her playmates, try using two puppets to enact a similar situation. Name your puppets something like Tong-Talk-Back and Fronz-Friendly. Put one on each hand and enact a play situation where Tong argues with Fronz over something, with the result that the play is discontinued. Ask the child what Tong could have said to keep the play going. Ask what she would have done.

▪ Coach the Child on How to Act

Sometimes you need to go to a child and coach her on how to act or what to say in a situation. You must make it clear to children that you will not let them hit anyone or hurt anyone or call them names. When they are upset about something, children must learn to express their feelings in words. You may need to coach those who do not know how.

> *Teresa, tell Jenny how you feel because she took your eggbeater. Don't call her names. Tell her why you are upset. Say it in words. Say, "Jenny, you took my eggbeater. That makes me feel bad. I wasn't finished using it. Please give it back."*

▪ Do a Group Role Play

Sometimes the play group itself doesn't know how to resolve conflicts peacefully. In that case, you can consider having a group role play sometime after the children have settled down. The players should be other children, so that the children having conflicts can watch. Take a role yourself if it seems appropriate. Then you can help direct the play. Give a few other children names and roles to play. Describe a brief conflict situation. Then have the children act it out. Stop the play at any time to discuss what has happened, and whether there is a better way to resolve the conflict. Try each of these techniques to see which ones work best with your particular children.

■ Read a Book

There are other ways for children to get what they want besides aggressive actions. Read to one or two children at a time *Move Over, Twerp* by Martha Alexander (New York: Dial Press, 1981) about little Jeffrey who is finally big enough to ride the bus to school, but the big boys won't let him sit where he wants to. Jeffrey's family members give him advice on what to do, but it is Jeffrey's own clever strategy that finally helps him get his way. Ask your children what they would do. Could any of them apply a strategy like Jeffrey's to anything that happens in your classroom?

OBSERVING, RECORDING, AND INTERPRETING SOCIAL PLAY

How should you use the "Social Play" *Checklist* with your children? The following description shows how one classroom team put the checklist to use.

When 3-year-old Lionel entered the classroom as a new child in January, he seemed to have a great deal of trouble interacting peacefully with the other children. By the end of the third week he still had not joined any of the group games. The staff members decided to make a running record of Lionel during the free play period for several days and then transfer the results to the *Child Skills Checklist*, as illustrated in Figure 5.1. Here is a typical example of a running record made on Lionel:

> *Lionel gets two little cars from box in block corner & sits on floor moving cars around, one in each hand. Makes car noises with voice. Plays by himself with cars for 5 minutes. Moves closer to block building that two other boys are constructing. Plays by himself with his cars. Then L. tries to drive his cars up wall of building. Boys push him away. L. waits for a minute, then tries to drive car up wall of building again. Boys push him away. L. crashes one car into building & knocks down wall. One of boys grabs L's car & throws it. Other boy pushes L. away. L. cries. Teacher comes over & talks with all three. L. lowers head & does not respond. Boys say: "He was trying to knock down our building with his cars" and "We don't want him to play with us."*

When the staff members reviewed the running records and *Checklist* information recorded for Lionel, they concluded that he knew where to find materials and toys in the classroom and how to use them. They also interpreted his "Social Skills" *Checklist* results to mean that Lionel was beyond onlooker behavior, and that he played by himself and in parallel play as close as possible to other children because he wanted to join them. His methods for gaining access to a group (i.e., driving his car up the block building wall and crashing his car into the wall) were not successful or acceptable. Nor was his language development as advanced as many of the children in the classroom, which they determined from the language skills checklist results. That may have been the reason he did not express his wants verbally.

Figure 5.1

Social play observations for Lionel

Child Skills Checklist

Name _____Lionel_____ Observer _____Barb_____

Program _____Preschool – K 2_____ Dates _____1/20_____

Directions:

Put a ✔ for items you see the child perform regularly. Put *N* for items where there is no opportunity to observe. Leave all other items blank.

Item	Evidence	Date
3. Social Play		
_N_ Is unoccupied during free play (or follows teacher)	L. is beyond this level of play	1/20
_N_ Spends time watching others play	L. is beyond this level of play	1/20
_✔_ Plays by self with own toys/materials	Plays with little cars	1/20
_✔_ Plays parallel to others with similar toys/materials	Moves close to block building, playing with his cars	1/20
_____ Initiates activity/play with others	Does not initiate with others	1/20
_____ Gains access to ongoing play in positive manner	Tries to gain access by driving cars up building; then crashes car	1/20
_N_ Maintains role in ongoing play in positive manner	Does not gain access	1/20
_____ Resolves play conflicts in positive manner	Crashes car into building when boys won't let him play	1/20

The staff decided to try pairing up Lionel with Adrian, a more mature player, who might help Lionel get acquainted with the others and gain access to their play. They asked Lionel and Adrian (who also liked cars) to build a block garage for the little cars for the staff to photograph. Eventually two other boys joined them in this activity.

By using observing and recording in this manner, individual children can be assisted in their development of social play skills and helped to grow and learn in your program.

REFERENCES

Corsaro, W. (1981). Friendship in the nursery school: Social organization in peer environment. In S. R. Asher & I. M. Gottman (Eds.), *The development of children's friendships (pp. 207-241)*. New York: Cambridge University Press.

Fiarotta, Phyllis, & Noel Fiarotta. (1977). *Be what you want to be!* New York: Workman Press.

Hatch, J. Amos, & Lynn G. Johnson. (1991). Guiding the social development of young children. *Day Care and Early Education, 18*(4), 29–33.

Kemple, Kristen M. (1991). Preschool children's peer acceptance and social interaction. *Young Children, 46*(5), 47–54.

LeBlanc, Linda M. (1989). Let's play: Teaching social skills. *Day Care and Early Education 16*(3), 28–31.

Parten, Mildred B. (1932). Social participation among pre-school children. *Journal of Abnormal and Social Psychology, 27*, 243–369.

Rubin, Kenneth H. (1977). Play behaviors of young children. *Young Children, 32*(9), 16–24.

Smilansky, Sara. (1968). *The effects of sociodramatic play on disadvantaged preschool children.* New York: Wiley.

Smith, Charles A. (1982). *Promoting the social development of young children: Strategies and activities.* Palo Alto, CA: Mayfield.

OTHER SOURCES

Beaty, Janice J. (1992). *Skills for preschool teachers.* New York: Merrill/Macmillan.

Howes, C. (1992). *The collaborative construction of pretend: Social pretend play functions.* Albany: State University of New York Press.

Ramsey, Patricia G. (1991). *Making friends in school: Promoting peer relationships in early childhood.* New York: Teachers College Press.

Trawick-Smith, Jeffrey. (1988). "Let's say you're the baby, OK?" Play leadership and following behavior of young children. *Young Children, 43*(5), 51–59.

Wintre, Maxine Gallander. (1989). Changes in social play behavior as a function of preschool programs. *Journal of Educational Research, 82*(5), 294–300.

LEARNING ACTIVITIES

1. Use the "Social Play" section of the *Child Skills Checklist* as a screening tool to observe all of the children in your classroom. Which ones engage mainly in solitary play? in parallel play? in group play? Are there any who are unoccupied or onlookers?

2. Choose a child whom you have observed engaging in solitary play. Make a running record of the child on three different days to determine what kind of solitary play was performed. How could you involve the child in the next level of play? Should you do it? Why or why not?

3. Choose a child whom you have observed engaging mainly in parallel play. What kind of play does the child do? How can you help the child get involved in the next level of play? Use one of the suggested activities and record the results.

4. Choose a child whom you have observed as not being able to gain access to ongoing group play, and use one of the activities described in the text to help the child enter and play with a group.

5. Make a running record of a child observed in group pretend play. Afterward determine which of the strategies discussed on page 130 the child used to resolve conflicts. If the child is not successful, assist the child in resolving conflicts as described.

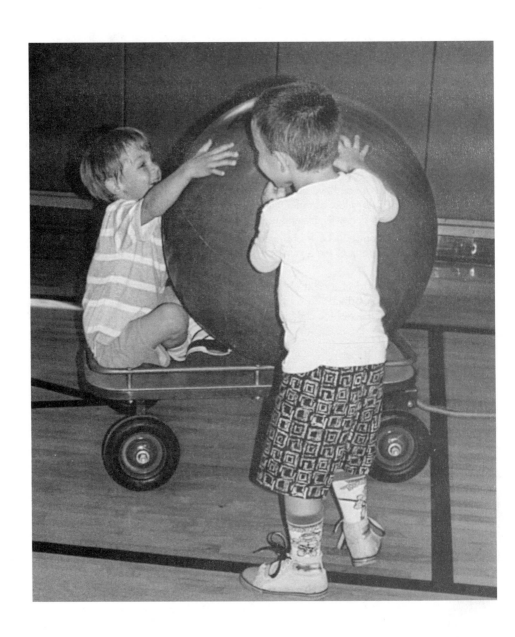

6 Prosocial Behavior

Prosocial Behavior Checklist

- ❑ Shows concern for someone in distress
- ❑ Shows delight for someone experiencing pleasure
- ❑ Shares something with another
- ❑ Gives something of his/her own to another
- ❑ Takes turns without a fuss
- ❑ Complies with requests without a fuss
- ❑ Helps another do a task
- ❑ Helps (cares for) another in need

A second area of young children's social development that is of great concern to early childhood caregivers is the positive aspect of moral development, better known today as *prosocial behavior*. It includes behaviors such as *empathy*, in which children express compassion by consoling or comforting someone in distress or by affirming a person's good fortune; *generosity*, in which children share or give a possession to someone; *cooperation*, in which children take turns willingly or cooperate with requests cheerfully; and *caregiving*, in which children help someone to complete a task or help someone in need.

These are some of the characteristics that help people to get along in society, that motivate people to interact with one another, and that help to make us human. Young children are not in the world alone. They are part of a family, a clan of relatives, a neighborhood, a community, a country, and a world of similar beings. To be an integrated member of the "human tribe," the young child needs to learn the tribe's rules of behavior from the beginning.

This learning, you may argue, should happen in the home, and it certainly does in an informal manner, whether or not parents realize they are teaching their children pro- or antisocial behavior. Children absorb everything that happens around them: what mom does when the baby cries, what dad does when someone upsets him, and what family members do when they disagree. Every emotional situation presents young humans with forceful patterns of behavior they can model. We know only too tragically that adult child-abusers often come from families where they were abused as children.

Prosocial behavior can be modeled as well. Both the home and the school should be aware of the powerful lessons taught by behavior modeling that children absorb so readily at this early age, especially in emotional situations. What do teachers do when they are upset by the behaviors of out-of-control children? It is so important for the other young children to see that the teachers do not allow their negative feelings to burst out.

The actions of adults in emotional situations can be used to demonstrate the prosocial feelings of caring, sharing, and consoling. As William Damon (1988) says,

> The social guidance that helps children refine their early moral emotions can come in many forms: as a conscious program of moral instruction offered by parents, teachers, and other adults; or as a spontaneous comment on one's conduct by friends, siblings and other peers. In each case, children *learn to know and interpret their own moral emotions in light of the moral reactions of others. (p. 29)*

Behavior also is taught by methods other than example both in the home and the preschool. Formal—often restrictive—rules for "proper" behavior have been drummed into children from time immemorial. Children are scolded or punished when they behave in an unacceptable manner. They may cry, sulk, or slink away, or they may try to behave correctly next time. But just as often, they stick out a tongue in defiance and grumble, Try and make me!

There is a better, easier way to teach appropriate behavior. Many early childhood specialists are focusing on the so-called prosocial behaviors in a search for ways to raise more humane members of the race. Not only does the learning of prosocial behaviors promise positive results, but it also offers more satisfying responses for both the child and the caregiver. Those who have tried this positive approach claim it is more effective than the negative method, and that as children learn prosocial ways to behave, negative behaviors seem to fade away.

Empathy, generosity, cooperation, caregiving—how do you teach such behaviors? They sound so elusive. Are not some children just "good" naturally?

If children seem to be good, they probably have maturity and a solid "home start." You can add to that maturity and home influence by the way you treat children in the early childhood classroom and by the way you model behavior yourself. But first, as with other areas of development, you should know where each of the children already stands concerning his or her development of prosocial behaviors. You will need to observe every child with regard to the eight checklist items and then make plans for individual support or activities that you will provide.

Each of the checklist items in this chapter is an observable behavior that shows whether the child possesses a particular prosocial capacity.

❑ SHOWS CONCERN FOR SOMEONE IN DISTRESS

Empathy

Empathy is the capacity to feel as another person does. Someone with empathy is able to understand another person's emotional response to a situation and to respond in the same way, in other words, "to feel" for that person. Empathy is a step beyond mere sympathy, in which one person can respond emotionally to another, but from his or her own perspective. With empathy, you respond from the other person's perspective, you participate in that person's feelings.

Some psychologists believe empathy is the basis for all prosocial behavior. Until children have this capacity, they will be unable to behave naturally in a helping, sharing, compassionate manner. Obviously, children can be forced to perform prosocially whether or not they understand what they are doing. But this forced performance is not empathy. Forced behavior has little to do with the prosocial skills of our concern. Behavior must be natural and spontaneous in order to show that children possess empathy.

Are children born with empathy, or do they learn it? Probably a little of both. Researchers have determined that capacities such as empathy have at least two different aspects that must be considered (Damon, 1983, p. 129). Empathy has an affective side that is the emotional response to another's distress or joy, and a cognitive side that allows the child to see things from another person's perspective.

Until this cognitive development has occurred (as discussed in Chapter 3), children will have difficulty expressing empathic concern for others because they still will be too egocentric and therefore unable to see things from another person's point of view. Because they lack this empathy, infants and toddlers often mishandle their animal pets. The youngsters have no idea that pulling a puppy's ear or squeezing a kitten might hurt it. These actions do not hurt the children themselves, therefore, why should the pulling or squeezing hurt their pet? This egocentric point of view eventually changes with cognitive maturity and experience, but until children can view things from another's perspective, they will have difficulty showing empathic compassion for another's distress.

When does this change take place? It happens gradually, of course, as does all development. Yet, some part of the human capacity to respond to distress must be built in, for even infants 1-day old will become upset and will cry when a nearby baby starts crying. Then, somewhere between 1 and 2 years of age, the cognitive change takes place. Toddlers, although they may not act appropriately, begin to show genuine concern for others. These youngsters have been observed giving up their favorite stuffed animal to an older sibling who is crying. They feel comforted by the animal, so why not give it to another in distress? The act of giving demonstrates their developing capacity for empathy.

From 2 to around 6 years of age, children begin to react more appropriately to the distress of others around them. The ages of the children in your class fall within this range. You will be observing them to determine which ones show concern for another child in distress. Distress may be displayed by someone who is hurt, sad, or sick. She may be crying or even screaming. It also could be less dramatically disclosed by a child who puts her head down on a table, goes into a corner, or leaves the room after an upsetting incident.

You will note that some children immediately come to the side of the upset child. Others do not. The children who display this empathic concern, of course, may be special friends of the upset child. On the other hand, highly sensitive children who have no particular friendship with the child also will come close. Some youngsters just stand by the side of the distressed child and look at him or look for the teacher. Others actively console the child, touching or speaking to him.

If a teacher causes the distress, a similar thing may happen. A child being reprimanded or scolded often will attract a circle of observers. In this case you will have more difficulty determining empathic behavior because some of the observers are more concerned for themselves and how the teacher feels about them. Others are simply curious. Before you check this item about them, watch and see who comforts the child after the teacher leaves. The children who comfort the child are not necessarily taking the distressed child's side against the teacher. If they stay with the child after the teacher leaves, they more than likely have true compassion for the child.

The classroom worker should know that family life and cultural background have a definite influence on empathic response in children. If families stress prosocial behavior, then their children will exhibit it more than children from families who do not teach or demonstrate it.

Some cultures stress consideration of group members more than others. Communal-type cultures, such as the Native American, Pacific Island, and Asian cultures, often stress concern for group members more than the American culture does. Our culture seems to stress competition among individuals more often than cooperation. The individual is glorified in our society, sometimes at the expense of the group. As a child caregiver in the multiethnic, multicultural society that makes up America, you need to be aware of such differences.

Research has shown that community size and the role of women also influence a child's prosocial inclinations. Children from a rural rather than urban setting, from a small rather than large city, or from a society where women have an important economic function outside the home are more inclined to show concern for others (Damon, 1983, p. 132). If the mother works outside the home, the children often learn to take on responsibilities at an early age. Learning helping and caretaking tasks so early obviously inclines children toward prosocial behavior. Thus, the teacher must know something about the individual child's background in order to make a more accurate assessment of the child's behavior.

If You Have Not Checked This Item: Some Helpful Ideas

If you have not checked this item for many of your children, do not be alarmed. Showing concern for someone in distress is one of the more difficult prosocial behaviors for preschoolers to learn. Distressful situations that happen to others upset onlookers too. Before the onlookers can respond, they often need to overcome their own anxieties. They thus are more apt to step back and let the adult show the concern. You, however, can involve your children in this humane act.

■ Model Empathic Behavior in the Classroom

You must serve as a model for the children. When something distressful happens to a child, you should show your own concern by going to her, touching, hugging, or holding her if this is appropriate. Talk to the child and give her time and space to feel better again.

A second way to model this behavior is through your actions in distressful situations that happen outside the classroom. If someone is hurt or dies, if a tragic event is shown on television, or if something upsetting happens within their families, then you must let the children know you are concerned, too.

■ Help the Children to Show Their Own Concern

Talk to the children both privately and in the group about distressful happenings that have occurred. Encourage the children to ask questions about things they do not understand. Show the youngsters that it is all right to cry and express emotions openly. When a class member is in the hospital, have the class make and send a card.

When children are pretending in dramatic play about people or pets being hurt, listen to see if the youngsters express compassionate feelings even in pretend. You can model a concerned role in pretending, too, by expressing your own sympathy when one of the players is pretending to be hurt.

■ Read a Book

Maybe a Band-Aid Will Help by Anna Grossnickle Hines (New York: Dutton, 1984) is a sensitively illustrated first-person narrative of little Sarah's concern and help for her doll Abigail when its leg comes off.

Don't Worry I'll Find You by Anna Grossnickle Hines (New York: Dutton, 1986) is a follow-up story about Sarah and Abigail, both of whom get lost when they go shopping in the mall. Sarah's concern for her doll and Mama's concern for Sarah are cleverly demonstrated.

I Have a Sister My Sister is Deaf by Jeanne Whitehouse Peterson (New York: Harper & Row, 1977) is a first-person narrative by a young girl about her younger sister, who is deaf. The girl tells all the things her sister can—and cannot—do in a manner showing great concern and sensitivity.

❏ SHOWS DELIGHT FOR SOMEONE EXPERIENCING PLEASURE

Empathy

Why are we humans always more aware of the bad things than the good? Is it because negative emotions are stronger or more upsetting to us, or because they occur more frequently? Whatever the reason, we seem to give negative emotions more of our attention. Giving negative emotions more attention in the presence of young children can be harmful. We are behavior models for the children, and if the youngsters see us showing more concern over the negative than the positive emotions, they may get the notion that bad is more important to us than good.

If we want children to learn a full range of empathic responses, then we ourselves need to be aware of and respond to the delightful things that happen to the people around us. How many gratifying things have happened to the children and adults in your classroom recently? Could any of the following be counted?

A new baby arrived at Sandra's house.

Richie got new sneakers.

Jeffrey found the mitten he lost.

Ken and Donnie finally finished their huge block building.

The bus driver won a lottery.

The teacher's assistant passed her CDA.

Michelle got a new dress.

Rhonda's grandmother is visiting her.

How would you have responded to these happenings? As a behavior model, you need to show the children that you care deeply about their successes as well as their troubles. Hug the children, exclaim over them, shake their hands, and laugh and dance around the room if this is appropriate. When children do the same to show their delight in someone else's success, make a point of thanking them for showing someone their pleasure. Celebrate happy occasions. Make your center one that rejoices in the good fortunes of its members.

We do not need to be like some newspapers that feature only bad news. Look for the good things that happen to individuals, and help your children to share in another person's pleasure by showing him they are happy for him.

Researchers looking at prosocial behavior in preschoolers report that friendly behaviors, in fact, occur more frequently than aggressive behaviors among peers in the group, and that friendly interactions increase at a faster rate than aggressive behavior during the preschool years, especially among the older children (Moore, 1982, p. 76).

If You Have Not Checked This Item: Some Helpful Ideas

■ Look for Reasons to Rejoice About an Individual's Happiness

Make a list of the good things that have happened to people you know. Make sure you model the prosocial behavior of rejoicing with the person yourself. Then invite individual children to do the same. They could make a congratulatory phone call to the person. They could take the person a flower or a finger painting. They could invite an outside person to the classroom and sing a song for the person.

■ Talk About Successes During Circle Time

Ask children to report on the nice things that have happened to people they know during group time. Start a ritual of going up to one of the children in the circle and shaking his or her hand in congratulations for anything positive that has happened to the child or the child's family.

❏ SHARES SOMETHING WITH ANOTHER

Generosity

Sharing and helping may be the easiest prosocial behaviors for young children to learn because these behaviors occur most frequently in the early childhood class-room, which is understandable when you consider the many opportunities children in a group have to learn to share materials with one another. Sharing also is easier to do than some of the other prosocial acts because the child only suffers a temporary loss. The youngster must give up something, but only temporarily.

Again, the child's ability to perform such an action depends upon her cognitive maturity as well as the lessons she has learned from those around her. The younger the child, the more inclined she is to consider the toy she is playing with as her per-sonal possession, whether it is or not. Children who still retain this egocentric view also will try to take the toys they want away from others, and they will be upset if the others do not comply. According to their reasoning, the fact that these egocentric children want the toy makes it theirs.

William Damon's study of the development of a child's sense of justice involved findings about what children considered to be fair in sharing or dividing up candy. The younger children (ages 4 and 5) gave themselves more candy than the older children gave to themselves. A scale that Damon derived to indicate children's levels of positive justice showed children at the first level (4 years and under) justified their choices simply on the basis of their wishes: They should get something because they want it. Children at the second level of the scale (ages 4 and 5) justified their actions on the basis of their size, gender, or whatever characteristic would get them the most candy. The next level of children (ages 5–7) preferred to share equally in order to prevent squabbles. Thus older children must realize that preserving the peace is more important than getting an extra piece of candy (Damon, 1983, p. 136).

In order to prevent squabbles, early childhood teachers need to establish rules governing "property rights" at the outset. When children first enter the classroom, they are confronted with a treasure house of materials to enjoy. The youngsters need to understand that these materials belong to the center, not to specific children. Individuals can use the materials, but the items must be shared, which means letting other children use the items either at the same time (as with paints), or one after another.

Nevertheless, some squabbles over equipment can be expected. The primary way young children learn rules is to test them. Who gets the favorite toy first? Favorites are often trikes and eggbeaters. Some teachers believe it is best to have several of the favorites in order to avoid problems. Other teachers believe that such problems afford good opportunities for children to learn how to share and take turns.

Researchers find that older children are more likely to share than younger ones. Sharing with peers, in fact, increases dramatically between the ages of 4 and 12 (Damon, 1983, p. 128). If a toy belongs to the center, young children are more likely to share the item than if it belongs to them personally. Most teachers ask children to keep toys from home in their cubbies. The youngsters can show the toys to the class at circle time, but afterwards the toys must be put away until it is time to go home.

Because sharing is such an important prosocial skill in the preschool center, everyone must spend time helping individuals to learn the skill. You may want to start by observing the prosocial behavior of every child in your class to see which children already know how to share and which ones may need help in learning this skill. Some children will share toys, food, and turns when asked by another child, but many still need the teacher to make the request.

If You Have Not Checked This Item: Some Helpful Ideas

■ Model Sharing

Sharing behavior of children is definitely influenced by adult modeling behavior. Adults often ask children to share with their peers, but how often do adults ask a child to share with them? Try it. Set up a situation where a child who has had difficulty in sharing must share a seat, a piece of equipment, or an activity with you. For example, invite him to paint at your table. Then, set out one jar of paint that the two of you must share. Verbalize as you work on your painting. Let the child know he is doing well sharing the paints.

■ Use Group Toys

Encourage a small group of two, three, or four children to construct a building using one set of table blocks. Have several children work on a large puzzle together. Have one child hold the wood while another saws at the woodworking table. Tie a wagon to the trike and let one child pedal while another rides in the wagon.

■ Set Up a Food-Sharing Experience

Bring in one apple, one orange, or one melon for each small group at your snack tables. Discuss with the children how they can share the piece of fruit. Let them help you divide it equally.

■ Read a Book

Sharing by Taro Gomi (South San Francisco: Heian International, 1981) is a simply illustrated book about two little girls who find ways to share an apple, colored paper, a ribbon, toys, and the love for their cat.

❑ GIVES SOMETHING OF HIS/HER OWN TO ANOTHER

Generosity

A great deal of research has been done on this aspect of prosocial behavior, perhaps because researchers find it easy to measure whether or not children are willing to give one of their possessions to someone else. Most studies show that as children increase in age their generosity also increases. What is not so clear is the reason for it.

We assume that as children become cognitively more mature they will be less concerned with themselves as the center of everything, and more aware of others and their needs. We also expect that as children grow older they will have more experiences with social customs through the teachings of their family, friends, school, and church. In other words, the children will have learned how society expects them to behave.

Other things also affect young children's giving. Length of ownership is one. Children seem more willing to give up a possession they have had awhile than something they have just obtained (Smith, 1982, p. 210). Perhaps the novelty of a recent acquisition eventually wears off.

The item the children are willing to give also makes a difference. It may be a toy, an item of food, a piece of candy, or money. Whether they have more of the same also makes a difference. Reasons for the giving have a bearing, too. Is the item given out of friendship, because someone asks for it, because someone has a need, or because an adult suggests that it might be a nice thing to do? Older children are more apt to respond to adult suggestions or pressure.

Children are more likely to share a favorite toy rather than to give it up totally. Formal occasions for giving such as birthdays or religious holidays teach children about giving. Their egocentric nature often shows itself when they want to give mom a toy truck or doll for her birthday.

Teaching generosity, however, is tricky in our society. We send children mixed messages. We tell children it is a good idea to give to people in need, but then the youngsters see us turn away charity solicitors at our front doors. Children hear us refuse to lend a lawn mower or power tool to a neighbor who has a need. Let him buy his own, we say. Let him work as hard as I did to buy this one.

Ours is a very materialistic, possession-oriented culture. Children learn this from television and our responses to the messages it sends us. Children witness how strongly we feel about our cars, stereos, and microwave ovens. It is an interesting commentary on our values to see families with fewer material possessions being much more generous with them.

Not all cultures value personal material possessions so highly. People of many Pacific islands, for instance, teach their children from the start that giving is more important than possessing. These people practice what they preach by simply giving a possession to a neighbor or relative who admires or has need of it. These people believe that their lives are enhanced by the person accepting something from them.

Nevertheless, as preschool teachers we need to be aware of how this prosocial behavior works with children in our classroom, regardless of our society's confusion over the issue. Use the *Child Skills Checklist* to determine which children will give a possession to someone else. Are these the same children you have checked for the other prosocial behaviors? What other characteristics do these children share? Do they come from families where they have been given a great deal of responsibility? Prosocial behavior such as generosity is often more evident in such children. Are they children who seem more mature in all areas of development? We know that generosity increases with age and maturity.

If You Have Not Checked This Item: Some Helpful Ideas

■ Be a Model of Generosity

Let children see you give up something of yours to someone in need: an item of clothing, a book, food, or money. How do you feel about this? In our society we are often reluctant as adults to begin this kind of giving ourselves. Will it get out of hand? Will people take advantage of us? How genuine is your own generosity? We have been conditioned to acquire material possessions and guard against losing them. Perhaps we need to learn to let go of something in order to get something else back.

■ Articulate Generosity

When situations arise where giving is appropriate, talk to your children about it. Maybe they could donate some money or services to help someone in need.

■ Read a Book

In *Jamaica's Find* by Juanita Havill (Boston: Houghton Mifflin, 1986), a little African-American girl named Jamaica finds a stuffed dog in the park and takes it home for her own. Her family helps her to realize that another girl like herself might have lost it. Jamaica returns the dog to the park lost-and-found, by chance finds the girl who lost it, and then shares the girl's delight over the recovery of her favorite toy.

Maebelle's Suitcase by Tricia Tusa (New York: Macmillan, 1987) is a whimsical story about 108-year-old Maebelle who lives in an exotic tree house she has built because of her fascination with birds. Maebelle makes hats to sell and also to enter in the town's annual hat contest. When her bird friend Binkle asks for her suitcase to take on his trip south, Maebelle gives it to him without hesitation. But when Binkle loads it too heavily to lift, she invites him in to watch her make her contest hat. Somehow all of the decorations she needs can be found in Binkle's suitcase; he gives them to her one by one, including the suitcase. Her hat does not win the contest but is chosen for the town museum. Both friends are proud and happy: Maebelle because she gave up her real hat to help her bird friend, and Binkle because he gave Maebelle the contents of the suitcase to make the hat.

❑ TAKES TURNS WITHOUT A FUSS

Cooperation

Cooperation includes a wide range of prosocial behaviors, including turn taking, alternating the use of toys, equipment, or activities, complying with requests, coordinating actions to accomplish goals, accepting other children's ideas, and negotiating and compromising in play. Certain of these behaviors were discussed in Chapter 5,

"Social Play." Here we are specifically looking at alternating behaviors—that is, going in a certain order, first one and then another; waiting for another child to have a turn; or alternating the use of toys and equipment with other children.

Opportunities for learning and practicing these particular prosocial behaviors occur much more frequently in the early childhood classroom than do occasions for giving. In order to maintain a smoothly running program, you must help children learn at the outset how to take turns and wait their turns in the group situation.

Those children with brothers and sisters at home may have learned this already, although it is sometimes the inappropriate behavior they learn, such as the biggest or strongest gets the first turn. Research has also shown that authoritarian parents do not necessarily help children to learn this prosocial behavior. When parents strictly control their children's actions, the children have less motivation and fewer opportunities to develop moral reasoning and turn taking on their own (Eisenberg, Lennon, & Roth, 1983, p. 854).

In order to grow from an egocentric being whose only concern is satisfying his own wants, to someone who understands the wants of others, the young child must learn to see things from another person's perspective. To do this, the child needs the freedom to be able to function on his own in an open environment. His parents can support this development best by helping him to understand the views of others and by encouraging him to participate in decision making about his own behavior. Following the dictates of authoritarian parents gives the child little opportunity to develop these skills.

Warm, supportive mothering also makes a difference in the development of prosocial behaviors in young children. As children move into elementary school the best support they can have at home is a nonauthoritarian mother who allows and encourages her children to act on their own.

In the preschool, however, the children must learn to take turns and wait for turns. You can help the children the most by setting up the environment so that it speaks to these needs. Arrange activity areas for three, four, or five children at the most, and put signs or symbols for these numbers in every area. Then children can regulate their own numbers during free play. Let children take tags to hang on hooks or pegboards, tickets to put in pockets mounted on the wall, or their pictures covered with clear contact paper to hang in the area where they want to work (Beaty, 1992).

Many centers start the day with circle time. The teacher lets the class know what activities are available, and the children choose activities by taking tags. If a child finishes playing in her chosen area before free choice time is over, then another child can pick up the tag and take his own turn. This is how children learn about taking turns and waiting their turn.

Nevertheless, the teacher must let them do it on their own. Directing individuals into particular areas is the same as the authoritarian parent telling his or her children what to do. If we want children to develop prosocial behaviors, we must not short-circuit the process by trying to do it for them. In order for them to learn the social interactions necessary, they must be allowed to experiment with turn taking on their own.

In the preschool, children must learn to take turns and wait for turns with materials.

Giving children this freedom requires forbearance on the part of the preschool staff. It is so much easier for adults to make choices for the children. After all, children take so long to make up their minds. But we must remember the purpose for the free choice period in the first place: to allow children to learn how to make their own decisions based on their own interests and needs, and how to deal with the consequences of their choices. Through freedom of choice children also learn that another child may have the same choice as theirs, and that they may have to wait their turn before their choice is available.

Children also learn by using timing tools, such as a kitchen timer or 3-minute hourglass-type timer, when several children want turns using favorite toys or equipment. One child can hold the timer while another uses the toy for 3 minutes. When it is the next child's turn, the child after her gets to hold the timer. Some children enjoy controlling the timer as much as playing with the toy!

Children can also learn to take turns by signing up for a turn. Put a list on a clipboard with a pencil near the activity, and have children sign up (print or scribble their names) one under the other. When their turn is finished, they can cross out their name. Some children whose names are far down the list may need to wait until another day, but then they find they are near the top of the list.

If You Have Not Checked This Item: Some Helpful Ideas

■ Have Children Practice Turn Taking in Dramatic Play

Set up a particular play area such as beauty shop or barber shop and put out two or three chairs for the customers. Then the children will have to wait their turn just as in real life. Or set up a bakery shop or other facility where people must take numbered tickets to be waited on. Have tickets available for the children to take. Perhaps one child could be the ticket taker.

Set up a traffic light in the classroom for the children to use in their big truck play. The light can be a cardboard milk carton with holes cut out and covered with clear plastic wrap colored red, yellow, and green. Not only will children learn safety rules, but they also will realize that cars and people must wait their turns before using the road at a street crossing.

■ Bring in a Special Plaything or Activity to Teach Turn Taking

Introduce a new toy at circle time and have the children help set up the rules for playing with it such as the number of people who can use the toy at one time and for how long. The children may want to use the kitchen timer you have provided to keep track of the time. One child will surely want to keep the time. The teacher can also help children sign up for turns on a chart.

■ Read a Book

Everybody Takes Turns by Dorothy Corey (Chicago: Whitman, 1980) is a book with similar pictures on facing pages showing first one child, then another taking turns. A simple line of text tells whose turn it is.

❏ COMPLIES WITH REQUESTS WITHOUT A FUSS

Cooperation

A second aspect of cooperation involves complying with requests. This includes following directions, but more especially, it looks at how children cooperate with one another by complying with something another child or the teacher requests of them. For example, a child or the teacher may request another child to help, to wait, to give up something, to take a different role, to give information, or to do something in a certain way.

Complying with requests in a cooperative way is not blind obedience. Children should know the reason they are being asked to do something. They should be expected to behave in a reasonable way if the request is reasonable. For example, rather than request cooperation without an explanation—"Josh, move your truck."—make the request in a more reasonable fashion—"Josh, Anna Maria needs you to move your truck so that she can get her coat out of her cubby."

Nor is cooperative compliance a submission to a demand. Before you decide to check this item for a child or leave it blank, be sure it is compliance to a request and not to a demand that you are witnessing: not "Get out of the way, Josh," but "Anna Maria needs you to move your truck," or "It's pickup time, Andy. Please help Jerome pick up the blocks."

Once children have complied with a request, they can expect to be thanked for doing it. If you are the one who made the request, don't forget to thank the children. When you notice a child complying with another child's request, be sure the requesting child thanks the cooperator. Cooperative behavior like this implies reciprocal behavior on another's part. You may need to point this out in a pleasant, not correcting manner: "Anna Maria, Josh really moved his truck for you in a hurry. Don't forget to thank him."

If You Have Not Checked This Item: Some Helpful Ideas

■ Model This Behavior

Make a point of complying with reasonable requests a child makes of you. When you do this, be sure to articulate what you are doing so that other children understand it. For example, you might say aloud as you help pick up blocks, "Andy and Jerome asked me to help them pick up the blocks because they have to leave early today." This should help children understand that you comply with their requests just as you expect them to comply with yours. In addition, it gives them the reason for your response so that they will know that you may not always help everyone pick up blocks on a daily basis.

If children are demanding things of one another and not getting the desired results, you can also model the behavior that they should use: "Rhonda, why don't you say to Anne, 'Please give me my doll. It's time for me to go home. I'll bring it back tomorrow.'"

❏ HELPS ANOTHER DO A TASK

Caregiving

Along with sharing, this is by far the most common prosocial behavior exhibited in the preschool classroom, possibly because it is much less of a cognitive act. Children simply assist someone in doing a task. They may be asked or they may volunteer to help when they see that a peer or the teacher needs help with something. The children do not need to understand or to intellectualize about what is happening. They do not need to take another person's perspective. They just need to lend a hand, so to speak. Most children have already learned this activity at home, and they soon realize that the early childhood classroom is another place where they are expected to help out.

Research shows that this behavior may occur three times more than any other prosocial act. Even so, helping others do a task is not all that frequent in proportion to other behaviors. Seeking help occurs about six times more frequently than giving help among 3-year-olds (Moore, 1982, p. 77). But as children grow and develop through the early childhood years, helping behavior increases. Whereas slightly more than half of the youngest children assessed in one study (3-year-olds) gave some form of help, 100 percent of children 9 and 10 years old gave help (Smith, 1982, p. 216).

The youngest preschoolers, however, may have some problems with helping. They may not know when to help or how much help to give. Sometimes children overdo their help, becoming bossy and not knowing when to stop. Other times children don't do enough and simply stand around watching before the task is finished. The best way for them to learn the cues for appropriateness in such social behavior is to plunge in and try it. Other children are not shy about telling peers what they are doing wrong.

You need to set up activities that require children to give assistance in order to provide them opportunities to develop helping skills. Setting tables for snack and lunch is one, getting out cots or mats for naptime, getting out paints and mixing them, filling the water table, feeding the animal pets, and helping with cleanup are a few of the others. These tasks are multiple learning situations for cognitive concepts as well as learning when and how to help.

Children may have favorite chores as well as chores they try to avoid. Making a "helpers" chart gives every child a chance at every chore. Let the children help design the chart. It can contain pictures and titles for every job. Children can hang their name tags on it daily at circle time or once a week. New jobs can be added from time to time as needed. Use your creativity to invent the jobs. Here are a few you may want to include:

mail carrier: delivers notes to office

zookeeper: takes care of pets

aquarium attendant: feeds fish

door attendant: opens and closes door

chef: helps prepare snack

waiter/waitress: sets tables

gardener: waters plants

You cannot expect young children to do all the work in the classroom. Picking up the block corner is a case in point. One or two children can easily empty the shelves while building a complicated construction. Putting all the blocks back in proper order during cleanup time may be an overwhelming chore for two. A teacher should get down on the floor with them and lend her assistance, just as the children help her from time to time.

If certain children are not helping at all, you need to engage them in chores. Chores do not need to be drudgery. Children enjoy doing grownup things. Youngsters have no idea that pickup is any less interesting than getting toys out, unless adults make pickup seem less glamorous. In fact, you should make cleanup in your room a fun thing to do.

If You Have Not Checked This Item: Some Helpful Ideas

■ Invite a Helper to Your Class on a Weekly Basis

Anyone engaged in an occupation is a helper. Perhaps a different parent could visit the classroom on a weekly basis to talk to the children about how he or she helps.

One class created a new job on their helpers chart each week after the helper had visited. Sometimes the children had to stretch their imaginations to create the new job. After a telephone installer had visited the room they finally decided to add the job "telephone attendant," which allowed one child each day to answer the classroom phone.

■ Use Games for Pickup and Cleanup

Block shelves fill up much easier when they are hungry monsters waiting to be fed by the children, or when children do pickup to music, trying to finish before the song is over. Long blocks can be bulldozers pushing the blocks or toys over to the shelves. Have your children help you think up other pretend games at cleanup time.

■ Read a Book

Herman the Helper by Robert Kraus (New York: Windmill Books, 1974) tells the colorful underwater story of Herman the little octopus who helps his mother, father, brothers and sisters, friends, enemies, and finally himself.

❑ HELPS (CARES FOR) ANOTHER IN NEED

Caregiving

This particular behavior is perhaps the most difficult of the prosocial skills for young children to attain. Helping another in need is an extension of the first item, "Shows concern for someone in distress." Whereas showing concern involves compassion, a psychological support, helping another in need involves caretaking or nurturing, a physical act of giving help. The help may consist of giving affection (a hug, a touch), positive attention, (getting help, giving help), reassurance (verbalizing support), or protection (standing by, physically protecting).

For young children, these behaviors are difficult because the youngsters must first overcome their own anxiety caused by the stressful situation. Then they must have an understanding of how to act. In emergency situations even adults are often confused and have difficulty knowing what to do.

Even very young children have been observed taking action when another child or person is in distress, but the instances are rare compared to other prosocial acts. Toddlers have been seen giving their bottles or cuddly toys to siblings who cry in distress. Giving something to the victim seems to be the main response of young children. They more often seek help than give it, however. In addition, those who seek help in the preschool more often approach adults than peers, although older preschoolers are beginning to turn to their companions for help.

Crying and uttering distressful sounds are supposed to trigger an empathic response in others according to psychologists. Scientists look to the animal world and note the intricacies of response in many species. Have we humans lost much of this seemingly instinctive concern? We read in the newspaper and see on television the instances of adults ignoring victims who call for help. Much of this inattention seems

Teachers can promote children's caring behaviors by involving them in helping situations.

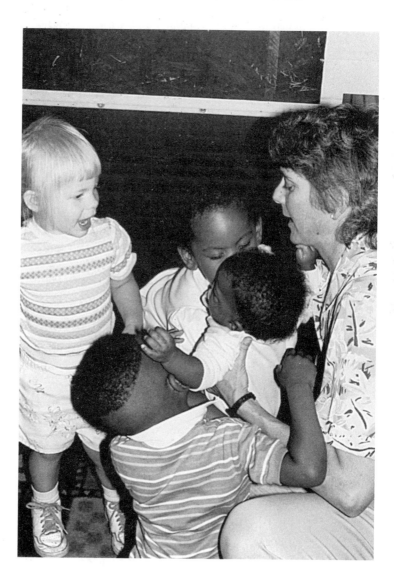

to be a defensive reaction on the part of people who do not want to get involved in the trouble, but also feel they might be victimized themselves.

Can helping be taught to children? Studies show that children can learn helping behaviors in pretend or symbolic situations, but when the real thing occurs, they still may not respond. Children with nurturant caregivers do give more help and express more sympathy. So it seems that modeling behavior does promote prosocial helping (Yarrow, Scott, & Waxler, 1973, p. 254).

What kinds of situations requiring help might occur in the classroom? Injury is one such occurrence. Children and adults may fall and hurt themselves, cut themselves, or burn themselves. The loss of something is another situation that requires help. Children may lose mittens, money, a toy. Accidental damage also necessitates assistance. Children may spill paint on themselves, fall in the mud, or spill milk or other food. They may drop and break a dish, a record, a toy.

How can other children help? Depending upon the situation, they could go for help if an adult is not in the immediate vicinity. They could comfort the victim by talking or touching. They could clean up spills, look for lost things, or give information to help an adult solve the problem.

Children are more likely to give help to others when with someone. Teachers should take advantage of this by involving the children in helping situations whenever possible, rather than doing all the helping themselves. When children are involved on their own, teachers should step back and allow the youngsters to do what they can.

This caregiving item can also be checked if you observe children giving care in pretend situations to their dolls or the classroom pets. Does someone put a blanket around their doll saying that she is cold and might catch the flu? Does someone notice that the guinea pig is out of water? If elderly people or babies visit your classroom, watch which children show signs of caring. Does someone get a chair for the guest without being asked?

If You Have Not Checked This Item: Some Helpful Ideas

■ Discuss Helping with the Children

When helping behavior occurs spend time in small and large groups talking to children about it. Sometimes television events seen by children make good discussion topics.

■ Read a Book

Swimmy by Leo Lionni (New York: Knopf/Pantheon, 1963) is a favorite of children. It tells about a little black fish, Swimmy, who helps a school of other little fish to swim unafraid like the biggest fish in the sea.

Who's Going to Take Care of Me? by Michelle Magorian (New York: Harper & Row, 1990) tells the story of little Eric, whose older sister Karin will not be going to day care with him this year because she is going to kindergarten. Who will take care of him? When Eric arrives at day care he discovers that he already knows how to do things for himself, but he spots a little newcomer over in the corner and takes it upon himself to help the new little boy.

Shy Charles by Rosemary Wells (New York: Dial Books, 1988) tells the story of little Charles mouse who cannot seem to please either his mother (with thank-you's) or his father (with football heroics), but when the baby-sitter, Mrs. Block, falls down the stairs, Charles knows how to help her up and call the emergency service.

Wilfrid Gordon McDonald Partridge by Mem Fox (Brooklyn: Kane/Miller, 1985) is a story about a little boy who knows all of the people in the old folks home next door because he visits them on their front porch. When he hears that one of the residents, Miss Nancy, has lost her memory, he helps her to find it by gathering together just the right collection of things.

■ When You Model Helping Behavior, Talk About It

You will be helping children all year long. Talk aloud to the other children about what you are doing, and help them find ways to assist you.

OBSERVING, RECORDING, AND INTERPRETING PROSOCIAL BEHAVIOR

Sandra is a 4-year-old who rarely performs any of the prosocial behaviors on the checklist unless forced to by the teachers, for example, sharing a toy or waiting for her turn. (See Figure 6.1.) The teachers have noted that she also seems immature in the area of social skills, and has played only by herself, not parallel to the others or with a group. The teachers have concluded that Sandra may not have developed the ability to see things from a perspective other than her own. Therefore, she has little or no empathy for others who need help or who are in distress. A suggestion to help Sandra develop empathy is to give her two hand puppets: one with a bandage on its arm and one to use as a helper. You can put the bandaged puppet on your hand. Ask her to find out what happened to the injured puppet. If she likes this kind of play, she may be willing to branch out and play helping puppets with a second child.

Figure 6.1
Prosocial behavior observations for Sandra

Child Skills Checklist

Name ___Sandra_____   Observer ___Angie_____

Program ___Pre-K_____   Dates _____11/5_____

Directions:

Put a ✔ for items you see the child perform regularly. Put *N* for items where there is no opportunity to observe. Leave all other items blank.

Item	Evidence	Date
4. Prosocial Behavior _____ Shows concern for someone in distress	Moved away from Mark when he got hurt	11/5
_N_ Shows delight for someone experiencing pleasure		
_____ Shares something with another	Would not give up her doll to Betty	11/5
_____ Gives something of his/her own to another	She has not done this	
_____ Takes turns without a fuss	Cried when she could not be first on the swing	11/5
_____ Complies with requests without a fuss	Always says "I can't" or "I don't know how" when asked to do something	11/5
_____ Helps another to do a task	Same as above	11/5
_____ Helps (cares for) another in need	Would not help when Mark got hurt	11/5

REFERENCES

Beaty, Janice J. (1992). *Preschool appropriate practices*. Ft. Worth, TX: Harcourt Brace Jovanovich.

Damon, William. (1983). *Social and personality development*. New York: Norton.

Damon, William. (1988). *The moral child: Nurturing children's natural moral growth*. New York: Macmillan.

Eisenberg, Nancy, Randy Lennon, & Karlsson Roth. (1983). Prosocial development: A longitudinal study. *Developmental Psychology, 19*(6), 846–855.

Moore, Shirley G. (1982). Prosocial behavior in the early years: Parent and peer influences. In Bernard Spodek (Ed.), *Handbook of research in early childhood education (pp.65-81)*. New York: Free Press.

Smith, Charles A. (1982). *Promoting social development of young children: Strategies and activities*. Palo Alto, CA: Mayfield.

Yarrow, Marian Radke, Phyllis M. Scott, & Carolyn Zahn Waxler. (1973). Learning concern for others. *Developmental Psychology, 8*(2), 240–260.

OTHER SOURCES

Bergin, Christi A. C., & David A. Bergin. (1988, April). *What it means to be prosocial: Caretakers' descriptions of prosocial 2- and 5-year olds*. Paper presented at the Annual Meeting of the American Educational Research Association, New Orleans. (ERIC Document Reproduction Service No. ED 294 687, pp. 1–25)

Edwards, Carolyn Pope. (1986). *Promoting social and moral development in children*. New York: Teachers College Press.

Goffin, Stacie G. (1987). Cooperative behaviors: They need our support. *Young Children, 42*(2), 75–81.

Melson, Gail F., & Alan Fogel. (1988). The development of nurturance in young children. *Young Children, 43*(3), 57–65.

Stockdale, Dahlia F., Susan M. Hegland, & Thomas Chiaromonte. (1989). Helping behaviors: An observational study of preschool children. *Early Childhood Research Quarterly, 4*(4), 533–543.

LEARNING ACTIVITIES

1. Use the *Child Skills Checklist* section "Prosocial Behavior" as a screening tool to observe all of the children in your classroom. Which ones demonstrate the most prosocial behavior? Do they also have friends in the class? Which children show few prosocial skills? How do these children get along with the other children in general?

2. Choose a child who exhibits few of the prosocial skills. Make a running record of the child on three different days to determine how the child works and plays with the others. Do an activity with the child to help promote sharing, taking turns, or helping. Record the results.

3. Choose a child who is a good helper and try to involve that child in getting another child to participate in helping. Discuss the results.

CHAPTER 6

4. Try two of the ideas under "If You Have Not Checked This Item" with a child who shows few prosocial skills. Discuss the results.

5. Read one of the children's books mentioned in this chapter with a group of children or do an activity with the group to promote prosocial skills. Discuss the results.

7
Large Motor Development

Large Motor Checklist

❑ Walks down steps alternating feet

❑ Runs with control over speed and direction

❑ Jumps over obstacle, landing on two feet

❑ Hops forward on one foot

❑ Climbs up and down climbing equipment with ease

❑ Moves legs/feet in rhythm to beat

❑ Claps hands in rhythm to beat

❑ Beats drum alternating hands in rhythm to beat

P hysical development for young children involves two important areas of motor coordination: movements controlled by the large, or gross, muscles and those controlled by the small, or fine, muscles. This chapter will focus on large motor development, involving movements of the whole body, legs, and arms.

Because motor development is so obvious and visible an aspect of children's growth, we sometimes take it for granted. Of course children will grow bigger, stronger, and able to perform more complicated motor tasks as they increase in age. But do all children develop these abilities? What about the awkward child who seems to trip over his or her own feet? What about the child who never can keep up with the others? Is the accident-prone child overeager or underdeveloped? How can we tell, and can we do anything to help such children?

Yes, children do develop physically in a predictable sequence of skills that can be observed, although there are individual differences in this growth as well as developmental lags in some children. And, yes, there is something we can do to help.

First, we need to become familiar with the entire sequence of normal large motor development. We need to know its origins, patterns, and range for individuals. Then we need to apply this knowledge to the children in order to determine whether they are developing predictably within the normal range, or whether they may need special help. Finally, we should assemble a repertoire of activities to help the child who is lagging behind in this development.

MOTOR DEVELOPMENT IN INFANCY

The infant uses motor skills as tools to explore himself and then the world around him. His initial movements are reflexive and involuntary. He sucks when his mouth touches something. He jumps at a loud noise.

Soon after birth, however, three types of rudimentary movement abilities appear. The nonlocomotor, or stability, skills involve developing control of the head, neck, and trunk, and eventually the ability to sit and stand. Manipulative skills involve reaching for, grasping, and releasing. Locomotor skills involve creeping, crawling, and eventually walking (Gallahue, 1982, pp. 5–6).

Muscular maturation follows both a predictable sequence and a direction. Large muscle coordination develops before small muscle synchronization. In other words, the infant or young child develops arm movement control before finger control. Development is also cephalo-caudal in direction—that is, it begins at the head and progresses to the feet. Control of the head and upper trunk occurs in the infant before control of legs and feet. Development also occurs in the proximal direction—from close to the trunk out to the extremities (Allen & Goetz, 1982, p. 130).

Many of the infant's first movements are random. She lies on her back in a bassinet or crib and kicks her legs and waves her arms. Should she happen to strike a mobile or rattle with either arms or legs, she will usually try to repeat the movement to cause the same interesting sound and touch effect. By repeating the movement over and over, she begins to gain control over her muscles, so that the movement eventually becomes voluntary and controlled.

Motor development occurs in a predictable sequence and is related closely to the maturation of the central nervous system, the integrating agent. Even though an infant's motor skills cannot develop until the neuromuscular system is ready, a rich environment filled with stimulating sights, sounds, and people motivates the child to initiate and to practice movements.

Are we saying that the environment and the infant's experience with it can improve her motor development? Yes, when the required maturation level has been reached. If there had not been a mobile in the baby's bassinet, she would not have struck it with her arm and then would not have continued to practice this movement. Even if her neuromuscular system was not mature enough for her to control this movement, the mobile's presence might still keep her trying until the proper maturity had developed.

Fraiberg's work with blind infants shows the importance of such environmental factors in the development of motor skills. The blind babies developed trunk control and sitting stability within the same time range as sighted children. Blind babies even could support themselves on hands and knees. But they never learned to creep. They lacked the visual stimuli the sighted babies had to motivate them to move across the floor. Their caregivers had to find other means to stimulate them to attempt locomotion (Fraiberg, 1975).

This is one of several studies that has proved the importance of sensory stimuli, especially sight, sound, and touch, in the development of large motor skills. We also know that caring adults must interact with infants from the beginning. Adults must encourage, support, and praise children for the accomplishment of motor skills, as they do in all aspects of children's development.

Because such encouragement tends to happen almost automatically in many families, we often think infants and young children develop these skills on their own with little support from adults or the environment. A look at infants and children in institutions where little or no human or material support was offered proves otherwise. J.

McVicker Hunt and several other American psychologists visited orphanages in Iran that had an infant:caregiver ratio of 40:3. Many of the 2-year-olds could not sit up and most of the children in their 4th year could not yet walk alone (Pines, 1979, p. 59). The quality of early child care does indeed make a difference.

The range for mastery of a particular skill varies from 1 or 2 months to 4–6 months in young children. Developmental delays may result when early reflexive movements somehow fail to become integrated into higher level voluntary movements (Allen & Goetz, 1982, p. 131). Birth defects, handicapping conditions, certain illnesses or injuries, and neglect may cause this lack of integration. Children whose early movement patterns have not become integrated into voluntary responses either do not learn the higher level skills or learn to compensate in some atypical manner.

Large motor skills, then, play an important part in the infant's learning first about himself by moving his body parts, and then about his world as he responds physically to the people and materials around him. His environment plays an important part as well in stimulating this development. He gains more and more independence through the movements he is able to master, and when he finally walks, the world is his to explore.

What about the preschool child, the 3–5-year-old? We also need to assess his large motor development to determine how far along he has progressed in this predictable growth. The eight items under "Large Motor Development" on the *Child Skills Checklist* are neither a complete list of large motor skills nor a sequence of skills, although one skill may precede the other. Instead, these eight items represent a sample of important motor behaviors that children should have acquired by age 5.

It is important to screen all the children in your class at the outset using this or a similar list of skills in order to identify children needing special help. Knowing that large motor development precedes small motor growth, you should help all of your children to be prepared in this first area in order to be successful in the small motor tasks expected of them in the reading and writing soon to come.

❑ WALKS DOWN STEPS ALTERNATING FEET

Three-Year-Olds

Most 3-year-olds walk in adult fashion. Their trunk is no longer top-heavy as it was a year ago, and they have mastered walking to the extent that they no longer need to watch their feet or balance with their arms. They swing their arms as they walk, just like adults. They still may fall occasionally on uneven ground, but they are not so far from the ground that falling hurts very much. Now they can walk up steps alternating feet unaided, although most 3-year-olds put two feet on a step coming down. The balance of some children this age is good enough to allow them to walk a straight line one foot in front of the other.

Although growth occurs in a predictable chronological sequence, it seems to happen in spurts. It's almost as if the body has to stop and assimilate all the development

With practice, 3-year-olds can walk a homemade block balance beam.

that has occurred before it can go forward again. This "assimilation stop" often happens at the half-year point. Children who walked and ran smoothly at 3 years may seem to have a "relapse" at 3-and-a-half. They suddenly act uncertain with their large motor skills and may even seek the hand of an adult as they walk along. This happens especially going up or down stairs. They may have good days when everything about their bodies seems to work well, and bad days when they stumble and fall (Caplan & Caplan, 1983, p. 177).

Four-Year-Olds

Four-year-olds have control of their bodies and take great pleasure in using them. Children age 4 walk confidently in many ways: forward, backward, sideways, tiptoeing, and striding along. They are able to walk a circular line for the first time without losing their balance. Most can walk both up and down stairs alternating their feet. Although their skipping is not at all perfected (most can do it only with one foot), some start to roller-skate.

Four is an age of great exuberance and expansiveness. If you do not provide enough walking, running, and climbing activities in your center, 4-year-olds may make their own. They definitely need an opportunity to practice their large motor skills both inside and outside of the classroom.

Five-Year-Olds

Five-year-olds are at the adult stage in walking. This age is another period of great growth when children shoot up as much as 2 or 3 inches in a year. Much of this growth occurs in the legs, which lengthen more quickly than the other body parts. Boys may be a bit taller and heavier than girls, but they are about a year behind them in physiological development (Caplan & Caplan, 1983, p. 237).

Children of this age can walk a straight line for about 10 feet without stepping off it. Most can skip with alternating feet now. Even the less active 5-year-olds can walk down stairs alternating their feet. Five-year-olds are less expansive and more controlled than 4-year-olds in all of their actions, but children age 5 still love to use their large motor abilities in play.

If You Have Not Checked This Item: Some Helpful Ideas

■ Practice Walking

Studies show that children between the ages of 2 and 6 demonstrate observable improvement in basic motor patterns after repeated performance with adult encouragement. Instruction in the movement doesn't seem to help, but practice does (Flinchum, 1975, p. 28).

Play follow-the-leader in the classroom and outside with yourself as the leader who sets the pace. Do all kinds of walking motions and be sure everyone has a chance to copy you before you change to the next movement: march, shuffle, stride, giant-step, tiptoe, bunny hop, skate.

Set up a walking-hopping-sliding trail in your classroom or large motor room with contact footprints stuck to the floor in various patterns of movement, some for one foot and some for two.

■ Practice Step Climbing

If your room is at ground level in a building with a second story, make it a practice to take children up and down the stairs every day. If you have no stairs, go for a field trip to a building that has stairs, or get a rocking-boat-steps piece of large motor equipment for the children to practice on. Some playground equipment also has stairs, but ladders do not provide the same type of developmental practice.

■ Play Charades

Have two or three children demonstrate how an animal walks and let the others guess what animal it is.

■ **Read a Book**

One of the most impressive picture books about walking is surely *Mirandy and Brother Wind* by Patricia C. McKissack (New York: Alfred A. Knopf, 1988). It is an old-time African American story about a young girl, Mirandy, who wants to win her first cakewalk and decides to catch Brother Wind to help her. Although long for preschoolers, Jerry Pinkney's elegant full-page illustrations can be "read" to individuals or a small group close to the teacher. If children like the story they may want to have their own cakewalk.

Many preschool teachers already involve their children in various kinds of walking when they take them "on a bear hunt," walking in place. Now this imaginative experience is available in a lively picture book, *We're Going on a Bear Hunt* by Michael Rosen and Helen Oxenbury (New York: Margaret K. McElderry Books, 1989).

Children also enjoy acting out a story like *The Three Billy Goats Gruff* as retold by Paul Galdone (New York: Clarion Books, 1973). Turn over your rocking-boat piece of equipment to make it into steps, and have the children billy goats trip-trap over the step "bridge."

❏ RUNS WITH CONTROL OVER SPEED AND DIRECTION

Running may be the large motor skill you think of when you consider young children. They seem to be perpetual motion machines. For some children this is their principal method of movement. For others, their running is somehow awkward and they spend much less time doing it than the rest of your children. What should you expect of the 3-, 4-, and 5-year-old children in your program? As with walking, you will need to know the whole range of development for this skill before you can decide where each of your children stands and how you best can help.

Three-Year-Olds

Running is smoother for 3-year-olds than it was when they were younger. Their body proportions have grown and changed from a top-heavy appearance. Their legs are now longer and more coordinated in their movements. They have more control over starting and stopping than 2-year-olds, but they still have not mastered this skill completely. Because their large motor skills are so much more automatic, they can abandon themselves to the pure enjoyment of running.

Then at about 3-and-a-half, many children go through the previously mentioned awkward stage where some of the smoothness of their large motor movements seems to disappear. Teachers need to be aware of these "disequilibrium" times in order to support children during their bad days, knowing they will return to their normal smoothness of motion sometime soon.

Such children should not be confused with the truly awkward child. Cratty's studies have found many so-called awkward children are boys who seem to show a developmental delay in motor coordination. They exhibit an exaggerated awkward behavior. Some of this behavior may be the result of "learned helplessness" obtained possibly from parents who overreact to their every little problem (Cratty, 1982, p. 36). On the other hand, the physical awkwardness of these boys may be more in the eye of the beholder, especially if a teacher compares them with the most coordinated boys in the class.

A wide range of individual differences exists in physical development as in every other aspect of development. Some children simply will never be highly coordinated. Others may grow up to be professional athletes. The sensitive teacher needs to work with each child, encouraging and supporting him to accomplish all he is capable of. Pressure and ridicule simply have no place in the early childhood classroom. The teacher needs to find interesting motor activities in which the awkward child can succeed, and to avoid those activities that pit one child against another in competition.

Can awkward children be helped? Whether they can be assisted seems to depend upon their age and the severity of their problem (Cratty, 1982, p. 37). Providing a wide range of interesting motor activities that are fun to participate in seems the best answer. Three-year-olds are at an ideal age to begin such a program. And because some so-called awkward children are simply beginners in the skill development, it is useless to label them as abnormal. Children are children; they are all different in looks, likes, and abilities. Each of them needs your special affection and support as he or she progresses through the sometimes rocky road of physical development.

You need to be aware of these ages and stages as they apply to your children. Take time to visit this year's class next year and you may see some surprises. This year's awkward boy may be the best runner around. The sedentary girl who will never join in may be the leader of the physical activities. A year makes such a difference in the development of young children.

Four-Year-Olds

Expansive 4-year-olds are good runners. Their movements are strong, efficient, and speedy. They can start and stop without difficulty, and they like to zoom around corners. They seem to know what their bodies can do and to enjoy putting them through their paces. Give these children space and time to run.

Some 4-year-olds are labeled *hyperactive* because they never seem to stop moving. Be careful of such labels. Only a doctor can diagnose this condition of hyperkinesis. Some children are just more active than others, often wearing out parents and teachers in the process. The age of 4—with its characteristic exuberance and surplus energy—is the period that causes parents the most worry about hyperactivity. Surely, these parents reason, there is a way to slow down such children. Maybe a doctor can put the children on drugs.

Using drugs to combat so-called hyperactivity is a very serious decision to make for such young children. Really active children probably always have been that way, but as 4-year-olds, their activity seems exaggerated. Parents should get more than one medical opinion before deciding what to do. True hyperactivity is sometimes difficult to distinguish from the normal surplus energy of an active 4-year-old.

Five-Year-Olds

As mentioned before, five-year-olds seem to sprout up in height, mostly in their legs. They are more mature runners than 4-year-olds, and many love to join in games that test their abilities. Their speed and control has increased, and they seldom fall when running across uneven surfaces as 4-year-olds sometimes do. Their running games, like the rest of their actions, are usually not as noisy and out-of-bounds as those of 4-year-olds.

If You Have Not Checked This Item: Some Helpful Ideas

■ Use Simple Running Games

Preschool running games should not be competitive. The awkward child may give up trying if he or she is always last. Instead, use simple circle games. Old classics like Duck, Duck, Goose are still favorites of 3- and 4-year-olds; they walk around the outside of the circle and tap someone who then chases them around to the empty space. No one wins or loses. Games with rules are often too complicated for preschoolers, but they learn to make the right responses in simple circle games like this, and enjoy the running it affords.

■ Employ Directed Running

You can make up all kinds of inside and outside running activities. For instance, one child at a time can run to the tree and back until all have had a turn. Make the activity more complicated by having them follow a second instruction: Run to the tree, run around it once, and then run back.

■ Have the Children Run to Music

Have children run to music in the large motor area. Ask them to run fast or slow, loudly or quietly, according to the music being played.

■ Involve the Children in Running to Chants

Young children need to run. If you do not have the inside space or if the weather outside is bad, have them run and hop in place to a simple chant you have made up:

> I'm a kangaroo-roo-roo
> See me run-run-run
> Have some fun-fun-fun
> In the sun-sun-sun
> Watch me hop-hop-hop
> Never stop-stop-stop
> Then I run-run-run
> In the sun-sun-sun

■ **Try Imaginative Running**

Let the children pretend to be cowboys and cowgirls riding their horses or jet planes going down the runway. Have them pretend to be animals that run such as deer or dogs. Put up pictures of animals that run and have the children imitate them.

■ **Read a Book**

Read *Mother Goose, If Wishes Were Horses, and Other Rhymes* illustrated by Susan Jeffers (New York: Dutton, 1979) with its rollicking verses about riding on horses. Then bring in stick horses for your children to run, trot, and gallop with as you read each verse.

❑ JUMPS OVER OBSTACLE, LANDING ON TWO FEET

Jumping is a skill that involves taking off with one or two feet and landing on both feet. Jumping is sometimes confused with leaping, which is taking off on one foot and landing on the other, and hopping, which is done all on the same foot. The checklist item mentions landing on two feet, so that observers will not confuse jumping with leaping or hopping. The obstacle to jump over can be anything—a mark or masking tape on the floor, a block, a toy, a stick, a low barrier, a book, a rug, a box—any item the child perceives as something that can be jumped over.

Jumping as a large motor skill, however, can be done in place with the child springing up and landing in the same spot, jumping forward landing on both feet, jumping from the floor or ground over an obstacle, or jumping from a height such as a step or a chair and landing on the floor.

Three-Year-Olds

Some children become quite proficient jumpers by age 3, but many do not, and we should not expect them to. They must have developed the strength first, and then must be encouraged to practice the skill. (Most parents do not encourage their children to jump off steps or from furniture!)

Three-year-olds, though, are becoming more long-legged and coordinated. If they are not too heavy, most probably will be able to do some jumping with practice. When jumping over an obstacle most children start by leading with one foot. Springing up with both feet simultaneously is more difficult, but possible for some children.

Four-Year-Olds

Four-year-olds are much more proficient jumpers, and by age 4-and-a-half, most can accomplish any type of jumping: up, down, forward, and over. They may not be able to do a sequence of different actions—such as hopping, skipping, and jumping—although they can perform some or all of these actions separately. One study showed only 42 percent of preschool children jump well by age 3, whereas 72 percent jump well by 4-and-a-half (Zaichkowsky, Zaichkowsky, & Martineck, 1980, p. 39).

Some, but not all, children are proficient jumpers by the age of 3 years.

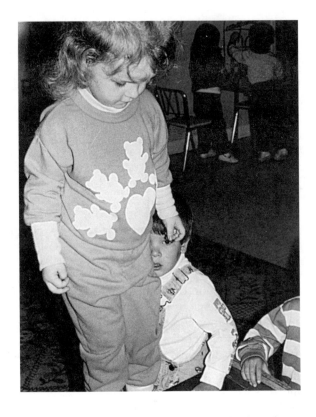

Four-year-olds can jump higher up in the air and farther down from higher elevations than they could before. The second step from the bottom of the stairs is now their big challenge, one you may want to redirect because of its potential for injury.

Five-Year-Olds

Five-year-olds, of course, are long, high, far jumpers, if they have had practice. Maturity is important, as previously noted, but just as necessary is practice of the skill, along with encouragement and praise from adult caregivers. If children have been ridiculed because of their awkwardness or lack of physical accomplishment in the past, then you may have to spend much of your time helping them improve their self-image.

They may not want to try because they have performed so poorly in the past. This may have been due to undeveloped muscular strength and/or coordination, lack of practice, or a half-year relapse stage. Now they need to try again to prove to themselves they really do have physical skills. Have them jump over a line on the floor. If they succeed, draw two parallel lines for them to jump over, or use masking tape to make the lines. As they become successful, let them move the taped lines farther and farther apart. They can do this on their own in a corner of the room if they don't want an audience, particularly in the beginning. Most 5-year-olds soon will feel secure enough to jump anywhere.

This is the age when jumping rope begins. Girls may try to make it their exclusive sport, but teachers can be the rope turners so that every class member who wants to participate can have a turn. Again, do not force the awkward child. Before you introduce a jump rope to 5-year-olds, be sure to check out the jumping skills of all of your children individually, so that no one will be embarrassed in front of peers if he or she tries to jump rope and fails. This failure sometimes happens, and it may prevent a child, especially a boy, from ever putting himself in such an embarrassing situation again, which means he may not participate in group sports in school.

Competition has no place in the early childhood large motor program, but neither do total group activities that play up the weaknesses or inabilities of individual children. Total group games such as jump rope seem like such innocent fun, but they are not for the awkward child. It is better to let three children at a time play with a small jump rope than to insist that all children have a turn on a big jump rope, if one of those children will be embarrassed by lack of ability. Your observations and records of the large motor abilities of individual children will help you to decide what new activities to introduce.

If You Have Not Checked This Item: Some Helpful Ideas

■ Work with Individual Children Who Show Poor Skills

If 4- and 5-year-olds still cannot jump, then you should try an activity such as jumping over lines, as mentioned under "Five-Year-Olds." If children are 3 years or younger you do not need to be so concerned, because jumping may not be well developed yet.

■ Chair Jumping

Have a "chair jumping day," when individuals or small groups get to jump from one of the small chairs in the room and have their jumps measured. Keep a record of each child's jumps on a chart or notebook so individuals can see how well they do each week. Do not measure the results against the others in the class; otherwise it becomes a competition. Let each child try three jumps, for instance, and have a different child be the measurer for each jumper.

You might want to measure with sticks you have color coded to certain lengths, a yard stick, or a piece of string you mark off and later measure against a ruler. Whether or not you want to record in inches, centimeters, or merely red sticks will be up to you and the cognitive developmental level of your children. You do not need to be absolutely exact with the youngest children. They will be delighted to find they jumped for two red sticks and a blue stick the first time, and three red sticks the second time.

It is good to have a special chair that you cover with contact paper to keep the seat from being scratched. Let the children know that this is the only "jumping chair," and put it away when not in use.

■ Try Concept Jumping

When children are learning the concepts *up*, *down*, *over*, *forward*, and *in place*, you might try having them act out the motions by jumping. Ask the others to guess what kind of jump a child made. Or let one child call out a concept and another child try to demonstrate it by jumping it.

■ Utilize Jumping Animals

Put pictures of jumping (leaping or hopping) animals on the walls at child eye level: kangaroo, kangaroo rat, frog, toad, rabbit, deer, for example. Have the children try to imitate the animals.

■ Read a Book

Jump, Frog, Jump by Robert Kalan (New York: Mulberry Books, 1981) is a simple cumulative story of a frog in a pond that has to "jump, frog, jump," to catch a fly and to escape from a fish, a snake, and a turtle. After reading the book, put contact paper lily pads on the floor and have the children jump from one to another.

Moon Jump by Mustapha Matura (New York: Alfred A. Knopf, 1988) is about a little boy, Cayal, who loves to jump and spends his days and nights jumping on chairs, sofas, and the playground, but especially on his parents' bed. One night he jumps so high he lands on the moon, and the moon man jumps with him until it is time to jump back home.

No Jumping on the Bed! by Tedd Arnold (New York: Dial Books, 1987) is the riotous story of Walter, who lives up high in an apartment building, and what happens when he disobeys his father and takes one last jump on the bed. Down he goes through apartment after apartment, taking everything with him until he ends up asleep in his own bed.

❏ HOPS FORWARD ON ONE FOOT

Hopping is the large motor "bounding" skill in which the child takes off and lands on the same foot. Jumping uses both feet together, and leaping uses alternating feet to take off and land. A child can hop in place or hop forward for one or more steps. This checklist item asks you to identify the children in your class who can hop forward (obviously on one foot because they are hopping).

Children need balancing skills before they can hop. They also need the leg length and strength to do jumping first. This means that not many will be truly hopping before 3 years of age, and maybe not until 3-and-a-half. In fact, hopping for most children is not well developed before the age of 4 years. There are large individual differences in this skill like there are in other areas of development, but the largest difference of all is in gender. Girls 4 and 5 years old almost always hop more and better than boys. At first we may reason that, of course, girls are a bit more physically mature than boys of this same age. Still, someone else may argue that boys generally have a greater proportion of body muscle tissue throughout their lives than girls, and therefore should be able to hop as well as girls.

The truth seems to lie instead in the differences in opportunities and encouragement for hopping between girls and boys. Hopping is a girl's skill in our society. Games such as hopscotch and jump rope, which appear among 5- and 6-year-olds, are examples. These games are played principally by girls, not boys. Challenge a boy to play hopscotch and he soon finds that girls his age are much more skilled hoppers, just as girls are better jump rope jumpers.

There is no reason why a boy could not also become skilled at hopping if he practiced. But until some new hopping challenge appears that appeals to boys, this improvement probably will not occur. Check the children in your class. How do the boys compare with the girls? Ask the children about the hopping games they play. Preschool children who play few or no hopping games will probably have great difficulty doing any hopping, whether they are boys or girls.

If You Have Not Checked This Item: Some Helpful Ideas

■ Create a Hopping Trail

Make a hopping-tiptoeing-walking trail in your classroom or large motor room. Place contact paper footprints on the floor that show hopping steps on one foot, then walking steps with both feet, then hopping on the other foot, tiptoeing, and jumping.

■ Hop to Music

Find a bouncy but slow record and let children try to hop and jump to it. Most 4-year-olds will not be able to do more than four or five hops at a time, but the children can change back and forth from hopping to jumping.

■ Hop to Drumbeats

Let children make different movements to different drumbeats you play. A one-thump beat can mean to walk, a two-thump beat can signify to hop, and a quick-time beat can indicate to run. See if the children can follow your rhythm. Don't change your beat too quickly because most children are beginners when it comes to moving to rhythm.

❏ CLIMBS UP AND DOWN CLIMBING EQUIPMENT WITH EASE

Climbing involves use of the arms as well as the legs. It is, in fact, an outgrowth of creeping. Most children begin climbing as soon as they can creep over to an item of furniture and pull themselves up. If they are allowed, they will creep up the stairs. They will try to creep down, too, and soon find out that a backward descent is the only kind that works!

Many 3- and 4-year-olds enjoy climbing on all sorts of things: jungle gyms, ladders, ladder climbers, dome climbers, slides, rope climbers, trees, rocks, poles, and drain pipes. By the time they are in your program, children this age should be able to climb down as well as up with ease.

Although it takes some bravery in addition to muscle strength and coordination to be a successful climber, many of your children will be able to accomplish this skill if they have the opportunity. You should consider providing climbing equipment and climbing possibilities both inside and outside your classroom. Safety factors, of course, should be considered. Since falling is the main concern with climbing, be sure that floor or ground surfaces are cushioned. Padding can be used inside. Sand or wood chips are preferable to grass or hard surfaces outside.

Not all children will attempt to climb. Do not force the reluctant ones. You can encourage them and help children if they try to climb, but if they refuse, they should not be forced to try. Not all children will want to accomplish climbing skills, which is perfectly acceptable. Children have as much right to their own personal choices and interests as adults. Were you a climber when you were 4 years old?

Table 7.1 shows the sequence of large motor development for children 8 months to 6 years old.

If You Have Not Checked This Item: Some Helpful Ideas

■ Provide a New Piece of Climbing Equipment

A packing crate (with splintery edges sanded down) is often a tempting piece of climbing equipment that can be used either inside or outside. Ladder steps can be fastened to the outside of the crate if necessary, or children may use a step-stool to climb up the crate. Cargo netting is also an excellent piece of climbing equipment. Fasten it to a classroom wall with padding underneath or to a horizontal bar outside on the playground.

■ Build a Loft

Lofts not only give preschool children extra space for various new activities, but lofts also provide a new perspective on climbing activities. Some lofts use ladders to reach their tops, others use steps. Some have several means of entrance and exit. Even nonclimbers often learn to manage all of the methods of access because being up in the loft is such fun.

■ Provide a Multiple-Access Slide

A multiple-access slide is perhaps the most valuable piece of large motor equipment you can purchase if your center can afford only one piece of equipment. Children are motivated to learn to climb in order to get to the platform at the top of the slide. There are usually steps, bars, or ladders to help children reach the top, and the youngsters soon know how to use them all. If you have space inside, an indoor multiple-access slide can serve as a loft as well as a large motor device.

TABLE 7.1
Large motor skills

Age	Walking	Running	Jumping	Climbing
8 months–1 year	Walks in a wide stance like a waddle			Climbs onto furniture and up stairs as an outgrowth of creeping
1–2 years	Walks in a toddle and uses arms for balance (arms are not swung)	Moves rapidly in a hurried walk, in contact with surface	Uses bouncing step off bottom step of stairs with one foot	Tries climbing up anything climbable
2–3 years	Walks upstairs two feet on a step	Runs stiffly, has difficulty turning corners and stopping quickly	Jumps off bottom step with both feet	Tries climbing to top of equipment, although cannot climb down
3–4 years	Walks with arms swinging; walks upstairs alternating feet; walks downstairs two feet on step	Runs more smoothly, has more control over starting and stopping	Springs up off floor with both feet in some cases, jumps over object leading with one foot	Climbs up and down ladders, jungle gyms, slides, and trees
4–5 years	Walks up and down stairs alternating feet; walks circular line; skips with one foot	Displays strong, speedy running; turns corners, starts and stops easily	Jumps up, down and forward	Climbs up and down ladders, jungle gyms, slides, and trees
5–6 years	Walks as an adult; skips alternating feet	Shows mature running, falls seldom, displays increased speed and control	Jumps long, high, and far; jumps rope	Displays mature climbing in adult manner

- **Make an Obstacle Course**

Use planks, sawhorses, barrels, ladders, and boxes to create an obstacle course for climbing. Rearrange them frequently. Children can climb up, over, and under.

- **Read a Book**

The classic book on climbing, of course, is *Jack and the Beanstalk*. There are many versions. You might try the one by Paul Galdone (New York: Clarion Books, 1974).

❏ MOVES LEGS/FEET IN RHYTHM TO BEAT

The acquisition of musical skills by preschool children crosses several areas of development, including physical, cognitive, language, and creative. But because music itself involves both rhythm and sound (tempo and tone), we will look first at young children's development of rhythm, partly a large motor ability. Later, in Chapter 9, we will consider musical sound, partly a cognitive ability; and in Chapter 10 we will consider musical memory, another cognitive skill.

All of we humans are rhythmical beings whether or not we recognize it. Rhythm, in fact, is the essence of our life: Witness the beating of our hearts and the breathing of our lungs. It is not so surprising to find, therefore, that even infants can make rhythmical responses with arms, hands, legs, and feet. These claps, kicks, and wavings seem to be triggered by internal stimuli and not by external sounds or motions; although Cratty mentions that in cultures where dance is important, infants too young to stand have been observed picking up the beat of nearby adult dancers with their own bodies and limbs (Cratty, 1986, p. 257).

Nevertheless, the first voluntary rhythmical movements of young children are stimulated by sounds rather than visual cues. As with other physical development, the young children's rhythmic development proceeds in an observable sequence. First to appear are movements of arms and hands and then legs and feet that can follow a regular and rather slow rhythmic beat. Next, the young child's movements are able to replicate an irregular beat. Finally, children can learn to follow sound cues of different intensities. Horizontal movements are acquired before up and down movements of the arms. Rhythmic movements of one leg or one arm appear before the ability to move both limbs rhythmically.

But regardless of development, most young children love to dance and sing. They will make attempts to imitate any rhythmic activity around them. Young children also will follow their own internal rhythms with moving and singing on their own. If we want children to continue the natural development of their musical abilities, then the next move is ours. Adults who notice young children moving rhythmically must compliment them, must encourage them to continue their creative movements, and must call attention to the children's accomplishment.

Children very quickly pick up on the values of the adults around them. If the adults show interest in children's dancing, then the youngsters will continue to dance. On the other hand, if adults disregard this action or reprimand children for moving around so much, then children will stop.

You need to provide the stimulus in your program for young children to move rhythmically. That means you must praise children for any impromptu creative moving they do. Then you must schedule creative movement activities in the daily life of your classroom. Be creative yourself and think of the curriculum areas that might include creative movement. An excellent book to follow is *A Moving Experience: Dance for Lovers of Children and the Child Within* by Teresa Benzwie (1987).

Creative Movement

An entire class of preschool children can gain tremendously from creative movement and dance activities if the activities are led by a sensitive teacher and held in a creative environment. A drum, tom-tom, tambourine, or simply hand clapping may be used by the teacher for the beat, but she or he must be sensitive enough to pick up the pulse or rhythm of the group, instead of imposing a rhythm on them. Records or tapes also can be used but, again, the teacher needs to rely on the group rhythm, which is usually different—often slower—than that of a record.

The environment should be attractive, orderly, and comfortable. If a gymnasium is used, it should be uncluttered. If the preschool classroom is large enough, clear a space for expansive movements. Preschoolers need to be able to run, leap, and gallop.

The teacher should be the leader—a sensitive and creative leader. If a child does not want to participate, don't make her. You can take her hand and swing it gently to the music. The teacher should be prepared with a series of simple movement activities for the children to try. Children do not like to be told, "Do whatever you want to do," or "Move any way you want to the music." This leads only to confusion.

Instead, you should lead the children into creative movement activities through the stimulus of a steady, rhythmic beat. They need to master the basic locomotor movements of walking, running, crawling, leaping, and galloping to music or to a beat. Start by beating the tom-tom slowly and having children walk across the floor to the beat. Then increase the tempo of the beat and have them come back across the floor a bit faster. Try other movements, at first slowly and then faster.

The children also should master some of the nonlocomotor movements such as swinging, swaying, rocking, bending, and stretching. Continue using a drum or tap on a tambourine to set the beat for movement. Have seated children tap their feet to the beat. Then have them sway or rock or bend while still seated. Change the beat, making it faster or slower, louder or softer. Then have the children stand up and make the same movements while you change the beat. Whatever you do with rhythm, make it fun and do not expect perfection from these developing children of yours.

The short attention span of preschoolers makes it necessary to keep the sessions short (20 minutes), and include a variety of movements and dance activities. Young children like activities that take place on the floor, so be sure to include "snake" and "worm" dances where children can wriggle and crawl. Four-year-olds especially love to run. You will want to include a "jet plane zoom" or a "race car rally" where children can run to music or a beat.

You could do a follow-the-leader activity in a line where you as leader set the pace. You can march, tramp, slide along, trip along on tiptoes, or walk in cadence, calling out a beat (one-two buckle your shoe, three-four shut the door, etc.). Use music as well as a drum to help children move their legs and feet to the beat. Put on a record with a strong beat, and have the children move around the room keeping time. You may want to wind down your session with a slower record. Choose an appropriate tune for a "monster shuffle" or a "dinosaur clump." Children are usually happily exhausted after such a creative movement session.

Researcher Barbara Andress finds that music-related creative movement responses increase among young children in a preschool classroom when three techniques are used: modeling, describing, and suggesting (Andress, 1991, p. 24). Modeling is done by a respected adult who moves to music, expressing his or her own ideas of what he or she hears. This does not mean the child will imitate the action, but that the youngster will be motivated to move independently. The adult can, however, encourage a child to move through what is called *tactile modeling*. Using this technique,

> The adult can extend the two index fingers for the child to grip (thus allowing the child to release at any time) and then begin to gently sway or otherwise guide movements to music. (Andress, 1991, p. 26.)

For instance, the two can sway side-to-side while singing "Hickory Dickory Dock" or they can face each other and make rowing movements while singing "Row, Row, Row Your Boat."

Describing is also an effective way to promote creative movement. Here the teacher makes statements describing what the child is doing while the youngster is doing it. One statement Andress used was, "I see Gregory slide his feet with the soft music. Now Gregory is stamping when the music is very loud" (Andress, 1991, p. 26).

Suggesting is a third technique that teachers can use in combination with the previous two, so long as it is not overdone. In this instance the teacher suggests movements as she or he begins to model them: "Let's fly a kite," or "See how my kitty can waltz around" (Andress, 1991, p. 26).

If You Have Not Checked This Item: Some Helpful Ideas

■ Use a Tape Recorder

After tramping, stamping, or tiptoeing, children may want to create some "foot music" of their own. Have everyone sit while one child taps out a rhythm with his or her feet. Record it. Play it back and let the other children try to imitate this rhythm with their own feet.

Children may want to tape-record other rhythms they hear. Have them listen for rhythms in the classroom. Can they hear the bubbling of the aquarium, the dripping of water from a faucet, the clicking of keys in the office down the hall? If you tape-record such sounds and play them back, children may be able to stand and move their feet to these rhythms.

■ Walk to Music

Play different records or pieces of music with different rhythms, and have your children try to walk around the room keeping time with the beat. Then have them walk to the rhythm of your drumbeats or to a clicker. If you do not have a percussion instrument, tap on a glass. Speed up the tempo. Slow it down. Make it syncopated.

- ## Use a Rock or Rap Album or Tape

Rock and rap music are characterized by their strong beat. Bring in several albums or tapes with a beat and let children move and dance to them in the classroom.

- ## Move to Chants or Poems

Books with chants and body action rhymes, such as *Move Over, Mother Goose! Finger Plays, Action Verses & Funny Rhymes* by Ruth I. Dowell (Mt. Rainier, MD: Gryphon House, 1987), are wonderful sources of verses with a beat that children can move to. So is a book like *Arroz Con Leche: Popular Songs and Rhymes from Latin America* by Lulu Delacre (New York: Scholastic, 1989).

- ## Read a Book

Read a story about dancing or movement and then put on a record or tape that seems appropriate for children's dancing. *Barn Dance!* by Bill Martin Jr. and John Archambault (New York: Henry Holt, 1986) is a night story in rhyme about some animals and a skinny kid who hears "plink, plink, plink on the wind's violin." The boy leaves his bed in the farmhouse to join the animals at a barn dance.

Ayu and the Perfect Moon by David Cox (London: The Bodley Head, 1984) is a story about an old woman, Ayu, who tells a little Balinese girl the story of how she danced the Legong dance near the banyan tree in the village square when she was young.

Bravo, Tanya by Satomi Ichikawa and Patricia Lee Gauch (New York: Philomel Books, 1992) tells how little Tanya and her ballerina bear, Barbara, go to dancing class. Tanya tries her best but doesn't always dance as well in class as she does in the meadow by the brook, where she moves to music only she hears.

❏ CLAPS HANDS IN RHYTHM TO BEAT

Most preschool children have participated in hand-clapping activities from infancy. They have imitated mother doing pat-a-cake, they have imitated others around them who applaud a performance by clapping. Now they are asked to perform a musical activity with their hands: clapping to a beat.

As discussed in the previous item, rhythm is a natural part of all of us. Our heart goes on beating whether or not we think about it. Our fingers may tap out a rhythm automatically. But can preschool children clap their hands in rhythm to a beat created outside of their body? They can if their physical skills have developed normally and they have had practice clapping in rhythm.

The developmental sequence of head to foot (cephalo-caudal) and trunk to extremities (proximal-distal), also applies to the physical maturity necessary for children to perform rhythmic movements. In other words, arm control in children occurs before hand control; and hand control occurs before finger control. A second sequence of development begins with control of one arm and hand independent of the other arm and hand (as in waving); next comes the simultaneous use of both arms and hands (as in clapping); and finally comes alternate movements of the two arms and hands (as in drumming).

Although the clapping ability appears early in a child's development, the ability to clap with control comes later. Two-year-old children, for instance, enjoy clapping but usually cannot clap in a pattern without a great deal of help and practice. The concept of clapping in a rhythm or clapping out the syllables of a name is beyond most of them. Children 3, 4, and 5 years old also may have some difficulty at first in following a clapping pattern. Most of them can learn to clap the syllables of words or names, however, and enjoy repeating the activity (Moomaw, 1984, p. 44).

Once they have reached this maturity, children need to have practice in order to follow external rhythms. The creative movement activities discussed previously should give the children practice in moving their feet and bodies to rhythm. At the same time, they hear you, the teacher, providing the beat with your hands. Now it is their turn.

When you sing songs or play records in your classroom, give children practice clapping to the rhythm. Or use familiar folk songs to practice clapping on different beats. For instance, in "Paw Paw Patch," children can clap on every other beat (capital letters) at first:

WHERE, oh, WHERE is SWEET little SUsy?
WHERE, oh, WHERE is SWEET little SUsy?
WHERE, oh, WHERE is SWEET little SUsy?
WAY down YONder in the PAW paw PATCH.

When children are able to follow this regular rhythm without difficulty, let them try to clap on every beat. Nursery rhymes and jump rope rhymes also are excellent for clapping practice. Let children follow the irregular rhythm of

Rain, rain, go away,
Come again another day,
Jill and Betsy want to play.

or

One for the money,
Two for the show,
Three to get ready,
And four to go!

If You Have Not Checked This Item: Some Helpful Ideas

■ Try Name Clapping

Focusing on a child's name is the surest way to interest a young egocentric child in almost any activity. At circle time or small group time you can introduce name clapping: clapping out the syllables in each child's name as the children say the name aloud. Make the activity more interesting by adding other words, such as "Hello" or "My name is." Now the children can chant and clap:

Hel-lo-Bob-bie.
My-name-is-San-dra.
Hel-lo-Ver-on-i-ca.

Finally, as the children become more adept, add their last names to this clapping activity:

My-name-is-Mel-is-sa-Brad-ley.

■ Use a Tape Recorder

Children may want their own clapped rhythms recorded on the tape recorder and then played back for others in the group to try to imitate. Have each child say his or her name and then clap out a rhythm.

■ Read a Book

Mother Goose books, nursery rhyme books, and books containing jump rope rhymes can be used for clapping in unison. *The Lady with the Alligator Purse* adapted by Nadine Bernard Westcott (Boston: Little, Brown, 1988) is a hilariously illustrated version of this well-known jump rope rhyme. Children will enjoy the pictures, the rhyming words, and the rhythm. Let them clap in unison when you read the book a second time.

❏ BEATS DRUM ALTERNATING HANDS IN RHYTHM TO BEAT

Moving their two arms and hands alternately in a vertical motion, such as beating on a drum, indicates a more mature development of children's arm and hand control than does clapping the hands together. Young children enjoy beating on drums, pans, wooden blocks, and almost anything that will make a noise. For beaters they use their hands (fingers, palms, knuckles, fists), drumsticks, mallets, building sticks, ladles, and anything else they can pound with. In this item you are observing children to see whether they can use both hands alternately to beat out a rhythm.

The developmental sequence of drumming with the hands follows that of clapping, but children will have more success in beating a drum in a particular rhythm if they first have had many clapping experiences. When your children demonstrate that they can clap in rhythm, it is time to introduce the drum.

Instruments used in preschool programs fall into the same categories as those used by professionals: sound makers, rhythm, melody, and harmony instruments. Sound makers for young children include pots, pans, seed pods, stones, and cans with seeds.

Rhythm instruments include rhythm sticks, tone blocks, coconut shells, bells, triangles, gongs, cymbals, tambourines, sand blocks, rattles, maracas, and drums, to name a few. Melody instruments include xylophones, marimbas, tone bells, tonettes, fluto-phones, and ocarinas. Harmony instruments include the autoharp, harmonica, guitar, ukelele, banjo, mandolin, accordion, piano, and electric keyboard.

Rhythm instruments such as the drum need to be taken seriously in the preschool: that is, a drum is not a toy but a real instrument, and should be treated as such. Perhaps because teachers forget that rhythm instruments are serious instruments used in real bands and orchestras, they allow children to treat these items as toys. Instead, each rhythm instrument should be introduced to children separately with directions on how to use it properly, and limits on using it improperly. In this way children get the most from the experience: They learn how to use the instrument, to appreciate the sound it makes, and to practice the physical skills the instrument affords them.

Unfortunately, rhythm instruments are often used in "rhythm bands" in the preschool classroom, with all of the instruments played at once as the children march around to music. The youngsters, of course, may have fun with such an activity, but it adds little to their enjoyment of music, their skill development, or their appreciation for the instrument they hold. Instead, children tend to bang as loud as they can all at once, creating a cacophony—noise—that drowns out the sounds of the individual instruments, the music, and the rhythm they are supposed to be following.

Drums are available in all sizes and shapes. Some are intended to be played with the hands, some played with two drumsticks, some played with one. Commercial drums are usually wooden or plastic with a skin or plastic head over one or both ends. Have several drums and drumsticks available in your classroom. Take time to introduce their use to the children, rather than merely putting the instruments on a shelf. Talk to the children about the drums. Demonstrate what each one sounds like and how it can be played. Let the children try out each drum.

After the children have tried the drums, have them sing a song while you clap out the beat. Next, have the children clap the beat themselves as they sing. Finally, let them try beating the drums to accompany the song. They can use drumsticks or their hands. Pass the drums around until everyone has a chance.

Be sure to continue this drumming activity for several days in order to give the children practice. You can use different songs, records, or tapes with different rhythms, and a variety of activities. Some children may want to beat the drums while the others march around the room.

If You Have Not Checked This Item: Some Helpful Ideas

■ Use Drums in Clapping Activities

Drums can be used alone or with clapping for any of the activities described under the previous checklist item on clapping.

■ Send Messages

Children enjoy sending drumbeat messages. If they have learned to clap out names by syllables, they will be able to send drum messages the same way. Let them try sending their names ("My-name-is-Ran-dy") with drumbeats. Can the other children guess what they are saying on the drum?

■ Make Your Own Drums

Making drums is an activity for the teacher, not the children, in the preschool. Various types of drums can be made depending on the material. Use large cans, ice cream containers, oatmeal boxes, round plastic containers, plastic bleach bottles, coffee cans, margarine containers, or wooden or metal buckets for the body. For the head use animal parchment (from repair departments of music stores), inner tube rubber, goatskin, heavy plastic, or canvas. Remove one or both ends of the can or container. Cut one or two circular head pieces larger than the container opening. Punch holes around the edge of the drum head material about 2 inches apart to accommodate a cord or rawhide lace. If you are using parchment or goatskin, soak it in water for half an hour. Place the drum head material on either end of the container and lace it tightly around the drum body. Or place the drum head material on the open end and tack it to the drum body.

To make drumsticks, glue small rubber balls on the ends of sticks—pencils, building sticks, wooden dowels. You can also wrap cloth around the ends of wooden ladles, or insert sticks into spools and wrap cloth around the spools.

■ Read a Book

I Like the Music by Leah Komaiko (New York: Harper & Row, 1987) is a city story about a little girl who likes street music, but her grandma feels that the symphony's the place to be. Told in rhyme with a strong beat, the story takes them both to a night concert in the park where both are involved in a treat.

Ty's One-man Band by Mildred Pitts Walter (New York: Scholastic, 1980) takes place long ago in the South. Ty, a little African-American boy discovers Andro, a wandering man with a peg leg and the ability to make music from two wooden spoons, a washboard, a tin pail, and a comb. The book is full of word sounds and rhythms as Andro fills the night with music. After reading this book, your children can try their own skill with these instruments.

OBSERVING, RECORDING, AND INTERPRETING LARGE MOTOR DEVELOPMENT

It is important at the beginning of the year to screen all of your children using the "Large Motor Development" section of the *Child Skills Checklist*. List the name of each child along the left side of a lined sheet of paper. Across the top of the paper, indicate the eight items of the checklist. Draw vertical lines separating the eight items. Check off the large motor skills you observe for each child. For children who have few check marks, you may want to do an in-depth observation on each of the items.

Lionel, whose social play observations are shown in Figure 5.1, was observed for large motor development and the information in Figure 7.1 was gathered. This observational data gathered for Lionel was helpful to the classroom staff. They could see that Lionel spent more time in sedentary activities. He seemed more at ease sitting and playing than running around in large motor activities. During a parent conference, the teachers learned that Lionel lived in a large apartment building, and had little opportunity to run outside and play. The staff was also concerned because the program itself offered few large motor experiences for the children. The *N* designation, meaning no opportunity to observe, was listed for most of the children because the preschool program does not have a playground, gymnasium, or indoor climbing equipment. Children are taken for walks, weather permitting, and are allowed to run around on the lawn outside the building. But it is obvious that additional large motor activities need to be provided.

Because Lionel and many of the other children showed skills and interest in rhythm activities, the classroom team decided to incorporate creative movement and dance activities at one end of the large classroom on a daily basis. As children become accustomed to moving to music and drumbeats, the teachers plan to take the children outside on the lawn for more expansive creative movement activities.

FIGURE 7.1

Large motor development observations for Lionel

Child Skills Checklist

Name _Lionel_   **Observer** _Barb_

Program _Preschool – K2_   **Dates** _1 / 20_

Directions:

Put a ✔ for items you see the child perform regularly. Put *N* for items where there is no opportunity to observe. Leave all other items blank.

Item	Evidence	Date
5. Large Motor Development	Holds onto rail & puts 2 feet on each step when going down stairs	1/20
___ Walks down steps alternating feet		
___ Runs with control over speed and direction	Does not run often	1/20
_N_ Jumps over obstacle, landing on two feet		1/20
_N_ Hops forward on one foot		1/20
_N_ Climbs up and down climbing equipment with ease		1/20
_✓_ Moves legs/feet in rhythm to beat	Taps feet when he beats drum	1/20
_✓_ Claps hands in rhythm to beat	Claps in time to records.	1/20
_✓_ Beats drum alternating hands in rhythm to beat	Uses drum during rhythmn activities	1/20

REFERENCES

Allen, K. Eileen, & Elizabeth M. Goetz. (1982). *Early childhood education: Special problems, special solutions.* Rockville, MD: Aspen.

Andress, Barbara. (1991). From research to practice: Preschool children and their movement responses to music. *Young Children, 47*(1), 22–27.

Benzwie, Teresa. (1987). *A moving experience: Dance for lovers of children and the child within.* Tucson, AZ: Zephyr Press.

Caplan, Theresa, & Frank Caplan. (1983). *The early childhood years: The 2 to 6 year old.* New York: Putnam.

Cratty, Bryant J. (1982). Motor development in early childhood: Critical issues for researchers in the 1980's. In Bernard Spodek (Ed.), *Handbook of research in early childhood education (pp. 27-46).* New York: Free Press.

Cratty, Bryant J. (1986). *Perceptual & motor development in infants & children.* Englewood Cliffs, NJ: Prentice-Hall.

Flinchum, Betty M. (1975). *Motor development in early childhood: A guide for movement education with ages 2 to 6.* St. Louis: Mosby.

Fraiberg, S. (1975). Intervention in infancy: A program for blind infants. In B. Z. Friedlander, G. M. Sterritt, & G. E. Kird (Eds.), *Exceptional infant* (Vol. 3). New York: Brunner/Mazel.

Gallahue, David L. (1982). *Developmental movement experiences for children.* New York: Wiley.

Moomaw, Sally. (1984). *Discovering music in early childhood.* Boston: Allyn & Bacon.

Pines, Maya. (1979). A head start in the nursery. *Psychology Today, 13*(4), 56–68.

Sullivan, Molly. (1982). *Feeling strong, feeling free: Movement exploration for children.* Washington, DC: NAEYC.

Zaichkowsky, Leonard D., Linda B. Zaichkowsky, & Thomas J. Martineck. (1980). *Growth and development: The child and physical activity.* St. Louis: Mosby.

OTHER SOURCES

Beaty, Janice J. (1992). *Preschool appropriate practices.* Fort Worth, TX: Harcourt Brace Jovanovich.

Beaty, Janice J. (1992). *Skills for preschool teachers.* New York: Merrill/Macmillan.

Gabbard, Carl. (1988). Early childhood physical education. *Journal of Physical Education, Recreation and Dance, 59*(7), 65–69.

Haines, Joan E., & Linda L. Gerber. (1988). *Leading young children to music.* New York: Merrill/Macmillan.

Munro, June Gustafson. (1986). Movement education: Balance. *Day Care and Early Education, 14*(2), 28–31.

Poest, Catherine A., Jean R. Williams, David D. Witt, & Mary Ellen Atwood. (1990). Challenge me to move: Large muscle development of young children. *Young Children, 45*(5), 4–10.

LEARNING ACTIVITIES

1. Use the *Child Skills Checklist* section "Large Motor Development" as a screening tool to observe all of the children in your classroom. Which ones are the most physically accomplished? Which need the most help? What are their ages?

2. Choose a child who seems to need a great deal of help in large motor development. Do a running record on three different days to determine what the child can do physically. Do an activity with the child to promote a skill he or she needs help with. Record the results.

3. How do the girls and boys of the same age in your program compare with one another in each of the Large Motor Checklist items? How do you explain any differences or similarities? Can you form any conclusions about gender differences based on your observations?

4. Choose a child who needs help in moving to rhythm. Involve the child using one or more of the rhythm ideas from the text. Discuss the results.

5. Have a staff member involve children in a new large motor game while you observe and record. Discuss your results as compared with the original screening you did. What conclusions can you draw?

8 Small Motor Development

Small Motor Checklist

- ❑ Shows hand preference (which is _____)
- ❑ Turns with hand easily (knobs, lids, eggbeaters)
- ❑ Pours liquid into glass without spilling
- ❑ Unfastens and fastens zippers, buttons, Velcro tabs
- ❑ Picks up and inserts objects with ease
- ❑ Uses drawing/writing tools with control
- ❑ Uses scissors with control
- ❑ Pounds in nails with control

S mall motor development involves the fine muscles that control the extremities. In the case of young children we are especially concerned with control, coordination, and dexterity in using the hands and fingers. Although this development occurs simultaneously with large motor development in children, the muscles near the trunk (proximal) mature first, before the muscles of the extremities (distal) that control the wrists and hands.

Thus it is important for young children to practice use of the large muscles before they become involved in small motor activities to any extent. Delays in developing large motor coordination may very well have a negative effect on the development of small motor skills. But once small motor involvement is possible for the children, preschool caregivers should encourage them to engage in all types of manipulative activities so that they can learn and then practice the skills needed to use their hands and fingers with control and dexterity.

REFLEXES

If infants and toddlers use their hands and fingers without much previous experience, why do 3-, 4-, and 5-year-olds present a different situation? The difference is important. It involves voluntary versus involuntary movements. Infants move their arms, hands, and fingers through reflexes, not voluntary movements. These involuntary movements are assimilated by the nervous system as it matures in order for children to be able to control their movements in a voluntary manner. As these initial reflexes disappear, children must purposefully learn to replace them by using and controlling their hands and fingers in a voluntary manner.

A very large number of reflexes are present in the infant. They include the Moro, or startle, reflex in which the infant throws out his arms with a jerk and lets out a cry; the rooting reflex in which the infant turns her head and opens her mouth when touched on the side of the cheek; the sucking reflex in which the infant sucks if his lips or mouth are touched; the walking reflex in which the infant makes stepping movements when held in an upright position on a surface; the swimming reflex in which the infant makes swimming movements when held in the water with her head supported. Many more reflexes also exist in infancy (Zaichkowsky, Zaichkowsky, & Martineck, 1980, p. 37).

The reflex most connected with small motor hand skills is the grasping reflex, or palmar grasp, in which a baby clamps his fingers around anything put in his palm. This grasp is so strong in the beginning that it will support the infant's weight and can be used to lift him entirely off the surface on which he is lying. It is difficult, in fact, for the infant to let go. You may have to pry his fingers apart.

Involuntary responses such as this have their origin in the lower brain stem and spinal cord, and eventually come under the control of the higher brain centers of the nervous system as the child matures. This higher part of the brain inhibits these initial reflexes after they have finished their task of aiding the survival of the helpless newborn, and the higher brain center then allows voluntary movements to replace them.

The initial reflexes fade away within their own recognized timetable, depending on individual differences, of course. Rooting and sucking usually disappear after 3 months, walking and swimming after 5 months, and Moro—the last to go—usually disappears after 9 months. When such reflexes persist after their allotted time, it may be an indication of brain impairment (Zaichkowsky et al., 1980, p. 37).

The grasping reflex lasts until about 9 months. Thus infants cannot start to control hand and finger actions voluntarily before this. Infants may reach for things—but not very accurately—before age 6 months; then letting go becomes a big problem. They can grasp an object easily but find it extremely difficult to let go. Even 1-year-old children may struggle to release an object voluntarily, and some do not gain control of letting go before a year-and-a-half of age.

READINESS

We understand that, like the large motor skills, voluntary small motor skills do not simply happen; they must be learned naturally and then practiced by young children. But is there a certain time period when particular skills can be learned best? Again we face the problem of readiness. When are children's neuromuscular systems mature enough for them to control their movements and perform certain actions? Should we wait until they are ready? Not necessarily. As with large motor skills, we should encourage children to use their small muscles as soon as they can. Because each child's development is different, this time period may differ for each.

All of us carry within us a biological time clock that we have inherited. For some of us, small motor development occurs in textbook fashion, just as the charts for average physical growth indicate. For others, this development happens just a bit behind or ahead of the charts. This staggered individual development will exist in all of the children in your program. Each child has his or her own built-in biological clock. But you do not know what time it is for a child except in general terms, and neither does the child. Since everyone's development occurs in the same sequence but at different rates, the best we can do is to assess the child's development, and then provide him or her with appropriate activities, materials, and encouragement.

Is there a critical moment, then, when small motor skills must be learned or it will be too late? Not really, except in broad general terms. The best time to learn a small motor skill seems to be when the skill is changing most rapidly (Zaichkowsky et al., 1980, p. 36). Because this point in development is not easy to determine, it is best to offer many types of activities for all of your children and to help them get involved with those activities that offer both success and challenge.

In order to know where your children stand in their small motor development at the outset, you may want to screen them using the eight Small Motor Checklist items. These items are observable behaviors that demonstrate acknowledged small motor skills of young children in the areas of rotation, manipulation, and dexterity, as well as handedness.

❏ SHOWS HAND PREFERENCE (WHICH IS ____)

Many, but not all, of your children will have developed a hand preference by age 3. You may want to take note of this preference, but you should not be concerned about it. A great deal of interest and controversy—as well as incomplete understanding—surrounds the development of handedness, or *lateral dominance* as it is called. Lateral dominance also includes the development of a foot preference and eye preference, which may or may not be the same as the hand preference.

Infants tend to use both hands in the beginning. This behavior is due to reflexive rather than voluntary movements. As the neuromuscular system matures enough for voluntary movements to occur, infants may begin to show a preference for one hand. At first this preference may not be very strong, and because involuntary movements do not disappear all at once, infants may use both hands for many months.

This seems to be the case for 1-year-olds. By the age of 2 years, the child may begin to prefer using one hand over the other. At 2-and-a-half years, about 58 percent of American children have established a dominant hand, and by age 3 about 70 percent have established dominance. Then this percentage does not increase much until 8-and-a-half years. By the age of 11 years, 94 percent have established a preferred hand and the remaining children are ambidextrous, or have mixed dominance (Zaichkowsky et al., 1980, p. 75).

Not all children in the world exhibit the same pattern of development in hand dominance. Hand preference development in Japanese children is similar to that of American children until about age 2-and-a-half. But between then and 4-and-a-half, development slows down considerably. Only 50 percent of Japanese children establish hand dominance by the age of 4-and-a-half years (Zaichkowsky et al., 1980, p. 75).

This is an important finding because we know that children develop in the same sequence and within the same timetable around the world. Differences, therefore, must be due to cultural influences: in other words, the child's environment. In America we are particularly concerned with handedness, and many parents go out of their way to make sure their children develop right-handedness. They put emphasis on using the right hand by handing things to the right hand and encouraging children to use their right hand to eat, hold, and throw. When the children are successful, the parents praise them and offer positive feedback.

Such practice accompanied by feedback and positive reinforcement is of course the best way to develop any motor skill. Perhaps the Japanese are not so concerned with hand dominance at an early age and have allowed their children to develop it naturally. In the end, parental influence seems to make little difference, because 90 percent of the human race eventually uses the right hand for small motor activities. More boys, by the way, are left-handed or ambidextrous than girls.

Foot dominance is somehow different from hand dominance. Even infants often show a clear-cut preference for one foot over the other. By the time they are 5 years old, 94 percent of children have developed foot dominance.

Our concern over handedness has always centered around children's ability in learning to read and write. Will lefties have more trouble? Will children with mixed dominance have learning problems? Should you try to change a child's hand preference from left to right? The answers are not all that clear. A great deal of controversy exists regarding the relationship between perceptual-motor development and learning disabilities. There is still so much we do not know about human development.

The best advice at the moment, it seems, advocates helping young children develop small motor dexterity, no matter what their hand preference. Children need to succeed. A strong hand preference may help them perform small motor tasks with dexterity. If you know what that preference is for each of your children, you can help them to develop it with practice and positive feedback.

If You Have Not Checked This Item: Some Helpful Ideas

■ Do Not Make a Fuss

You may want to know if a child has established handedness, and with which hand, but keep your efforts at a low key. Encourage the child to use whichever hand she prefers, so that she will become more skillful in using it.

❑ TURNS WITH HAND EASILY (KNOBS, LIDS, EGGBEATERS)

Twisting or turning movements done with the wrist, hand, and fingers by rotating the wrist and/or forearm take several different forms. The child may enclose a doorknob with her hand and try to twist and then pull it to open the door. Depending upon the size and stiffness of the knob and door, she may or may not succeed at first. Or she may not be tall enough to make her small motor skills work effectively. Turning a key in a lock involves this same type of motion.

Another form of small motor rotating involves vertical turning at the wrist or rotating the forearm while the fingers are gripping an implement: a cranking type of movement. The operation of eggbeaters, food mills, and can openers requires this motion. Still another type of small motor rotating uses the fingers to twist a nut onto a bolt, turn a screw into a hole, or twist a lid onto or off of a jar or bottle.

Children at an early age can accomplish this particular motor skill. Children 2 and 3 years old, for instance, can turn a doorknob if they can reach it. They love to screw and unscrew lids or caps on jars and bottles. Ask parents to collect empty plastic bottles and containers of all sizes along with their screw-top lids, and keep the items in a box in the manipulative area of the classroom for the children to practice on. Small motor control is far from perfect in the preschool years, especially with the younger children; things have a way of slipping out of their fingers from time to time. It is very important to use only unbreakable containers such as plastic—never glass—in the classroom.

This same hand-rotating skill is also used by 3-year-olds and older children as they try to put together a puzzle. Whereas 2-year-olds will often try to jam a puzzle piece into place and will give up if it doesn't fit, older children will rotate the piece to try to match the shape of the hole.

Watch and see how your children make puzzles. Obviously, perceptual awareness is also at work in this instance, but children first need the small motor rotating skill in order to use their shape-recognition ability. Puzzles of differing complexities should be an item on your shelves of manipulative materials. These puzzles offer excellent practice for finger dexterity and eye-hand coordination, as well as the cognitive concepts of matching, shapes, and part-to-whole relationships.

Three-year-olds can turn an eggbeater, and they love to do it. Be sure to have more than one eggbeater at your water table, because it is usually a favorite implement and the focus of many squabbles if only one is available. Children like to try turning food mills and can openers as well, but sometimes youngsters do not have the strength to succeed if the items to be ground or opened are too difficult.

Research has found that objects of differing shapes and objects that permit the child to modify them are more interesting to children than objects that are rigid and unchangeable. Novelty is also an important quality in encouraging children to handle and manipulate objects. When the novelty wears off, children are less interested in playing with the items. Teachers should respond to such findings by including a variety of items in the manipulative area, and by changing them from time to time (Cratty, 1986, p. 214).

In addition, teachers should include cooking experiences in the classroom on a daily or weekly basis. Children can help with "cool cooking," that is, food preparation without heat, such as fixing daily snacks. They can scrape carrots and cut celery for dips; mix cream cheese with flavorings; grind peanuts into peanut butter; whip cream into butter. They can also help with "hot cooking" by whipping eggs with eggbeaters for scrambled eggs or grinding cooked apples or cooked pumpkin with a food mill.

More and more teachers are making food preparation a part of their curriculum because of convenient appliances such as hot pots, electric skillets, microwaves, and toaster ovens. Cooking is an activity with special significance for children's development of small motor skills. As Cosgrove (1991) points out,

Many kinds of learning are involved in cooking; motor, sensory, conceptual, and social skills all play an important part in food preparation. All five senses are involved. Stirring, beating, and rolling improve muscle control. Measuring, boiling, and freezing illustrate change. Following directions requires listening. Sharing, cooperation, and good manners encourage social skills. And waiting for someone to say "OK, it's done—let's eat" develops patience. (p. 44)

If You Have Not Checked This Item: Some Helpful Ideas

■ Provide a Collection of Food Utensils for Cooking and Play

Visit a hardware store that has a large assortment of food-preparation utensils and stock up on all kinds of grinding, squeezing, and cranking types of implements. Better still, visit a flea market and buy the same sort of things secondhand. Some of the old-fashioned hand tools of great-grandma's kitchen will make a big hit in your classroom. Keep some of the items in your housekeeping area for pretending, and some near the water table or on your manipulative shelves for small motor practice. But be sure to let the children themselves use these utensils when you do real cooking.

■ Make a Nuts-and-Bolts Board

Fasten bolts of different sizes to a well sanded board, and provide a box of nuts for the children to screw onto the bolts. The children will need to use their size-sorting as well as small motor skills.

■ Get Sample Doorknobs

Ask a building supply company for sample doorknobs, door locks, bolts, and other similar items when the particular model is no longer on display. Put them in your manipulative area. Other sources for doorknobs and other similar hardware are companies that regularly deal with used building materials, such as wreckers and demolition firms.

■ Collect Old Locks and Keys

Have a box of old locks and keys available for children to experiment with. The youngsters will need persistence as well as motor skills to match up the locks and keys and make them work, but it is an exciting challenge for them.

■ Get a Toy Hopper with a Hand Crank for the Sand Table

Children love to play with sand. Toy stores and toy catalogs sell sand implements for sifting and grinding that certain children will use for hours if you let them.

■ Try a Citrus Reamer

Bring in a citrus reamer that works by hand, and let your children take turns twisting half an orange on it to make their own juice for snack.

■ **Read a Book**

Pancakes for Breakfast by Tomie de Paola (New York: Harcourt Brace Jovanovich, 1978) is a wordless picture book about a little old woman who tries to make pancakes but can't seem to get the ingredients together. Illustrations show a flour sifter with a grinding handle as well as a butter churn. Be prepared to make pancakes with your children after reading this book.

The Best Peanut Butter Sandwich in the Whole World by Bill MacLean (Windsor, Ontario: 1990) shows little Billy gathering the ingredients and then making the best peanut butter sandwich in the whole world. Your children may want to grind peanut butter for their own best sandwiches.

❑ POURS LIQUID INTO GLASS WITHOUT SPILLING

Two-year-olds are able to hold a glass of milk, at first with two hands and then with one. Most parents are not really concerned that their children do more than this sort of holding. Pouring tends to be an adult activity that mothers do even for their preschool children. Many nursery school teachers and day-care personnel feel the same way. Why should children learn to pour? Won't they just make a mess if they spill? Isn't it much quicker and more efficient if the adults in the classroom do the pouring?

Children should learn to pour not only as a helping activity, but to acquire and practice small motor coordination. Pouring is an excellent real activity that children can participate in, and it is both helpful to others and, more importantly, helpful for their own small muscle development. Long ago, Maria Montessori, the renowned Italian early childhood educator, recognized the value of pouring by including all sorts of pouring activities in her "daily living exercises" that taught children small motor skills such as eye-hand coordination. Today, Montessori children still learn by pouring rice before they finally pour liquids successfully from small pitchers.

The size of the pitcher is the key to successful pouring. Three-year-olds may need to use both hands for pouring, but if the pitcher is small enough, 4- and 5-year-olds can often handle it with one hand. Put a small pitcher on each snack or lunch table, and let your children help themselves to juice or milk. If they should spill, they can help clean up with a soft sponge, another good small motor exercise.

Allowing children to pour may not be as efficient as having an adult pour the drinks, but you need to think about the purpose for your program. Is it to take care of a group of children, or is it to *help young children develop their own skills* and learn to take care of themselves? Young children take a great deal of pride in being able to do adult-type tasks. Performing these tasks not only makes them feel grown up but also gives them a real sense of self-worth and accomplishment.

There will be accidents. Spills are part of the price our children pay for the complicated task of growing up. Remember the problem of releasing the grip, in which children actually have to learn how to let go because some traces of the palmar grasp reflex may still remain. If they do not have their minds on what they are doing, they

If children spill, they can help clean up with a sponge, another good small motor exercise.

may release their grip without meaning to. Again, make spilling a learning experience, not an embarrassment. They will enjoy squeezing out the cleanup sponge.

If You Have Not Checked This Item: Some Helpful Ideas

■ Have Pouring Implements in Your Water Table

Have several sizes and types of plastic pitchers in your water table. Some can be large with lids on the top; some can be small and open at the top. All should have handles. Children can do much of their initial pouring practice here without worrying about spilling.

■ **Use Pouring Implements on Your Food Table**

Provide small plastic or ceramic pitchers that the children can use to serve themselves. You can fill these small-sized containers as they empty. Again, a flea market is a good source for interesting pouring implements such as vinegar cruets and small metal pitchers.

■ **Read a Book**

Sunshine by Jan Ormerod (New York: Lothrop, Lee & Shepard Books, 1981), another wordless book, shows a little girl getting up by herself in the morning, pouring milk on her breakfast cereal, helping her father get her mother's breakfast, brushing her teeth, dressing herself, and finally getting her parents going so they won't be late. Children enjoy seeing a child like themselves behaving so independently. Have them "read" the book to you.

❏ UNFASTENS AND FASTENS ZIPPERS, BUTTONS, VELCRO TABS

Unfastening and fastening zippers, buttons, and Velcro tabs are other self-help skills we want children to accomplish in order to take care of themselves, but also to develop small motor dexterity. Young children want to do things for themselves. Often they have trouble accomplishing unfastening and fastening tasks because their motor coordination has not developed sufficiently. But just as often their difficulty has to do with lack of practice because the adults around them do everything for them.

It is interesting to note that economically disadvantaged children frequently develop small motor dexterity before middle-income children do. Economically disadvantaged children often have more practice. In fact, preschoolers in many large one-parent families are expected to help dress themselves when the working mother has her hands full getting herself ready for work every morning, the baby ready for the sitter, and breakfast ready for everybody before she has to leave.

If mothers and fathers do all the buttoning and fastening of clothing for their preschoolers, the children miss an excellent opportunity for learning how to do it on their own. They may even resist when the preschool teacher encourages them to try, wanting the teacher to perform the same function as their parents.

Three-year-olds are able to unbutton first—always an easier task—but many can also button large buttons on clothing if given the chance to practice. Most 3-year-olds also can fasten regular snaps, but may have trouble with the heavy-duty jeans-type snap. Even 4-year-olds seldom have the finger strength necessary to make these heavy-duty snaps work.

Four-year-olds should be able to button and unbutton clothing with little difficulty. They can unzip zippers, but often need help getting started with jacket zippers that come apart completely.

Many shoes and articles of clothing are now equipped with Velcro-type fasteners, which seem to be the easiest kind for children to handle. A Velcro fastener is pulled apart by gripping the end between the thumb and forefinger and pulling; it is fastened merely by pushing one Velcro-covered tab against the Velcro backing. Preschoolers have the strength and coordination to do this with ease.

If You Have Not Checked This Item: Some Helpful Ideas

■ Use Buttoning/Zipping Boards

Make or purchase several boards that will help your children acquire and practice these skills. If you make your own boards, keep each skill separate: buttoning on one board, zipping on another, snaps on another. Then the children can practice one of these skills at a time. Have these boards available in the manipulative area of your classroom.

■ Talk with Parents

Talk with parents about the importance of their children's development of small motor coordination. Let them know the kinds of activities their children will be doing in your class. Suggest some of the activities the children could be doing at home, such as self-help skills like dressing themselves—including buttoning, zipping, and snapping clothing—or helping to dress younger members of the family.

■ Read a Book

I Love My Baby Sister (Most of the Time) by Elaine Edelman (New York: Viking Penguin, 1984) is a first-person story by a little girl who tells about the things her baby sister can do and the things she does to help her sister, such as showing her how to dress herself. Self-help skills are featured with intriguing illustrations. Your children should be motivated to talk about their own experiences along this line.

❑ PICKS UP AND INSERTS OBJECTS WITH EASE

Manipulative Materials

Picking up and inserting objects is the small motor skill most frequently promoted in the early childhood classroom. This skill involves manipulation of items by gripping them between thumb and fingers and inserting or placing them somewhere else. Using puzzles, pegboards, and stacking toys; lacing, sewing, weaving, stringing beads, and sorting small items call for this skill. Playing with building bricks, geoboards, formboards, bristleboards, and many plastic table games also requires picking up and inserting skills.

All classrooms should have a permanent space for manipulative activity of this sort. Put shelves equipped with many materials at children's level for easy selection and return. There should be a table in the area next to the shelves as well as floor space for playing with the larger toys.

The selection of materials should cover a wide range of children's abilities. Wooden puzzles, for example, should include simple single pictures with pieces showing an entire part of the picture for beginners, as well as more complicated pictures with many pieces for older or experienced children.

Teachers should plan to check all of the manipulative materials at least once a week to be sure all the parts and pieces are there. If some pieces are missing, either replace the piece or remove the material. It does not help beginners to try to make puzzles or play games that have pieces missing; many beginners soon give up.

It is not necessary to put out all of the manipulative materials that the program owns at once. Add a few new ones to the area every month and remove some of the old ones. Remember that the novelty of materials motivates children to use them. Save some of the more complicated table toys for challenging the experienced children later in the year. If you have a limited supply of materials, consider trading with other programs.

Children's Skills

You will want to know which children visit the manipulative area during your free play period. Use the Small Motor Checklist as a screening device to help you find out. Are children avoiding the area because they are not comfortable with small motor skills? Do mainly boys avoid the manipulative materials?

Once you know which individuals avoid manipulative activities, you will be able to sit down at a table with a single child and challenge him or her to make a puzzle with you, stack blocks, or sort shapes into a formboard. If you are keeping file card records of each child, you can add this information to his or her card. You or your co-workers may need to spend time every day with children who need extra practice with small motor skills. You may need to encourage these children to complete some of the small motor activities on their own.

Gender Differences

Our society seems to encourage girls to engage in small motor activities more than boys. Even the women's movement has not changed the way many parents raise their children. Boys are still encouraged to run outside and climb trees or play ball. Girls are given manipulative-type toys for their play. As a result many girls are more dexterous with their fingers, and boys are more skillful in large motor activities such as running and throwing.

In the end, all children need to be skillful and at ease with both large and small motor activities. Once involved with formal education, both genders will need to handle writing tools and reading activities. Girls who are more skillful with finger dexterity and eye-hand coordination have an edge over boys in writing and reading at present. Is this skill imbalance perhaps the reason more boys than girls have problems in learning to read?

If You Have Not Checked This Item: Some Helpful Ideas

■ Use Bead Stringing

Provide all kinds of materials for both boys and girls to use in making necklaces. Have macaroni and all sorts of pasta shapes available. The children can paint them before stringing. Bring in little sea shells with holes drilled in them (hobby shops do this), as well as acorns and horse chestnuts in the fall, plastic or wooden beads, and any other small items you can find. Save tops from plastic bottles and tops of magic markers; punch holes in them and use them for stringing necklaces and bracelets.

■ Make A Geoboard

Make a 1-foot-square wooden board at least $1/2$ inch thick and pound in headless nails over the surface of the board in rows 1 inch apart. Allow the nails to extend above the surface about 1 inch. Let the children string colored rubber bands over the tops of the nails, making all kinds of designs.

Older children can try to copy design cards you have made. Make 1-foot-square cardboard cards on which dots indicate the exact arrangement of nails as on the geoboard. On each card, draw around the dots the outline of a red square or a blue triangle or a yellow rectangle, and let the children try to copy each shape with similar colored rubber bands on the geoboard. These designs must be simple for 3- and 4-year-olds, because their copying skills are still at an early level. Kindergarten children will have an easier time copying geoboard designs.

If this play becomes a favorite activity, you will want more than one geoboard. Such boards can also be purchased.

■ Make Pegboards

Ask a building supply company for scraps of pegboard that would normally be thrown away. You can cut the scraps to child-size shapes and sand down the edges. The pegboards do not have to be squares. Triangular pegboards are just as useful and appealing. Provide boxes of colored golf tees for pegs and let the children use the tees the same as colored rubber bands are used on the geoboards. You may also want to make simple designs on paper or cardboard for the children to copy on their pegboards. Graph paper is helpful if you do not want to spend time measuring spaces.

■ Ask Parents to Help

Have a parent "board-making bee" to help stock your classroom as well as make enough extra boards to take home for their children. You can almost always attract parents or other family members to come to your program to help like this if they know they will be making educational games they can also take home. Besides helping their children both at home and at school, the parents themselves can be learning the importance of small motor activities for their children. Too often adults tend to look upon all children's activities as play, an unimportant entertainment. Parents need to be aware that play is essential to their children's physical, mental, and social development as human beings. Such parent group activities may change parents' outlook.

■ Read a Book

The Balancing Girl by Berniece Rabe (New York: Dutton, 1981) is the story of Margaret, a handicapped girl in leg braces and wheelchair, who nevertheless is a whiz at manipulating books, blocks, and dominoes. A domino maze, her outstanding creation, not only helps the school carnival succeed, but also reconciles her problems with Tommy, her chief competitor. Be sure to have at least one set of dominoes on hand after reading this story.

❑ USES DRAWING/WRITING TOOLS WITH CONTROL

Preschool programs for 2-, 3-, and 4-year-olds should not be concerned with "teaching" children how to draw pictures or write words. Some of your older children may—and probably will—progress to this stage of development, and may be able to do some pictorial drawing and word-writing naturally. Don't expect all of your children to reach this more advanced stage. Instead, you should provide children with opportunities to use writing and drawing implements of all kinds to encourage development of their small motor finger strength and dexterity and their eye-hand coordination.

The first time preschoolers use crayons, pencils, or magic markers they usually hold them in the so-called *power grip:* that is, with all of the fingers clamped fistlike around the implement. This grip does not give them much control over the marks they will make, because the entire hand, wrist, and arm is involved in the movements rather than the fingers. As their motor skills develop and they have the chance to practice, they will eventually switch to the *precision grip:* that is, holding the implement between the thumb and fingers.

Young children go through predictable stages in their development of writing skills. Cratty has noted that the earliest stage is a grasp (as mentioned) in which only the pencil touches the page, with the arm and hand unsupported in the air. Next, the little finger and elbow side of the hand are rested on the page of paper, but the hand and fingers are moved as one unit. Finally, children learn to use their hand and fingers separately, with the hand as an anchor on the paper and the fingers moving the pencil. The final stage, however, may not be reached until between 5 and 7 years of age (Cratty, 1986, p. 224).

Watch and see which of the children are using a mature grip on their writing implement and which still seem to prefer the fist clench. Ask their parents what writing or coloring tools they have at home. Some children may not have had the same practice as others because they have no materials. You may want to send home a few crayons and paper for those who need more drawing and writing practice.

Are your children using these tools with their preferred hand? Check and see. Children often pick up an implement with either hand and start to use it whether or not the hand works well. For those whose handedness you have already identified, you might have them try switching hands if they are coloring with the nondominant hand.

The stubby fingers of preschoolers sometimes have more success gripping a thick tool, although some youngsters prefer regular pencils and crayons. Felt-tip markers are thick and easy for them to use. Many preschoolers prefer markers to any other writing or coloring implement. The problem for teachers is reminding the children to keep the markers capped so they don't dry out. Most preschoolers just can't remember. Clemens (1991) offers a clever solution:

> You can make a mound of plaster of Paris, take the caps off your markers, and sink the caps upside-down into the wet plaster, so their open ends are flush with the surface. After the plaster dries, the markers, inserted in their caps, stick out like porcupine quills. Children easily return the markers to the mound when they are not using them. (p. 7)

Easel paintbrushes are thick enough but usually too long for young children to control readily. You may need to cut off a few inches of the brush handle and sand the rough end. Day-care supply houses have finally got the message and are coming out with properly proportioned paintbrushes for preschoolers.

Art and writing skills for preschoolers will be discussed more fully in Chapter 12, "Prewriting and Prereading Skills," and Chapter 13, "Art Skills."

If You Have Not Checked This Item: Some Helpful Ideas

■ Use Coloring Books

Coloring books are quite controversial with preschool educators. There is great concern that the stilted, stereotyped pictures will be a substitute in the classroom for creative art. It seems we have missed the point. Coloring books have little to do with art, but a great deal to do with small motor skills. Coloring books should be kept on the shelves with manipulative materials. Children love to fill in the outline pictures with various colors. At first children merely scribble over them with one color. As they gain control of the crayons, the youngsters work more carefully using different colors. Finally, they are able to stay within the lines, a very satisfying accomplishment for children struggling to control the use of their fingers.

Using coloring books, in fact, is an excellent prewriting activity for young children if books contain simple pictures with large spaces. Children can color in the pictures, trying to stay within the lines, or they can trace over the outlines of the pictures with a crayon or marker.

■ Provide a Writing Table

Place a small table in your library corner. Provide primary pencils, regular pencils, markers, ballpoint pens, crayons, and notebooks and tablets of various sizes to scribble on. Let the children pretend they are writing.

■ **Read a Book**

We Are Best Friends by Aliki Brandenberg (New York: Greenwillow Books, 1982) is the story of Robert, whose best friend, Peter, moves away. The two boys write letters to one another and finally make new friends. Your children may want to write a letter—with your help—to someone who has moved away.

❑ USES SCISSORS WITH CONTROL

Learning to cut with scissors takes a great deal of coordination and practice. Children who have had practice with this activity at home may be way ahead of those who have not, regardless of age. Sometimes the scissors themselves make it difficult for youngsters to learn how to use them. The blunt scissors found in many preschools are often dull and difficult to manipulate even by adults. Try the scissors yourself; loosen and sharpen them before giving them to the children. Really good scissors cost money, but they are a worthwhile investment when you consider what fine practice they give children in developing strength in their hands and coordination in their fingers.

For children who have not learned to cut, you can help them in several ways. Show them how to hold the scissors with their favored hand. As with crayons, children sometimes pick up scissors with either hand, but will not have much success if they are trying to use the nondominant hand. Hold a narrow strip of paper stretched taut between your two hands for the child to cut in two. Once she can do this cutting without difficulty, get another child to hold the paper and let each take a turn holding and cutting. Give them a task such as cutting all the yellow strips into small pieces.

On another day, show the child how to hold the strip of paper in her own hand and cut with the other hand. She needs to keep her scissors in her dominant hand. Let her practice on different kinds of paper, including construction paper, typing paper, and pages from magazines. Finally, draw a line on a sheet of paper and let the child practice cutting along a line. Be sure to have at least one pair of left-handed scissors.

Most 4-year-olds can cut along a straight line without difficulty, but many have trouble turning corners and following a curved line. Children need to practice all kinds of cutting. Whenever you are preparing art materials for the children to use, especially cutouts that need to be pasted, try to involve the children in helping to do the cutting.

If You Have Not Checked This Item: Some Helpful Ideas

■ Use Paper Ribbon

Let children practice cutting paper ribbon (for gift wrapping) into confetti. This type of ribbon has more body than ordinary paper and so is easier to cut. Save the confetti for a celebration.

▪ Read a Book

Let's Make Rabbits by Leo Lionni (New York: Pantheon Books, 1982) is a simple story about a talking pencil and pair of scissors who get together and decide to make rabbits. The pencil draws a rabbit and the scissors cuts out a collage rabbit, and the two rabbits immediately become best friends. The teacher can trace the circular pieces that make up the rabbit and help the children to cut out their own collage rabbits.

Paper Boats by Rabindranath Tagore, illustrated by Grayce Bochak (Honesdale, PA: Boyds Mills Press, 1992), is a delightful story of a boy from India who cuts out paper boats, writes his name and the name of his village on them, and sets them afloat. Simply and beautifully presented with lines by the Indian poet Tagore and unique full-page illustrations that are paper cutouts themselves, this story seems almost three-dimensional. Let children sit close to see Bochak's cutouts. Can they then cut out their own simple paper boats and set them afloat in the water table?

❏ POUNDS IN NAILS WITH CONTROL

Holding a nail with one hand and pounding it with a hammer held in the opposite hand is the most complicated small motor skill thus far discussed. Many children will not be able to do it well until they are older and more coordinated. Even adults often have difficulty. Try it yourself and find out.

Handedness makes a difference. So does arm and wrist strength. Small toy hammers should not be used. They are not heavy or strong enough to have much effect other than frustrating the pounder. A small adult hammer is better.

Both boys and girls should be encouraged to pound. It is an excellent activity to develop small motor strength and coordination. If you do not have a carpenter's bench in your room, you can set up a woodworking area by hanging tools on the wall from a pegboard and using several tree stumps as pounding surfaces. Building supply companies often will provide wood scraps when asked.

To get children interested in this or any activity area in your classroom, simply go into the area yourself and begin pounding something. Pounding always attracts attention, and soon children will want to do the same thing the teacher is doing. Again, you should make sure the children are holding the hammer in their favored hand. You can control for the safety factor by limiting the number of hammers or tree stumps available for pounding. Also be sure the pounders wear safety goggles.

If You Have Not Checked This Item: Some Helpful Ideas

▪ Use Soft Materials

Do not start your pounding activities with wood. Children need to acquire the skill before they will be able to drive a nail through wood. Start with a softer material such as fiberboard, ceiling tile, or Styrofoam. Children also love to pound nails through the holes in Tinkertoys.

Holding a nail with one hand and pounding with the other is a complex small motor skill that many preschoolers can learn.

■ Use Large-Headed Nails

The children should use large-headed nails at first. Most tacks are too short for the pounder to hold, but roofing nails or upholstering tacks are large enough and long enough to work well.

■ Read a Book

Tool Book by Gail Gibbons (New York: Holiday House, 1982) is a simple but effective introduction to tools for your children. Tools are categorized by their function and illustrated with careful, colorful drawings showing their use. Be sure to bring to class real tools like the ones shown, when you read this book.

Building a House by Byron Barton (New York: Penguin Books, 1981) shows carpenters, masons, plumbers, electricians, and painters putting together a house.

OBSERVING, RECORDING, AND INTERPRETING SMALL MOTOR DEVELOPMENT

As you did with the Large Motor Checklist items, you should also screen your entire class on the eight Small Motor Checklist items. Make a similar chart with the children's names on one side, and the eight items across the top. Check off the accomplishments for all of your children based on your observations. Then at a glance you can see by the blanks which of the children may need special help in order to accomplish small motor skills.

Observe each of the children who need special help separately during the free choice period, recording their actions in a running record. Later you can transfer this information onto the entire *Checklist* for an individual by checking off items and writing in evidence. Finally, you should make an individualized learning prescription for each child who needs special help. The activities you choose to help the child in "Areas Needing Strengthening" should be based on his or her "Areas of Strength and Confidence." For example, Figure 8.1 shows the Small Motor Checklist for Lionel, the new boy discussed at the end of Chapter 5 and Chapter 7. Using these observations and the information they gathered on the Social Play Checklist and Large Motor Checklist, the staff put together the learning prescription for Lionel shown in Figure 8.2.

Because Lionel shows the ability to make puzzles and to fasten and unfasten zippers and buttons, the staff felt he could use his small motor skills to work with another child in a class project. He likes art activities such as play dough and finger painting, but does not use paintbrushes, writing tools, or scissors. Could this be because he is left-handed? We will provide him with left-handed scissors and give him support in the activity of cutting out pictures of cars for the class scrapbook. We have not had a woodworking bench, but Lionel says he has helped his grandfather pound nails. Perhaps he and other children could make rhythm instruments from wood, paint them, and then use them in a rhythm activity (Lionel excels at rhythm). Using things Lionel likes to do and is good at doing may help him get involved with the other children.

FIGURE 8.1

Small motor development observations for Lionel

Child Skills Checklist

Child Skills Checklist

Name _Lionel_   **Observer** _Barb_

Program _Preschool – K2_   **Dates** _1 / 20_

Directions:

Put a ✔ for items you see the child perform regularly. Put *N* for items where there is no opportunity to observe. Leave all other items blank.

Item	Evidence	Date
6. Small Motor Development		
✔ Shows hand preference (which is _left_)	Uses left hand to eat, turn things	1/20
✔ Turns with hand easily (knobs, lids, eggbeaters)	Plays with eggbeater at water table easily	1/20
✔ Pours liquid into glass without spilling	Pours own milk at lunch	1/20
✔ Unfastens/fastens zippers, buttons, Velcro tabs	Dresses & undresses self with ease	1/20
✔ Picks up and inserts objects with ease	Makes puzzles with ease	1/20
_____ Uses drawing/writing tools with control	Does not use paintbrushes or writing tools	1/20
_____ Uses scissors with control	Does not use scissors	1/20
_N_ Pounds in nails with control	Woodworking not available	1/20

FIGURE 8.2

Learning prescription for Lionel

Learning Prescription

Name ___Lionel_____ Age __3__ Date __1/20__

Areas of Strength and Confidence

1. _Does manipulative activities well by self_
2. _Performs or participates in music and rhythm activities_
3. _Has good small motor coordination_

Areas Needing Strengthening

1. _Needs to develop large motor skills_
2. _Needs to learn to play with others_
3. _Needs to develop small motor skills of writing, drawing, cutting_

Activities to Help

1. _Bring in pair of left-handed scissors and have Lionel cut out pictures of cars from magazine to make a car scrapbook with one of the other boys._
2. _Bring in hammer, nails, and tree stump; ask Lionel to help another child with pounding nails to make rhythm instrument shaker._
3. _Have Lionel and other children paint the rhythm instruments they make._

REFERENCES

Clemens, Sydney Gurewitz. (1991). Art in the classroom: Making every day special. *Young Children, 46*(2), 4–11.

Cosgrove, Maryellen Smith. (1991). Cooking in the classroom: The doorway to nutrition. *Young Children, 46*(3), 43–46.

Cratty, Bryant J. (1986). *Perceptual and motor development in infants and children.* Englewood Cliffs, NJ: Prentice-Hall.

Zaichkowsky, Leonard D., Linda B. Zaichkowsky, & Thomas J. Martineck. (1980). *Growth and development: The child and physical activity.* St.Louis: Mosby.

OTHER SOURCES

Beaty, Janice J. (1992). *Skills for preschool teachers.* New York: Merrill/Macmillan.

Caplan, Theresa, & Frank Caplan. (1983). *The early childhood years: The 2 to 6 year old.* New York: Putnam.

Dunn, M. L. (1979). *Pre-scissors skills.* Tucson, AZ: Communication Skill Builders.

Paul, Aileen. (1975). *Kids cooking without a stove: A cookbook for young children.* Garden City, NY: Doubleday.

Schickedanz, Judith, David I. Schickedanz, & Peggy D. Forsythe. (1982). *Toward understanding children.* Boston: Little, Brown.

Thompson, David. (1981). *Easy woodstuff for kids.* Mt. Rainier, MD: Gryphon House.

LEARNING ACTIVITIES

1. Use the *Child Skills Checklist* section "Small Motor Development" as a screening tool to observe all of the children in your classroom. Pay special attention to which hand each seems to favor. Also note which ones spend time in small motor activities and which do not.

2. Compare the children in your classroom on their *Checklist* results in both large and small motor development. Do you see any relationships?

3. Choose a child who seems to need a great deal of help with small motor skills. Do a running record of the child on three different days, concentrating on small motor skills. Do a learning activity with him based on the results.

4. How do the girls and boys of the same age compare with one another in small motor skills? What conclusions can you make based on your observations?

5. Put out a new small motor activity for the children to use. Observe and record the results. What conclusions can you draw?

9 Cognitive Development: Classification and Seriation

Classification and Seriation Checklist

❑ Recognizes basic geometric shapes
❑ Recognizes colors
❑ Recognizes differences in size
❑ Sorts objects by appearance
❑ Recognizes differences in musical tones
❑ Reproduces musical tones with voice
❑ Arranges events in sequence from first to last
❑ Arranges objects in series according to a rule

C ognitive development of preschool children is concerned with how they develop their thinking abilities. We are only at the beginning of our understanding of how this takes place. The early work of researchers like Swiss psychologist Jean Piaget in his investigation of how knowledge is created (see Table 9.1), and psycholinguist Noam Chomsky in his exploration of how language is acquired, have given us new insights into how children think as well as how their thinking evolves. The learning theories of psychologist Jerome Bruner have helped us to apply this information to the classroom. Work with computer models of children's thinking have added even more understanding of how the brain works and of its unimagined complexity.

Today an information-processing approach is currently being used to study children's thinking. Researchers in the field employ tools such as *error analysis* to reveal children's conceptual understanding, *eye-movement analysis* to reveal how children process visual information, *chronometric methods* to study children's reaction times, and *production systems* (a type of computer language) to model thinking patterns (Siegler, 1986, pp. 5, 102).

Technological advances in video- and audiotaping and other laboratory devices have combined to give us an entirely different perspective on child development. We now understand that infants display previously unsuspected intelligence in early activities. We also realize that young children's thinking is not the same as that of adults. Still, we are only at the threshold, the mere frontiers of understanding about intellectual ability and how it develops.

What we do know is something quite startling to those unfamiliar with recent findings: that *children create their own knowledge.* Using the physical and mental tools they are born with, children interact with their environment to make sense of it, and in so doing, they construct their own mental images of their world. The brain seems to be conditioned to take in information about objects and their relationship to one another. What do things look, feel, taste, sound, and smell like? What can they do? How are they like one another? How are they different? What happens if you touch, push, or throw them?

TABLE 9.1
Piaget's stages of cognitive development

Sensorimotor Stage (Birth to age 2)

Child thinks in visual patterns (schemata).
Child uses senses to explore objects (i.e., looks, listens, smells, tastes, and manipulates).
Child learns to recall physical features of an object.
Child associates objects with actions and events but does not use objects to symbolize actions and events (e.g., rolls a ball but does not use ball as a pretend car).
Child develops object permanence (comes to realize an object is still there even when out of sight).

Preoperational Stage (Age 2–7)

Child acquires symbolic thought (uses mental images and words to represent actions and events not present).
Child uses objects to symbolize actions and events (e.g., pretends a block is a car).
Child learns to anticipate effect of one action on another (e.g., realizes pouring milk from pitcher to glass will make level of milk decrease in pitcher as it rises in glass).
Child is deceived by appearances (e.g., believes a tall, thin container holding a cup of water contains more than a short, wide container holding a cup of water).
Child is concerned with final products (focuses on the way things look at a particular moment, "figurative knowledge," and not on changes of things or how things got that way, "operational knowledge"), and he cannot seem to reverse his thinking.

Concrete-Operational Stage (Age 7–11)

Child's thoughts can deal with changes of things and how they got that way.
Child is able to reverse her thinking (has ability to see in her mind how things looked before and after a change took place).
Child has gone beyond how things look at a particular moment and begins to understand how things relate to one another (e.g., knows that the number 2 can be larger than 1, yet, at the same time, smaller than 3).

Formal-Operational Stage (Age 11 +)

Child begins to think about thinking.
Child thinks in abstract terms without needing concrete objects.
Child can hypothesize about things.

NOTE: Some information adapted from *The child's construction of knowledge: Piaget for teaching children (pp. 69–93)* by G. E. Forman and D. S. Kuschner, 1983, Washington, DC: NAEYC.

USING PLAY

Another startling finding, for those new to the field, involves the method that preschool children use to create this knowledge. They do it by *playing* around with things, people, and ideas. Most people think of play as something recreational, something we do for enjoyment, and something rather inconsequential. For adults, this definition of play may be true, but for infants and young children, play is a way of trying out and finding out. Children fool around with toys, their clothing, their hands and feet, sounds, words, and other people. Youngsters use their senses of taste, touch, sound, sight, and smell in a playful manner with anything and everything they can get their hands on, in order to find out what an object is, what it feels like, what it sounds like, what can be done with it. The fact of the matter is that *child's play is practice in thinking.*

From the time he is born, the human infant pursues such information with a single-minded determination. At first, everything goes into the mouth. Then the infant bangs objects against the side of the crib to see what sounds they make, to see what they will do, and to find out what will happen. The toddler has an extra advantage. He has expanded his field of exploration by learning to walk. Suddenly the world's objects are his to touch, pick up, shake, throw, taste, and take apart. He uses his senses to "play" with his world in order to find out what it is about. And as soon as he can talk, he plays with words and word sounds as well.

All of the information extracted through this playful exploration of the environment is filed away in predetermined patterns in the brain, to be used to direct or adjust the child's behavior as he continues to respond to the stimuli around him. We now know that this knowledge is organized by the brain in predictable patterns from a very early age. Some of these patterns may even be inherited. Highly sophisticated research with 2- and 3-year-olds has convinced psychologists that children may be born with the ability to make distinctions between animate and inanimate things, and to understand cause and effect (Pines, 1983, p. 48).

Nevertheless, if children do not have the opportunity to explore their environment, if their environment is uninteresting or sterile, if their caregivers are harsh or controlling or neglectful—they may not develop their intellect to the same extent as children without these handicaps. We mentioned in Chapter 7 the apathetic children in the Iranian orphanages who hardly could walk at 4 years. Yet when Dr. Hunt trained their caregivers to use vocal play with newly arrived infants, an overwhelming change took place in the infants. Not only did these youngsters learn to walk and talk on schedule, but even their appearance and their facial features changed for the better (Pines, 1979 p. 63).

ASSESSING DEVELOPMENT

How have your children fared in the construction of their own knowledge? They need to have built up mental representations of objects: ways to differentiate things by their appearance or by their sound, ways of telling how things are alike or different, and ways to decide how things fit together as a part of a sequence or a series. These are the types of patterns or concepts the brain forms in organizing the data it takes in.

You will need to assess each of your children by observing his or her ability to accomplish the eight *Checklist* items at the head of this chapter. The first six of these items refer to classification skills the child needs to know, and the last two items involve skills for arranging things in a series. Once you have made your assessment, you should plan activities or playful exploration periods for children to use in order to continue developing their thinking skills.

❑ RECOGNIZES BASIC GEOMETRIC SHAPES

The development of thinking begins with the infant's seeing, hearing, and feeling things in her environment: her mother's face, the nurse's face, and her bottle or mother's breast. Her brain takes in these important visual perceptions and stores them in particular schemes or patterns that are mental representations for the objects and events she experiences. Her brain seems to be conditioned to pay attention to certain things in her environment and to ignore the rest.

Research has shown, for instance, that an infant looks longer at the human face than at anything else around her (Schickedanz, Schickedanz, & Forsythe, 1982, p. 152). The infant seems, in fact, to prefer visual stimuli that have a contour configuration. She is beginning her construction of knowledge.

The first aspect of this knowledge is called *figurative knowing* because it deals with shapes and configurations, as well as the patterns of movements, tastes, smells, and so on (Saunders & Bingham-Newman, 1984, p. 117). The infant will have to recognize these objects and shapes again and again. He will need to respond to his caregivers, his bottle, his rattle, and other environmental objects in an appropriate manner. Perceptual recognition, then, is the earliest form of the infant's store of knowledge. As early as 3 months old, infants can perceive an object's shape as being constant (Siegler, 1986, p. 150).

The first checklist item, on shape, is concerned with refinement in the child's perceptual recognition. In order to think, reason, and problem-solve, the child needs to know and discriminate among basic shapes of things. We start with geometric shapes because the concept of shape is one of the first concepts to emerge in the child's cognitive development. He needs to distinguish among a circle, a square, a rectangle, and a triangle—not to do math problems, but to be able to categorize and to distinguish mentally among the objects in his environment.

Adults are often surprised to learn that some young children view all enclosed figures as being similar. In other words, these youngsters think that a circle and a square are the same! How can that be? Researchers say that these young children are operating geometrically in the *topological* domain, which views

> circles and squares as being equivalent figures, both figures having closed boundaries. Children have difficulty differentiating one figure from the other until they begin to be aware of features of the boundaries of the figures themselves. At this time, work with shapes should begin. (Richardson, Goodman, Hartman, & LePique, 1980, p. 67)

This learning takes place not just by a teacher telling the child, This is a square, or, This is a circle, but more effectively by the child's hands-on playing and exploring with all of his senses about what makes a particular object a circle and what makes another shape a square. Children in this preoperational stage of development (see Table 9.1) learn best from three-dimensional objects first, and then from pictorial representations, before finally recognizing more abstract symbols. Seeing pictures of the various shapes is helpful, but it is too abstract to be the only method for young children to learn. Youngsters first need hands-on activities with concrete materials.

Your program should provide the children with many such experiences. Because children learn these classification skills through the senses, you should give the youngsters all kinds of sensory play opportunities. Playing with dough, for instance, allows children to make dough balls, which they flatten into circles with their hands or roll flat with a rolling pin and cut into circular cookies. Sensory learning involves taste, touch, smell, and sight in this instance. Playing with clay and play dough provides similar experiences.

Building with blocks is an excellent medium for creating circles, squares, rectangles, and triangles. In the beginning you will need to name the shapes the children are making. They probably already know circle and perhaps square, but rectangle and triangle are interesting new grown-up words. Can the children build a triangle, one of the most difficult shapes for youngsters? Their triangles may be rather rounded in the beginning, because corners are hard for the children to deal with. Put masking tape on the floor in the shapes of circles, squares, rectangles, and triangles, and let children try to build these shapes with their blocks.

The diagonal line is the last concept to appear in children's learning about shapes. For this reason triangles and diamonds are very difficult for children to copy. See the discussion about space in Chapter 10, and Chapter 13, "Art Skills," for further information on shapes.

If You Have Not Checked This Item: Some Helpful Ideas

■ Start with One Shape at a Time

Children need to focus their attention on one concept before expanding it to include other aspects. The circle is a good shape to begin with because children are used to the roundness or ovalness of the human face. They need to experience examples of all kinds of circles. Let the youngsters find out how many circles they can discover in the classroom. Did they find the wheels on toy vehicles, the casters on the doll bed or office chair, the clock, or the mark on the table made by a wet glass?

How long should you concentrate on this shape before including a second shape in their explorations? It depends on your children and their interest. Be sure every child has a chance to have enough sensory involvement with circles so that he or she can internalize it. The internalization may take several weeks, depending on the age and experience of your children. Bring in a collection of things that contains some circular shapes, and let each child try to sort out the circles. Include items such as bottle tops, coasters, jar lids, and rings. Then have the children try sorting blindfolded. Can they sort circles by feel alone? If some children are frightened by having a blindfold tied over their eyes, let them simply shut their eyes or hold their free hand over them.

■ Have the Children Make Their Own Circles

Use circle-making activities that involve molding clay, shaping dough, finger paint-ing, cutting out circles, cutting out jack-o-lantern tops, stamping circular shapes on paper, and tracing around circular objects. When the children finally have a strong sense of "circleness," introduce the square as the next shape.

■ Read a Book

Wheels Go Round by Yvonne Hooker (New York: Grosset & Dunlap, 1981) is an interesting cardboard book of large colorful pictures of vehicles and their wheels. From steamrollers to go-carts, their wheels are cut out of every other page of the book, each wheel increasingly smaller. On the page opposite each illustration is a four-sentence rhyming description of the vehicle. Children will enjoy feeling the roundness of the cutout wheels, and may want to trace the wheels on paper.

Round in a Circle by Yvonne Hooker (New York: Grosset & Dunlap, 1982) fol-lows a similar cardboard book format with squares, circles, and triangles cut out of every other page from things like an artist's easel, a television, a balloon, and a tepee.

Tatum's Favorite Shape by Dorothy Thole (New York: Scholastic, 1977) is the story of little Tatum, an African-American boy who has trouble in school distinguish-ing the different shapes until his mother plays a shape-finding game with him at home.

■ Use a Computer Program

Preschool children can learn to use a computer with ease, and love to do so (see Beaty & Tucker, 1987). *Learning Shapes* (Houston: Access Unlimited, 1988) is one of the simplest programs using four basic shapes. Children must find the shapes hid-den within colorful scenes in *Inside Outside Shapes* (Heightstown, NJ: McGraw-Hill Media, 1986) and *Stickybear Shapes* (Norfolk, CT: Optimum Resources, 1983). Let the children discover on their own by trial and error how each program works.

❑ RECOGNIZES COLORS

Another way the brain classifies things is by color. Research shows that infants as young as 4 to 6 months of age begin discriminating colors (Richardson et al., 1980, p. 123). Children develop color perception shortly after shape recognition, although they seem to talk about colors first. More reference is made to color than shape by adults, and children quickly pick up this fact. Your children may, in fact, be able to name many colors just as they name numbers, without truly knowing what the name means. Just because a child tells you she knows red does not mean that she can identify the color. Ask the child the color of her shirt. Ask her to find something red in the classroom.

Color, like shape, is an aspect of visual perception that the child's brain uses to help him classify objects and discriminate their differences. Although the child sees colors from the beginning, he now needs to put a name to each different one.

Again, concentrating on a single color at first and then adding other colors is the best approach. Basic colors such as red, yellow, green, and blue, plus black and white, are usually easier for children to recognize at first. But you must take advantage of seasonal and holiday colors as well. Orange should certainly be a part of your classroom during the fall Halloween season, and pink as well as red for Valentine's Day.

Allow children to play with colors as they do with blocks. Give them things like poker chips or golf tees and let the children see if they can find all the reds. Some children will be able to sort out all of the items by color, but don't expect everyone to be so accurate at first. Let the children experiment with the look and texture of "redness" in all of its shades as they mix red and white paint. Give the children plenty of time to experience one color before you focus on another.

As your group begins its investigation of other colors, you can add colors one by one to the easel. Provide color lotto cards, colored plastic blocks, and many other table games featuring colors. Be sure to bring in many different items of the color you are exploring. If you have bilingual children, be sure everyone learns color names in both languages.

Children with handicapping conditions can learn color concepts along with all of the others youngsters. Set up your activities so that children with physical and mental disabilities can participate. If you keep concept games in the manipulative area, be sure the shelves are low enough for everyone to reach.

If You Have Not Checked This Item: Some Helpful Ideas

■ Let the Children Mix Colors

Let children experience the fun of mixing colors. Put out squeeze bottles of food coloring, spoons for stirring, and plastic cups or muffin tins full of water. You may want to use only one or two colors at first, or you may want to let children discover how mixing blue and yellow together makes green, since this is such a dramatic change. At another time, use cups of premixed colors, medicine droppers, and muffin tin cups full of clear water.

There are many different ways for children to play with mixing colors. The youngsters can finger paint with the color you are focusing on. When the children add a new color to their repertoire, add the same one to the finger paint table. Have them mix the old and new colors together to see what happens.

■ Cut or Tear Colored Paper

Colored construction paper can be used in many ways. When children have learned two or three colors, let them cut up or tear pieces of construction paper of these three colors for a sorting activity or for making collages. Do not confuse children by combining shape and color activities when they are first learning color or shape concepts.

■ Play Concept Games

Children love to play any game that focuses on them. A game that asks them to identify the color of their clothing makes an excellent transition between activities:

"The boy with the blue and white sneakers may go to lunch; the girl with the red and white top may go next; all the children with brown pants may go."

■ Do a Color Dance

Bring in filmy, see-through cloths of three different colors: red, blue, and yellow. Give the children each a color to hold as they dance or sway to music. Turn the lights off and shine a spotlight (projector or strong flashlight) through the colors. What happens when blue and yellow dance together? Read children the book *Color Dance* by Ann Jonas (New York: Greenwillow Books, 1989) to see what other secondary colors they can make with the cloths.

■ Read a Book

Many picture books feature colors. One of the most simple yet dramatic is Leo Lionni's classic *Little Blue and Little Yellow* (New York: Astor-Honor, 1959), in which a little blue circle and little yellow circle want to play together but are not allowed to by their respective blue and yellow families. When the two circles finally do come together, a dramatic change takes place: They, of course, become green.

Early Childhood Specialist Sue McCord has added a most effective activity for demonstrating the blue-yellow change as she reads *Little Blue and Little Yellow*. She covers two flashlights with colored cellophane, one with blue and one with yellow. Then she reads the story at naptime with the room darkened and the blue and yellow lights from the flashlights playing on the ceiling as the children watch from their cots. The yellow circle and blue circle on the ceiling turn just as green as paint when they finally come together.

Another classic color story is Margaret Wise Brown's *The Color Kittens* (New York: Golden Press, 1977). Brush and Hush, two kitten painters who have all of the colors in the world *except green*, spend the story trying to find green.

Other favorite books featuring colors include the following:

Eric Carle, *The Mixed-Up Chameleon* (New York: Harper & Row, 1984)

Lois Ehlert, *Planting a Rainbow* (San Diego: Harcourt Brace Jovanovich, 1988)

Kathy Feczko, *Umbrella Parade* (Mahwah, NJ: Troll, 1985)

Don A. Freeman, *A Rainbow of My Own* (New York: Puffin Books, 1978)

Tana Hoban, *Is It Red? Is It Yellow? Is It Blue?* (New York: Greenwillow Books, 1978)

Bill Martin, Jr., *Brown Bear, Brown Bear* (New York: Holt, Rinehart & Winston, 1984)

Kathy Stinson, *Red Is Best* (Toronto: Annick Press, 1983).

■ Use a Computer Program

Color and Shapes (Dimondale, MI: Hartley Courseware, 1984) contains four simple activities based on matching colors and shapes.

❑ RECOGNIZES DIFFERENCES IN SIZE

As young children construct their own knowledge by interacting with the objects and people in their environment, their brains seem to pay special attention to the relationships between things. Size is one of those relationships. Is an object big? Is it small? Is it bigger or smaller than something else? The property of size, like the properties of shape and color, is an essential understanding that children need in order to make sense of their world.

There are various orders of size, usually thought of in terms of opposites: big-little, large-small, tall-short, long-short, wide-narrow, thick-thin, and deep-shallow. Direct comparison of objects based on one of these aspects seems to be the best way for young children to learn size.

Natural Curiosity

The children already should be making sensory explorations of objects in the classroom. Are they? We know that infants are born investigators. They are not only predisposed to explore their surroundings with their senses, but they seem to be driven by some inner urge to try out, to get hold of, and to get into everything that is within reach. We call this natural curiosity when its results are positive. But we say other, less pleasant things about it when infants, toddlers, and preschoolers get into things that they should not touch.

All investigations by children are part of the same natural urge to find out. We should cultivate this drive in children, for it is their principal motivation for learning. Many parents encourage this exploration, some do not. You can see parental influence—or lack of it—in the behavior of your preschoolers. Some children seem to have retained their natural curiosity; others have not, maybe because their original investigations were stopped by their parents.

Rather than stop such investigations, some parents realize it is better to childproof the house by putting dangerous and breakable items away, covering electrical outlets, and blocking off stairs and cupboards. Then the child can explore without negative consequences for anyone.

If, instead, children have been constantly scolded, punished physically, or restrained from exploring their environment, many eventually give up. You may have to talk with their parents about how children learn, and to work with the children in trying to reactivate their natural curiosity.

Bring in some new, interesting, but unknown item and watch to see which of your children tries to find out about it. For instance, seal an onion in a box covered with colored wrapping paper and punctured with several holes. Put it on a display table in your classroom with a sign reading: Guess what's inside! Then observe and record which of your children is curious enough to try to find out.

The children will have to ask what the sign says. You can tell them, but do not give them any other hints. Does anyone shake the box, smell it, or try to see through the holes? Does anyone ask another child or another classroom worker about it?

Let each explorer tell his or her guess to the tape recorder, saying why he or she thinks the guess is correct, and giving his or her name. Later at circle time you can play the tape, discuss it, and then open the box to see if anyone guessed its contents correctly.

This activity can help you in two ways. First, you can determine who are the curious children and which ones never seem to notice things or do not have the courage to make a guess. Second, it should motivate your children to do sensory exploration. This activity may even remotivate those who seem to have lost their natural curiosity.

Repeat this activity every few days for several weeks (with different objects, of course) and see if it makes a difference in your children's sensory exploring abilities, their guessing abilities, and their interest in new things. In addition, you should take the lead in modeling the behavior you want your children to exhibit. When you yourself come to something new, explore it with your senses and make your own educated guesses. Shapes, colors, and now sizes are some of the properties you and your children should be focusing on.

Comparisons

Comparing one object with another is one of the best ways to investigate the properties of something new or different. This is, in fact, how the brain works. It focuses on, takes in, and evaluates data about the new object on the basis of what the brain has previously processed about a similar object. Information-processing researchers mention three functions that the brain must complete in order to process new perceptions: (a) attending, (b) identifying, and (c) locating.

> *Attending* involves determining what in a situation is worthy of detailed processing. *Identifying* involves establishing what a perceptual pattern is by relating the pattern to entries already in memory. *Locating* involves determining how far away an object is, and in what direction. (Siegler, 1986, p. 135)

When you are first using comparisons with your children that focus on the concept of size, be sure to use objects that are alike in all of their properties except size. This is not the time to use different colored or different shaped items. Instead, try using two similar items, one that is large and one that is small. Then talk to the children about how the objects are alike and how they are different.

Using Opposites

Making a direct comparison of two objects that are similar in every aspect except size is one of the best methods for helping children learn the concept of size. Use things such as two apples (a big and little one of the same color), two cups, two blocks, two books, or two dolls. Be sure to talk in positive terms ("This one is big. This one is little."), rather than in negative terms ("This one is not big") that may only confuse the child. Also be sure the children are making comparisons of the two objects themselves and not of their position in space. Some children look at two similar objects and say that the closest one is biggest because it looks larger than a more distant object.

Use the size opposites *big* and *small* in all sorts of comparisons in your classroom before you move on to another aspect of size such as *tall* and *short*. Be sure that you yourself use the words for size opposites whenever you can in the classroom: "Look, Alice has built a tall building and Bonnie has made a short one." "Who can find a thick pencil? Who can find a thin one?"

If You Have Not Checked This Item: Some Helpful Ideas

■ Play Size Transition Games

When you are waiting with the children for lunch to be served, for the bus to come, or for something special to happen, it is a good idea to have a repertoire of brief transition games, finger plays, or stories to tell. This time provides an excellent opportunity for concept games: "The girl wearing the skirt with wide stripes may stand up." "The boy wearing the T-shirt with narrow stripes may stand up." Or play a guessing game with your fingers. Hold your hands behind your back and ask your children to guess which hand has a big finger held up and which has a little finger held up. Then show them. Can one of your children then be the leader of this game?

■ Read a Book

Some children's books feature size. A favorite one is Steven Kellogg's *Much Bigger Than Martin* (New York: Dial Press, 1976), in which Martin's little brother fantasizes about what it would be like to be much bigger than his brother. The illustrations are hilarious.

A funny book of opposites is P. D. Eastman's *Big Dog . . . Little Dog, A Bedtime Story* (New York: Random House, 1973). It features Fred and Ted, a big dog and a little dog, who go on a skiing trip to the mountains where they do everything in an opposite manner except sleeping in their mixed-up beds.

Children also have a lot of fun with the imaginative story *When You Were Little and I Was Big* by Priscilla Galloway (Toronto: Annick Press, 1984), in which a little girl pretends to be the mummy and tells her mother what it was like "when you were little and I was big."

■ Use a Computer Program

Many "opposites" programs are extremely simple to operate by pressing the left or right arrow key. Each key controls one of the two opposites (e.g., big and little). A colorful animated sound graphic grows or shrinks with the press of a key in *Stickybear Opposites* (Norfolk, CT: Optimum Resources, 1986) and *City Country Opposites* (Heightstown, NJ: McGraw-Hill Media, 1986).

❏ SORTS OBJECTS BY APPEARANCE

Once they have begun to notice the similar properties of objects, children can begin to group or classify the objects. The ability to classify is necessary in cognitive development in order for the brain to sort out and process the wealth of incoming data obtained through the sensory activities of the child. Sorting objects and materials gives children practice in this skill and involves identifying the similarities of objects as well as understanding their relationships. The more we learn about young children's development of thinking abilities, the more we realize that thinking is concerned primarily with information processing and retrieval.

Piaget and other researchers have noted that children progress through a sequence of sorting skills, and that each skill is more complex than the previous one. The earliest sorting skill to appear is simple classification, which many 2-year-olds and most 3-year-olds can do. Children doing simple classification can sort or group objects that actually belong together in the real world. For example, they can group together all of the toy animals that live on the farm in one set and all of the toy animals that live in the zoo in another set, if the youngsters have had the appropriate experiences concerning such animals. This activity is not quite true classification

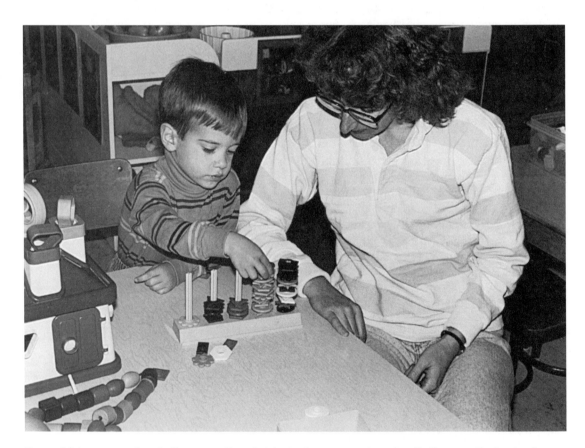

Once children recognize similar properties of objects, they can sort or classify them on the basis of color, shape, or size.

because it is based on associations between the animals and their homes rather than likenesses or differences of the animals.

Another type of simple classification that young children can do is to place things that "belong together" into a group. For example, they can put all of the toy trucks, cars, and motorcycles together in a group because you can drive them, or put the proper hats on all of the dolls, or group all of the blocks together because they make a house.

Less verbal children seem to do as well in simple classification tasks as verbal children (Richardson et al., 1980, p. 181). These simple classification tasks do involve real classification skills. In order to perform them, children need to understand the rule for sorting and to follow it with consistency. In addition, the youngsters must discriminate likenesses and differences based on function or some other rule in order to place objects in the correct group. The main difference between this kind of sorting and real classification is that simple classification is based on something other than appearances only, and the groups formed are not true classes.

A more mature type of classification that many 3-year-olds and most 4- and 5-year-olds can do involves classifying objects into separate sets based on a common characteristic like color, for instance. You can ask the children to place all the red blocks in one set and all the blue blocks in another.

The problem most young children have in doing this kind of sorting involves consistency. They have difficulty keeping in mind the rule upon which the sorting is based. Often, they will start sorting objects on the basis of color but will switch in the middle of the task to some other property, like shape, and even may switch again before they are finished.

Children need to practice with all kinds of sorting games, activities, and collections—and the youngsters love this practice. Give a child a box of mixed buttons and let him sort it out in any way he chooses. Talk with the child afterwards, and ask how he decided on which buttons to put in each pile. Look around your classroom for other objects to sort: things such as dress-up clothing, blocks, and eating utensils. By age 5, children with experience can sort objects into intersecting sets based on more than one characteristic: color as well as size, for instance.

If You Have Not Checked This Item: Some Helpful Ideas

■ Use Block Sorting

Have children help sort out a certain size of the unit blocks during cleanup before putting them back on the shelves. This activity will give you an indication of which children can and which cannot sort objects based on appearances. Make the activity a game, though, and not a task.

■ Play with Lotto Cards

Make or purchase simple lotto cards that the children can match. You can mount different colored construction paper onto cardboard, cover it with clear contact paper, and cut it into playing card size pieces. Make at least four cards for each color. Mix up the cards, and let the children try to sort them out.

Get several duplicate catalogs from companies such as car dealers. Cut up the catalogs, mounting four similar car pictures on each set of four cards.

■ Make Collection-Sorting Games

You will need a shoe box, three empty margarine cups that have a hole cut in their lids, and a collection of three kinds of seeds. You can use three varieties of beans, three sizes of paper clips, or any other similar collection to store in the shoe box. Let the child dump the collection into the top of the shoe box and sort it piece by piece into the margarine cups. This activity provides good small motor practice as well.

■ Read a Book

Dear Zoo by Rod Campbell (New York: Viking Penguin, 1982) is a simple book with large type and pop-up containers on every other page, hiding an animal that the zoo has sent to a child as a pet. The child rejects each of the animals based on a particular animal characteristic. Although this is not a sorting book, it can help children think about animals based on their appearances. Perhaps they can name other animals with the same characteristic.

Another animal book with a similar theme, *Is Your Mama a Llama?* by Deborah Guarino (New York: Scholastic, 1989), is a rhymed story about little Lloyd Llama who goes from one animal to another asking each if its mother is a llama, and hearing in return descriptions of each mother before the page turns to show the mother.

■ Use a Computer Program

Several computer games include sorting items into classes. *Animal Photo Fun* (Allen, TX: DLM, 1985) has six games in which children match animals with their habitats. Children use a joystick to move Grover to one of four environments in *Sesame Street Grover's Animal Adventures* (New York: Hi Tech Expressions, 1985). Then they place different animals in their proper location in the sky, land, or water. In *Dinosaurs* (Berkeley, CA: Advanced Ideas, 1984) children classify six dinosaurs by what they ate and where they lived. Be sure to have animal and dinosaur figures for children to play with when these programs are in use.

❏ RECOGNIZES DIFFERENCES IN MUSICAL TONES

Music for young children—indeed for all of us—is a language. It is a natural means for communicating our feelings and our ideas. This language uses musical sounds (tones) and rhythm (beat) for its expression. In Chapter 6, under large motor moving of feet, clapping of hands, and beating of drums, we considered the rhythm part of music. Here we will consider the sound. Musical tones have several different aspects, including their intensity (loud-soft), their duration (long-short), their pitch (high-low), and their quality (timbre). For preschool children the most important aspects of musical tones are loudness-softness and highness-lowness. The concepts of loud-soft and high-low should fit in easily with activities about sizes and opposites that the children are already pursuing.

Young children recognize musical sounds very early in their development. Even infants respond to music by turning their heads in the direction of the sound or clapping their hands to music. If bells or tone-producing mobiles are accessible, infants will hit them again and again to reproduce the sound. Toddlers continue this tone-producing activity by hitting toy instruments such as xylophones or by rolling jingling toys across the floor with great gusto. Toddlers will also try to imitate the singing they hear around them by humming or chanting.

Thus, preschool teachers need to include all sorts of musical experiences in the curriculum in order for young children to continue their development of the language of music. Teachers and children should sing songs, chant chants, do musical finger plays, play records and tapes, play simple instruments, listen to guest instrumentalists, and explore sounds and sound making in every way possible. Not only should teachers model an interest in music, but most especially, they should make music *fun* for children. Teachers can make music a pleasurable experience for both children and themselves if they develop an understanding of what music really is, why it is attractive to human beings, and how its attractiveness can be preserved.

Young children have a tremendous interest in sounds and sound making. They are surrounded with sounds from the very beginning. Their natural curiosity motivates children to explore new sounds to find out what they are. Children do this playfully by imitating the sounds they hear, and then by inventing their own sounds. Some of their sounds are pleasant to the ear, some are pure noise. We wonder how they can possibly stand the noise. But we must remember two things: Sounds of all kinds are the raw materials of music, and people like sounds best when they are the sound-makers.

Thus, the preschool teacher's role is to provide opportunities and direction in helping young children convert their enthusiastic sound making into music making. For example, set up a "sound table" in your science corner with various types of sound-making objects from time to time. When you are exploring the concept of loud-soft with the children, have the table set up with shakers (sealed boxes, jars, Band-Aid boxes, margarine cups, and other plastic containers filled with materials that make loud or soft noises when shaken). The materials inside the shakers could be pennies, pebbles, beans, rice, paper clips, sand, rock salt, or table salt. Children can try to identify which of the containers makes the loudest noise and which the softest. Then they can shake the containers to the beat of music that you play.

Another time provide a variety of empty glass containers and let children tap them with a "soft tapper" such as a Popsicle stick or paintbrush. A "hard tapper" could be made of metal (a spoon, for example) but children must go easy so the glass does not break. For safety's sake, remove the glass containers immediately after this demonstration.

Have children explore only one aspect of sound at a time. When they are concentrating on loud and soft sounds, try to use sounds that are all on the same pitch. Otherwise, children may confuse *loud* with *high* or *soft* with *low*. Have them beat drums loudly and softly. Let them blow a whistle loudly, then softly. Can they chant a nursery rhyme loudly and then softly? Let them choose how to sing a favorite song: loudly or softly.

Do your children enjoy performing like this? They should. Pleasure and not perfection always should be your goal with developing children. Do not force reluctant children to participate. If the activity is interesting enough, they will join on their own. These musical sound activities can be done with the total class, a small group, or individuals. Sometimes we think that music must be performed with everyone at one time. Instead, let the type of activity determine how many children should be involved. Chanting calls for a group, but sound-makers on a table are for individuals.

When children are thoroughly familiar with the concept of loud and soft musical tones, you can introduce high and low sounds. Your sound table can then display glass containers filled with water of varying amounts. Children can experiment by tapping to find out which glasses sound high, and which sound low. Melody and harmony instruments can also be used to demonstrate high and low sounds. Let individuals tap on a xylophone or blow on a tonette or harmonica. (Be sure to wipe clean the mouth instruments after each use with disinfectant to prevent the spread of germs). Montessori materials include "sound tablets" with graduated sounds like a xylophone. The "high" instrument players also might stand high (on a chair), while the "low" players sit low (on the floor).

These musical concepts involve auditory discrimination. It is possible that your sound-making activities may point out children who do not discriminate loud-soft or high-low because of a possible hearing impairment. If you think that this is the case, arrange with a child's parents for a professional hearing examination.

If You Have Not Checked This Item: Some Helpful Ideas

■ Listen to Sounds in the Environment

Children can listen for animal sounds and try to determine whether they are loud or soft, high or low. Have them listen to birds, dogs, squirrels, or a guinea pig. Other interesting environmental sounds are car and truck horns, bicycle bells, church bells, squealing brakes, and sirens. Tape-record these sounds and play them back for later discussion.

■ Play Sound Games

Have children demonstrate with their voices a sound they know and let other children try to guess what it is. Examples: buzzing bee, zooming jet plane, racing car, dripping faucet, blowing wind, pouring rain, mooing cow, growling bear. Another time have children demonstrate only soft sounds—or only high sounds.

■ Do a Whistling Activity

Can any children in your class whistle? Let them try. Then read them the Ezra Jack Keats classic story, *Whistle for Willie* (New York: Viking Press, 1964), in which Peter learns, after many attempts, to whistle for his dog Willie. Can you yourself whistle? You will need to when you read this book! Talk about whistles with your children. Listen for factory whistles and train whistles. Tape-record them. Bring in whistles for the children to blow (e.g., a referee whistle). Can anyone's grandfather make a "willow whistle"?

■ **Read a Book**

Music, Music for Everyone by Vera B. Williams (New York: Greenwillow Books, 1984) is a heartwarming story about four neighborhood girls who play accordion, violin, flute, and drums. Their own enjoyment of music helps them share it with others by forming a neighborhood band. Although the story features children older than preschoolers, the lively action and colorful illustrations will hold the attention of younger children, too.

Ben's Trumpet by Rachel Isadora (New York: Mulberry Books, 1979) is a 1930s story of young African-American Ben who listens to the music from the Zig Zag Jazz Club down the street, and makes his own music on his imaginary hand trumpet. Striking black-and-white illustrations seem to blow the music right off the page as Ben is ridiculed by peers but finally taken under wing by a real trumpeter from the band.

❏ REPRODUCES MUSICAL TONES WITH VOICE

Young children's first sound-maker is their own voice, and they soon recognize its importance in communicating their wants and needs. Because they learn how to use things through playful exploration, infants and young children are soon playing around with the sounds their voice can make. Some of the sounds are crying or laughing; some are speech sounds; and some finally become musical sounds or singing.

Children learn to sing very early if they are around adults who sing. Some mothers sing nursery songs to babies, make up tunes and words as they bathe or dress their youngsters, and sing lullabies when they put their children to bed at night. Preschool and nursery school teachers can continue this beneficial tradition of communicating to children through song. They can sing greeting songs in the morning to individuals or the group; they can sing directions at transition times; they can play concept games with children through songs.

Children who are comfortable with the give and take of "song-versation" between themselves and an adult soon may be answering your song questions with song replies of their own. The traditional finger play song "Where Is Thumbkin?" (tune: "Are You Sleeping?") asks the whereabouts of a child's thumb and the other fingers one by one. It is up to the child to answer in song, "Here I am, Here I am."

The voices of toddlers do not have much range. In other words, it is difficult for children from 1-and-a-half to 2-and-a-half years old to sing very high or very low. Preschoolers, on the other hand, not only have greater vocal range, but also the ability to discriminate musical sounds and match them with their own voices. The belief that young children have high singing voices is a myth. Their voices average around middle C to an octave above. Thus, songs for young children should be sung in this middle range.

Many preschool teachers depend upon records and tapes for the music in their programs. Children enjoy almost any kind of music, but they truly show their appreciation for an adult who takes the time and effort to sing with them on her or his own, and who teaches them new songs to sing on their own. After all, it is the music maker who enjoys music the most.

When should you and the children sing in the classroom? Any time! It is better to sing when you are happy, when you are feeling good, or when the children are busy at other activities than during a formal music period. If you wait for a formal period before singing, then that period is probably the only time vocal music will be heard in your classroom. On the other hand, if you sing when you feel like it, then vocal music may set a happy tone for the whole day—month—year!

If You Have Not Checked This Item: Some Helpful Ideas

■ Make Up a Simple Song for Children to Sing

If you do not know any new songs, take old traditional tunes and make up new words. You may know these tunes:

"Row, Row, Row Your Boat"	"Three Blind Mice"
"Here We Go Round the Mulberry Bush"	"Are You Sleeping?"
"Twinkle, Twinkle Little Star"	"London Bridge"
"Do You Know the Muffin Man?"	"A Tisket, a Tasket"
"Ring Around the Rosy"	"Ten Little Indians"
"Sing a Song of Sixpence"	"This Old Man"
"Mary Had a Little Lamb"	

A change in the weather, a happy occasion, or a visitor may inspire you to make up new words to an old tune like "Sing a Song of Sixpence":

Come with us together
We'll all go down the hall;
Someone's here to see us
And he is very tall;
He has some news to tell us,
And it's a nice surprise;
So keep your ears wide opened up
And do not close your eyes!

■ Make Comb Harmonicas

Provide combs and squares of wax paper for every child. Have them fold the wax paper over the comb, put the comb between their lips and hum. Once they have mastered the skill, have them hum a simple tune. They can hum individual songs or all hum together on a song the class knows.

■ Read a Book

This Old Man illustrated by Carol Jones (Boston: Houghton Mifflin, 1990) presents the traditional nursery song/finger play/counting rhyme in picture book style with a see-through hole in every other page that shows where the old man plays his drumsticks. The children can sing or chant the words as you turn the pages.

The Happy Hedgehog Band by Martin Waddell and illustrated by Jill Barton (Cambridge, MA: Candlewick Press, 1991) shows a happy hedgehog named Harry, who loves noise, making a big drum and banging on it. He is soon joined by Helen, Norbert, and Billy, hedgehogs with their own drums. But when the forest animals want to play, too, nobody knows what they can do except Harry. He gives each of them a part to hum, hoot, buzz, whistle, clap, click, or pop. Give each of your children a similar part to play when you read this book, and have your own hedgehog band!

❏ ARRANGES EVENTS IN SEQUENCE FROM FIRST TO LAST

In observing children to determine their cognitive development, we have been concentrating thus far on the classification aspects of what is known as *logico-mathematical knowledge*. Children display three aspects of this knowledge:

1. *Classification abilities:*   The ability to understand particular characteristics or properties of objects and the ability to group things into classes with common properties.

2. *Seriation abilities:*   The ability to understand "more than" or "less than," and the ability to arrange things systematically in a sequence or a series based on a particular rule or order.

3. *Number abilities:*   The ability to understand the meaning and use of numbers, and the ability to apply them in counting and ordering. (Saunders & Bingham-Newman, 1984, p. 120)

The last two checklist items in this chapter involve seriation abilities in children, and the first two items in Chapter 10 deal with number abilities. These aspects are part of children's *operative knowing*, that is, the system of knowledge they have constructed about their world through the organization of their perceptual experiences.

In order to arrange events in a sequence, the child first has to recognize their properties and relationships. How are they alike? how different? What is the common thread that creates their relationship to one another? Then the child must understand order: that something comes first, something happens next, something occurs last. Her practice in sorting things by appearances should help her to note both properties and relationships among events as well.

But just as the young child often changes the rule she is using as she sorts a number of things, she also displays inconsistency in arranging events in a sequence. It is as if her immature mind cannot hold for long the rule upon which the sequencing is based. Or, perhaps, as Siegler (1986) notes, "Children's performance on relatively unstructured tasks, such as sorting, may reflect what they find interesting rather than what they know" (p. 267).

Cards with action pictures frequently are used in sequence games. The cards show sequences of an action from beginning to end, with one part of the sequence on each card. For example, one set of cards may have pictures of a pencil (a) lying on a desk, (b) rolling off the desk, (c) falling through the air, (d) hitting the floor, and (e) lying on the floor. Often 3- and 4-year-olds arrange only the first and last cards correctly. Another card set may show a baseball (a) being thrown, (b) going straight through the air, (c) being hit by a bat, (d) looping through the air, and (e) being caught by a person with a baseball glove.

Such sequence cards really are not appropriate for preschoolers because games with rules are beyond many of them at their developmental level, and because many of the cards depict events that are unclear and difficult even for adults to arrange. Some preschoolers will be able to arrange three easily understood sequence cards in their proper order. Kindergartners, with their increased maturity, are more successful. When asked to tell about a series of events in the order they occur, many young children can do it correctly if the events are familiar. But if the sequence is too long and complicated, the best most preschoolers can do is to identify the correct beginning and ending.

Ask your children to relate their favorite stories that you are familiar with. Do the youngsters get the plot sequence in the right order? Ask them to tell you what they would do in a fast food restaurant in order to get something to eat. Did they include all the essential steps?

If You Have Not Checked This Item: Some Helpful Ideas

■ Make Your Own Sequence Cards

Children learn best from their own actions. With an instant print camera, take a series of three photos of a child performing an action: for instance, bringing in a birthday cake, blowing out the candles, and eating the cake; or starting a block house, completing the house, knocking it down. Cover the photos with clear contact paper for protection and put the sets in envelopes for the children to play with. If youngsters understand number sequence, you can number the pictures on the back so that the children can check their sequencing accuracy.

Coloring books often show simple drawings of people or animals in a sequence. You can cut out each drawing and mount them separately on cardboard for use in your table games area. Comic books, of course, show pictures in a sequence. If you find any that are simple enough and appropriate for preschoolers, you can also cut and mount sequence pictures from comics in sets. In addition, you can buy duplicate paperback storybooks that you can cut out and mount into sets of three sequence cards of the favorite stories.

■ Use an Illustrated Recipe Chart in Cooking

Use a large chart with each step in the process numbered and illustrated in sequence. You can use drawn outlines of measuring cups and spoons, or actual three-dimensional plastic utensils mounted on a cardboard chart. Discuss each step with the children as they do it. Ask them which comes next, and then what.

You may discover that some of the preschoolers' problems with sequencing can be explained by their incomplete understanding of a particular process. For instance, children who had completed all of the steps in the recipe chart for making a birthday cake and were ready to put it in the oven were asked what to do next. Some said, "Eat it," others thought that candles should be put on, but nobody understood that the next step was to bake it.

■ Make a Pictorial Daily Schedule

Draw or paste pictures to illustrate the time blocks of your daily schedule in the order they occur. Display this pictorial schedule prominently, and discuss it with the children whenever the need arises, using questions such as, "What do we do first today?" "What comes next?"

■ Read a Wordless Book

All wordless books are illustrated in a sequence of events from first to last. You can "read" them to children; children can tell them to you. If children have trouble understanding the books, ask, "What comes next?" "And then what happened?" A current favorite is the bizarre wordless book *Tuesday* by David Wiesner (New York: Clarion Books, 1991). Around 8 o'clock on a Tuesday night, frogs on lily pads take off from the pond and sail through the air to the town, causing quite a commotion. The only text is the time that appears on blank white pages opposite the blue-black pages of floating frogs.

❏ ARRANGES OBJECTS IN SERIES ACCORDING TO A RULE

The final item involving seriation asks us to observe children to see if they can arrange objects in a series based on a certain rule. For example, can they order items from the biggest to the smallest, from the tallest to the shortest, from the hardest to the softest, or from the loudest to the quietest? Children's previous activities with opposites should prepare them for identifying the extreme differences in objects and events.

Young children are usually able to arrange items in a series if they are provided with cues. Montessori classrooms, for instance, provide cylinders that can be arranged in a board containing a series of graded holes. Children try to fit the cylinders from large to small in the increasingly smaller holes. They match the size of each cylinder with the size of each hole by trying out which cylinders do fit or do not fit. Once they have learned the concept, many children are able to line up the cylinders in the proper order without cues from the board.

Stacking blocks, boxes, and rings work on the same principle of arranging items in a series from the largest to the smallest. Even toddlers soon learn that the smallest ring will not go down all the way on the stacking column. Instead, they have to put the largest ring on first. Then, if one ring is left over, they will need to start over again to find their mistake. Russian *matreshka dolls*, a classic folk art, are a series of hollow wooden dolls, each smaller than the next, that fit inside one another. The point of these activities is that children play these learning games on their own, and thus come to discover the concept of sequencing through their own play.

It is true, though, that 3- and 4-year-olds have difficulty forming a consistent series from a large number of items when no cues exist, just as they have trouble in sorting out large collections or arranging a large number of action cards into the proper sequence. Although young children are able to compare two items on the basis of size, as soon as several other graded items are added, the youngsters have difficulty arranging the items in the proper order.

Most preschoolers understand the concept of bigger and smaller, but when this concept is applied to a series, the complexity of the many comparisons seems to confuse some youngsters. How can an object that is bigger than one item also be smaller than the item that precedes it?

You may find that you have not checked this particular checklist item for any but the most mature children. This finding is to be expected with 3- and 4-year-olds. Five-year-olds, on the other hand, usually are more successful. You may decide to add a number of new series games and activities to your manipulative or science/math areas in order to promote this skill. Be sure the new materials provide enough cues for your children to be successful. Most of all, be sure these activities are fun to do.

If You Have Not Checked This Item: Some Helpful Ideas

■ Arrange Children

Have groups of three children at a time arrange themselves from tallest to shortest. Mix up the children so that the shortest child in one group may not be the shortest in another group. Be sure everyone gets at least one turn.

■ Read a Book

The traditional classic stories of *Goldilocks and the Three Bears*, *The Three Little Pigs*, and *The Three Billy Goats Gruff* all feature a graduated series of characters from the smallest to the biggest along with their graduated series of furniture, cereal bowls, houses, and even noises. Children love these stories and will want to say aloud the repetitious dialogue or sounds as you read or tell the stories. The youngsters may want to act out the stories as well.

You can cut out the pictures of the three characters from extra paperback copies of each of these books. Then you can mount the cutouts on sandpaper and use them with your flannelboard activites. Can your children arrange the characters in proper order from smallest to biggest?

OBSERVING, RECORDING, AND INTERPRETING COGNITIVE DEVELOPMENT

Sheila, the girl who was recorded in Chapter 2, was found to have many items checked on this section of the *Checklist*, as shown in Figure 9.1. When the classroom staff reviewed Sheila's entire *Checklist*, they were not surprised to see her results in cognitive development. Sheila had already seemed to them to be a bright child with exceptional language and art skills, but she seemed to have difficulty in gaining access to group play. She preferred to play by herself, although often parallel to others. In fact, one of the staff members predicted that every one of the items for Sheila under cognitive development would be checked. The prediction was almost correct. Sheila does not play with sorting games, probably because of a personal preference and not because she could not do them.

It is important for staff members to look at the total picture when they observe and record a child's development, and also to talk together about the results. Not every child will accomplish every item in a section, although a girl like Sheila probably could have. All of us have personal preferences, even preschool children.

FIGURE 9.1

Classification and seriation observations for Sheila

Child Skills Checklist

Name _Sheila — Age 3_   **Observer** _Connie R._

Program _Head Start_   **Dates** _10-22_

Directions:

Put a ✔ for items you see the child perform regularly. Put *N* for items where there is no opportunity to observe. Leave all other items blank.

Item	Evidence	Date
7. Cognitive Development: Classification and Seriation		
✔ Recognizes basic geometric shapes	Can draw circles, squares, triangles	10/22
✔ Recognizes colors	Names all the colors she uses	10/22
✔ Recognizes differences in size	Plays size-matching games with ease	10/22
_____ Sorts objects by appearance	Does not play sorting games	10/22
✔ Recognizes differences in musical tones	Can play simple tunes on xylophone	10/22
✔ Reproduces musical tones with voice	Sings songs with accuracy	10/22
✔ Arranges events in sequence, first to last	Can follow a cooking chart with understanding	10/22
✔ Arranges objects in series according to a rule	Arranges dolls from biggest to smallest	10/22

REFERENCES

Beaty, Janice J., & W. Hugh Tucker. (1987). *The computer as a paintbrush: Creative uses for the personal computer in the preschool classroom.* New York: Merrill/Macmillan.

Forman, George E., & David S. Kuschner. (1983). *The child's construction of knowledge: Piaget for teaching children.* Washington, DC: NAEYC.

Pines, Maya. (1983). Can a rock walk? *Psychology Today, 17*(11), 46–54.

Richardson, Lloyd I., Kathy L. Goodman, Nancy Noftsinger Hartman, & Henri C. LePique. (1980). *A mathematics activity curriculum for early childhood and special education.* New York: Macmillan.

Saunders, Ruth, & Ann M. Bingham-Newman. (1984). *Piagetian perspective for preschools: A thinking book for teachers.* Englewood Cliffs, NJ: Prentice-Hall.

Schickedanz, Judith A., David I. Schickedanz, & Peggy D. Forsythe. (1982). *Toward understanding children.* Boston: Little, Brown.

Siegler, Robert S. (1986). *Children's thinking.* Englewood Cliffs, NJ: Prentice-Hall.

OTHER SOURCES

Barr, Kathryn Woodson, & John M. Johnston. (1989). Listening: The key to early childhood music. *Day Care and Early Education, 16*(3), 13–17.

Beaty, Janice J. (1992). *Skills for preschool teachers.* New York: Merrill/Macmillan.

Buckleitner, Warren. (1991). *High/Scope survey of early childhood software.* Ypsilanti, MI: High/Scope Press.

Cherry, Clare, Douglas Godwin, & Jesse Staples. (1989). *Is the left brain always right?* Belmont, CA: David S. Lake.

Pines, Maya. (1979). Head start in the nursery. *Psychology Today, 13*(4), 56–58.

Moomaw, Sally. (1984). *Discovering music in early childhood.* Boston: Allyn & Bacon.

Wadsworth, Barry J. (1989). *Piaget's theory of cognitive and affective development.* White Plains, NY: Longman.

LEARNING ACTIVITIES

1. Use the *Child Skills Checklist* section "Cognitive Development" as a screening tool to observe all of the children in your classroom. Which of your children did you check for most of the items? How did these children do on other areas of the *Checklist*, for example, "Small Motor Development"?

2. Choose a child whom you found did not have many checks under "Cognitive Development: Classification and Seriation." Observe that child on three different days, making a running record to help you get a more detailed picture of his or her cognitive skills. Plan an activity to help this child, and record the results when you use it.

3. What are the ages of the children who had the most checks on the Classification and Seriation Checklist? What are the ages of the children with the least checks? What are the

children's backgrounds? Can you make any inferences about cognitive development based on this information?

4. Choose a child who needs practice in discriminating likenesses and differences. Set up activities for him or her to practice this skill, or play some appropriate games with the child. Record the results.

5. Read one of the children's books from this chapter with a child you have identified as needing help in a particular area. Discuss the results.

10 Cognitive Development: Number, Time, Space, Memory

Number, Time, Space, Memory Checklist

❑ Counts to 20 by rote
❑ Counts objects to 20
❑ Knows the daily schedule in sequence
❑ Knows what happened yesterday
❑ Can build a block enclosure
❑ Can locate an object behind or beside something
❑ Recalls words to song, chant
❑ Can recollect and act on directions of singing game

T his second chapter on children's cognitive development continues the discussion begun in Chapter 9, but deals with several different aspects: children's learning to understand the concepts of number, time, and space, as well as the development of memory. There are two *Checklist* items devoted to each of these aspects. Observers will need to watch and listen to children *as they work and play naturally* in the classroom, displaying evidence of their cognitive development.

As with all of the *Checklist* items, those under "Cognitive Development" are not a test of children's abilities under structured conditions, but a listing of behaviors that are possible for children to accomplish in the normal classroom environment. As you interact with the children, watch for these behaviors to be performed naturally by individuals. If there is no opportunity to see the behaviors performed, the observer needs to record *N* rather than leaving the item blank. Teachers should then plan to provide more activities in these cognitive areas so that children have the opportunity to accomplish these skills.

❑ COUNTS TO 20 BY ROTE

Learning the concept of number is important for young humans to accomplish. They will be dealing most of their lives with the numbers involving size, distance, amounts, time, temperature, costs, money, and measurement. In their mind's quest to create its own knowledge, the children will be going through a predetermined sequence of development, internalizing the information gained from their sensory interactions with the world around them.

Even 2-year-olds display a rudimentary knowledge of numbers when they hold up two fingers to show you their age and count aloud one-two. For most, this counting is more of a parroting response than a true understanding of the quantity 2 years. However, some 2-year-olds can count to 10, and most 3- and 4-year-olds are able to count by rote to 20 (Siegler, 1986, p. 279).

Again, this rote counting does not mean that the children understand the concept of number. Often, in fact, children do not get the sequence correct in their counting and they may even leave out a number or two. These mix-ups and omissions are understandable because the children are performing a memory task, not a concept task. Their counting is really chanting, as in a nursery rhyme. If you ask them, you will find that many children do not know the meaning of each word. In fact, their chanting of numbers seems more like one long word instead of 10 separate ones: "onetwothreefourfivesixseveneightnineten."

Nevertheless, chanting like this is very important in the cognitive development of the child. Cognitive development proceeds from the general to the specific. Children first chant a line of numbers and then begin to understand specific number names from the line. Listen to the children as they chant. Are they getting the number names right and in the right order? Chant along with them to help them to hear the correct pronunciation.

This type of counting is due in part to the children's limited language experience. In order to understand the meaning of each number word, the child must form a mental image of it. You cannot expect this mental image formation in many 2-year-olds. By age 3 some children will have formed mental images of certain numbers because of their sensory experience with these numbers in their environment. It is therefore important for parents and other adults to use numbers frequently in the children's everyday living, and to involve children in the use of numbers with activities such as chanting, measuring, weighing, counting out items, counting out money, and playing games involving the counting of moves.

With infants and toddlers, the chanting of numbers and the singing of number rhymes, such as "One-two, buckle my shoe," is an important prelude to the understanding of number concepts. But before children of any age can be expected to know the meaning of each number, they must first accomplish several of the developmental skills mentioned in Chapter 9.

The children will need to be able to place objects in a series and to understand that the objects are more or less than one another. The youngsters will need to know the answers to questions such as Which group has the most? And, of course, they will need to know the names of the numbers. Some of these skills are just beginning in the preschool classroom, but many children will not fully grasp the concepts of seriation and number much before the age of 7 or second grade (Cowan, p. 181).

For children who can count to 20 but have no real understanding of numbers or of what counting really means, try having them count to 7 or to 13. The children will have to slow down and think about what they are doing. They may not be able to stop at a number other than 10 or 20 at first. Play games with individuals or small groups asking each to count to a number other than 10 that you will call out. Make such games exciting. Children who have not learned to count will soon be picking up this skill in order to play the game.

Be sure that bilingual children learn to count along with you. They can also count in their native language for the others to hear and even learn. Make counting by rote fun for all, but be sure to do it often. Familiarity with numbers can only happen for preschoolers if the numbers and number games are repeated frequently.

If You Have Not Checked This Item: Some Helpful Ideas

■ Play Number Chanting Games

Say or sing chants together, such as "One little, two little, three little Indians," using fingers or even children who jump up, sit down, or perform some other action. Use words other than *Indians*: for example, *children, kittens, butterflies*.

■ Chant Backwards

Use number chants in all sorts of ways. Children love to count down 10-9-8-7-6-5-4-3-2-1-0 before the space shuttle blasts off. Have them make shuttle models in their woodworking area or with clay, or ask them to bring in toy space ships, and then count down to blast-off.

■ Read Counting Books

Moo Moo Brown Cow by Jakki Wood (San Diego: Harcourt Brace Jovanovich, 1992) is a strikingly illustrated farm animal counting book with a double-spread picture of each animal and its number of babies. Kitty asks, with animal sounds, how many babies each has, and each animal replies in large print text.

Demi's Count the Animals 1-2-3 by Demi (New York: Grosset & Dunlap, 1986) counts from 1 to 20 all kinds of animals, from rhinos to water buffaloes on its brilliantly colored double-spread pages.

Arroz con Leche, Popular Songs and Rhymes from Latin America by Lulu Delacre (New York: Scholastic, 1989) contains one counting rhyme in Spanish or English, "The Graceful Elephant," that children enjoy repeating.

Moja Means One: Swahili Counting Book by Muriel and Tom Feelings (New York: Dial Press, 1971) gives the numbers 1 through 10 in regular number symbols along with the number name in the Swahili language on each double page. One sentence of text describes the African scene or custom portrayed. Children enjoy learning new names for things.

Children also enjoy saying big, unusual words such as the names of 10 different dinosaurs on the pages of *Count-A-Saurus* by Nancy Blumenthal (New York: Four Winds Press, 1989) as they count from 1 to 10.

Ten, Nine, Eight by Molly Bang (New York: Greenwillow Books, 1983) portrays a little African-American girl and her father counting down the objects in her bedroom before she goes to sleep.

❑ COUNTS OBJECTS TO 20

Children 3, 4, and 5 years old can master simple one-to-one correspondence, which is what we are asking them to do when they count objects. Learning that a number stands for an object is their next step in the sequence of learning number concepts. At first many youngsters try to rush through their counting without actually including all of the objects. The children seem more concerned with saying all of the numbers than with making sure each number represents an object. They eventually come to learn the key principles governing counting:

1. The number names must be matched one-to-one with the objects being counted.
2. The order of the number names matters, but the order in which the objects being counted are touched does not matter. (Resnick, 1989, p. 163)

Preschool children learn these principles not by being taught, but by being involved playfully in hands-on counting. As with learning shapes and colors, concrete objects should be used first, later pictures, and finally number symbols. From such activities children teach themselves (a) number names, (b) number names in order, and (c) one-to-one correspondence. Children become familiar with the names and the task by repeating it many times in many forms. Through repetition and trial and error, they finally get it right.

Most adults are not aware of the importance of learning to count. Cognitive scientists, on the other hand, believe that

Figuring out how to count is evidently a key ingredient in developing an understanding of number. In the skill of counting, the transition from novice to expert often occurs during early childhood. (Price, 1989, p. 55)

Thus, it is important that children count or hear you counting every day in the classroom, and that you provide youngsters with many opportunities for doing so on their own. Start with fewer items than 20 in the beginning, just as you did with number chanting. Then the children will learn to stop before they get to 20. Be sure that the children touch each item as they count. If they skip one, have them try again. Or have them hand you an item as they count it. Remember to make the activity fun or interesting for them, and not a task involving right or wrong.

Learning to sort, as discussed in Chapter 9, also is good preparation for counting things. Putting a cup with a saucer or a hat on a doll helps children understand one-to-one correspondence. Now they must apply their learning to numbers. They learn by their sensory actions that the number 1 represents the first object, that 2 represents the second, and so on. This learning is a first step. But counting in a progression still is not the same as understanding one-to-one correspondence.

Children may be able to count a row of 10 or even 20 children, and still may not be able to choose four of them. Give them practice. Once they are able to count up to 10 objects in a progression, the youngsters can practice picking out a particular number of items, such as three dolls, five blocks, or seven dominoes. Phrase your questions or directions to give the children practice with both activities. "How many red markers are there?" asks them to count in a progression. "Bring me eight napkins," takes them one step further in their development of number concepts.

It is also important that children count *on their own* in all sorts of unsupervised everyday activities. Cognitive scientists point out that

Only in this way is enough practice likely to be generated to produce a real effect on the rate of number-concept development. . . . Preschool programs can foster number-concept development mainly by providing many occasions and requests for quantification and by eventually tying these requests to situations of comparison, combination, and increase or decrease of quantities. (Resnick, 1989, p. 164)

Put out small collections of items in margarine cups on the tables of your manipulative area, and have children count them. They can do it on their own and record their number on the tape recorder if you have it set up for them. Have "Count Me" signs hanging around the room on objects like your fish aquarium, your painting easel paints, and the hats in your dramatic play area. What other things would the children like to count on their own? Ask them. If they want you to check on their accuracy, you will have to count these things, too—a good modeling behavior.

Using Marks, Picture Symbols, and Number Symbols

To support your children's number activities, you or your children can record their counting. You should not use number symbols at first, but simple marks to represent the numbers. For example, keep an attendance chart with all of the children's names and mark a symbol for each child present. Then the children can count the marks. Have children keep track with marks on a pad or punches on a card with a paper punch of how many times they feed the guinea pig or water the plants, or of how many cars pass by the building. Then they will have to count the number of marks or punch holes to get the total.

Use shape symbols, stick figures, or picture symbols for numbers, too. Put signs in each activity area with a particular number of stick figures or peel-off picture symbols to represent the number of children allowed in the area at once. Have a certain number of hooks on the wall with tags on them for use in each area. Have children take the tags while in the areas. Check from time to time with the children in the area, having them count how many participants are there to determine whether this is the proper number.

Use charts and bar graphs at appropriate times to record numbers. Hang a calendar chart near the guinea pig's cage and record the number of carrots he eats every day by pasting or drawing carrot symbols. Plant seeds and record how tall each child's plant grows every week. Post a chart with the children's names and have them measure the height with a ruler. Help each child count and record the height after his or her name every week. Or use a bar graph that can be colored in up to the height the plant has grown.

Later in the year when the children have shown that they understand one-to-one correspondence, you may want to use real number symbols along with the picture symbols. Numbers alone are often too abstract for many of the children at the beginning of the year.

If You Have Not Checked This Item: Some Helpful Ideas

■ Have Children Count One Another

Any activity is more meaningful to young children if it involves them directly with their peers. Have children help you take attendance in the morning by going around and counting how many children are present. Have the counting children touch each child. Give the counters help if they need it with numbers above 10.

■ Provide Many Counting Materials

Fill your manipulative or science/math area with counting materials or games. Use egg cartons for children to fill the sections with items and count how many there are. Use buttons, seeds, dominoes, spools, paper clips, and macaroni as items to fill the sections.

■ Do a Follow-the-Leader Counting Walk

Walk around the room with three or four children doing a follow-the-leader touch-and-count walk. Do it out loud the first time and then silently once children know how. For example, after touching three items silently yourself, stop quickly and ask, "How many did we touch?" Congratulate the ones who get it right, and continue your walk. When all of the children have caught on, let one of them be the leader.

■ Have Children Set the Table

Let the children set the table for meals and snacks. They will need the same number of knives, spoons, and forks for each table; the same number of plates, cups, and napkins. This real task is an especially powerful activity for teaching one-to-one correspondence.

■ Use a Computer Program

Preschool children can learn to use a computer with ease, and love to do so. Counting activities are especially well suited to computer programs, thus many computer math games for preschoolers include counting. Children will need to be able to find and use the number symbols 1 through 9 on the computer keyboard to work many of these programs. For children who have taught themselves to use the letter keys, this should present no problem. Show them the top row of the keyboard where the numbers are, and let them learn to use the programs on their own. Be sure you have a color monitor.

Stickybear Numbers (Norfolk, CT: Optimum Resource, 1987) responds to a child pressing a number key with a colorful scene showing a set of that number of objects appearing on the scene one at a time.

Charlie Brown's 1-2-3 (Heightstown, NJ: McGraw-Hill Media, 1985) shows a Peanuts scene when children press a number key, but then they must count out the number of objects with the space bar or number keys in order to animate the scene.

Children match numbers from 1 to 10 with sets of objects in *Counters* (Scotts Valley, CA: Wings for Learning, 1983), and from 1 to 20 in *Counting Critters* (St. Paul: Minnesota Educational Computing Consortium, 1985). In *Number Farm* (Allen, TX: DLM, 1988) children count not only farm animals in six entertaining games, but in one game they have the unique experience of counting the sounds the animals make.

■ **Read a Book**

How Many Stars in the Sky? by Lenny Hort (New York: Tambourine Books, 1991) is the ultimate counting book. It is the tender first-person story of a little African-American boy who can't sleep because his mama is away, so he goes outside to count the stars. After he fills up pages of his pad, his daddy joins him and together they go looking for a better place to count the stars, eventually ending up in the country and sleeping under the stars.

❑ KNOWS THE DAILY SCHEDULE IN SEQUENCE

Understanding Time

Time is the next cognitive concept we need to look for in young children. Youngsters 3, 4, and 5 years old are only at the beginning of their temporal understanding. We need to provide them with simple activities involving time, but we cannot expect them to develop a mature understanding of so abstract a concept during the preschool years.

Time comprehension for young children has a number of different aspects: (a) the ability to understand what comes *before* and what comes *after*; (b) the ability to describe past events; (c) the ability to anticipate and plan for future events; (d) the ability to describe the order or sequence of things; (e) the ability to understand the passage of time and how it is measured (with clocks, calendars); and (f) the understanding of units of time (seconds, minutes, hours, days, weeks, months, years, centuries).

The child's ability to arrange things in a sequence or series based on a particular rule or order was discussed in Chapter 9 under Seriation Abilities. This knowledge that events may occur in a particular order with something happening first, something next, and something last generally precedes a child's understanding of time intervals.

Because young children are still egocentric, looking at everything exclusively from their own point of view, they do not perceive time as adults do. To young children, time occurs because they are there. For example, snacktime and naptime do not happen unless they participate. They learn to understand the movement of the hands on the clock only very superficially: that two hands pointing straight up means lunchtime. Calendars likewise have little meaning for young children, although they can repeat the names of the days of the week.

Time is a very abstract concept. It is not something you can see. Even adults realize that the passage of time seems uneven in different circumstances. If we are occupied, time goes quickly; if we are bored, time seems to drag. For young children the present moment is the most important. Children's comprehension of past and future is limited to periods of time not too distant from the present.

Time is one of the basic organizing dimensions of the child's experience (Cowan, 1978, p. 126), and as such time needs to be considered an important part of the child's cognitive development. Although the young child will not develop a mature perception of time while in your classroom, you need to be aware of each child's present development in this area in order to provide activities and support for the continued growth of the time concept.

Using the Daily Schedule

Children learn best from things and events that involve them directly; therefore, using the daily schedule to help them understand the concept of time is a good place to begin. First of all, you must have a daily schedule that is clear and consistent. The activity periods can be of various lengths so long as they follow one another in the same order daily. A brief transition activity between each period helps children to understand that the next period is about to begin.

As an example, a full day's program might consist of

A.M.	*P.M.*
Arrival	Naptime
Morning circle	Free choice
Free choice	Snack
Snack	Afternoon circle
Outdoor play	Departure
Toilet	
Story	
Lunch	

If you follow this same schedule consistently day after day, children not only feel secure about what will happen, but they also come to an understanding about the sequence of things. The abilities to represent mentally and to remember the order of events are essential ingredients in the young child's development of the concept of time. Even if your morning free choice period varies in length from day to day, the children will still know that it comes after morning circle and is followed by snacktime.

The morning circle time is essential in bringing about awareness of this sequence, in helping children to make choices and plan for future activities, and in giving them an awareness of time in general. The *Checklist* observer should attend the morning circle in order to hear which children give appropriate answers to the teachers' questions about the activities to follow and which children do not seem to understand time intervals.

Although many teachers do calendar activities during morning circle time as well, they need to be aware of children's superficial understanding of calendars and clocks. We really cannot expect children to understand these abstract concepts much before age 7.

Four-year-olds are aware of established sequences and become upset if things are not done in the regular order. If one of your periods is to be omitted, this should be made clear at circle time. On the other hand, the length of the activity periods can vary without anyone seeming to notice. Teachers who have had to shorten their day by several hours report that the children hardly notice the difference so long as the activities follow one another in the established, regular sequence.

Giving children advance notice that a period is coming to a close is another method for helping them to understand the passage of time. "Five more minutes before cleanup time," may not have the same meaning for young children as it does for adults, because children still do not really understand *minutes*. But youngsters do know that this signal means that the free choice period is almost over and that they must soon help to clean up.

Having some kind of transition between each activity period also helps a child to order the day mentally. When everyone has finally arrived and it is time for morning circle, you can give a transition signal by playing a chord on the piano or singing a transition song such as:

(Tune: "Happy Birthday")
Good morning to you,
Good morning to you,
Good morning everybody,
Good morning to you.
Come sit in our group,
Come sit in our group,
Good morning everybody,
Come sit in our group.

When circle time is finished, you can play a concept game as a transition to send the children to their activities: "All the children with red on may go to their activity area." Free choice period usually ends with cleanup. When children are finished with that they go to the snack table on their own. The transition from snack to outdoor play could be a song that will send them to get their outdoor clothes on:

(Tune: "The Farmer In the Dell")
We're waiting to go out,
We're waiting to go out,
Jill and Joe and Rodney, too,
Get ready to go out.
We're waiting to go out,
We're waiting to go out,
All the girls at table one,
Get ready to go out.

When they come in from outdoor play, the youngsters already know that they go to the bathroom and wash their hands after hanging up their coats. From the bathroom they generally go over to the library corner, where one of the teachers will be waiting with a book to read. The transition activity to lunch can involve something from a story you have just read:

Harry, the Dirty Dog, is looking for a hungry boy or girl to go to the lunch table. Everyone close your eyes and wait for Harry to tap you on the head.

Activities such as these help the children to establish a meaningful order to the day. This order is more than an explanation in words, for the children must interact with their environment in order to construct mentally the concept of daily time sequences.

An afternoon circle time is important to help the children internalize these activities, and to help you realize their understanding of the things they have been doing. Now is the time to discuss what the children liked best about the day. Ask things like, "What did you make today that you can tell us about?" "What did you choose to do during free choice in the morning?"

Just as the morning circle asked them to look at the daily schedule and make plans for the future, so the afternoon circle asks them to look back at the past and think about what they accomplished. *Checklist* observers also need to be present at this group meeting in order to determine who really understands the daily schedule and can remember past events.

If You Have Not Checked This Item: Some Helpful Ideas

■ Play a Time Game

Because children learn best by playing, and especially by playing something that involves themselves, you might play a time game with them in which they pretend to be your various activity periods. For instance, you could have one child represent each of the morning periods: arrival, morning circle, free choice, snack, outdoor play, storytime, and lunch. Put a sign on each child. The sign could have both words and a symbol: a handshake for arrival, a circle for morning circle, blocks for free choice, a glass of juice for snack, a swing for outdoor play, a book for storytime, a plate for lunch. Then let the children arrange themselves in a line in the order the periods occur. To get the children started, ask which child should come first? Which one next? Do the same for afternoon activities.

■ Make a Pictorial Daily Schedule

Draw or paste pictures to illustrate the time blocks of your daily schedule in the sequence they occur. Display this pictorial schedule prominently and discuss it with the children.

■ Play Before and After Games

Make up brief transition questions that you ask the children while they are waiting for something else to happen. For example, you could ask them, "Does lunch come before nap or after nap?" "Does snack come before outdoor play or after outdoor play?" Have them make up similar questions of their own.

■ **Read a Book**

The following stories take place in a nursery school and show children engaged in a sequence of activities: Miriam Cohen, *Will I Have a Friend?* (New York: Collier Books, 1967); Miriam Cohen, *Best Friends* (New York: Collier Books, 1971); Harlow Rockwell, *My Nursery School* (New York: Greenwillow Books, 1984). After reading the books, you can discuss the order of the activities and how they compare with the activities in the children's own school.

Wordless books are especially good examples of time sequencing because their illustrations show a sequence of pictures that tell the story from first to last. Some seem to be better than others in illustrating what happens in a specific sequence.

Going Shopping by Sarah Garland (New York: Viking Penguin, 1986) shows a mother, baby, girl, and dog getting in the family car, driving to the supermarket, shopping for groceries, checking out the groceries, getting back in the car, driving home, and getting out of the car with the bags of groceries. After reading the story, see which of your children can reconstruct the sequence of events.

Moonlight by Jan Ormerod (New York: Penguin Books, 1982) shows a little girl, with her parents' help, eating supper, doing dishes, taking a bath, getting ready for bed, going to bed, getting up several times in the night, and finally being put to sleep for good—all in a series of sequential pictures across the pages.

❏ KNOWS WHAT HAPPENED YESTERDAY

One of the problems young children must face in learning time concepts is recognizing the fact that while they are involved in a present event, the memory of the preceding events has already disappeared. Thus the past may exist for a young child only vaguely. We all know that as we mature, recollections of the distant past fade away and are stored in the recesses of the brain, not to appear again unless tapped by hypnosis or jogged into life by some trigger event. For young children, memories of even the recent past may slip away unless they learn to be aware of them.

Just as all development is interrelated, so the formation of the cognitive concept of time is dependent for young children on the development of both language and memory. Children first of all need to understand the vocabulary of time words: before, after, during, next, today, yesterday, tomorrow, next time, after awhile, and soon. This understanding does not occur overnight. Psychologist Margaret Donaldson in fact believes that "we have tended both to underestimate children's competence as thinkers and to overestimate their understanding of language" (Donaldson, 1979, p. 60).

Recent studies are showing that although children seem astonishingly adept at making original spontaneous utterances, the youngsters' understanding of what is said to them is not always that clear. The first words they learn, in fact, are naming words—nouns—then action words—verbs. Prepositions and adverbs, which show place, order, and *time,* are much farther down the scale of words young children understand or use. It takes much longer for these seemingly "less important" words to become a part of the young child's vocabulary.

For children to conceptualize the past, they must first learn what *before, after, yesterday,* and *tomorrow* mean. Children learn these terms as they learn everything: through actual experiences. Your circle time discussions will help the children to focus on the good experiences they had the day before and the good things they can look forward to tomorrow. As such concepts become meaningful to the children, they will incorporate these time terms into their vocabularies as well.

Although most memories of their distant past already may be gone, they will be able to bring to mind the recent past if it is focused on as a part of their life in your center. In addition, memory and recall, to be discussed later in this chapter, play a part in their ability to know what happened yesterday.

If You Have Not Checked This Item: Some Helpful Ideas

■ **Play Today-Yesterday-Tomorrow Games**

Afternoon circle time is a good time to play games that involve events that happened yesterday, today, or will happen tomorrow. Make three signs, one for each of these days, with a stick figure of a person with hands on hips representing *today,* with hand pointing backward (left) representing *yesterday,* and with hand pointing forward (right) representing *tomorrow.* Then ask children questions about activities that actually happened: "Which day did we get new fish?" or "Which day was Bobbie's birthday?" or "On which day will we go to visit the farm?" Let children hold up the proper sign when they guess the correct day.

❏ CAN BUILD A BLOCK ENCLOSURE

Understanding Space

Space, like time, is another of the basic organizing dimensions of the young child's experience. Like the other basic dimensions, it has several aspects: (a) enclosure, (b) position of things, (c) closeness of things, (d) distance between things, (e) location of things, (f) order of things, (g) shapes and sizes, including body parts and body in space. The concept of space answers the question, Where? It is one of the three dimensions, along with number and time, that eventually merge to make up the basis for logical thought (Osborn & Osborn, 1983, p. 115).

Also like time, space is an abstract concept that young children cannot represent mentally until they experience *enclosure.* As with the other knowledge they create, the idea of space comes from their sensory exploration of things. Children see objects and perceive objects as being close to or far away from other things.

But in the beginning, the infant's only experience with space involves the nearness of objects. When the object is out of sight, it is literally out of mind for him until he develops *object permanence* at about 8 months. Before that time, the infant will not continue to search for an object that is out of his range of vision or one that has been hidden. He acts as though the object he cannot see is no longer there, as if it has disappeared completely and no longer exists.

With experience and maturity the infant comes to understand that objects in his environment are still there even though out of his sight. Yet even with object permanence, most young children cannot perceive objects from any point of view other than their own. Nor can most children imagine how an object will look if its position in their space is changed.

Because space is not perceived readily by a youngster unless it is enclosed, *Checklist* observers are asked first to look for this aspect of space perception in assessing a child's cognitive development in this dimension.

Using Block Building

One of the most effective activities for developing cognitive concepts about space involves playing with "unit blocks." These deceptively simple and plain wooden units, half units, double units, quadruple units, cylinders, curves, triangles, ramps, pillars, floorboards, and switches were invented before World War I by Carolyn Pratt for use by her children in the experimental City and Country School in New York City (Winsor, 1974, p. 3).

One of the most effective activities for developing cognitive concepts about space involves playing with unit blocks.

Unit blocks are found today in almost every nursery school, preschool, and in many kindergartens throughout the country. Children learn to sort and categorize during cleanup by putting the blocks back on the shelves that have the correct cutout block shape. The block building corner is a favorite area for children's play during free choice period. The youngsters build houses and farms and towers and hospitals and anything else their imagination can invent. Adults rarely think of block building as a primary activity for children to develop such an abstract cognitive concept as space.

Adults may not think this way because they often have trouble keeping in mind how children learn: (a) by constructing their own knowledge through sensory interactions with things in their environment and (b) through free play with such materials. Abstract concepts can come to life in children's minds when such versatile yet defined playthings as unit blocks represent these concepts.

Harriet Johnson, another pioneer early childhood specialist who worked with Carolyn Pratt and later founded the nursery school that still later became the demonstration school for the Bank Street College of Education, spent years observing children's use of building blocks. She eventually published her findings in the 1933 classic study, "The Art of Block Building" (Johnson, 1974, pp. 9–24). She found that children go through predictable stages in learning to use blocks, based on their maturity and experience, when they are given the freedom to use blocks naturally without adult interference. Sound familiar? Her observational data give strong support to much current research on child development.

Her block building stages serve us well today in our observation of children's cognitive development. What better way to determine if children understand spatial concepts and relationships than by watching how the youngsters use unit blocks? If the first understanding that children can grasp about space comes only when they can enclose it, then their block creations offer a fine way to witness whether they have mastered this concept.

The children Johnson worked with ranged from 2 to 6 years in age, and varied in their experience with blocks. She found that the older children with no experience still progressed through the same stages as the younger ones, but with greater speed. An amended version of her stages includes

1. carrying, filling, dumping
2. stacking and lining
3. bridging
4. enclosures
5. patterns
6. representation

Children 2 years of age or older who have no block building experience begin by massing the blocks together, *carrying* them around, *filling* up containers (or toy trucks) with them, and *dumping* them out—over and over—but not building. This manipulative action is typical of the novice child's approach to most new activities: getting the feel of the blocks, the heft of them, the way you can move them around, but not using them for their purpose (which the child has not figured out yet), then repeating the activity again and again. It is a pattern the child will use throughout her natural development of block building skills if she is given the freedom to proceed on her own.

Somewhere between the ages of 2 and 3 years, real building begins. The first real building stage is either *stacking* blocks into a tower or *lining* them up in a row. Some children do one activity first, some do the other. Some combine the tower and the row. Some learn to straighten their blocks neatly so that their towers will not fall. Others pay little attention to either vertical or horizontal alignment. When they have mastered this first attempt, they tend to repeat it again and again before moving on to the next stage (Johnson, 1974, pp. 11–12).

Eventually, the children are faced with the problem of *bridging*, or using a horizontal block to span the space between two upright parallel vertical blocks. If the youngsters are working without the help of a teacher or peers (and they should be), it may take a great deal of time to resolve this building problem. The children's concepts of size and distance are still somewhat hazy at this age, and they often make many trials and errors before they can get the right size block. The other solution to the bridging problem, of course, is to move the two upright blocks closer together so that the horizontal bridging block will fit. Some children discover one solution but never the other.

Even when peers at higher levels are building nearby, the novice builder usually does not try to copy their methods. Block building, like art, is a very personal and satisfying expression of a child's individual creativity. What someone else is doing matters very little. For that reason teachers should not interfere with children's block building. The youngsters truly will learn cognitive concepts only by struggling with building problems on their own and finding their own solutions. Once children have learned to bridge, this skill is incorporated into their own personal building style, to be used over and over.

The next stage to master in block building for most children is *enclosures*. Some may solve the problem of enclosing or encircling a floor space horizontally with block walls or fences before they learn to bridge, however.

Adults find it difficult to understand why children have trouble making an enclosure. A child will start out correctly by making two walls joined at a corner to enclose the corral for her toy horse, but somehow be unable to turn the next corner for the third wall, and thus the wall goes on and on. She seems to know what she wants to do but is unable to do it. It is frustrating indeed: something like the adult standing before the bathroom mirror trying to cut her own hair. The child needs your support but not your help in arriving at her own solution: her own understanding of space and how to manipulate the objects in it.

Many 3- and even 4-year-olds make incomplete enclosures for a long time before they perceive how to close the gap. Their enclosures tend to have some rounded corners as well, for children still have difficulty at this age either constructing or drawing a square (see Chapter 9). But once they have mastered the problem of completing an enclosure, they also incorporate this skill into their block building repertoire.

A few children begin naming their enclosures when they start to build, but most youngsters do this after they have finished the enclosures. It may be a garage for their car or a house for their doll or a house for the guinea pig. This structure may not have been in their minds as they started to build, but they know adults want them to name things, so these names sound reasonable.

Whether the name is reasonable depends upon whether the toy car, doll, or guinea pig fits into the building. You will have an additional opportunity to observe the children's conception of space and size when you see whether the object fits its enclosure. Often it does not. Children sometimes try to force a toy car into a block building without seeming to realize that the car is too big and will not fit. Why can't children see that it does not fit, we wonder? Their mental structures still are not refined enough to handle such details. Children need more practice as well as maturity. Playing with blocks on their own will help to correct these deficiencies.

With skill in towers, rows, bridging, and enclosures, children are ready to build in patterns—decorative, repetitive, often geometric—building either horizontally or vertically and incorporating the entire repertoire of building skills they have developed over the years. Children 4 and 5 years old use the same building styles they began with at ages 2 and 3, but in a more sophisticated and complex manner. You thought that block building was simple children's play? Now that you know it is neither simple nor play as adults know it, perhaps you will want to record with an instant print camera the children's stages of building over the year or two they are with you.

The final block building stage, as with art, is *representative*. Children start by building a structure and then giving it a name such as school, playground, house, store, fire station. Eventually they learn to name the building first and then build it according to their own inner design. Most early efforts at representation do not look much like the building they name. But practiced builders eventually are able to represent a wide range of structures. Their play now becomes less solitary or parallel and more of a group effort, as discussed in Chapter 5, "Social Play." Once children have mastered the skill of building with unit blocks, they are usually ready to contribute to another child's building or to invite other children to help them. At this point in development, they often want their structures to remain standing at the end of the period in order to play with them later. You may have to enlarge your block building area if you have many such skilled builders.

Keep magazine pictures of houses, stores, bridges, roads, barns, and office buildings mounted in your block building area at the child's eye level when seated on the floor. Where can you mount pictures when block shelves are in the way? Pull the shelves away from the walls and use them as room dividers for your building area. Then pictures can be mounted on the walls. Take photos of completed buildings and their creators, and mount the photos attractively in the same area to motivate further building.

If You Have Not Checked This Item: Some Helpful Ideas

■ Hold a Special Building Day

If boys tend to dominate the block building area, try having a special building day for girls only. Is this idea too sexist for you? Then try holding a special building day for all the children wearing red (or blue or sneakers or some other distinctive feature). If one child never seems to build, perhaps you could choose the feature from that child's clothing to identify a group that will then help him or her get interested.

■ Build Things Seen on a Field Trip

Take your instant print camera along on your next field trip. Snap photos of structures that children might want to represent in blocks when they return to the center: highways, bridges, towers, office buildings, stores, barns, and houses. Mount the pictures in the block area and watch what happens.

■ Supply Pictures to Motivate Building

Make photocopies of illustrations from a book that features buildings, and mount the copies in the block area to motivate building. The children will not copy in their block constructions the buildings in the pictures as adults view them, but from their own inner view of what buildings in the pictures look like.

■ Read a Book

Block City by Robert Louis Stevenson, illustrated by Ashley Wolff (New York: Dutton, 1988) is a modern version of Stevenson's classic poem "Block City" from *A Child's Garden of Verses.* The beginning pages show in large colorful drawings, a little boy building a block city to represent a medieval city in a storybook. Then follows pictures of the medieval city coming to life as the boy falls asleep. Finally the boy awakens and knocks down his block city.

Up Goes the Skyscraper! by Gail Gibbons (New York: Macmillan, 1986) is a tall nonfiction picture book showing how a skyscraper is constructed.

❑ CAN LOCATE AN OBJECT BEHIND OR BESIDE SOMETHING

The second checklist item that demonstrates your children's understanding of space asks whether they can locate an object that is behind or beside something. To respond accurately, children need to have constructed mental images of the position of things, the closeness of things, the distance between things, and the meaning of the spatial prepositions being used. This checklist item provides an especially good example of the interrelatedness of child development.

Children must have developed physically enough to be able to make sensory explorations of the objects in the environment. They need the mental maturity to convert this perceptual knowledge into cognitive concepts. They also need the language development and experience to put words to these concepts. Preschoolers and kindergartners are only at the beginning of such a synthesis, but your program is in an excellent position to help them create this knowledge.

Some of the prepositions children need to know in order to understand spatial relationships are shown in Figure 10.1. It must be a confusing task for youngsters to make sense of so many seemingly "unimportant" words. As mentioned previously, children first learn nouns, or naming words. These nouns are much easier to learn because children hear these words over and over in the abbreviated sentences used around them when they are first learning to speak. Nouns can be seen, touched, experienced in many ways. Next come verbs, the action words. These words, too, are used frequently in children's presence to describe what is happening to the noun.

Prepositions, however, are much more abstract. They do not represent a thing, but a location, which means that children must first learn the concept of location in space by experiencing the concept. Then the youngsters pick up a few of the location words, but the children's understanding of these words during the preschool years is still limited and incomplete. One of the difficulties may be that these words are so much alike. *Behind* and *beside* even sound alike. Children tend to learn one or two words for the same location, but they do not realize that there are still other words with the same meaning. For instance, *under*, *underneath*, and *below* can all mean the same thing. Most young children have trouble with such synonyms.

An interesting study of preschool children's understanding of the words *on, next to, in, underneath, behind, over, outside of, below, between, in front of, above, beside, inside, under,* and *out of,* was carried out by Holzman and her students in the form of a game. Each child was asked to put the Cookie Monster doll in a certain location involving a small red box inside a large one-shelved blue box. Twenty percent of the children made errors on the words *underneath, below, over,* and *under* (Holzman, 1983, p. 120).

The concepts of *inside* and *outside* evolve from the children's understanding of enclosure or surrounding. Observe how many of your children who can make an enclosure also understand the location of *beside*. What about the other children?

Because a child's awareness of space and location grows out of his own body in space, he will need to move physically around your classroom in order to determine the locations of *behind* and *beside*. The child's perceptual awareness of space develops more rapidly than the more abstract concepts involving space. But if the child

FIGURE 10.1
Prepositions children need to know in order to understand spatial concepts

behind	down	in
in back of	under	inside
beside	underneath	into
alongside	below	out
at the side of	over	outside
by the side of	above	out of
next to	up	
in front of	up above	
between	on	
in between	on top of	

has many meaningful sensory experiences with space in your classroom, his mental construction of location in space will eventually be created.

If You Have Not Checked This Item: Some Helpful Ideas

■ Play Location Games

"Where is the fish?" is a cumulative game that children enjoy. Play it during circle time by asking the children, "Where is the fish?" Have one child go to the location of the fish (or whatever), point to it, and respond, "The fish is in the fishbowl." Then ask, "Where is the fishbowl?" Another child must go and touch it and say, "The fishbowl is on the table" (or wherever). This game can continue as long as there is interest. Be sure the children answer in sentences containing a location preposition.

Unlike the concept of enclosure, which children learn best on their own, youngsters need more help understanding location prepositions. You should take the lead in games and questions.

■ Read a Book

Guinea Pigs Far and Near by Kate Duke (New York: Dutton, 1984) demonstrates location words very simply and effectively. Large pictures of guinea pigs are captioned with one word at the bottom of each: *apart, far, near, together, over, under, around, through,* and many more. The illustrations show the plot line of the story.

Use the book *Find the Cat* by Elaine Livermore (Boston: Houghton Mifflin, 1973) with one or two children at a time, because they must look closely at complex line drawings in order to find the cat. After the children have put a finger on the cat, ask them to tell you in words where it is located. This is a good whole-part game as well, for some of the pictures show only the cat's tail, or its head. *But Where Is the Green Parrot?* by Thomas and Wanda Lacharias (New York: Delacorte Press, 1968) can be used in the same way.

One Snail and Me by Emilie Warren McLeon (Boston: Little, Brown, 1961) is another book full of humorous animal antics. Children can be asked things like: "Where are the turtles?" (The turtles are on the rim of the tub, not in it.) "Where is the duck?" (Sometimes the duck is in the water, but other times it is on the girl's head, on the whale's back, on top of another duck.)

❑ RECALLS WORDS TO SONG, CHANT

Developing Memory

Memory, the last of the cognitive abilities to be discussed, is an integration of all of the others. It is the process of storing information in the brain for future use and of retrieving the information later. Memory depends not only upon children's development of classification and seriation abilities, as well as number, time, and space concepts, but memory also rests upon the children's previous experiences. The more children experience, the richer their memory becomes.

Children and adults do not necessarily remember things in a pure form, so to speak, but instead experiences are enriched by being built upon. In other words, every experience a person has changes every previous experience by building on it. For this reason it is essential for children to participate in numerous activities of every possible variety in your program.

The most basic experiences in the beginning, as we have reiterated, are perceptual: the sensory experiences of seeing, hearing, feeling, tasting, and smelling. The richness of perceptual learning will determine the meaningfulness of future experiences. According to Spitzer, "The most important single determinant of what we remember, is the meaningfulness of the information" (Spitzer, 1977, p. 64). Think about how this statement can affect what you do in your program. Are the activities you set up *meaningful* to a child?

If information must be meaningful to children in order to be remembered, then we need to provide all kinds of activities the children will participate in because they find them interesting, enjoyable, exciting, worthwhile, or fun. Then we must give the children the freedom to explore the activity on their own. The activities must be experiences the children choose because they want to try them and not because they are directed to them by an adult. It is no wonder that children have made spontaneous play their particular process for learning, and no wonder children have difficulty remembering information that has little meaning for them, or is dull or boring.

Why haven't adults made play the basis for their own learning throughout life? It is because the basis for learning shifts during the early elementary years from perceptual experiencing to language. As language facility increases, verbal functions take over the role of the senses and become the principal basis for learning. We should not forget, though, that the meaningfulness of verbal information is still the most important determinant of our ability to remember.

Due to the cumulative effect of past experiences (and even verbal experiences have to be built on the child's earlier perceptual experience), it is the child with the richest perceptual experiences who can develop the richest language and verbal memory.

Developing Recognition and Recall

Memory has three different aspects: recognition, recall (discussed here), and recollection (which will be discussed under the next checklist item). Recognition is the most basic of the three processes. It is the simple knowing that an object has been met with previously. The infant uses this form of memory to make sense of his world. As he experiences his environment over and over, he begins to recognize its forms and ingredients. By about 8 months his recognition of objects has developed to the point that he knows they exist even when he can't see them. The more experiences he has, the more material his memory has to build on in the future. Recognition seems to be the primary mechanism for remembering until about age 2 (Spitzer, 1977, p. 65).

At about 2 years of age, recall comes into play more and more. This is the memory process by which pieces of information are retrieved from the memory banks of the brain for use by the child. Recall is more abstract than recognition; recall does not depend upon an outside object, person, or event to trigger memory. Children who show understanding of the time concepts of past and future have the ability to recall this information. Until this process has developed, youngsters really cannot remember much of the past and have difficulty anticipating the future.

Recall is necessary in order for the child to learn language. Much of her early attempts involve imitating the words of others. She files these in her memory and then recalls them at the appropriate time in her speaking.

Recalling Songs and Chants

Observers using the *Child Skills Checklist* are asked to listen to whether children in your program recall the words to a song or a chant. Doing singing and chanting are excellent methods for practicing recall abilities. Such activities give children perceptual memory cues, making an appropriate bridge between sensory and language learning. For example, songs and chants are rhythmic. Children can tap their toes, clap their hands, or beat out a rhythm while they sing in unison or listen to a record. Songs and chants are also usually in rhyme, a good memory cue for later recall of words. Chants are usually done to finger plays or body actions. Thus sensory experiences provide memory cues for later recall of words.

Children as young as 1 and 2 years old may begin to chant using nonsense syllables. These children are usually unable to sing accurately at this age, but they enjoy musical sounds, especially the human voice. Between ages 2 and 3, children often chant or sing to themselves at play—often in a monotone—and try to keep time to the beat of music they hear. By age 3 youngsters can sing simple songs, play simple singing games like "Ring Around the Rosy," and move to the beat. Children 4 and 5 years old have improved all around if they have had practice (Greenberg, 1979, pp. 23–26). They still may not pronounce all the words of the songs accurately, but what does it matter? Singing is for enjoyment, not perfection, during the early childhood years.

To teach your children songs and chants, you need to repeat them over and over again with the children every day. Sing morning greeting songs; transition songs; finger plays at circle time; singing games in the large motor area; songs for the seasonal holidays of Halloween and Thanksgiving; songs for rainy days, sunny days, and snowy days; songs about animals; and, especially, songs and chants about the children themselves. Use nursery rhyme favorites of your own and make up words to familiar tunes, using the children's names whenever possible, and you will soon create an interested group of young singers. Records are fine for occasional use, but give your children a special cognitive memory boost by helping them learn their own words to songs and chants.

You do not need to be a good singer yourself. The children will never know the difference. If you cannot sing, then chant with the children in unison or in a monotone. Research shows that children who have experienced nursery rhymes in the preschool years have fewer problems learning to read in later years than those who have not encountered nursery rhymes.

To teach children songs, chants, and finger plays, you need to repeat them over and over.

If You Have Not Checked This Item: Some Helpful Ideas

■ Use Children's Names in Songs

Make up words to a familiar tune using children's names. For example,

> (Tune: "Are You Sleeping?")
> Where is Bridget?
> Where is Bridget?
> Here she is!
> Here she is!
> How are you this morning?
> How are you this morning?
> Nice to know,
> Nice to know.

Some other tunes you can use with your own words are the following:

> "Here We Go 'Round the Mulberry Bush"
> "Lazy Mary, Will You Get Up"
> "Row, Row, Row Your Boat"

"Sing a Song of Sixpence"

"This Old Man"

"Three Blind Mice"

"Twinkle, Twinkle Little Star"

■ Read a Book

There are several good children's books that may motivate your children to sing:

The Wheels on the Bus by Maryann Kovalski (Boston: Little Brown, 1987) is a rollicking version of the traditional nursery school song. Grandma takes Jenny and Joanna to town to buy them winter coats, and while waiting for the bus back home, they sing the song as Grandma remembers it—about a red two-decker London bus and all its funny people.

Old MacDonald Had a Farm illustrated by Glen Rounds (New York: Holiday House, 1989) puts large distinctive farm animals and huge words that almost leap off the pages into the sights and sounds of a unique barnyard in this traditional singing game. The music is provided on the last page.

■ Do Finger Plays

There are several excellent finger play books you may want to use with your children:

Finger Frolics by Liz Cromwell and Dixie Hibner (Livonia, MI: Partner Press, 1976) contains the words and actions to dozens of finger plays for seasons, holidays, animals, community helpers, and transportation.

Move Over, Mother Goose! Finger Plays, Action Verses & Funny Rhymes by Ruth I. Dowell (Mt. Rainier, MD: Gryphon House, 1987) contains dozens of original verses and finger plays about animals, seasons, people, food, games, colors, and numbers.

❏ CAN RECOLLECT AND ACT ON DIRECTIONS OF A SINGING GAME

Understanding Recollection

Recollection is the most advanced of the three aspects of memory. It is an information-retrieval process in which the brain groups and selects particular information and recalls it for use by the child. It includes recognition and recall but takes them a step farther. The child's mind must not only recognize things and recall information, but it must also group information in a meaningful way for use.

To be successful at recollection, the child first must be able to locate things and events in space and time. Researchers involved with the information-processing approach to studying young children's thinking and remembering talk in terms of short-term memory, long-term memory, and attention. Short-term memory is the storage of information that is received visually or auditorially by the brain. If the information is understood and useful, then it goes into long-term memory for storage. In order to receive any information at all, the person must attend. Attention refers to the sensory data that a person selects to process from all of the available incoming information (Schickedanz, Schickedanz, & Forsythe, 1982, p. 389).

Developing Attention

A young child has only limited attention. During the early years the child seems able to see only one aspect of objects or situations at a time. Therefore, the child's thinking skills lack the full range of information necessary to provide understanding for many events. Her long-term memory, which is called upon when she must recollect and act upon the directions of a singing game, is not capable of holding as much information as a mature mind. You may not be able to check this item for all of your children. Many are only at the beginning of this mature memory process. You will need to provide many experiences for children to use their memories for attending to the words and music of a singing game and then following its directions.

In order to follow even simple directions, children must first of all listen to and attend to the directions given. Sound games are good attention-getting activities to begin with. Children must listen to and understand the directions of the game; then they must use their auditory perception to accomplish the game successfully. For example, teachers can drop two different objects, one at a time, while children cover their eyes. Then children can be asked to compare the sounds of the objects. First, drop objects that are completely different sounding (e.g., a pen and a penny). Can the children tell the difference? Then drop two objects that are alike. Do the children recognize similar sounds? Next, play different rhythm instruments. Can the children tell what they are? Can the children tell when you play the same instrument over again?

Singing games ask for the children to listen carefully to the words of the song and then follow the actions called for. Many singing games are on records. Some of these are concept games such as "This is a Song About Colors," in which each child represents a particular color. The song asks each color to stand up or sit down at various times. The teacher should play the record first so the children can hear the directions, before acting them out. After repeating this singing game many times, children will be able to recollect the directions well enough to sing and act out the song without the record.

Traditional singing games are nursery rhymes that are sung without records and acted out by the group. The following are familiar examples:

"Here We Go 'Round the Mulberry Bush"

"Do the Hokey Pokey"

"Go in and out the Windows"

"London Bridge is Falling Down"

"The Farmer in the Dell"

"A Tisket, a Tasket"

"Ring Around the Rosy"

"The Grand Old Duke of York"

"Here We Go Looby Loo"

"This is the Way We Go to School"

"Bluebird, Bluebird on my Shoulder"

"Where, Oh Where, Is Sweet Little Susy?"

"Pass the Shoe from Me to You"

"Skip to My Lou"

Children learn to recollect the directions by repeating the games over and over. This is called *verbal rehearsal*. Some children do not understand the words they hear, but merely follow the other children around. Imitation like this is another effective learning method for young children.

Children can follow the prescribed motions in these games or make up their own motions. Most preschoolers, for instance, will not be able to skip in "Skip to My Lou." Let them make their own movements instead.

If You Have Not Checked This Item: Some Helpful Ideas

■ **Make Up a Singing Game**

Have the children make up new words to a singing game they already know, and then act it out. For instance, instead of "The Farmer in the Dell," they could sing "The Keeper in the Zoo," and then act out the zoo animals that the keeper takes in a descending order of size.

■ **Use a Music Book**

Music: A Way of Life for the Young Child by Kathleen M. Bayless and Majorie E. Ramsey (New York: Merrill/Macmillan, 1987) contains not only words and music to many singing games, but also chapters on music for children by age groups.

OBSERVING, RECORDING, AND INTERPRETING COGNITIVE DEVELOPMENT

Sheila, the child mentioned in Chapter 9 and earlier, had shown evidence of her self-identity, emotional development, and cognitive development when observed and recorded on the *Checklist*. Her Number, Time, Space, Memory Checklist results shown in Figure 10.2 indicate that she also displays development of number, time, space, and memory. The only items not checked seem to reflect her personal preference about an activity (blocks), plus her reluctance to enter group games. It is important to use the entire *Checklist* when attempting to interpret a particular section.

In this case, Sheila's needs are related not to cognitive development, but to social play and her difficulty in entering group games. Other children may well need your

FIGURE 10.2

Number, time, space, and memory observations for Sheila

Child Skills Checklist

Name _Sheila — Age 3_   Observer _Connie R._

Program _Head Start_   Dates _10-22_

Directions:

Put a ✔ for items you see the child perform regularly. Put *N* for items where there is no opportunity to observe. Leave all other items blank.

Item	Evidence	Date
8. Cognitive Development: Number, Time, Space, Memory		
✓ Counts to 20 by rote	Can count to 20 and beyond	10/22
✓ Counts objects to 20	Can count all the children in the class	10/22
✓ Knows the daily schedule in sequence	Is first to note when next activity starts	10/22
✓ Knows what happened yesterday	Often talks about events from yesterday	10/22
____ Can build a block enclosure	Never plays with blocks	10/22
N Can locate an object behind or beside something		10/22
✓ Recalls words to song, chant	Knows & sings many songs	10/22
____ Can recollect and act on directions of a singing game	Does not participate in group games yet	10/22

help in becoming involved in number, time, space, or memory activities to promote development of this aspect of cognition.

REFERENCES

Cowan, Philip A. (1978). *Piaget with feeling.* New York: Holt, Rinehart & Winston.

Donaldson, Margaret. (1979). The mismatch between school and children's minds. *Human Nature.*

Greenberg, Marvin. (1979). *Your children need music.* Englewood Cliffs, NJ: Prentice-Hall.

Holzman, Mathilda. (1983). *The language of children.* Englewood Cliffs, NJ: Prentice-Hall.

Johnson, Harriet M. (1974). The art of block building. In Elisabeth S. Hirsch (Ed.), *The block book.* Washington, DC: NAEYC.

Osborn, Janie Dyson, & D. Keith Osborn. (1983). *Cognition in early childhood.* Athens, GA: Education Associates.

Price, Gary Glen. (1989). Mathematics in early childhood. *Young Children, 44*(4), 53–57.

Resnick, Lauren B. (1989). Developing mathematical knowledge. *American Psychologist, 44*(2), 162–169.

Schickedanz, Judith A., David L. Schickedanz, & Peggy D. Forsythe. (1982). *Toward understanding children.* Boston: Little, Brown.

Siegler, Robert S. (1986). *Children's thinking.* Englewood Cliffs, NJ: Prentice-Hall.

Spitzer, Dean R. (1977). *Concept formation and learning in early childhood.* New York: Merrill/Macmillan.

Winsor, Charlotte B. (1974). Blocks as a material for learning through play—The contribution of Caroline Pratt. In Elisabeth S. Hirsch (Ed.), *The block book.* Washington, DC: NAEYC.

OTHER SOURCES

Barr, Kathryn Woodson, & John M. Johnston. (1989). Listening: The key to early childhood music. *Day Care and Early Education, 16*(3), 13–17.

Bayless, Kathleen M., & Marjorie E. Ramsey. (1987). *Music: A way of life for the child.* New York: Merrill/Macmillan.

Beaty, Janice J. (1992). *Skills for preschool teachers.* New York: Merrill/Macmillan.

Kail, Robert. (1990). *The development of memory in children.* New York: W. H. Freeman.

Kohl, Diane M. (1990). Math activities for young children. *Day Care and Early Education, 17*(3), 12–15.

Wolf, Jan. (1992). Let's sing it again: Creating music with young children. *Young Children, 47*(2), 56–61.

LEARNING ACTIVITIES

1. Use the *Child Skills Checklist* section "Cognitive Development: Number, Time, Space, Memory" as a screening tool to observe all of the children in your classroom. Which of your children did you check for most of the items? How do these children fare on other areas of the *Checklist*?

2. Make a graphic rating scale for block building and observe all of your children in this area. How do the results compare with the results for this chapter's section of the *Checklist*? Can you draw any conclusions from this?

3. Try to find out how many of the children whom you have checked on the item "Can build a block enclosure" also can locate an object that is beside something.

4. Play a singing game that your children already know, and record which children can recollect the actions.

5. Use one of the activities suggested under each item with a child who needs help in cognitive development and record the results.

11

Spoken Language

Spoken Language Checklist

- ❏ Speaks confidently in the classroom
- ❏ Speaks clearly enough for adults to understand
- ❏ Speaks in expanded sentences
- ❏ Takes part in conversations with other children
- ❏ Asks questions with proper word order
- ❏ Makes "No" responses with proper word order
- ❏ Uses past tense verbs correctly
- ❏ Plays with rhyming words

S poken language is one of the important skills that makes us human beings. We assume, without much thought, that our children will learn to speak the native tongue before they enter public school. Language acquisition cannot be all that difficult, we decide; otherwise, how could a little child accomplish it? After all, the child does not have to be taught; language acquisition just seems to happen. It is nothing to get excited about, we think, unless it does not happen on schedule.

As a matter of fact, the acquisition of a native language is one of the greatest developmental accomplishments and mysteries we may ever encounter involving the young child. It is a great accomplishment because the child starts from scratch, with no spoken language at birth, and acquires an entire native tongue by age 6. A child in a bilingual family may acquire more than one language. The acquisition of this complex skill is a great mystery because we are still not exactly sure how it takes place.

True, we may not show concern while all goes well, but we should learn all we can about the kinds of things that help or hinder the language acquisition process in order to smooth the way. The years from age 2 to age 5 are especially crucial in this process, when children's vocabulary suddenly expands from 250 words to 2,000 words, and they learn the rules of putting words together properly to speak in complex sentences. Children are often in an early childhood program during these years; thus the language environment you provide can have a significant effect on their progress.

In order to support your children's language development, you must know at the outset how accomplished they already are as speakers. Using an observation screening device such as the eight *Child Skills Checklist* items under "Spoken Language" to assess each of your children at the beginning of the year is a good way to start. Then follow up the observations with written or tape-recorded language samples of each child.

269

❏ SPEAKS CONFIDENTLY IN THE CLASSROOM

The first checklist item actually refers more to children's emotional adjustment to the classroom than to their speaking abilities. A child must feel at ease in the strangeness of the classroom environment and among her peers in order to speak at all. The so-called nonverbal child is frequently one who lacks confidence to speak outside the confines of the home. The child may have a shy nature or may come from a family that uses little verbal communication; or the child may have a physical disability such as a hearing impairment that has interfered with language development.

Spend time assessing this child using the entire *Child Skills Checklist*. The areas of "Self-Identity," "Emotional Development," and "Social Play" are especially important. Does the child have trouble separating from her parents when she comes to the center? Can she do things for herself with any confidence? Does she seem happy? Does she play by herself or with others?

Set up a meeting with her parents and discuss the *Checklist* results with them. If the results point toward some type of disability, then the parents will want to have the child tested further by a specialist for her particular problem. If the parents indicate that the child talks fluently at home, then the nonverbal child in your classroom may be demonstrating her feelings of insecurity in a strange new environment.

Your principal task with the shy or uncommunicative child will be to help her feel comfortable in the classroom. Using pressure to get her to talk before she is at ease may well produce the opposite results. You and your co-workers will need to take special pains to accept the child as she is and to try to make her welcome in the classroom. You can invite her to join appropriate activities, but if she refuses, then you need to honor her reluctance. It often takes a great deal of patience and forbearance on the part of an early childhood classroom staff to allow the shy child to become at ease in her own good time.

If the nonverbal child seems to feel comfortable with another child, then you may be able to have that child involve her with the others. On the other hand, sometimes the only solution is to leave the nonverbal child alone. If your environment is a warm and happy one, she eventually should want to participate.

The environment must be stress-free. For many children, speaking in a group of peers is a new and untried experience. To help them feel at ease about speaking, you need to help them feel at ease about themselves by accepting them as they are. Show you accept them with smiles, hugs, and words of welcome and praise. Show you are happy to see them every day and want them to participate.

In addition, you need to accept their language, no matter how poorly pronounced or how ungrammatical it is. Language is a very personal thing. It reflects not only the child's stage of development, but also his family life-style. You must be especially careful not to correct a child's language. Telling him he is saying a word wrong or using the wrong word is a personal put-down. He will learn the correct form himself when the time is right by hearing you pronounce the word correctly and by practicing it with his peers.

A stress-free environment means that your classroom is free from stressful situations for the young child. He should not be put on the spot and forced to perform verbally, creatively, or in any other way. Offer him opportunities and encouragement, but do not force the shy or unsure child to speak.

If You Have Not Checked This Item: Some Helpful Ideas

■ Use a Prop for Security

Many young children feel more secure when they have something in their hands, especially something soft and cuddly with the quality of a security blanket. You might want to keep several stuffed animals for children to choose from and hold when they feel out of sorts, or when they first come into the classroom and are not yet feeling comfortable. Your nonverbal child may even end up talking to her animal. It may be the beginning of her verbal integration into the classroom.

■ Use a Puppet

Almost every child likes the idea of putting a puppet on his hand. Have a box of various kinds of puppets and let the shy child choose a different one every day if he wants. Preschool children tend to play with puppets as if the puppets are a part of themselves rather than a separate toy like a doll. Because puppets have mouths, children often first experiment by trying to bite someone with the puppet—in fun, of course. Later the youngsters get the idea of having the puppet speak, perhaps in a whisper or in a different tone from their own voice. Shy children are often more willing to have a puppet speak for them than they are to speak for themselves. You might find yourself able to talk with a shy child's puppet through a puppet you put on your own hand.

Puppets can be played with alone, but they often lead naturally to involvement with other children. Thus, puppets are an excellent transition material to help the shy child integrate himself painlessly into the activities of the classroom. An excellent source to consult is *The Magic of Puppetry: A Guide for Those Working with Young Children* by Peggy Davison Jenkins (Englewood Cliffs, NJ: Prentice-Hall, 1980).

■ Read a Book

Louie by Ezra Jack Keats (New York: Scholastic, 1975) tells the story of Louie, an inner-city boy who has never been heard to speak a word. When he attends a neighborhood puppet show, he becomes entranced with the doll puppet, Gussie, and says his first word: Hello.

Maria Teresa by Mary Atkinson (Chapel Hill, NC: Lollipop Power, 1979) is about an unhappy little Hispanic girl who moves from her home in New Mexico to a new school where no one can even pronounce her name. She solves her problem by making a sheep puppet who speaks only Spanish and sharing him with the class during show-and-tell. This book is somewhat advanced for preschoolers, but bilingual classes and kindergartners should enjoy hearing the Spanish spoken by the puppet.

❏ SPEAKS CLEARLY ENOUGH FOR ADULTS TO UNDERSTAND

The pronunciation of the language, or articulation, may be another speech area of concern to the teacher of young children. When children first begin to speak, they try to imitate the speech sounds of those around them, but with limited success. As they listen and practice, their vocal organs become more adept at making the sounds of English consonants, vowels, and blends. At first children may use only 10 basic sounds: nine consonants and a single vowel. By the time they are completely mature speakers—usually by age 7—the children will have mastered 40 to 44 separate sounds (Eisenson, 1976, p. 75).

Most children with normal speech and hearing abilities are able by age 4 to produce most of these sounds. A few letters or blends such as *s, l, r, th,* and *sk* still give many children problems. Usually children substitute an easy sound for one they cannot pronounce: for example, p*wease* for p*lease.* By 7 or 8 years of age, even these difficulties have disappeared in most children, and the youngsters are able to articulate like mature adults. In fact, some children—more likely girls—may produce mature speech by age 5.

Nevertheless, language development, like the other aspects of growth, is highly individualized. Some children normally will be more advanced than others. Others are normally slow developers. One study showed that about 10 percent of 3-year-olds were slow language developers, but most of these children outgrew their problems within a year (Caplan & Caplan, 1983, p. 40).

Articulation, the way children pronounce words, is difficult for the layperson to evaluate. Whereas mispronouncing words is a common speech disorder, articulation problems with preschoolers tend to be developmental lags rather than disorders. Something may seem to be a disorder to you because you cannot understand the child, but the condition may be merely a delay in the child's normal development. If you have doubts, call on a speech specialist to evaluate the child. All aspects of the child's speaking—not just his articulation—should be taken into account.

In the meantime, you and your co-workers will need to serve as good language models for the child, helping and supporting him in classroom activities, but taking care not to correct his speech. Modern linguists now realize that it is pointless for adults to try to correct a preschooler's speech by making him repeat words according to an adult standard that he is not yet ready to use. Correcting, in fact, is a negative response that tends to reinforce the unwanted behavior and make the child feel there is something wrong with him personally. Instead of improving a child's language, correcting often makes the child avoid speaking at all in the presence of the corrector.

If the other children in your classroom can understand the child speaker, then you should be encouraged. It often takes longer for an adult with set speech patterns to become used to a child's speech idiosyncracies. Listen carefully and try to pick up what meaning you can without embarrassing the inarticulate child by making him repeat everything over and over.

Occasionally a child who has been pronouncing words normally will slip back into a kind of baby talk. He may also display other similar signs such as thumb sucking and wetting his pants. Since this tends to be an indication of an emotional upset, you will want to talk with the parents about the pressures in the child's life that may be affecting him adversely, causing the temporary regression. Is there a new baby in the family? a new father or mother? a death or a divorce? someone in the hospital? someone out of work? Young children feel these emotional upheavals in their families as severely as adults. Sometimes the first indication of such stress for a child is his slipping back to earlier speech patterns.

Because they are in a group of other child speakers, however, most young children will quickly pick up or revert back to the speech patterns and word pronunciations they hear around them. Their brains are programmed to do such copying at this stage of their lives. Even non-English-speaking children will soon join the mainstream of language with continued exposure to mainstream speakers. The common mispronunciations of preschoolers should be overlooked. As soon as the development of their vocal apparatus allows them to, they will be pronouncing English words just like everyone else.

If You Have Not Checked This Item: Some Helpful Ideas

■ Do Not Make a Fuss

Making a fuss about children's mispronunciation may cause more problems than it resolves. As previously pointed out, a person's speech is highly personal. If children are made aware they are doing something wrong, then they may stop trying altogether. Or in the case of children who are going through a period of disequilibrium in their development and begin to stutter, calling attention to their problem tends to make it worse. Have patience and have faith. Once through a stressful period, most children will continue their language development normally.

■ Help the Child to Feel Accepted

Children want to talk like the others around them. Their pronunciation trouble may already make them feel out of place. You will need to show by your actions and your words that you accept the child as she is, that you are happy to have her in the class, and that you will support and encourage her in all of her endeavors. Accepting the non-English-speaking child is just as important. Children from bilingual families may not speak English as the dominant language at home. Nevertheless, preschool age children have the ability to learn English quickly when they are surrounded by English speakers. Your acceptance of the way they speak their native language and the way they pronounce English is an important first step toward their success in learning English as a second language.

■ Help the Child Succeed at Something Else

All children need to experience success at this stage of their development. If they are having trouble speaking clearly, then help them to be successful in something else. Perhaps they can finger-paint or model with clay or play dough. Such art activities are also therapeutic for children under stress.

■ Try Singing

Sometimes children who have trouble saying words will be able to sing words. Do not single out such children, but include them with the others in your singing activities. Give verbal praise to your children for their singing just as you do their block building. They will be happy you liked what they did, and they may be more inclined to want to do it again another day.

❏ SPEAKS IN EXPANDED SENTENCES

Young children 3, 4, and 5 years old are just at the age when their speaking develops most rapidly. From the simple two-word sentences they uttered before age 2, they now are suddenly able to expand the subjects and predicates of their sentences into longer, more complex thoughts. Although their early communications included gestures—"Want more," they might have said while pointing at the milk bottle—they now speak in complete and expanded sentences, such as, "I want some more milk," with no necessity for gestures.

How did this expanded language come about? Linguists are searching for answers by audiotaping infants' utterances, videotaping their interactions with their caregivers, and comparing infants' development with deaf children, children from other cultures, and children from a variety of backgrounds.

We know that soon after infants walk, they talk. We also know that all human infants are predisposed to acquire their native language. Their brains are programmed to sort and store the information that will later be used in producing speech. Human infants give their attention to human voices, listening and then responding, at first in babbles, but as soon as possible in word sounds. Then sometime between 18 months and 2 years of age, the infants realize that everything has a name. Immediately, their vocabulary starts expanding as they begin to absorb the words for everything they see and touch.

This is the crucial time for meaningful caregiver intervention. The parent or caregiver can name objects and actions. The children will listen and try to imitate. The caregivers will listen to the children and respond; all of this interaction takes place in the natural give-and-take manner of parents playing with their children.

This is also the crucial time for an enriched physical environment and the child's freedom to explore it. As children learn names for things, the youngsters need to see them, feel them, hear them, try them out. The children will want to see the doggie, pet the doggie, and laugh at the doggie's funny antics with a rubber bone. Young children learn words by interacting with the things that are represented by words in their environment. The more things the child interacts with, the more words the child will have the occasion to learn, as long as support, encouragement, and good language models are also at hand.

Young children do not learn word meanings by having someone teach the meanings, but rather youngsters induce the meanings on the basis of hearing the words used in life experiences (Holzman, 1983, p. 65). Children hear a word being used and watch carefully what is going on while it is used. Their first words are names—mama, daddy, doggie, ball, bottle, bed—and other common words they hear—bye-bye, no-no, drink.

At first these words are used only in one way to mean one thing, but soon the infant discovers he can call, direct, demand, point out, play with, and ask things by the way he intones the word. "Ball" comes to mean, "There is the ball," "Where is the ball?" "Get me the ball." By this time, the child is putting two words together to make primitive sentences. "Mama, ball," may mean, "Mama, get me the ball," "Mama, see the ball," or "Mama, find the ball." He is beginning to learn the rules for producing sentences. In the meantime, Mama is hopefully responding not only by giving him the ball, but by repeating the child's sentence back to him—just a bit expanded: "Oh, the ball. Here's the ball. Mama's got the ball. See the ball? Baby want ball?"

Children seemed to be predisposed to learn language this way. Linguists find it surprising that adults and older children also seemed predisposed to "teach" children language this way. Observers watching mother-infant interactions soon picked up this behavior. The language behavior of the infant seemed to elicit the particular language behavior from the mother that was most appropriate to the infant's level of development. As the infant's ability improved, the mother's level of response expanded (Holzman, 1983, p. 87). Even more surprising is the fact that anyone playing with an infant seems to be able to adapt intuitively to the infant's language level.

Studies with 4-year-old boys who had no younger brothers or sisters showed that the boys were able to adjust their language to a 2-year-old with good language ability and another 2-year-old with poorer skills, in explaining how a toy worked. The boys listened to the toddler's responses to their own instructions, and made adjustments intuitively (Holzman, 1983, pp. 107–108). This result very well may indicate that not only are infants born with the method for acquiring their native language, but also that the speakers around them are endowed with a similar skill for helping them acquire it.

By around 2 years old, children are able to use the proper word order consistently in their primitive sentences. As they suddenly blossom into pretend play at this time, a parallel expansion seems to occur in their language. Their sentences grow longer and more complex, and their vocabularies increase (McCormick & Schiefelbusch, 1984, p. 72). Once they have absorbed the basic rules for forming sentences, they are on their way, for they then will no longer need to rely exclusively on imitating the language around them. Instead, they will be able to produce sentences they have never heard. For most children this mastery has occurred by age 4.

Obviously, it is important for children to be involved with competent speakers of the native language. If youngsters do not hear the language used or do not engage with someone in speaking it during these crucial years, they may have difficulty acquiring it. Language tends to be an activity carried on by the left hemisphere of the brain. The brain is programmed to acquire language during the early years. Recent evidence seems to indicate that if language acquisition has not occurred before puberty (as in the cases of extremely deprived children), then it is too late for the young person ever to learn it except at a primitive level (Holzman, 1983, p. 100).

It is important for you to know which children in your class are speaking in the expanded sentences that most 3-, 4-, and 5-year-old children should be able to use. Some children who are not speaking in sentences may be the shy or ill-at-ease children who have the ability but not the confidence to speak in the classroom. Others may come from homes where language is not used so extensively. Still others may have physical or mental impairments and need to be tested by a specialist in the appropriate area. For these and all of your children, you will want to provide rich language opportunities that allow the youngsters to hear sentences spoken and to respond.

If You Have Not Checked This Item: Some Helpful Ideas

■ Provide Dramatic Play Opportunities

Children's imaginative play is one of the best preschool activities to motivate and promote language growth in young children. Youngsters take on roles in which they must produce dialogue. Even the shy nonverbal child will learn by listening to the others. Be sure to schedule enough time for children to become involved in this pretending type of play. Take a role yourself in order to help the shy child join the others. But once he is involved, you should withdraw.

■ Go on Field Trips

Children need many real experiences with their world in order to process and use information in thinking and speaking. Give the youngsters many new things to think and talk about by going on field trips. These out-of-class experiences do not have to be elaborate or at distant locations. Have one adult take three children down to the corner store to buy something. Take a small group on a walk around the block to see how many different sounds they can hear. Be sure to take a tape recorder along to record sounds and play them back later. Go on a field trip to a tree every week in the spring or fall to see how it changes. You may want to take along an instant print camera to record the experience and to motivate talk about it back in the classroom. Be sure to use new vocabulary words to label the new things and ideas the children have experienced. Then use them over and over with the children.

Listen to children's own interests about their world. Have they ever really explored the building they are in? Do they know where the heat is produced? Young children are fascinated by things like furnaces, which adults take for granted. Take the children to see such things, and then listen to the sentences they produce.

❏ TAKES PART IN CONVERSATIONS WITH OTHER CHILDREN

If children feel comfortable in your classroom and have mastered the skill of speaking in expanded sentences, they also should be participating in conversations with the other children. As soon as they are able to converse with ease, their speaking ability will show even greater improvement from practice with their peers, some of whom may speak at a bit higher level. Once the basic rules of language are mastered, children improve in speaking most rapidly when in the presence of speakers whose abilities are just a bit higher than their own.

For this reason it is important to have mixed age groups in preschool programs. The younger children learn language skills from the older ones. The older children have an excellent opportunity to practice their skills with someone a bit younger. As noted previously, even children seem to be able to adapt their language level intuitively to less mature speakers, thus enabling younger children to improve their speech.

Just as the infant is predisposed to acquire her own language in a particular manner, she also seems to bring with her in life a preprogrammed way to learn the rules of conversation. Researchers have noted that infants as young as 10 weeks old are beginning to learn behaviors necessary for later conversation (Holzman, 1983, p. 3). For instance, in order to converse, speakers must listen to what someone says, speak one at a time, and then pause for the other speaker to have a turn.

Another interesting finding is that mothers seem to treat their baby's gestures, cries, coos, smiles, and babbling as meaningful contributions to a real conversation. An infant's arm may reach out toward her rattle. The mother responds by picking up and giving the rattle to the child, at the same time conducting the following conversation: "Oh, you want your rattle. Here it is. Here's your rattle." Baby takes the rattle and shakes it. Mother replies, "Yes, your rattle. Your nice rattle." Baby pauses to hear mother say this, shakes the rattle, and smiles. Then the baby pauses to hear the mother again respond: "Oh, you like your rattle. Shake your rattle." The baby shakes the rattle, and pauses once more for the mother's response. The mother smiles and nods her head in approval. "Shake, shake, shake," and so on. Thus the rules for conversation are learned long before the child can speak.

We may wonder, Who is reinforcing whom? The mother starts the conversation but the baby listens and replies with her physical response, which makes the mother say the next thing, and the baby responds again. It takes two to talk in conversations. Children learn this from infancy, unless there is no one to talk to or no one who will listen. Parents who do not talk to their children during this preverbal period of development make a great mistake. Children need to hear their native language being addressed to them from the moment they are born if we want to motivate them to become fluent speakers themselves.

You have undoubtedly heard that one of the best things caregivers of preschoolers can do is to read to their children. This is true. An even greater contribution to their development is to converse with children, to listen and respond to them in conversational speech. Because many mothers intuitively treat preverbal youngsters as real contributors to conversations, the youngsters eventually do become contributors.

You may have children who do not participate in peer conversations because they still are not confident enough. An additional reason could be the one just discussed: The children may not have learned to converse naturally at home in their earlier years.

Teachers need to spend time every day in conversations with small groups of children.

If You Have Not Checked This Item: Some Helpful Ideas

■ Converse with Your Children

Spend time every day in conversations with small groups of children. One of the best times is at snack or lunch. Be sure an adult sits at each of the children's tables and helps to carry on a conversation. Talk normally about anything that interests you or the children. You do not have to be the "teacher" who is teaching them the names of the fruits on the juice can. Instead, relax and enjoy your snack or meal with the children. Say the kinds of things you would at your own meal table at home. "Whew, isn't it hot today? I think summer is coming early." "What's that you say, Jamie, you like summertime best of all? Me, too. I love to swim and picnic." "You like to do that too, Jill?" " Yes, you are lucky to live next to the park."

■ Encourage Dramatic Play

Children's own conversations often take place in dramatic-play situations. Bring in props to encourage imaginative play in the housekeeping area, the block building area, and the water or sand table. Take props outside to encourage dramatic play there too.

■ Read a Book

Anna Maria's Blanket by Joanne Barkan (New York: Barron's, 1990) is an imaginary tale about a little girl's blanket that gets upset and talks back to her because she is going to nursery school and plans to leave the blanket behind. The story is one long conversation between Anna Maria and her blanket. Colorful realistic illustrations show Anna Maria playing with and caring for her doll and stuffed animal toys. She finally resolves the situation by showing the blanket how to be a baby-sitter when she is away.

❏ ASKS QUESTIONS WITH PROPER WORD ORDER

This language skill is another good indication that your children's command of language is developing normally. Most children are able to ask questions as adults do by about 4 years old. Before that they go through a predictable sequence in learning to ask questions, just as they do in other areas of development (McCormick & Schiefelbusch, 1984, p. 74).

Children usually do not learn to ask questions until they have learned to answer them. Between 18 months and 2 years of age, when they are putting a few words together to form primitive sentences, they also ask their first questions, if caregivers have been asking them questions first. The word order of these first questions is the same as a statement but with a rising intonation at the end: "Bobbie drink milk?" meaning, "May Bobbie have a drink of milk?" or "Should Bobbie drink his milk?"

Next they begin to learn the use of the "wh" words at the beginning of questions, words like *what, where,* and *who*: "Where Mama going?" meaning "Where is Mama going?" This type of question becomes quite popular because the adult generally responds, and suddenly the child realizes he has stumbled onto another way of controlling an adult: asking a question that the adult will answer. This is not always true with mere statements. Because he delights in the attention of adults and their responses to things that he originates, he will often burst into a period of questioning. It is not only that he wants to know the answer, but also that he wants the adult's attention.

The next stage in learning to ask questions comes as he expands his sentences to include auxiliary verbs such as *can* and *will*. These questions, though, are often expressed in inverted word order: "Where Daddy will go?" instead of "Where will Daddy go?"

The final stage is the expanded question in proper word order, which most children are able to ask at around 4 years: "Can I go with you?" "What are you doing?" "Why doesn't the light go on?"

If you discover through your observation that certain children have not yet attained this level, what will you do? Will you sit down with them and teach them how to ask a question correctly? If you have been reading this text carefully, you know that the answer is No. Young children do not develop language skills or most other developmental kinds of skills by being taught formally. How do they learn? They learn language just as they learn to develop their perceptual skills. They teach themselves proper word order by hearing the proper language forms spoken around them and by practicing it themselves when their physical and mental development has progressed to the point where it is possible for them to do so.

If You Have Not Checked This Item: Some Helpful Ideas

■ Ask Questions

If children do not ask questions correctly until they have learned to answer them, then you need to include your own asking of questions in your activities with the children. Circle time is a good time for everyone to hear the proper word order of questions, and to volunteer to answer the inquiries if so inclined. Even the children who are not at the point of answering questions in front of a group will learn by listening.

■ Ask Children to Help You Gather Answers to Questions

You can ask a child to question three or four other children for some information you need. For example, if you are planning a field trip, you might ask several children to go around asking others if one of their parents would like to come along. This may not be the most accurate way to gather this information, but it provides excellent practice in questioning skills, and you can always check the accuracy of the information with the parents later.

■ Read a Book

A number of children's picture books have questions in the title or the text. Read these books with your children and give them a chance to answer the question asked or to make up similar questions of their own.

Where Does the Butterfly Go When It Rains? by May Garelick (New York: Scholastic, 1961) is a rhyming story about where various animals, birds, and insects go to get out of the rain. The book contains many questions that are asked and answered, with the exception of the question in the title. This format should motivate a discussion of how people find out such answers.

Whose Footprints? by Molly Coxe (New York: Crowell, 1990) shows a little country girl and her mother going out into the snow and wondering whose footprints they are seeing. They follow different footprints one after the other and find a cat, a rooster, a mouse, a pony, a sheep, a dog, and themselves.

The 2 Ton Canary & Other Nonsense Riddles by Polly Cameron (New York: Coward, McCann & Geoghegan, 1965) is a wonderfully crazy riddle book full of riddle questions on every other page. Most are elephant jokes or animal riddles such as, What is grey, has four legs and a trunk? Answer: A mouse on vacation. Many of the children may not have the cognitive understanding to get the point of the answers, but it really does not matter. The book with its outlandish grey and red illustrations is so much fun, and the children love to repeat the riddle questions, which is the real point for reading it to them.

Hey, Riddle, Diddle! by Rodney Peppe (New York: Puffin Books, 1971) is a more traditional riddle book in rhyming verses and questions with clear illustrations that give clues to the answers. Children love to guess, What has a face but cannot see? Answer: A clock.

❏ MAKES "NO" RESPONSES WITH PROPER WORD ORDER

As with questions, making "No" responses with proper word order is another sentence cue that can help you determine whether children are on target in their language development. By about 4 years of age, they should be producing statements containing negatives just as adults do.

The child's development of negative sentences parallels that of questions, because many questions must be answered in the negative. As soon as she understands the use of *yes* and *no*, the young child usually includes them in her utterances. *No* is especially popular when she finds out—probably to her great astonishment—that she can cause adults to respond with vigor when she says, "No". Using *yes* has a lesser effect, so she delights in saying no, no matter what she really means.

The discovery of the effect of using *no* happens around 2 years of age. Much of the theme song of "the terrible 2s" is based on the toddler's use of *no*. What would happen if adult caregivers refused to respond as they usually do to such negative declarations? What would happen if the adult caregivers just ignored the 2-year-old's *no* declarations? Why don't you try it and find out!

Once they understand the use of *no* and *not* at around 2 years, children begin to use these negatives in simple phrases: "No do it," meaning, "I won't do it." "Not more milk," meaning, "I don't want any more milk."

By age 3 or 3-and-a-half many children have learned contractions: *don't, can't, won't, isn't, ain't.* Children often use such contractions in sentences with inverted word order: "Why me can't go out?" instead of, "Why can't I go out?" (McCormick & Schiefelbusch, p. 75). Through hearing others speak with proper order and by practicing it themselves, children come to learn the mainstream manner of speaking.

If children are not exposed to standard English in their homes, however, they will come to your center speaking the language or dialect used at home. Again, it is not up to you to correct their speech. Instead, you will be providing them with many opportunities to listen to and engage in the speaking of standard English. Table 11.1 summarizes the language accomplishments of children from birth through age 6 years.

If You Have Not Checked This Item: Some Helpful Ideas

■ Have Question-and-Answer Discussions

At circle time, or with a small group, ask "why" questions containing negatives such as: "Why can't cats get down out of trees as easily as cats climb up?" "Why don't we

TABLE 11.1
Language development

Age	Articulation	Expanded Sentences	Questions	Negative Responses
0–1	Pronounces first word near end of first year or beginning of second year	Uses one word to express different meanings		
1–2	Uses only 10 basic sounds at first	Realizes everything has a name; expands vocabulary; speaks in two-word sentences	Asks first questions; uses same word order as for statements (e.g., "Bobby go?")	Uses *no* alone
2–3	Uses only 10 basic sounds	Uses telegraphic speech (e.g., "Me go store.")	Uses question words *what*, *where,* and *who*	Uses *no* and *not* tagged onto simple phrases
3–4	Has mastered most sounds but may have problems with a few: *s, l, r, th,* and *sk*	Uses proper word order consistently in statements	Uses *can* and *will* in questions, sometimes with inverted word order	Uses negative contractions *don't, can't, won't, isn't, ain't;* inverts word order sometimes
4–5	Has mastered most sounds but may have problems with a few: *s, l, r, th,* and *sk*	Has mastered basic rules for expanding sentences	Asks questions in adult manner	Produces negative statements in adult manner
5–6	Most children of this age speak in a mature adult manner.			

usually see the moon in the daytime?" "Why can't you ride a two-wheel bike as easily as you ride a trike?" Some of their answers should contain the proper use of negatives. Make up your own questions with negatives, based on your children's interests.

■ Read a Book

Pierre by Maurice Sendak (New York: Harper & Row, 1962) is one of the tiny Nutshell Library books. It tells a rhyming story about a little boy, Pierre, who "doesn't care." His parents ask him to do many things, all of which he refuses by saying, "I don't care."

❏ USES PAST TENSE VERBS CORRECTLY

Linguists have learned how children construct their own knowledge about language by listening to the particular errors children make at the various stages of their development. Because the errors are different from those of mature speakers, and because the language of young children is different from the language they hear from adults, we know that children learn language by methods other than pure imitation. Cognitive scientists believe that young children spontaneously extract rules about language from the language they hear around them. Then they apply those rules to all similar situations.

A case in point is the rule in the English language for putting *ed* at the end of regular verbs to make them past tense. A child hears adults in his environment saying walk*ed*, dress*ed*, look*ed*, hop*ed*, want*ed*, and need*ed* when speaking about past actions. He somehow comes to understand that they are talking about past time. His brain encodes this information as a rule to be applied when you talk about something that happened in the past. Then he begins applying this rule to every past tense situation he talks about, without realizing there are many exceptions in English to the adding-*ed*-for-past-tense rule.

He says things like "I eated," "I runned," "She goed home," "I seed the man," "My leg hurted"—forms he never heard an adult say. From this construction, we learn that children do indeed create their own grammar rules. The children do not create their own grammar rules from imitating mature speakers, because mature speakers do not talk this way. Because all children make these same errors in the same sequence and at about the same time during their language development period, we realize that the human brain must be preorganized to take in language information and sort it out like this. Applying a past tense rule like this to every past tense verb, even the irregular ones, is called *overgeneralizing* or *overregularizing*.

Young children do the same thing with other general rules their brains have extracted. Once they learn that plurals are formed by adding *s*, they say "boys" and "girls," but then they overgeneralize the rule, also saying things like "tooths" instead of "teeth" and "foots" instead of "feet."

Children's brains seem to be preconditioned to absorb information about things, then to extract rules from the way the information seems to work, and finally to apply the rules to similar things. This process is called *inductive reasoning*. Preschool children who are allowed to play with computers also learn to use the computers in the same way. The youngsters induce rules about how a computer program works from working with it. Then they play around with the program, making mistakes, trying again, and finally figuring out what to do. This process is an effective method for self-learning. Perhaps this is the reason that many adults, who tend to think deductively, have trouble learning to use the computer, whereas children seldom do.

When children are at the overgeneralizing stage in language production, there is not much adults can do—or should do—to correct the youngsters. You can ask a child to say "ran" instead of "runned" over and over, but somehow it always comes out as, "I runned home." To learn the proper formation of past tense verbs, the child will need more than just hearing verbs used correctly at this stage; she will need time.

Be patient. When the brain matures, the child will discriminate more finely with word use, just as she does with motor coordination. Provide her with a rich language environment where she will hear competent speakers and will participate in all kinds of speaking activities herself.

If You Have Not Checked This Item: Some Helpful Ideas

■ Use Tape Recorders

Help children learn how to listen to and record tape cassettes on their own. Then provide the youngsters with some motivation for taping. You could start a story on the tape and ask an interested child to finish it. Have several tapes for as many as want to record. Play the tapes to a small group later. You might start something like: "As I was coming to school today, I heard a very strange noise. It sounded a little like a train. It sounded like it was coming around the corner. I felt like running away, but I didn't. Instead, I. . . ."

■ Use Toy Telephones

Have at least two toy telephones in your classroom for children to use for pretend conversations.

■ Read a Book

Children eventually learn the correct English forms by hearing them spoken. Reading books or telling stories aloud is yet another way to fill the environment with the spoken language. *Cloudy with a Chance of Meatballs* by Judi Barrett (New York: Atheneum, 1978) is a hilarious tall tale of a world where food falls from the sky. The story might motivate your children to make up their own tall tales. They may want to record their own stories.

❑ PLAYS WITH RHYMING WORDS

Just as they play with blocks, toys, and each other, children also play with words. Youngsters make up nonsense words, repeat word sounds, mix up words, say things backward, make up chants, and repeat rhyming words. Most people pay little attention to this activity, because it seems so inconsequential. What we have not seemed to realize is that through this playful activity, children are once more at work creating their own knowledge. This time the content is language rather than cognitive concepts, and this time the child is manipulating the medium (words) with his voice rather than his hands or body. Once again, he is structuring his experiences by finding out what words do and what he can do with them. Play is once more the vehicle because of the pleasure it gives him.

All children play with words, especially in the early stages of language development, but of course there are great individual differences in the amount of language play you will witness among your children. We do know that children who are involved in rhyming activities at an early age carry over this interest in poetry into adult life (Caplan & Caplan, 1983, p.41), and that children who have had early experience with nursery rhymes are more successful later in reading than children who have not. It behooves us, then, to observe children's language play and to provide encouragement and support for all youngsters to become more involved with word play.

Although mothers often promote language play with their infants by playing word and action games with them such as patty-cake and peekaboo, much language play is solitary. Children carry on monologues in which they manipulate sounds, patterns, and meanings of words. These three areas (i.e., sounds, patterns, and meanings) have, in fact, been identified by specialists as common types of word play (Schwartz, 1981, pp. 16–26).

Infants from 6 to 18 months often "talk" to themselves before going to sleep, repeating rhythmic and rhyming sounds. The infants sound almost as if they are really talking, only with nonsense words. With older children, sound play contains more meaningful words, consonants, and blends. The children often repeat these words in nonsensical fashion: "Ham, bam, lamb, Sam, wham, wham, wham."

Pattern play is a common form of play that involves manipulating the structure of the language. The child begins with a pattern and then substitutes a new word each time he says it: "Bobby go out; Mommy go out; Daddy go out; doggie go out." or "Bite it; write it; light it; sight it; night it; fight it."

Meaning play is not as common among younger children, but it is really more interesting. Here the child interchanges real with nonsensical meanings or makes up words or meanings. An interesting example Schwartz found was children doing water play with floating and sinking objects, and telling the objects to "sink-up," meaning *float*, or "sink-down" (1981, pp. 19–20).

Piaget describes much of the talk of 3- to-5-year-olds as egocentric. It is as if much of their speaking is not directed to anyone in particular, but produced for their own pleasure. Some children go around muttering to themselves most of the day, especially when they are involved in an interesting activity. The muttering seems to disappear by the time they enter public school, but it may become inner speech instead (Caplan & Caplan, 1983, p. 41).

Are any of the children in your class engaged in word play? They will be if you sponsor or promote it. Do finger plays and body-action chants with the children during circle time or for transitions between activities. Read children's poems and nursery rhymes to the youngsters. Use tape recorders to stimulate the children's own made up rhymes.

If You Have Not Checked This Item: Some Helpful Ideas

■ **Read a Book**

Rhymes and Verses

There are many traditional nursery rhyme books on the market. Children still enjoy hearing and repeating nursery rhymes.

Mother Goose illustrated by Aurelius Battaglia (New York: Random House, 1973) is a traditional Mother Goose with illustrations of medieval people and animals.

The Bedtime Mother Goose pictures by Ron Himler (New York: Golden Press, 1980) has some seldom heard Mother Goose rhymes with illustrations of early American children.

Old Mother Hubbard and Her Wonderful Dog illustrated by James Marshall (New York: Farrar, Straus & Giroux, 1991) is a nineties' version of the traditional nursery rhyme with hilarious illustrations showing dog and dame in their various posturings.

Dogs & Dragons, Trees & Dreams by Karla Kuskin (New York: Harper & Row, 1980) is one of a number of poetry books by this popular author. Long and short, rhyming and not, the poems in this collection are full of word plays, questions and answers, and humor. Children will enjoy listening to and repeating the poems.

Ride a Purple Pelican by Jack Prelutsky, illustrated by Garth Williams (New York: Greenwillow, 1986) shows Cincinnati Patty, Kangaroos from Kalamazoo, and 26 other rollicking rhymers with a full-page picture of each opposite their verse. Prelutsky is another favorite children's poet.

Sound Play

Certain children's books are especially attractive to their audience because of one or two words that sound funny to children. The youngsters often go into spasms of laughter upon hearing them, and want the book read again and again.

Mert the Blurt by Robert Kraus (New York: Simon & Schuster, 1980) is one. Little Mert can't keep anything to himself, but goes around blurting out fanciful family secrets to a colorful host of neighbors.

My Orange Gorange by Judith Fitzgerald (Windsor, Ontario: Black Moss Press, 1985) is a nonsense poem by a little girl who can't find a word to rhyme with *orange*.

A Snake is Totally Tail by Judi Barrett (New York: Macmillan, 1983) is a book of illustrations of animals, with an alliterated line of text at the bottom of each picture, similar to the title. Children enjoy playing with the funny descriptions such as, "A skunk is oodles of odor."

Pattern Play

My Name Is Alice by Jane Bayer (New York: Dutton, 1984) is an alphabet book containing a pattern verse for each letter, much like a jump-rope rhyme. For example: "A. My name is Alice and my husband's name is Alex. We come from Alaska and we sell ants."

Silly Sally by Audrey Wood (San Diego: Harcourt Brace Jovanovich, 1992) is a hilarious pattern play story of Silly Sally walking backwards, upside down to town through shining fields of yellow buttercups, meeting a pig, a dog, a loon, and a sheep, who join her silly capers.

Meaning Play

Rugs Have Naps (But Never Take Them) By Charles Klasky (Chicago: Children's Press, 1984) is a book of nonsense phrases and illustrations with funny double meanings.

The Surprise Party by Pat Hutchins (New York: Collier Books, 1969) is a delightfully mixed-up communication muddle like the game Gossip. Here, rabbit whispers to owl that he is having a party tomorrow and it's a surprise. The message is passed on from one animal to another in such a garbled form that it truly is a surprise for all in the end. Children love the nonsensical phrases that the animals repeat, and may want to try them on their own.

OBSERVING, RECORDING, AND INTERPRETING SPOKEN LANGUAGE

The Spoken Language Checklist results for Sheila, as illustrated in Figure 11.1, were much as the teachers in her classroom had predicted. Every item was checked except for "Takes part in conversations with other children." Although Sheila spoke to other children, it was rarely in the form of conversation, but more often a command or a complaint. Because Sheila showed evidence of "Speaks confidently in classroom," the staff members felt that Sheila eventually would join in with other children in classroom activities, including conversation. In fact, Sheila's language skill could be used to help her become involved with the others. The teachers made plans for Sheila to tell several other children, one at a time, how to use the computer program *Stickybear ABC* (Norfolk, CT: Optimum Resource, 1982) that the preschool had recently acquired.

FIGURE 11.1

Spoken language observations for Sheila

Child Skills Checklist

Name _Sheila — Age 3_ **Observer** _Connie R._

Program _Head Start_ **Dates** _10-22_

Directions:

Put a ✔ for items you see the child perform regularly. Put *N* for items where there is no opportunity to observe. Leave all other items blank.

Item	Evidence	Date
9. Spoken Language ✓ Speaks confidently in the classroom	Makes loud statements and talks to teacher with confidence	10/22
✓ Speaks clearly enough for adults to understand	Adults can understand her clearly	
✓ Speaks in expanded sentences	"She ate my orange crayon so I can't finish my pumpkin."	10/22
___ Takes part in conversations with other children	Speaks to others but does not converse	10/22
✓ Asks questions with proper word order	Yes	10/22
✓ Makes "No" responses with proper word order	Yes	10/22
✓ Uses past tense verbs correctly	Yes. Says "Becky painted yesterday"	10/22
✓ Plays with rhyming words	Likes to repeat rhyming verses — "See you later, alligator."	10/22

REFERENCES

Caplan, Theresa, & Frank Caplan. (1983). *The early childhood years: The 2- to 6-year-old.* New York: Putnam.

Eisenson, Jon. (1976). *Is your child's speech normal?* Reading, MA: Addison-Wesley.

Holzman, Mathilda. (1983). *The language of children.* Englewood Cliffs, NJ: Prentice-Hall.

McCormick, Linda, & Richard L. Schiefelbusch. (1984). *Early language intervention.* New York: Merrill/Macmillan.

Schwartz, Judith I. (1981). Children's experiments with language. *Young Children, 36*(5), 16–26.

OTHER SOURCES

Beaty, Janice J. (1992). *Skills for preschool teachers.* New York: Merrill/Macmillan.

Berk, Laura E. (1985). Why children talk to themselves. *Young Children, 40*(5), 46–52.

Dumtschin, Joyce Ury. (1988). Recognize language development and delay in early childhood. *Young Children, 43*(3), 16–24.

Genishi, Celia. (1988). Children's language: Learning words from experience. *Young Children, 44*(1), 16–23.

Hughes, Fergus P. (1991). *Children, play, and development.* Boston: Allyn & Bacon.

Mussen, Paul Henry, John Janeway Conger, Jerome Kagan, & Aletha Carol Huston. (1990). *Child development and personality.* New York: Harper & Row.

Siegler, Robert S. (1986). *Children's thinking.* Englewood Cliffs, NJ: Prentice-Hall.

Soto, Lourdes Diaz. (1991). Understanding bilingual/bicultural young children. *Young Children, 46*(2), 30–36.

LEARNING ACTIVITIES

1. Use the *Child Skills Checklist* section "Spoken Language" as a screening tool to observe all of the children in your classroom. Which of your children seem to need help in more than one of the items? How do these children fare in the various areas of cognitive development (Chapters 9 and 10)?

2. Choose a child who seems to be having difficulty with spoken language and observe him or her on three different days, keeping a running record of the child's language activities. Compare the results with the Spoken Language Checklist results. How do you interpret the evidence you have collected? Are there any pieces of evidence that are still missing about this child's language performance?

3. Choose a child whom you have screened as needing help in several of the Spoken Language Checklist items, and carry out one or more of the activities listed. Record the results.

4. Teach the children a finger play or rhyming game. How did the children perform whom you noted as needing help in this area?

5. Do a tape recorder activity with a small group of children. Have them tape-record their own words and then play them back. They may want to tell about themselves, tell a story, or say a verse.

12 Prewriting and Prereading Skills

Prewriting and Prereading Checklist

❑ Pretends to write by scribbling horizontally

❑ Includes features of real letters in scribbling

❑ Writes real alphabet letters

❑ Writes words with invented spelling

❑ Retells stories from books with increasing accuracy

❑ Shows awareness that print in books tells story

❑ Attempts to match telling of story with print in book

❑ Wants to know what particular print says

W hy should a chapter on children's writing and reading skills be included in a book on observing the development of preschool children? Surely learning to write and to read has little to do with early child development, does it? Teaching children to write and read should come later, when children are in first grade, shouldn't it? The answers to all of these questions are quite different today from what they would have been as recently as 15 or 20 years ago.

A great deal of research has been completed about how writing and reading are learned, about how children make sense of their world through playful exploration, and about how children's brains take in this information and extract rules from it to help the children use it. Such research has changed our minds forever about the way children develop and how we can best support their growth.

We know now that writing and reading are outgrowths of the same communication urge that drives children to express themselves orally and even pictorially. We also know that, given the proper tools and support, all children everywhere go through the same sequence of stages in teaching themselves to write and to read. Learning to write and to read is indeed as much a natural part of a child's development as learning to talk. Child development specialists are finally coming to realize that "learning to write is largely an act of discovery," as one specialist puts it (Temple, Nathan, & Burris, 1982, p. 2).

The term used currently to describe children's natural development of writing and reading skills is *emergent literacy*. Scholars studying child development have this to say about it:

> In both oral and written language systems, children construct personally meaningful rule systems based on their developing understandings of oral and written language surrounding them in their daily life experiences. (Schrader & Hoffman, 1987, p. 9)

From these personal rule systems, children teach themselves to talk (see Chapter 11) and also to write and read, as we will discuss in this chapter.

Thus, writing and reading join language, thinking, emotional, social, and motor skills as other aspects of development that children can arrive at *on their own* by playfully experimenting with the materials in their environment.

This does not mean, however, that writing and reading development always occurs naturally in all children. Many youngsters come from families with few toys, let alone books for reading or the tools for writing. Furthermore, most parents are unaware that their children can develop these skills without being taught. Children need their parents' encouragement as well as their parents' expectations that they can develop writing and reading skills naturally. But in addition, children need to practice writing and reading skills over time, just as they do running or speaking.

Without tools to write with at home, preschoolers can do little more than make marks on steamy windows or scratches in the dirt. Without books to look at, preschoolers have little motivation to try reading. Without parent expectations that they should be experimenting with writing and reading on their own, children may never try it.

On the other hand, this does not mean that teachers should sit down with preschool children and formally teach them how to write and read, any more than they should formally teach them how to walk and talk. Cognitive scientists worry that preschool teachers who are in a critical position for nurturing in young children the "roots of literacy," may not know how to do it.

> When teachers are unfamiliar with current knowledge about the natural development of literacy in young children, they impose skill-oriented expectations and tasks on these youngsters—copying and tracing standard adult print, for example. Such activities not only are stressful for three-, four-, and five-year-old children, but they do not afford children the opportunity to use their self-constructed knowledge in meaningful ways. (Schrader & Hoffman, 1987, p. 13)

Instead, we should be filling the children's environment with examples of written language and books; we should serve as models by doing a great deal of writing and reading ourselves in the presence of the children; and we should provide them with the tools and encouragement to attempt writing and reading on their own.

Although the natural development of writing and of reading occurs simultaneously in children, this chapter discusses writing first and then reading.

Do any of your children pretend to write, perhaps at the easel, by scribbling rows of markings? Make an assessment of all of the children in your classroom by using the first four items of the Prewriting and Prereading Skills Checklist. Then set up a writing table, an easel, or a writing area complete with a variety of writing tools, and watch what happens.

❏ PRETENDS TO WRITE BY SCRIBBLING HORIZONTALLY

The first natural attempts to write by young children are usually scribbles. Initial scribbling is also done at the outset in art, you may point out. Yet children as young as 3 years seem to recognize the difference between writing scribbles and drawing scribbles. In fact, some children do drawing scribbles on one part of the paper and writing scribbles that "tell about the picture," on another part (Vukelich & Golden, 1984, p. 4). The two kinds of scribbles look completely different.

Writing scribbles are usually done in a horizontal linear manner across the page, something like a line of writing. The children who make writing scribbles seem to understand that writing is something that can be read, and they sometimes pretend to read their scribbled writing. This is the first step in the natural acquisition of writing. Once their scribbles have become horizontal lines instead of circular or aimless meanderings, they are indicating they understand that writing is something different from drawing.

Their first scribbles do not resemble letters or words at all. The children, in fact, seem to have extracted only the broad general features of the writing system: that it is arranged in rows across a page and that it consists of a series of loops, tall sticks, and connected lines that are repeated. Only later will children differentiate the finer features of the system: the letters and words.

Where have they acquired this knowledge of written language so early in life? Look around you. They, like all of us, are surrounded by written material in newspapers and magazines, on television advertising, on food product labels, in letters in the mail, in the stories read to them, on store signs, on greeting cards, on car bumper stickers, and on T-shirts. The printed word is everywhere. In the terminology of reading specialists, this writing is called *environmental print*.

Some families, of course, encourage their children to print their own names at an early age, and may even take time to write out creative stories their young children tell them. Some children have older brothers or sisters who bring written material home from school. Some children come from homes with computers. These children see family members engaged in writing or reading and want to become involved themselves.

Observe to discover which of your children do pretend writing, this first step in the writing process. Which ones have progressed beyond this beginning? Which have not yet started?

If You Have Not Checked This Item: Some Helpful Ideas

■ Set Up a Writing Area

Most children will not try to become involved in writing if there is no evidence of writing in their environment. Set up a special writing table with all of the necessary implements, and you will soon have a group of budding writers.

It is best to provide unlined sheets of paper for the children. They will be placing their scribbles and pretend letters all over the page, and lined paper may inhibit this free-form exploration of how writing works. Use typing paper or stationery as well as tablets and pads of different sizes and colors. You may want to have an individual notebook for each child with his or her name on the front.

Include a variety of writing tools. We sometimes think of pencils first, but research with beginning writers shows that pencils are the most difficult of all writing implements to manipulate effectively (Lamme, 1979, p. 22). Children themselves choose colored felt-tip markers as their favorites. You should also include colored chalk and a small chalkboard, crayons, and a few pencils in addition to the markers. It is not necessary to have only the large primary-size pencils. Some preschoolers have great difficulty handling these thick pencils and much prefer to use regular pencils. Put out a variety of writing tools, and children will find out on their own what works best for them.

Voluntary participation in writing activities should, of course, be the rule in your program. Some children need to develop better eye-hand coordination before they engage in writing. They might learn more from painting at the easel or playing with the utensils you have put out at the water or sand tables instead. If the youngsters can build a tall block tower without its toppling over, can drive a nail straight into a piece of wood, or can use a pair of scissors with ease, then their eye-hand coordination is probably developed enough for them to use a writing implement—as long as they choose to.

■ Encourage Children to Write Messages

Children can write messages in "pretend writing" to other children, to their parents, or to you. Have youngsters write notes to their parents inviting them to visit the classroom, or write a block corner sign asking other children to leave their buildings standing. If you want (or if the children ask), you can write the real words under the scribble writing. This is not necessary, though. Most children know what their scribbled messages say, and they can tell this to the message recipients. Specialists who are studying young children's emergent literacy call these early writing attempts *personal script*, whereas mature writing is known as *conventional script*. By using these terms, you can avoid telling children their writing is not real or is nothing but scribbles.

■ Support the Children's Efforts

You need to praise the children for their efforts in all the writing they do, just as you praise them for their art. Mount samples of their writing on the wall as you do for the children's art. You also may want to save samples of this stage of their writing, keeping it in a portfolio or the scrapbook you are making to show each child's accomplishments. Be sure to date these samples so that you will be able to compare them with later samples.

❏ INCLUDES FEATURES OF REAL LETTERS IN SCRIBBLING

Just as an infant's babbling finally begins to take the sound of real talking, so a child's first linear scribblings eventually begin to look like real writing. For many children the lines of their scribbles become somewhat jagged and then finally take on features of real letters such as straight, curved, and intersecting lines, although no real letters are formed (Schickedanz, 1982, p. 243). Linguists call this *linear mock writing* (Temple et al., 1982, p. 29). This advanced scribbling happens as a natural developmental sequence when children have the freedom and opportunity to experiment with writing on their own. Teaching, in fact, has little or no effect at this point in the children's development.

Children extract the elements of writing from their environment and play around with these elements using markers and paper. Once again, youngsters are manipulating the medium (writing) until they have learned how to handle it, what it can do, and what they are able do with it. Just as they do when they first learn to climb stairs, put together a puzzle, or ride a trike, they want to practice over and over. Many children fill pages with this pretend writing, and take great satisfaction in doing so. This activity provides wonderful practice for them in learning to control the writing tool as well.

Children often think this scribbling is something meaningful. If this is writing, they reason, then someone who knows how to read should be able to read it. Often they will take a piece of mock writing to an adult and ask her to read it. How should you respond? Be honest about it. "Oh, Sharon, your writing is beginning to look almost real. Can you tell me what it says?" Some children really have a story in mind when they do their mock writing, and they will be able to tell it to you. Others think that their "words" must speak only to someone who can read.

Researchers, however, see something very important when they analyze children's mock writing:

> Though mock letters clearly are not alphabet letters, they do reveal progress in children's development from scribbling to writing. DeFord (1980) carefully analyzed mock letter forms and found that they reveal the following concepts of letter form: symmetry, uniformity of size and shape, inner complexity, left-to-right directionality, linearity, and appropriate placement. (Hayes, 1990, p. 62)

Observe to see which of your children are at this stage in their experimental writing. What can you do to help them progress further?

If You Have Not Checked This Item: Some Helpful Ideas

■ Use Sand or Salt Trays or Finger Painting

Put out small trays of sand or salt in your writing area so that children can practice "writing" with their fingers. It is easy to "erase" this writing simply by shaking the tray. Finger-painting on tabletops or paper also gives the children practice doing linear mock writing with their fingers.

■ Have Children Sign Up for Turns

Children can use their mock writing to sign up for turns to use the computer, to play with blocks, to paint at the easel, or to ride a wheeled vehicle. Put small clipboards or sign-up sheets at the entrances to your activity areas, next to the computer or easels, or wherever children need to take turns in the classroom. Tie a pencil to each clipboard and tell the children to put their names under the one above. Have them cross off their names after they have finished their turns, so that the next person can have a turn. Some children can already print their name or initials. If other children say they cannot write their names, tell them to try. Tell them to use their personal script just as they do at the writing table. They will remember which personal scribble is theirs when it is time for their turn. It is important that children understand that you consider their scribbles as real writing. Then they will continue in their developmental sequence on their own.

■ Be a Writing Model

Do a lot of writing in the presence of the children. If they see that writing is important to you, they will want to do it too. If you are doing *Checklist* recording or running records in their presence, children will often want to use your pen and paper to do some pretend writing themselves. Don't give up your writing tools; instead, be sure you have a well-equipped writing table from which they can get their own recording notebook. Serving as a writing model will almost always stimulate certain of your children to try their own hand at writing.

■ Read a Book

We Are Best Friends by Aliki Brandenberg (New York: Mulberry Books, 1982) tells the story of Robert and his best friend, Peter, who moves away. They communicate by printed and illustrated letters. Books showing written communication like this help motivate children to try their own letter writing. How is theirs different from Peter's and Robert's?

Dear Zoo by Rod Campbell (New York: Viking Penguin, 1982) is an action book in which a child has written to the zoo to send him a pet, and each page has a different kind of container that the reader has to open to see what the zoo has sent. The containers all have white tags that read, "From the zoo."

❑ WRITES REAL ALPHABET LETTERS

Just as the 1-year-old begins to say wordlike sounds that parents recognize as words, the preschooler begins to make letterlike scribbles. When adults see this, they often point it out: "Oh, Hilary, you made an *l* in your writing, see! Yes, you did it again. Do you know that you have an *l* in your name?" Many children have been taught to print the letters in their names. This is different. Scribbles evolve more like cursive writing. But as the child realizes that her scribbles are being recognized by adults as real letters, she tries to make real letters by printing them.

Although adults often intervene at this point, children still learn alphabet letters on their own by being surrounded by letters and hearing them used. The youngsters' own names are often the first source. Children may learn to say the letters in their names soon after they recognize their name sign on their cubby. Many children are then able to identify those particular letters wherever they see them.

Reciting or chanting the ABCs is not the same. Just as children can chant the numbers from 1 to 10, but not understand what any of the numbers mean, so preschoolers often chant the alphabet without the slightest idea of what they are saying. Programs like "Sesame Street," of course, teach children the letter names, and some youngsters may have learned letters from this technique, although it is a more passive and formal method.

Other children may have learned alphabet letters from a personal computer at home or in the classroom. A number of software programs feature alphabet games for children 2 to 6 years of age. In many ways, computers are superior to television as a learning tool because children are actively and playfully involved in their own learning. Computers should be used playfully with young children, rather than in formal lessons. Children should be allowed to use a classroom computer during free choice period just as they are allowed to use blocks or dolls or the water table.

Also be sure to have alphabet games on the shelves of your manipulative area; alphabet letters mounted on the wall at children's eye level; alphabet books in the book area; and wooden, plastic, sandpaper, or magnetic alphabet letters available for the children to play with. Play alphabet games with the youngsters, but do not teach the alphabet formally. You will find that if you have filled the children's environment with letters, children will teach themselves alphabet letters. Formal teaching, even of the alphabet, is not appropriate during the preschool years because this is not how young children learn.

In recognizing alphabet letters, children progress through a particular sequence just as they do in learning to make speech sounds naturally. The first distinctive feature children seem to recognize is whether the line that makes the letter is straight or curved. Letters that are round, such as *O* and *C,* are distinguished first. Then letters with curved lines, such as *P* and *S,* are noted. Next, curved letters with intersections, such as *B* and *R,* are distinguished from curved letters without intersections, like *S* and *J.* Letters with diagonal lines, such as *K* and *X,* are among the last to be recognized (Schickedanz, 1982, p. 311). This pattern follows the one we noted earlier in Chapter 9, that young children also have difficulty distinguishing shapes with diagonal lines and so they are the last ones to be identified.

As children begin to print letters, their first attempts are usually flawed. Youngsters make the same mistakes in writing letters that they do in recognizing letters; that is, they often overlook the letter's distinguishing features. Development of children's written language, as with their other aspects of development, progresses from the general to the particular. Until they are able to perceive the finer distinctions in letters, they will have difficulty making letters that are accurate in all the details.

Let the children practice on their own. Pointing out errors is not really productive, just as it was not in their development of spoken language. In time their errors will become less frequent as the children refine their perception of individual letters and gain control over their writing tools.

One of the children's problems in printing letters correctly has to do with the orientation of the letters in space. Children are often able to get the features of the letters accurate, but not the orientation of the letters. Children reverse some letters, and some they even write upside down. Occasionally their letters are facing the right

The first distinctive feature that children recognize naturally is whether a letter is curved or straight. Round letters such as *C* and *O* are distinguished first.

direction, but just as often their printing may be a complete mirror image of the real thing.

Part of the answer may lie in the fact that children have already learned that an object's orientation—that is, the direction it faces—makes no difference in identifying the object. For instance, a cup is a cup no matter whether the handle is pointing toward or away from a person. A flashlight may be lying horizontally or standing on end, but it is still a flashlight. Objects, in other words, do not change their identity when they face a different direction.

Letters do, however. Letters made with the same features are completely different depending on the direction they face and whether their vertical lines are at the top or bottom. If children's brains have not extracted these orientation rules for distinguishing letters, they are sure to have trouble identifying and printing such letters as *d, b, p,* and *q.* All four of these letters are made with the same curved and straight lines. Yet it may take some years for children to get their orientation straight. Children often reverse letters even into the elementary grades.

One of the problems in children's playing with three-dimensional alphabet letters is the fact that the letters can be reversed or turned upside down. If you have such letters in your writing area, be sure to have real alphabet letters mounted on the nearby wall at child's eye level so that the youngsters can easily see the letters' proper orientation. Magnetic letters are better than letter blocks or plastic letters in this respect. At least the magnetic letters cannot be turned back to front when placed on a metal backing.

Another detail children sometimes overlook when they first print letters is whether the letters are open or closed: for example, the difference between O and C. This visual discrimination problem may have to do with children's perception of space and their difficulty in making enclosures as discussed in Chapter 9. The youngsters, in fact, may not really see this detail at first. With practice and maturity, children resolve these problems themselves unless they have a learning impairment. Your best strategy is to fill the environment with words, letters, and occasions to write, as well as to support and encourage the children's own attempts at writing. But do not formally teach them.

If You Have Not Checked This Item: Some Helpful Ideas

■ Make Alphabet Letters Personal

Children always learn in a more meaningful way if the subject is somehow connected to them. Help children to recognize the first letter in their own first name by playing games with it. You can have letter cards on string necklaces that the youngsters can hang around their necks. Let the children find their own letters. Then let the youngsters see if they can find any other child with a letter like theirs. Be sure to have enough similar letters, and make them big enough so that everyone can see them easily.

■ Provide Alphabet Cards

Let children play with alphabet cards having a picture of an object on them. In that way the youngsters will be seeing the letter in the proper orientation. The object on the card will also give them a clue to the name of the letter. It is best to show both upper- and lowercase letters on the cards. Then children will see that each letter can be written in two different ways. It is not helpful for children to use only capital letters, since they will need to write in lowercase in the elementary grades.

■ Provide a Typewriter

Bring in a manual typewriter for the children to experiment with. Children love to play with letters and words that they can type. Let the youngsters teach themselves how to use it. They will need to investigate the keyboard to find each letter they want, and then learn to press one key at a time to print their letters.

■ Use Computer Alphabet Games

Computer alphabet programs are good introductory programs for young children who need to learn to locate letters on the computer keyboard. Be sure the programs are simple, colorful games, not lessons, using single letter keys from the entire keyboard to bring up an appropriate animated graphic on the color monitor screen when the letter key is pressed. *Stickybear ABC* (Norfolk, CT: Optimum Resource, 1982), *Mickey's ABC's* (New York: Walt Disney Computer Software, 1990), and *Talking Alpha Chimp* (Pound Ridge, NY: Orange Cherry Software) are simple alphabet games. *Muppets on Stage* (Pleasantville, NY: Sunburst Communications, 1984) consists of letter recognition games; *Sesame Street Letter-Go-Round* (New York: Hi Tech Expressions, 1984) is a letter matching game with a ferris wheel.

■ **Read an Appropriate Alphabet Book**

There are many good alphabet books on the market, but you first will need to review any you plan to use with your children to see if the books are appropriate to the youngsters' age level. Some alphabet books are for very young children. Looking at the simplicity of the pictures may help you to determine the age level. If there are pictures of children in the book, are the children in the book the age of yours?

Some alphabet books are too sophisticated for young children. These books often display the talent of the artist rather than teaching the letters. Other alphabet books are confusing because of the unfamiliar objects used as illustrations. Alphabet books are most effective if they

1. use both upper- and lowercase letters
2. have simple illustrations that children can recognize
3. use illustrations with only one common name (not *cat*/*kitten* or *rabbit*/*bunny*, for instance)
4. use words starting with a single consonant (*cow, sail, ball*) rather than a blend (such as *church, ship,* or *brown*, for instance)
5. have a theme, a simple story, or rhyming verses

Two examples of appropriate alphabet books are *Eating the Alphabet: Fruits & Vegetables from* A *to* Z by Lois Ehlert (San Diego: Harcourt Brace Jovanovich, 1989) and *The Icky Bug Alphabet Book* by Jerry Pallotta (Watertown, MA: Charlesbridge, 1986).

These books are more effective when read to one or two children at a time rather than a group. The children need to sit close to the teacher to identify the objects being named and to see the shapes of the letters. Have the books on your bookshelves so children can look at the books by themselves. Chall's extensive study on learning to read in America found that children's ability to identify letters was an important predictor of reading achievement in first and second grades (1967, p. 141).

■ **Serve Alphabet Soup**

Serve alphabet soup for lunch and see if the children can identify any of the letters.

■ **Have Fun with Pretzels**

Serve pretzels for snack and see what letters your children can make by breaking off pieces before eating the pretzels.

❏ WRITES WORDS WITH INVENTED SPELLING

Even though children may print their own names and write lines of mock writing, they may know very little about the concept of symbolization: that words are symbols representing objects. Children need to have many meaningful experiences with print in their everyday lives before this concept becomes clear. Reading picture books to individuals and filling the room with printed signs, labels, and charts can give them this experience.

In addition to labeling the children's cubbies and seats with their names, you should have each activity area labeled with its name. Other labels can include job charts, attendance charts, experience charts, weather charts, and recipe charts; names of animal and fish pets; labeled pictures of community helpers and of buildings in the block area; first aid kit and emergency directions; records of children's height, of how much their plants have grown, of how far children can jump, of which children have pets at home; stories the children have dictated; favorite songs and finger plays; signs for the play supermarket. There are many, many opportunities for using printed words in your classroom. Be sure these labels and signs are mounted at the children's eye level.

From this exposure to printed words, children will learn several things about words:

1. Written words convey messages that can be read.
2. Words are arranged in horizontal rows. (Be sure you do not use vertical labels.)
3. Words are made up of letters with a space between each word.
4. Some letters are repeated, but never more than two together in a word. (Temple et al., 1982, p. 51)

Such concepts are internalized subconsciously by the children, and you do not need to point them out. Your role is to fill the environment with printed words. The children's interaction with this printed material will make certain impressions on their minds. Some youngsters will realize, just as they did when they first learned to talk, that everything has a name, and that this name can be written. So they will begin experimenting with writing down words.

Their first written words should be just as exciting to those around them as their first spoken words, but adults are sometimes disappointed because children have not spelled the words correctly. Of course not. Spelling has little to do with children's writing of their first words—just as correct pronunciation has little to do with children's first spoken words. Proper spelling comes later, with experience and refinement.

Instead, youngsters are putting together letters that sound like the word. First words are often made up mostly of consonants: *skwl* for *school; das* for *days* (Sansone, 1988, p. 14). Linguists call this *invented spelling*. Do not correct the children. With experience and maturity they will eventually transfer from invented spelling to conventional spelling on their own.

Your role at this point is to focus on the meaning of children's words rather than on the mechanics of writing. Letters may be backward or missing a leg. Words may be spelled wrong or spelled more than one way in the same message. Never mind. The child has written his first words. Hurray!

Directionality or orientation is also a problem with the first words of beginning writers just as it is with their letters. Adults take for granted that words start at the left and go to the right. Young children have not established that directional perspective at first. They may print a word such as *book* by starting with a *b* in the middle of the page, and going both ways: *koobook*. They may be merely "manipulating the medium" (letters) like they do with paint and unit blocks to find out how they work.

Children may also write words from bottom to top or from right to left as frequently as from left to right. Most youngsters go through a stage of writing their names backward in a perfect mirror image. Children seem to see things from a number of different perspectives, in fact, before they finally learn a single linear orientation.

You may think that lined paper would help them to establish this baseline. During these early formative years, the children's experiments with letters and words just do not fit between lines, and the youngsters are better off with unlined paper. Later in elementary school, as they learn to control their pencil movements and refine their perceptions of letters and words, a line can be very helpful to the children.

But wouldn't it be better just to print out the words correctly for the children to copy, you may wonder? Not at all. Then they would not be creating their own knowledge—extracting their own rules about how writing works. You must be careful, in fact, not to take over the writing process from the children at this point. For emergent writing to occur, children must maintain control of the process themselves (Schrader & Hoffman, 1987, p. 11).

Instead, you should give each child support, encouragement, and plenty of writing activities to become involved with. Can he make a sign for his block structure saying Please Keep Off? (It may well turn out as *PLS KP AVF* in invented spelling.) Can she make a list of things she wants to do in school tomorrow?

Not all youngsters arrive at this level of development in the preschool years. In fact, it may well be kindergarten before many will produce their first written words. Do not try to force the process. It emerges in its own good time with patience, support, and encouragement.

If You Have Not Checked This Item: Some Helpful Ideas

■ Write Signs for Children to Use

Be a writing model for the children and write out signs for them on the spot to be used in their classroom activities. Signs for the block area could include Garage, Hospital, Bridge, Please Do Not Touch, Block Area Closed Today. In the book area you could make a sign saying Sign Out Books Here. In the science area, Please Feed Guinea Pig. At the children's cubbies, Don't Forget Permission Slips Tomorrow. What other signs would the children like to see? Ask them.

■ Ask Children to Make Their Own Signs

Set up a table in the class for producing signs. Have cutout cardboard strips, file cards, cellophane tape, masking tape, peel-off pictures, markers of different colors, stamp pad and letter stamps, animal stamps, and alphabet letters on the wall nearby. Encourage children to use this area to make their own signs. If they ask for your help, give it to them, but don't make the signs for them.

■ Have Individual Mailboxes

Put your written communications to children or their parents in each child's mailbox. Make the mailboxes out of shoe boxes or other compartmentalized boxes with the child's name clearly visible. You may want to take a field trip to the post office or have a mail carrier visit and talk to your class.

You should plan on writing one note to each child on a weekly basis. It should be simple and nice: "Rob, I love your new sneakers!" or "Shirl, thanks for helping Carol today." When the child receives the note, one of the adults in the class can help him or her to read it. This modeling behavior on your part should stimulate children to want to write notes to classmates or answer your notes on their own.

■ Read a Book

The Postman by Rosalinda Kightley (New York: Macmillan, 1987) shows simple colorful pictures with a rhyming line of text at the bottom of each page telling where the postman is delivering mail.

The Post Office Book: Mail and How It Moves by Gail Gibbons (New York: Harper & Row, 1982) is an illustrated nonfiction book for young children about the process of how mail is sorted and delivered.

The Signmaker's Assistant by Tedd Arnold (New York: Dial Books for Young Readers, 1992) is the story of a young man, Norman, the signmaker's assistant, who learns an important lesson about signs after he mixes up the whole town by making his own signs for things (No School Today on the school, Open for Swimming on the town fountain, for example).

Ruby by Maggie Glen (New York: Putnam, 1990) is the touching story of Ruby, a little stuffed bear in a toy factory, who is made differently from the other bears by mistake, and so is stamped with an *S* on her paw, meaning *second*. Ruby believes it means *special*, and helps the other bears marked *S* to escape. Eventually, Ruby ends up being purchased by Susie, a little girl with a silver *S* hanging from her necklace.

❏ RETELLS STORIES FROM BOOKS WITH INCREASING ACCURACY

At the same time that young children are pretending to write and beginning to identify letters, they are also involved in the natural emergence of reading skills. They are asking parents and teachers to read them stories, and scribbling their own stories in mock writing. They are drawing their own primitive illustrations, scribbling mock stories about them, and "reading" them back to the teacher. To children, reading and writing are all the same thing. You write something and you read it back; you read something and you write about it. And it is very exciting to "read" your own "words"!

Nevertheless, until recently most educators somehow never made the connection that writing and reading emerge naturally and develop simultaneously in preschool children. Even teachers who noted that many more "early readers" were entering kindergarten these days still believed that writing was different. Maybe some children could develop reading on their own, but surely children had to be taught to write, didn't they?

Perhaps it is because writing and reading have always been taught as distinct subjects in primary school that educators had just not looked closely at what was actually happening with younger children. But now the evidence is in. Studies over two decades by child development specialists in the United States, Argentina, Australia, Germany, Great Britain, Israel, and Mexico agree that

> The young child's reading and writing abilities mutually reinforce each other, developing concurrently and interrelatedly rather than sequentially. . . .Furthermore, reading and writing have intimate connections with oral language. Truly, the child develops as a speaker/reader/writer with each role supporting the other. (Teale, 1986, pp. 3–5)

Child development specialist Judith A. Schickedanz (1986) poses several sequential stages in young children's natural development of reading based on her research with preschool children. These stages are converted here into *Checklist* items:

1. retells stories from books with increasing accuracy
2. shows awareness that print in books tells story
3. attempts to match telling of story with print in book
4. wants to know what particular print says

It is assumed that children in your classroom have had a great deal of experience with books before you can check them on this first item. Hopefully, parents have read to them. Surely, you and your staff have read to them on a daily basis. Certainly, books abound in your classroom: in the book area, in the dramatic play area, in the science area, in the block area—wherever children need to read for pleasure or read to find out. If this is not the case, then you should make it so as soon as possible. You need to bring children and books together—quickly—happily. It is one of the most important things you can do for the children in your program. A number of books that you can read to children are suggested in each chapter in this book.

Then you need to observe the children's interaction with books and stories, in order to determine where each child stands on this checklist item. Perhaps the best approach is to become involved directly in the process. When a child asks you to read a story, have her choose a favorite story, one she has heard before. After you have finished, tell her it is now her turn, that she should tell the story to you. She can turn the pages if she wants and "read" the story to you. Make it fun, so that she will want to repeat the activity again and again. This means, of course, that you will need to spend much of your reading time on a one-to-one basis with individuals rather than reading to a whole group. Most teachers find this very rewarding, and so do children.

Schickedanz (1986) notes that the child's accuracy in retelling book stories is influenced by four factors:

1. characteristics of the child's language
2. structure of the book
3. familiarity with the book
4. past experience with books in general (pp. 51–52)

Children tell the story in their own language, at their own developmental level, with the same articulation they use when they speak. If they speak a dialect, they will retell the story in this dialect. If they are learning English as a second language, they will retell the story the way they speak English rather than the way the story is written in the book. The more times the child hears the story, the more accurate she will become in her retelling.

The structure of the book also influences the accuracy of the child's story retelling. Research has found that the best beginning books for helping children learn to read are *predictable books*, those that "contain selections with repetitive structures which enable children to anticipate the next word, line, or episode" (Bridge, 1986, p. 82). If children are familiar with a story and can anticipate what comes next, they will have a much easier time retelling the story themselves.

Repetitive structures in children's picture books are patterns such as the following:

1. certain phrases or sentences repeated at various points in the story
2. repetitive words, phrases, or sentences in a cumulative sequence
3. repetitive pattern based on numbers, the alphabet, days of the week, or months of the year
4. repetitive events children can predict
5. repetitive pattern based on rhymes (Bridge, 1986, p.82)

If the child is familiar with the book you are reading, and is familiar with books in general, then she can follow the story more easily. If the book is written in a predictable pattern, then it is also easier for the child to remember the story line and to recall what comes next. The following books contain patterns that make them excellent predictable books to use with preschoolers and kindergarten children.

1. Certain phrases or sentences repeated

Caps for Sale, Esphyr Slobodkina (New York: Scholastic, 1968)

If You Give a Mouse a Cookie, Laura Numeroff (New York: Harper, 1985)

Lizard's Song, George Shannon (New York: Greenwillow, 1981)

Moo Moo, Brown Cow, Jakki Wood (San Diego: Harcourt, 1992)

Nine-in-One, Grr! Grr!, Blia Xiong (San Francisco: Children's Book Press, 1989)

Owl Babies, Martin Waddell (Cambridge, MA: Candlewick Press, 1992)

Rum, Pum, Pum, Maggie Duff (New York: Macmillan, 1978)

Stone Soup, Ann McGovern (New York: Scholastic, 1968)

The Surprise Party, Pat Hutchins (New York: Collier, 1969)

The Three Bears, Paul Galdone (New York: Scholastic, 1972)

The Three Billy Goats Gruff, Paul Galdone (New York: Clarion, 1973)

Tikki, Tikki, Tembo, Arlene Mosel (New York: Scholastic, 1968)

We're Going on a Bear Hunt, Michael Rosen (New York: McElderry, 1989)

Whose Footprints? Molly Coxe (New York: Crowell, 1990)

Wild Wild Sunflower Child Anna, Nancy Carlson (New York: Macmillan, 1991)

2. Repetitive words, phrases, or sentences in cumulative sequence

Bringing the Rain to Kapiti Plain, Verna Aardema (New York: Dial, 1981)

Drummer Hoff, Barbara Emberley (Englewood Cliffs, NJ: Prentice-Hall, 1967)

Fiddle-I-Fee, Melissa Sweet (Boston: Little, Brown, 1992)

The House That Jack Built, Jenny Stow (New York: Dial, 1992)

Jump, Frog, Jump! Robert Kalan (New York: Mulberry, 1981)

The Turnip, Janina Domanska (New York: Collier, 1969)

3. Repetitive pattern based on numbers, alphabet, days, or months

Chicken Soup with Rice, Maurice Sendak (New York: Scholastic, 1962)

Ten, Nine, Eight, Molly Bang (New York: Greenwillow, 1983)

This Old Man, Carol Jones (Boston: Houghton Mifflin, 1990)

The Very Hungry Caterpillar, Eric Carle (New York: Putnam, 1981)

4. Repetitive events that children can predict

Edward the Emu, Sheena Knowles (New York: Angus & Robertson, 1988)

Leo the Late Bloomer, Robert Kraus (New York: Windmill, 1971)

Milton the Early Riser, Robert Kraus (New York: Windmill, 1972)

The Wheels on the Bus, Maryann Kovalski (Boston: Little, Brown, 1987)

Whose Mouse Are You? Robert Kraus (New York: Collier, 1970)

5. Repetitive patterns based on rhymes

Brown Bear, Brown Bear, What Do You See? Bill Martin (New York: Holt, 1967)

Each Peach Pear Plum, Janet & Allan Ahlberg (New York: Puffin, 1978)

Half a Moon and One Whole Star, Crescent Dragonwagon (New York: Macmillan, 1986)

Is Your Mama a Llama? Deborah Guarino (New York: Scholastic, 1989)

The Lady with the Alligator Purse, Nadine Bernard Westcott (Boston: Little, Brown, 1988)

Old Mother Hubbard, James Marshall (New York: Farrar, Straus, & Giroux, 1991)

Pretend You're a Cat, Jean Marzollo (New York: Dial, 1990)

If You Have Not Checked This Item: Some Helpful Ideas

■ Use Predictable Books from Category 1

Some of the books in this category ("Certain Phrases or Sentences Repeated") are favorite fairy tales the children may have heard before. In *The Three Billy Goats Gruff*, children who know the story remember the size of the goats, where they were going, how they went across the bridge ("trip, trap, trip, trap,"), what the troll said to each goat ("Who's that tripping across my bridge?"), and many more details of the story. They can tell it almost by heart. If they want to tell you the story by pretending to read as they turn the pages, let them. Also ask them to tell the story afterwards without looking at the book. You try it first and let them correct you if you leave out anything.

Children who are not as familiar with books and reading may still agree to tell you the story, but their story may be created by them as they look at the pictures. Your acceptance of any story they tell is important. As they progress in their experience with stories and books, their retelling will become more accurate. On the other hand, some children who know stories very well may after a time become reluctant to retell them. Schickedanz (1986) points out that

> a decrease in a child's willingness to tell a story may indicate an increase in the child's understanding about the exactness and stability of the story that is printed in a book. Reluctance, in this case, indicates progress, not regression." (p. 56)

❑ SHOWS AWARENESS THAT PRINT IN BOOKS TELLS STORY

The next developmental step in prereading skills involves print awareness. If you are reading to children on a one-to-one basis, they already may have indicated some thing about their print awareness or lack of it. At first, children believe that th tures in the book tell the story. They may not pay any attention to the text. when they do, they may not understand that it is the print and not the picture the reader is reading.

Some children are so unaware of the purpose of print that they may cover it tentionally with their hands if they are holding the book. Others may understand

At first, children believe that the pictures in a book tell the story.

the reader needs to read the print, but they may also think that the reader still needs the pictures to know what the words say (Schickedanz, 1986, p. 57).

Books that contain both print and wordless pages often confuse youngsters who are beginning to be aware of print. *Where the Wild Things Are* by Maurice Sendak (New York: Harper & Row, 1963) has text on every page except for six pages in the center of the book that depict the wild things having their wonderful wild rumpus. Some unaware children insist that the reader read the words for these textless pages.

Look What I Can Do by Jose Aruego (New York: Scribner's, 1971) has only two pages of one-line text at the beginning and one at the end, as one water buffalo challenges another to "look what I can do." *Do You Want to be My Friend?* by Eric Carle (New York: Crowell, 1971) has a mouse asking a horse's tail the title question, and then going through a series of wordless pages with animals seen from their tail ends, to the conclusion of the book where another mouse answers "yes." Unaware children may feel that you are skipping pages if you do not read something for every page.

The many wordless books on the market today also require that you or the children make up the words for the story to go along with the pictures. Using such wordless or partially wordless books with preschool children may help to clarify for you the listener's level of print awareness.

Eventually many of the children may come to realize that it is the print in the book that tells the story and not the pictures. You can determine who these children are by asking them where you should look in the book when you read it to them. Again, you will need to be reading to individual children.

If You Have Not Checked This Item: Some Helpful Ideas

■ **Make Experience Chart Stories**

Bring an experience chart into the book area and have children dictate stories to you that you write on the chart. Can they read them back?

■ **Have Children Dictate Stories for Wordless Books**

Children can dictate words for the wordless pages of the books previously mentioned. You can write them down and read them back when the books are in use. Wordless books about children like themselves can be the motivation for your children to dictate stories to go along with the wordless pages for books like *Sunshine* by Jan Ormerod (New York: Lothrop, Lee & Shepard, 1981), *Moonlight* by Jan Ormerod (New York: Puffin Books, 1982), and *A Boy, a Dog and a Frog* by Mercer Mayer (New York: Dial, 1967).

■ **Fill the Children's Environment with Print**

As mentioned earlier in the chapter, you need to fill the classroom with print: charts, place cards, books, magazines, newspapers, telephone directories, labeled food containers, and signs of all kinds. Have the children help you make the signs. Ask them what should be labeled in the classroom and then spell the words aloud as you print them on the signs: aquarium, door, table, chair, telephone, dramatic play area, and so on. Then have them help mount the signs on the appropriate objects.

❑ ATTEMPTS TO MATCH TELLING OF STORY WITH PRINT IN BOOK

This particular behavior occurs late in the prereading developmental sequence of preschool children. First must come the children's interest and knowledge of the stories themselves, then their print awareness. Children will not try to match the telling of the story with the print in the book until they recognize the story, and are aware that the print tells the story (Schickedanz, 1986, p. 58). The attempts that children make to match the oral story with print in the book are just that: attempts. Don't expect the children to be wholly successful. Learning specific words comes later.

If the adult reader runs his or her finger along under the print, the child may imitate this behavior. Young children are still not seeing words as such. A line of print is much like their line of mock writing: all of a piece. They may say it aloud as if it is a line of words, but they do not recognize printed words as being separate entities. Their first perceptions of writing, as discussed earlier in the chapter, are general in nature. They see whole lines, but not separate words or letters. As they become more familiar with the concept of separate words, their brains assimilate shape and space details that help them to distinguish words. Again, it is not up to you to "teach" them this concept. Furthermore, teaching does little good. Emergent literacy is a natural process that children themselves accomplish.

As with other new and complex concepts, it may take many months for a child to become relatively accurate in matching words with print. He needs time and practice with books, both with adults and on his own. Be sure that a great deal of individual story reading takes place on a daily basis. Also fill the shelves of your reading area with the children's favorite books. Predictable books in which the children can tell what's coming next and in which the pictures match the text closely are the best kinds.

If You Have Not Checked This Item: Some Helpful Ideas

■ Use Predictable Books from Categories 2 and 5

The simple story *Jump, Frog, Jump!* is a cumulative tale of a frog in a pond who has to jump during each event: to catch a fly, to get away from a fish, to escape from a snake, to get away from a turtle, to escape a net, and to get out of a basket. This colorful story is filled with double-spread illustrations of the frog jumping out of each new dilemma, and words in large yellow print saying, "Jump, Frog, Jump!" If children enjoy this story and begin repeating the words when you read it, they may very well come to realize that the yellow words actually represent the words they are saying. You will know when this happens if they repeat the phrase before you do, every time they see the words.

Pretend You're a Cat, on the other hand, is a delightful but more complex book of verses about moving like an animal: cat, dog, fish, bee, bird, squirrel, pig, cow, horse, seal, snake, and bear. Each double-spread page shows a large, sensitively drawn picture of multiethnic children pretending to be the animal on one page. On the opposite page are two verses and a separate line about pretending below each poem that asks, "What else can you do like a ____?"

If children enjoy these verses, they themselves may want to pretend to be the animals at first. As they hear the story over and over and look at the pictures by themselves, some of them may try to match the words, "What else can you do like a ____?" with the print.

■ Use a Computer Program

Computer programs with animated pictures and a minimum of text also help children make the story-print connection. In *Jack and the Beanstalk* (Cambridge, MA: Tom Snyder Productions, 1988) an adult needs to read the story as the child presses the key to "turn the pages." Children can also press a key to make choices for the character. In *The Milliken Storyteller* (St. Louis: Milliken Publishing, 1989) the program itself tells the story of "The Ugly Duckling," "Henny Penny," and "Little Red Riding Hood," while children click a mouse to see the next screen. An adult must also do the reading for *The Princess and the Pea* (Acton, MA: Bradford Publishing, 1989), *Stone Soup* (Acton, MA: Bradford Publishing, 1989), and *The Three Little Pigs* (Acton, MA: Bradford Publishing, 1989). Then the children can use the nonverbal part of the program to create their own stories using animated objects. These last three stories can also be printed out in color with an ImageWriter II. Storybooks of these traditional tales should be available in the classroom whenever these computer programs are in use.

❑ WANTS TO KNOW WHAT PARTICULAR PRINT SAYS

Once children have made the connection between the oral story and the printed text, they soon begin to shift their attention almost exclusively to the print. They may no longer even pay attention to the orally read story, but instead want to know what a particular word of print says. If the child knows the story really well, he may want to know which word tells the character's name or where does it say, "trip-trap, trip-trap." Then he may want to spend the rest of the time going through the book to find those words again.

The same type of behavior occurs with a child using a computer program having both animated graphics and a simple text. After the child discovers the text and induces the rules for how it works, he no longer seems much interested in the pictures on the screen. In this author's study of teams of 3- and 4-year-old children using exploratory play to discover the workings of selected computer programs, one of the children, Jeremey, taught himself how words were formed on the mixed-up animal program *Jeepers Creepers*. After that, he lost interest completely in scrambling and unscrambling the mixed-up animal pictures, and concentrated instead on making new words—and pronouncing them.

> At the bottom of the screen is the name of the mixed-up animal that the children have created: catowlfish, for example. A few of our children realized that the long word represented a combination of three animal names and tried to sound out the word. Jeremey, for instance, became so involved in trying to decipher the crazy animal names that he let his partner completely control the keyboard during his turn. It was a marvelous discovery for him to crack the reading code. While it is not necessary or appropriate for every preschool child to learn to read such words, it is an additional challenge for children who have induced the rules for unscrambling the animal pictures, to apply their learning to the unscrambling of the mixed-up animal names, as well. (Beaty & Tucker, 1987, p. 148)

Not all of your children will arrive at this last item in the "Prewriting and Prereading" section of the *Checklist*. You should not be concerned. Natural writing and reading development occurs slowly in children over a lengthy period of time. Many children will not exhibit this last behavior before kindergarten or even first grade. Your concern, instead, should be directed at filling the classroom with print, with books, with numerous writing and reading activities, with opportunities for children to prewrite and preread, and with support and acceptance for every aspect of development that the youngsters accomplish.

If You Have Not Checked This Item: Some Helpful Ideas

■ Use Predictable Books from Category 3

The books from this category are based on numbers, the alphabet, days, or months. The books often feature a particular word on each page, illustrated by the picture of the word. Children who have arrived at the mature prereading behavior of wanting to know what particular print says may well be motivated to ask what certain words say when you read them one of these books.

In *This Old Man* many children have the added advantage of knowing this rhyme as a finger play. When they hear the same words in a book, and see illustrations to match, they are often intrigued by the concept that the finger play they already know can be in a book. In Carol Jones's book version of this rhyme, she shows a little girl and her grandfather on one side of a double-spread page, and one line of the verse on the opposite page, above and below a cutout hole. Children look through the hole in the page to see what "this old man" played "nick nack" on.

On the first page children see a drum through the hole, but the reader must turn the page to complete the sentence: "He played nick nack on my ____." The next page shows the word *drum* in large print. Children enjoy the participation aspect of this book and may spend some time going through it just to see the fascinating illustration details. You may need to read the book a number of times, in fact, before anyone asks about particular words. Be patient. You know that prereading skill development takes time. If no one wants to know what the particular print says, you will realize that the children are not yet at that point in their development.

■ Bring in the Daily Newspaper

Why would anyone bring in the daily newspaper for preschool children, you may wonder? Early childhood specialists who have used newspapers with young children have this to say:

> The daily newspaper is an ideal support for young children's emerging literacy skills. First, the newspaper is an example of printed material that is familiar and available in many young children's homes. It is the source of reading for a purpose by parent and adult models whom the children are likely to observe. . . .The newspaper's large size and format invite children to examine it in pairs or small groups. . . . Finally, the newspaper supports literacy development through its contents. Helping young children better understand their world outside the classroom is a major goal in early childhood education. (Richie, Foster, & Johnston, 1991, p. 29)

These researchers suggest clipping pictures, cartoons, and advertisements from the paper and displaying them on a bulletin board to introduce the newspaper. Afterward, the teacher can help children locate the different appropriate information that can be found in a newspaper: weather report, pictures of other children, stories about animals, comics, advertisements for stores in the neighborhood, letters to the editor, lost-and-found. These items can be circled with a highlighter. Then the newspaper can be placed in the book area for the children to peruse on their own, or in the dramatic play area for the children to pretend with. Obviously, preschool children cannot read the newspaper. But they can come to understand that the newspaper communicates important information to everyone, including them. It is a prime motivation for paying attention to print, and eventually for learning to read.

■ Use Old Experience Chart Stories

The old stories that you have written down on experience charts that the children have dictated—about field trips, visits from community helpers, events they have witnessed, activities they have enjoyed, things they have accomplished, the latest news on the birth of the baby guinea pigs, and so on—should not be thrown away. They can be torn off the pad of easel paper and given to children in the writing center or book area.

These are stories you have read back to the children many times. Some of the children may have tried to read them themselves by remembering what happened. Don't throw old stories away. Instead, give them to the children as if they were their own newspapers. Let them use them as they like. Some children will pretend to read them. Others may ask you to come into the area and read them again. Still others will use them for their own purposes: maybe as a pretend report from outer space, or as the daily newspaper. Children who are at the level of the last Prewriting and Prereading Checklist item may ask you what particular words say.

OBSERVING, RECORDING, AND INTERPRETING PREWRITING AND PREREADING SKILLS

Although young children develop prewriting and prereading skills at the same time and in much the same manner that they develop spoken language, we realize that the same emphasis has not been placed on the natural development of preschool writing and reading by the adults around them. Therefore, there may be children who can produce mock writing and letters, but have not practiced it. There may be some children who are aware of print and try to read it, but have not been noticed. If you screen your entire class using the *Child Skills Checklist* items on writing and reading skills, you may find certain children who exhibit these skills.

After observing the 4-year-old boy Jeremey previously referred to, the teacher was able to complete the *Checklist* section "Prewriting and Prereading" as shown in Figure 12.1. Jeremey's accomplishments helped this teacher to understand that Jeremey was showing real progress in his prewriting and prereading skills. In fact, she had not realized how far he had progressed.

The teacher decided to work on a one-to-one basis with Jeremey, using predictable books. After he had heard the story repeated, perhaps he could retell it. If he

FIGURE 12.1
Prewriting and prereading observations for Jeremey

Child Skills Checklist

Name __Jeremey — Age 4__   Observer __Betsy__

Program __Pre – K__   Dates __5/5__

Directions:

Put a ✔ for items you see the child perform regularly. Put *N* for items where there is no opportunity to observe. Leave all other items blank.

Item	Evidence	Date
10. Prewriting and Prereading Skills		
_N_ Pretends to write by scribbling horizontally	He no longer scribbles but tries to write real words	5/5
_N_ Includes features of real letters in scribbling	Same as above	5/5
✔ Writes real alphabet letters	Prints his name. Copies other words	5/5
✔ Writes words with invented spelling	Writes words on easel: PLS DON TCH	5/5
✔ Retells stories from books with increasing accuracy	Likes to repeat stories from books	5/5
✔ Shows awareness that print in books tells story	Seems to understand, but still points to pictures	5/5
____ Attempts to match telling of story with print in book		5/5
✔ Wants to know what particular print says	Points to word & asks if it says " ___ "	5/5

really liked the story, she would ask him if he knew which particular print represented certain words. She also decided to encourage him to "write a story" about what he was building in the block area.

This teacher also decided that now was the time to expand her writing table to an entirely new and separate classroom writing area with an old rolltop desk, many writing tools and paper, a small table with a manual typewriter, and magnetic alphabet letters to play with. Who knows which other children would *emerge* with self-taught knowledge of letters and words!

REFERENCES

Beaty, Janice J., & W. Hugh Tucker. (1987). *The computer as a paintbrush: Creative uses for the personal computer in the preschool classroom.* New York: Merrill/Macmillan.

Bridge, Connie A. (1986). Predictable books for beginning readers and writers. In Michael R. Sampson, *The pursuit of literacy: Early reading and writing* (pp. 81–96). Dubuque, IA: Kendall/Hunt.

Chall, Jeanne. (1967). *Learning to read: The great debate.* New York: McGraw-Hill.

Hayes, Anne Haas. (1990). From scribbling to writing: Smoothing the way. *Young Children, 45*(3), 62–68.

Lamme, Linda Leonard. (1979). Handwriting in an early childhood curriculum. *Young Children, 35*(1), 20–27.

Richie, June Rose, Janet E. Foster, & John M. Johnston. (1991). Using the newspaper to support children's emerging literacy. *Day Care and Early Education, 19*(2), 28–31.

Sansone, Rosemary M. (1988). SKWL DAS: Emerging literacy in children. *Day Care and Early Education, 16*(1), 14–19.

Schickedanz, Judith A. (1982). The acquisition of written language in young children. In Bernard Spodek (Ed.), *Handbook of research in early childhood education.* New York: Free Press.

Schickedanz, Judith A. (1986). *More than the ABCs: The early stages of reading and writing.* Washington, DC: NAEYC.

Schrader, Carol Taylor, & Stevie Hoffman. (1987). Encouraging children's early writing efforts. *Day Care and Early Education, 15*(2), 9–13.

Teale, William H. (1986). Written language development during the preschool and kindergarten years. In Michael R. Sampson, *The pursuit of early reading and writing* (pp. 81–95). Dubuque, IA: Kendall/Hunt.

Temple, Charles A., Ruth G. Nathan, & Nancy A. Burris. (1982). *The beginnings of writing.* Boston: Allyn & Bacon.

Vukelich, Carol, & Joanne Golden. (1984). Early writing: Development and teaching strategies. *Young Children, 39*(2), 3-8.

OTHER SOURCES

Cashion, Marie, & Ruth Eagan. (1989). Developmental considerations in learning to read. *Day Care and Early Education, 16*(3), 10–12.

Cratty, Bryant. (1986). *Perceptual and motor development in infants and children.* Englewood Cliffs, NJ: Prentice-Hall.

Dyson, Anne Haas. (1990). Symbol makers, symbol weavers: How children link play, pictures, and print. *Young Children, 45*(2), 50–57.

LEARNING ACTIVITIES

1. Use the *Child Skills Checklist* section "Prewriting and Prereading Skills" as a screening tool to observe all of the children in your classroom. Compare the children who have checks at the higher levels of prewriting skills with their results in the spoken language category. Can you draw any conclusions?

2. Set up a writing area with paper and writing tools and make a running record of how children use it on three different days.

3. Observe and make a running record of children using a typewriter or computer on three different days. How do they go about teaching themselves how to use the instrument or programs? Are they using trial and error to teach themselves? Do they learn from their errors? How?

4. Read a well-known predictable book to an individual child. Does the child show any awareness of the print? Can he or she retell the story?

5. Bring in a newspaper for a small group of children to look at. Circle headlines and pictures that contain information appropriate for preschoolers. Read the headlines aloud, and discuss the articles. Do any of the children show awareness of print, try to match words with print, or ask what particular print says?

13 Art Skills

Art Skills Checklist

- ❑ Makes random marks or covers paper with color
- ❑ Scribbles on paper
- ❑ Forms basic shapes
- ❑ Makes mandalas
- ❑ Makes suns
- ❑ Draws human as a circle with arms and legs attached
- ❑ Draws animals, trees, flowers
- ❑ Makes pictorial drawings

This chapter on the development of children's art skills and the following chapter on the development of imagination focus on the growth of creativity in young children. Too often creativity is not included when the major aspects of children's development—emotional, social, physical, cognitive, and language—are discussed. Yet it is as notable a drive in the development of the young human being as thinking or speaking.

The unfolding of the creative urge in the young child is a joy to behold for most sensitive early childhood caregivers. To help foster and not suppress such development is just as important here as it is for speaking and thinking skills. Yet somehow we equate creativity with special talent that not everyone displays; we downplay or ignore the development of creativity as more of a frill than a necessity for getting along in life.

By downplaying or ignoring creativity, we deprive the developing human of a basic aspect of his or her expressional capacities. Every child, surprising as it may seem, has the capacity to become an artist, a musician, a writer, or an inventor, if his interests carry him in that direction, and if his caregivers and teachers give support and not control for his urge. The fact that not many people become artists is evidence of society's low priority for creativity and high priority for conformity.

Creativity connotes originality and novelty. To create, one brings into existence a new form of some kind. Creative people have original ideas, do things in new and different ways, see things from unique and novel perspectives. Creative people do not imitate, they do not follow the crowd. In a word, they are nonconformists.

Who are they? Artists, inventors, poets, writers, actors, musicians, interior decorators, chefs, architects, clothing designers, to name a few, and young children. They are all people who follow their own bent, and who use their ingenuity to design something new. Young children are naturally creative because everything they do, make, or say is completely new to them. They explore, experiment, put things together, take things apart, and manipulate things in ways no adult would ever think of, because the youngsters don't know any better.

Children come into the world uninhibited and with an entirely fresh point of view, their own. They continue to follow its bent until "they learn better," until they learn how society expects them to behave. Only those youngsters with strong enough psyches or strong enough outside support to resist society's inhibitions become the artists or creators whom we value as adults.

Could the children in your classroom become such creative adults? If their natural-born creativity is supported and valued by the adults around them, and if it is given an opportunity to blossom and grow, the children have the chance to escape the smothering pressure to conform, and to be able to enrich their own lives and those of others with the products of their talent.

This chapter on creative development deals with art skills, not only because art is an important curriculum area in most early childhood programs, but also because many early childhood caregivers need help in restructuring their art programs. Too many activities in such programs suppress rather than support creativity.

The chapter just as well could deal with the development of science skills, which are also dependent on children's natural exploratory inclination. Yet science at the preschool level has somehow escaped the controlled approach that many teachers take with art. It seems good for children to explore plants and animals in all sorts of ways. But drawings should be done only in the manner prescribed by adults, because of course adults "know better."

This traditional point of view needs to be challenged. We need to step back and take a good look at the development of creativity. When does creativity appear in human beings? What are its characteristics? What can we do to help it grow? How can we keep from suppressing it?

This chapter looks at an eight-step developmental sequence in drawing skills that appears in all children everywhere in the world in the same order. Even blind children exhibit the beginning steps of the sequence until the youngsters' lack of visual feedback discourages them from continuing. You will note that this sequence is similar to the steps children take in developing physical skills, cognitive skills, and even writing skills.

It is obvious that the brain is programmed to accomplish all kinds of development in this particular order, from the general to the specific, as youngsters have the opportunity and materials to interact with their environment in a playful manner and thus discover what it and they are able to do.

❑ MAKES RANDOM MARKS OR COVERS PAPER WITH COLOR

During their first year of life, children really do not draw. If they have access to a crayon, they are more apt to put it in their mouths than to put a mark on a paper. Around the age of 13 months, according to Piaget, children's first scribbling begins (Lasky & Mukerji, 1980 p. 9). The first marks they make are usually random. These marks have more to do with movement, in fact, than with art. The toddler is surprised to find that a crayon, a pencil, or a paintbrush will make marks. The youngsters are often captivated by watching the lines that their movements can make on a surface. The surface is not always paper, much to their caregivers' dismay. Children will mark on walls, tabletops, or anything else that will take a mark.

We need to be careful about scolding the child for her mistake. She was only investigating the properties of a strange new implement; she had no idea she was damaging anything. We want her to understand that the exploring and the marking were all right to do, but not on the walls and table. Harsh punishment at this stage may abort the budding creator's continued exploration of art. Have her help you clean off the marks with a child-size sponge, give her a tablet to mark on, and put a newspaper under it to control slips.

This first stage of art skill development is purely mechanical and manipulative. The child is gaining control over the art tool whether it is a crayon, paintbrush, pencil, felt-tip marker, or chalk. The child makes random marks or covers the paper with color without using eye control. Even blind children make the same kind of random marks. The urge to express oneself through drawing seems to be inborn, because young children with no art materials will make marks anyway on frosty windows or in the dirt.

Older children in your program who have had no access to art supplies or who have been suppressed in their attempts at home still go through these same checklist stages, but more quickly. It will take these children far less time to learn manipulation of the materials, for instance. The youngsters soon will be scribbling.

If You Have Not Checked This Item: Some Helpful Ideas

■ Have Art Materials Available Daily

Creativity blooms only when children have the freedom to try things on their own. Have paints available at one or two easels all the time. Provide colored chalk and a small chalkboard, sets of watercolor felt-tip pens and markers, sets of primary crayons, soft pencils, and various kinds of drawing paper on low shelves next to art tables. Let children select and use their own materials in a spontaneous manner.

■ Make Only Positive Comments on Children's Art Efforts

Beginning drawers will often produce art that is smudgy and uninteresting from an adult point of view. Refrain from negative comments. You need to know that the children are not trying to draw a picture, but only to manipulate the medium. Your comments should reflect this: "You really worked hard in art this morning, Jeff. I'm glad you enjoy it so much."

❏ SCRIBBLES ON PAPER

From about 2 years of age on through 3 and 4 years, and sometimes later depending on the child, an individual will mark on paper in a scribbling manner. At first the scribbles may be endless lines done in a rhythmic, manipulative manner. Eventually the child will use eye control as well as hand/arm movement to make her scribbles and direct their placement on the paper. One scribble often is placed on top of another until the paper is a hodgepodge of lines and circles. Painters may cover over their painted scribbles with layers and layers of paint before they are finished. These scribbles are different from the writing scribbles discussed in Chapter 12.

The product she has produced has little meaning to the child at first, for she is not trying to create something, but merely experimenting by moving colors around on a paper. The process is important to her, not the product. Adults, however, think of art mainly in terms of creating a product. Their response to scribbling is often either to dismiss it as unimportant and worthless, or to ask children to tell them what they have drawn. Once children learn that adults expect this sort of information, the youngsters often begin naming their scribbles. This behavior does not mean that they really had anything in mind when they began moving the brush or crayon around on the paper. Our comments should focus on their efforts in the process of drawing, not on the imperfect products they first create.

Scribbling is hardly worthless. It is the first step in the self-taught process of learning to draw. In many respects, scribbling is the equivalent of babbling in the process of learning to speak. We support children in their babbling and congratulate them when they finally make sounds that seem to be words. Think what might happen to their language development if we forced them to stop making such worthless sounds, just as some adults force children to stop wasting their time making "worthless" scribbles.

Children work hard at scribbling. Only they know when a scribbled "drawing" is finished. Actually, not the drawing, but the process is finished. Some youngsters go over and over and over the lines they have made, almost as if they are practicing the way to make a straight or curved line. Their early products seem to show a greater proportion of vertical lines, especially in easel paintings (Smith, 1982, p. 301). But the children are able to make multiple horizontal lines, diagonal lines, and curved lines as well. Back and forth the youngsters work, sometimes changing their hand direction when they get tired and sometimes even changing hands. Two-year-olds place one scribble on top of another, whereas 3- and 4-year-olds frequently put a single scribble on one paper (Kellogg, 1970, p. 18).

Rhoda Kellogg, an art specialist who collected and analyzed hundreds of thousands of children's drawings from around the world, identified 20 scribbles that children make. Not all children necessarily make all 20 of the scribbles that they are capable of producing. Individuals tend to concentrate on a few favorites and to repeat them in many variations. The fact that all children everywhere, taken together, produce the same 20 scribbles spontaneously—and no others—seems to indicate, though, that this early form of art somehow must be inborn in the human species.

Kellogg considers these scribbles to be "the building blocks of art" (1970, p. 15). The individual's scribble "vocabulary" most easily can be read in his finger painting. He will draw his "designs" with one or more fingers, and then "erase" them before starting over. Because they do not pile up one on top of the other as with opaque paint or crayons, it is easier to see which of the 20 basic scribbles he favors.

It is not necessary for the early childhood teacher to identify a child's scribbles, only that he or she understands the importance of scribbles in the sequence of art skills development. Many children continue to go back to scribbles even when they have progressed beyond them to shape drawings. This is a perfectly natural progression. All child development tends to occur in a spiral rather than a straight line. We can expect children to slip back even while they are progressing forward.

If You Have Not Checked This Item: Some Helpful Ideas

■ Provide Controllable Materials

Beginners will not be able to progress much beyond scribbling unless they can control the materials. Be sure to provide fat, kindergarten-size crayons for children to grip well. Children can use thin crayons, too, but sometimes the youngsters bear down so hard they break them. Mix your tempera paints with just enough water to make them creamy but not drippy. Cut off the ends of long easel paintbrushes so that youngsters can manipulate brushes easily. Wrap ends of colored chalk with masking tape to help gripping and prevent smearing.

In the beginning, provide easel painters with contrasting colors rather than complementary colors in order to prevent muddy results. Children have more control when they start with only two contrasting colors instead of several different kinds. Avoid putting red and green together, yellow and purple together, and blue and orange together. Haskell (1979, p. 74) recommends any of the following combinations instead: (a) yellow with blue or red or green or brown, (b) orange with green or purple or brown or red, (c) white with blue or red or green or purple.

■ Be Nondirective

Allow children to explore and experiment with paint and chalk, finger paint and crayons, and felt-tip markers and pencils completely on their own. Put the materials out for their use during free play, or have materials invitingly placed on low shelves near art tables for the youngsters' own selection.

❏ FORMS BASIC SHAPES

As children's physical and mental development progress and they are able to control the brush and paint more easily, their scribbles begin to take on the configuration of shapes. Kellogg (1970, p. 45) has identified six basic shapes in children's early art: rectangle (including square), oval (including circle), triangle, Greek cross (+), diagonal cross (X), and odd shape (a catchall category). These shapes do not necessarily appear separately, but rather are mixed up with scribbles or with one another.

If children have had the freedom to experiment with art as toddlers, they usually begin to make basic shapes spontaneously by the age of 3 years. Children's perceptual and memory skills help them to form, store, and retrieve concepts about shapes quite early if they have had appropriate experiences (see Chapter 9, "Cognitive

As children's natural art skills develop, their scribbles begin to take on the configurations of basic shapes.

Development"). The particular shapes a child favors seem to evolve from his or her own scribbles. Attempts at making ovals and circles usually appear early. This form seems innately appealing to young humans everywhere, perhaps because of their preferred attention to the human face.

Circular movements in their scribbling eventually lead children to form an oval. Then the youngsters often repeat it, going round and round over the same shape. Visual discrimination of the shape and muscle control of the brush or crayon finally allow them to form the shape by itself instead of intertwined within a mass of scribbles. Memory comes into play as well, allowing the children to retrieve the oval from their repertoire of marks and to repeat it another day.

In this manner the child's capacity to draw shapes seems to emerge from his capacity to control the lines he makes in his scribbling. In other words, he makes one of the basic shapes because he remembers it from creating it spontaneously in his scribbling, not because he is copying the shape from his environment. As he experiments, he stumbles onto new ways to make new shapes. But certain ones seem more appealing, and individual children return to them again and again.

Children 3 and 4 years old first create rectangles by drawing a set of parallel vertical lines and then later adding horizontal lines at the top and bottom, rather than drawing a continuous line for a perimeter (Smith, 1982, p. 301). We understand why when we remember the problem children first have trying to make an enclosure with blocks (see Chapter 10). Thus we see why it is important to give them many opportunities and much time to practice. The children are teaching themselves to draw, just as they did to block build, walk, talk, think, speak, write, and read.

If You Have Not Checked This Item: Some Helpful Ideas

■ Provide Materials Children Can Use on Their Own

Easels always should be available. They are one of the best motivators for spontaneous drawing that you can provide. Children soon find out that all they need to do to paint is to put on a painting smock and go to the easel. There is no need to get out paints, for they are already mixed and waiting. There is no need to ask for help or direction from the teacher. If an easel is free during free choice time, they can go to it and paint.

For children who are experienced easel painters, it is always good to challenge them with a new activity. Perhaps they would like to try flat table painting with paints in a muffin tin. Or you might make a table easel with two sections of cardboard taped together to form an inverted V over a table. Paper can be fastened to it with masking tape. Paint can be mixed and waiting in muffin tins or jars taped to the table so they will not tip over.

❏ MAKES MANDALAS

The next step in the sequence of children's self-taught art skills involves combining two of the shapes they have made. Kellogg has observed and written a great deal about this behavior. The Greek cross and the diagonal cross are favorite shapes. These are often combined with an oval or rectangle to make what is called a *mandala*. Mandalas don't necessarily stand alone on a sheet of paper, but are usually repeated by children in a balanced way. Groups of these shapes or others form the bulk of art for 3- and 4-year-old children.

Pictorial drawing eventually evolves out of particular combinations of shapes. One of the first representations to occur in children's art is the human being. This representation seems to evolve naturally from the child's first experiments with an oval shape combined with a cross inside it (the mandala), which leads to an oval with lines radiating from its rim (the sun), which evolves into an oval with two lines for arms, two for legs, and small circles inside the large head/body oval for eyes (the human).

From mandalas to suns to humans is the natural sequence found in much of children's spontaneous art. Watch for this development in the children in your program. Talk to parents about the spontaneous way art skills develop in children if youngsters are given the freedom to explore on their own. Both you and the parents may want to save children's scribbling and early shape drawings to see if you can identify the sequence of their development. Be sure to date the art.

Because the mandala shape combination is a key part of this sequence, it is treated as a separate checklist item for observers to look for. The circle with a cross inside is a symbol found throughout the world. In oriental religions it is the symbol of the cosmos. Obviously, young children are producing it spontaneously without any notion of its symbolic meaning. But there must be an inborn appeal for such a shape for it to appear as a natural sequence in children's art. Kellogg feels that its overall balance is what makes it so appealing to the human species (Kellogg, 1970, p. 68).

Early scribblings show many examples of crossed lines as well as ovals and rectangles. It seems only natural that children eventually would experiment by trying to put the two together. Many scribbles show early attempts at placing a cross over a circle, possibly because children make scribbles this way: one on top of the other. As children gain control of their drawing implements and remember how to make the shapes they like, a shape like the mandala emerges naturally. If this shape is appealing to them, then they will repeat it endlessly.

Perhaps this method reveals how early humans came to include the mandala in their repertoire of symbols. Circles and squares with crosses inside them are found on rocks throughout the world in the form of petroglyphs and pictographs created by ancient humans.

Not all children make mandalas, but most of them do. These basic shape combinations are never really lost once they have become a part of a person's art vocabulary. Take a look at the doodles adults make in a nonthinking, spontaneous fashion. You yourself still may draw the mandalas you first discovered as a child!

If You Have Not Checked This Item: Some Helpful Ideas

■ Provide Variety in Your Art Materials

Not all children may enjoy painting at an easel. You should include other possibilities as often as possible. Finger painting is one. It can be done on a smooth paper, a tabletop, or a cookie sheet. Paper finger paintings can be hung to dry and are thus preserved if the child wants to save them. Tabletop finger paintings can also be preserved before the table is cleaned by pressing a paper onto them and rubbing the paper.

The finger paint itself can be homemade in several ways: Pour liquid starch onto paper, shake powder paint into it, and mix; mix wallpaper paste with water and poster paint to the proper consistency; or mix soap powder with a little water and paint powder. Soap powder can also be whipped with water until stiff and used as white paint against colored construction paper.

❏ MAKES SUNS

A combination of an oval with lines radiating from its rim is often the next step in the child's natural sequence of drawing a pictorial representation. We call this shape combination a *sun* because it looks like the symbol adults use to represent the sun. Children do not call their sun-shape a sun unless adults or more experienced peers first give it the name. The youngsters are not drawing a sun, but merely experimenting with shapes. If this combination appeals to them, they will repeat it many times. When they finally do begin to draw pictorially, they sometimes will call this figure a spider.

Although the figure seems quite simple to draw, the sun does not appear spontaneously in children's drawings in the beginning. Two-year-olds can make curved and straight lines, but children rarely produce suns before age 3 (Kellogg, 1970, p. 74).

The sun figure may well emerge from the children's experimentations with the mandala figure. Most of children's early attempts at sun figures include some kinds of marks in the center of the figures, either lines, dots, or ovals. Once the children have begun to make a sun with a clear center, they have progressed beyond the mandala to something new. These early suns with center marks are not forgotten, however. When children begin to draw "sun-faces," their first humans, they include the center marks for eyes, nose, and mouth.

We see sun figures in primitive rock art as well. Early humans must have followed the same sequence in their progression to artistic representation.

If You Have Not Checked This Item: Some Helpful Ideas

■ Draw with Chalk

Colored chalk is very appealing to children if they can grip it and control its smeariness. Wrap the upper end with foil or masking tape to make gripping easier. Soft, thick chalk (sidewalk chalk) is preferred. The regular size breaks too easily with the pressure some children apply.

Chalk should first be used dry by the children so they become used to its properties. Then you can wet either the paper or the chalk for a richer effect. Use either a water-sugar solution (4 parts warm water to 1 part sugar) or liquid starch as the wetting medium. Apply it directly to the paper for children to draw on with dry chalk, or use the liquid as a dip in which the children wet the chalk but draw on a dry surface. Many children like the rhythm of dipping and drawing (Haskell, 1979, p. 45).

Dry chalk marks on paper can also be smeared around to create different effects. Draw on brown paper grocery bags for still more variety.

■ Draw with Felt-tip Markers

Water soluble felt-tip markers are always favorites with children. They seem to be able to control them more easily than paintbrushes and crayons. The thick size of the pens and their smooth marking ability make them especially well suited to preschool art. Some markers have brush tips rather than the more rigid felt tips. These have the spreading capacity of watercolor paint. It is not necessary or even desirable to give each child an entire set of markers of all colors. Give the youngsters only one or two colors at a time until they express the need for more.

■ Keep Art Activities Spontaneous

Do not use pictures, figure drawings, or models for your children to copy. This is not how spontaneous art develops. Even children who have reached the pictorial stage do not need to copy. You will find that they draw what they know rather than what they see.

■ Read a Book

When the Snake Bites the Sun by David Mowaljarlai and Pamela Lofts (San Diego: Mad Hatter Books, 1984) is an Australian aboriginal folktale about how the day and the night came to be. Its illustrations are adapted from aboriginal children's art and done in brilliant primary colors.

How the Birds Got Their Colors by Mary Albert and Pamela Lofts (San Diego: Mad Hatter Books, 1983) is another Australian aboriginal folktale done in the same blazing colors with the brush strokes visible.

Draw Me a Star by Eric Carle (New York: Philomel Books, 1992) is a simply done but striking book in large format, showing the artist as a boy, a young man, a mature man, and an old man drawing large pictures against a white background: a star, a wonderful double-page, orange-yellow sun, a tree, a woman and a man, a house and a dog, and more. The figures are brilliant collage cutouts pasted on white, and at the end on a blue-black night sky.

❏ DRAWS HUMAN AS A CIRCLE WITH ARMS AND LEGS ATTACHED

One of the first pictorial figures that young children draw is a person. They draw it as one large head-body oval or circle with two lines coming out of the bottom for legs, a line from either side for arms (sometimes these are omitted), and circles or dots inside the head circle for eyes and sometimes a nose and mouth. All children everywhere seem to draw their first humans in this spontaneous manner. They are known in the art world as *tadpole drawings* because of the obvious resemblance.

To adults unfamiliar with the sequence of children's development, these are strange humans indeed: all head and no body, with arms and legs attached to the head. Surely children age 3 and 4 can see that a person's arms and legs are attached to the body and not the head, you may say. Adult concepts about art, however, are entirely different from those of the beginning child artist. Adults tend to look at the product of children's art, that is, the drawing or painting, as the most important thing. As a matter of fact, to the young child, it is the process that is more important. In the beginning, they are not drawing a picture but developing a skill. Their efforts progress through an observable sequence of development from general to specific, from holistic to detailed drawings.

Their production of a human is the transition to pictorial drawing for most young children. The method they apply is the same one they used for making shapes and symbols. They draw *what they know how to make, and not what they see.* Out of their practice with mandalas and suns comes this sun-face human with a few of the "sun's rays" for arms and legs.

It is not surprising, in fact, that their first humans are all face. We remember that even infants attend to this image most frequently. The human brain seems to be programmed to take in details about faces. This, after all, is the most important part of the human being.

As children first create their circle humans, they do not always repeat their drawings in exactly the same way. All children make armless humans at one time or another, even though the youngsters may have drawn arm lines earlier. This behavior does not indicate that a child is regressing or is cognitively immature. It may appear simply because the child decided that the proportion of two parallel legs to head is more appealing alone than with arms sticking out at the sides. Children rarely draw legless humans (Kellogg, 1970, p. 101). The behavior of omitting arms may also result from the brain's tendency to overgeneralize in early categories. Later in the children's development, they will be more discriminating about details.

Without a great many examples of a single child's drawings, it is risky to try to determine where he or she stands in this developmental sequence. Schools or psychologists who try to evaluate a child's maturity on the basis of only one drawing of a person (such as the Draw-a-Person Test) are basing their findings on extremely sketchy information. Kellogg found that one-third of 2,500 public school children who were asked to "draw a man" each day for five days drew such different humans that their scores on the Draw-a-Man Test varied as much as 50% (Kellogg, 1970, p. 191).

As children have more practice drawing their early people, they often add hair or hats, hands or fingers, feet or toes. The additions may be lines, circles, or scribbles. Children may identify their persons as being themselves or someone else. The actual size of the person named in the drawing is usually not considered by young children. Instead, they often draw the most important person in the picture as the biggest. The so-called stick figure is not a part of children's spontaneous art; the figure seems to be learned by children at age 5 or 6 by copying the work of adults or older peers (Kellogg, 1970, p. 108).

Eventually, children will add a body to their head drawings. They often do this by drawing two extremely long legs and putting a horizontal line part way up between them. You may remember that this is the common method they used earlier to draw rectangles. The youngsters often will draw a belly button in the middle of the body. By this time, they frequently are drawing other pictorial representations as well. These representations, as you will note, are based on the children's previous experience, showing once again how development proceeds in a continuous sequence from the general to the specific, so long as children have the freedom to learn naturally.

If You Have Not Checked This Item: Some Helpful Ideas

■ Record Children's Stories About Their Drawings

Some children verbalize a great deal about their drawings. Others do not. You should take your lead from the child. If he or she likes to tell you stories about the people in the drawings, you may want to record these. Children may want to have their stories displayed along with their art on the classroom walls. On the other hand, they may want to make a scrapbook of their art or to take their art home.

If children do not want to talk about their art products, then you can support them best by comments like, "You surely put a lot of effort into your drawing today, Sheila." Keep in mind that much early children's art is not pictorial, so there really are not any stories to tell about it, unless, of course, adults press children to make up something.

❏ DRAWS ANIMALS, TREES, FLOWERS

Animals

Once children have discovered the way to draw a person, they will often begin drawing animals as well. Youngsters' first animals are hard to distinguish from humans. It is obvious that the animals are based on the same practiced form: a head with eyes, nose, and mouth, a body with arms sticking out from the sides and legs coming out from the bottom. Often the animal is facing frontwards like a person and seems to be standing on two legs. What makes the drawing an animal instead of a person are the two ears sticking up straight from the top of the head. Sometimes these are pointed like cat ears and sometimes circular like mouse ears. This is a transition animal.

Eventually, the young artist will find a way to make her animal horizontal with an elongated body parallel to the bottom of the paper, four legs extending from the bottom of the body in a row, a head at one end, and often a tail at the other end. The features of the face are still in a frontal pose, not a profile. Most animal head profiles do not appear in children's drawings until around age 5 years or later.

In fact, many children do not draw animals until they go to kindergarten. This behavior—or lack of it—may be due to their progress in their own developmental sequence, but drawing animals is also influenced by the kindergarten curriculum. Often kindergarten teachers give children outline animals to copy that may, in fact, short-circuit the youngsters' spontaneous development. Kellogg (1970) believes that many teachers seem to feel that a child's self-taught system differs too widely from adult drawing, and therefore the child needs to be taken in hand and taught how to draw "correctly" (p. 114). Children often abandon art in elementary school because of lack of teacher approval for their natural art.

Trees and Flowers

The first trees children draw are also transitional representations based on the human figure they have taught themselves to draw. The first trees look like armless humans with two long legs for the trunk and a circular head for the treetop, which often contains small circles or dots that may be leaves but look more like fruit. The trees are not drawn to scale. They may be similar in height to the humans in the picture or even smaller. A few 4-year-olds may draw trees, but most children are 5 years old before they begin doing so.

As children have practice and freedom to draw, more details evolve on their trees. The tops of some trees resemble the sun, with the rays as branches and balls at the ends of the branches as leaves. Other children make branches coming out from the trunk like arms on a human. The first flowers are also drawn to a familiar model: a sun with a stem.

The children in your classroom may not have advanced to this level. In this case, you should leave the checklist item blank. Given the freedom to develop art skills spontaneously, children will make their own progress as individuals. It is not your role to push the youngsters ahead, but to provide materials, time, and support so that the children may make their own progress according to their own biological timetables.

If You Have Not Checked This Item: Some Helpful Ideas

■ Add New Art Activities

Your children may want to try drawing with liquid glue from a plastic squeeze bottle. They may want to draw with a pencil or other marker first and then follow the lines with glue. Or they can try the glue without guidelines. Because some glue is transparent when it dries, you may want to add food coloring to the bottles. Colored glue is also available. This liquid glue is a much more free flowing medium than the children are used to; they will need to play with it for a while to see how it works and how to control it. They will need to squeeze and move the bottle at the same time, a trick of coordination that may be difficult for some. Don't expect pictorial designs from glue drawing.

■ Read a Book

Planting a Rainbow by Lois Ehlert (San Diego: Harcourt Brace Jovanovich, 1988) tells a simple story in large bold type of a little girl and her mother who plant bulbs and seeds for flowers that grow in rainbow colors. Brilliant flower cutouts against a white background, with color-coded pages of flowers in the center of the book, clearly display the shapes and color categories of the blooms. Be sure you use this book for reading only, and not as a model from which children would be expected to draw their flowers. Young children's art does not evolve from copying models.

Let's Make Rabbits by Leo Lionni (New York: Pantheon Books, 1982) is the simple story of a scissors and a pencil who say to one another, "Let's make rabbits." So they do—a pencil-drawn rabbit and a cutout collage rabbit. The two rabbits become friends, become hungry, and eventually become real. Again, allow the children to look closely at the illustrations but not copy them.

❏ MAKES PICTORIAL DRAWINGS

A few of the children in your classroom may begin doing pictorial drawings at 3 years and a few more at 4 years old. Do not expect all of the youngsters to. Let them progress through their own sequences of development at their own individual rates. Those who do draw pictorially will be using the previously discussed repertoire of figures that they have developed. Their drawings will be representations and not reproductions, for the young child draws what she knows, not what she sees. This principle is especially apparent in children's spontaneous drawings at age 6 when many youngsters go through a stage of so-called X-ray drawings that show both the inside and outside of objects at the same time. The children's drawings show things as the youngsters know them, rather than just what can be seen. People are shown inside drawings of houses that are seen from the outside, for example.

The children in your classroom probably will not have reached this stage; nor will they have developed a baseline in their drawings much before 5 years old. Objects are still free-floating on their art papers just as their first spontaneous letters are (see Chapter 12). This different perspective used by young children is sometimes used by adult artists as well.

Children also interpret their pictorial drawings differently from adults. Often youngsters do not start out to draw a particular thing. Instead, they describe their art more by the way it turns out than by what they had in mind. The way it turns out may have more to do with the materials they are using than anything else. Runny paint in easel drawings may remind the youngsters of smoke, rain, or fire, for instance.

On the other hand, the children purposefully may make a picture of the post office that the class visited on a field trip. The picture will look just like the building shape they have learned to do spontaneously, of course, and not at all like the post office itself. Children first draw buildings by combining mostly rectangular shapes in various ways and not by looking at buildings. The drawing often has a door in the middle and at least two square windows above it. Roofs may be flat or pointed and often have a chimney with smoke coming out. The drawing catches the essence of the building, not the reality. Some 4-year-olds also draw cars and trucks, as well as boats and planes. Often it is hard to tell the difference between early cars and trucks.

Once children have a repertoire of figures that the adults around them seem to accept, they will begin to put the figures together into scenes. The size and color of their objects will not be realistic. The more important the object or person, the larger the child will make it. Colors will have little relation to the object being depicted. Color choice depends more upon the particular brush the child happens to pick up, or a color the child happens to favor at the moment. Objects will be free-floating, as mentioned, and not anchored to a baseline. But the effect will be balanced and pleasing, nevertheless.

Those children who verbalize about their art may tell you things about their drawings that have little to do with what your eyes seem to show you. The youngsters must be speaking about an inner vision of their world, you decide. You are right, of course. Never forget that from inner visions come creative ideas. Let's support this beginning urge toward creativity in all of the children by giving it the freedom to grow spontaneously.

Table 13.1 shows the sequence of the development of art skills in children from 1 to 6 years old.

If You Have Not Checked This Item: Some Helpful Ideas

■ Encourage Children to Draw About Field Trips

Not all of your children can or want to draw pictorially. For those who do, you can suggest they draw a picture about a trip you have taken together. Children find it satisfying to be able to represent things they know about. They can tell about the things in words, have you write down their words, or record their words on tape.

It is also good to make a drawing or build a block structure about new things the children have encountered. Their products help you as a teacher to find out what is important to them and how they conceptualize the new ideas they have gained.

■ Have the Children Draw About Things in Their Repertoire

If you know that the children can draw people, houses, trees, and animals, they may want to draw a picture of their house and family. Those who want to can have you write down their story about the drawing.

■ Read a Book

Emma by Wendy Kesselman, illustrated by Barbara Cooney (New York: Doubleday, 1980) depicts lonely 72-year-old Emma, whose family gives her a painting of her village across the mountains for her birthday. The picture is not what Emma remembers, so she buys art materials and paints her own vision of the village. Soon Emma is filling her house with paintings, attracting the attention of people from everywhere, and surrounding herself with the people and places she loved.

TABLE 13.1
Development of art skills

Age	Art Skills
1–2	Makes random marks on paper Begins scribbling
2–3	Makes scribbles one on top of the other May cover paper with layers of color
3–4	May put a single scribble on a paper Makes basic shapes
4–5	Combines two shapes, often the circle and the cross to make mandala Draws suns Draws human as circle with arms and legs
5–6	Draws head of animals in profile Draws trees Makes pictorial drawings Includes baseline in pictures

OBSERVING, RECORDING, AND INTERPRETING ART SKILLS

Screen all of your children using the eight items of the Art Skills Checklist as shown in Figure 13.1. If you find that most of your 3- and 4-year-olds have not progressed beyond the random marks or scribbles stages, then ask yourself if your program has allowed the children the opportunity and the freedom to pursue art on their own. Do you have at least one easel in the classroom? Do you have an art area where children can get their own supplies and do their own work without teacher directions? Give children this opportunity and freedom to explore and experiment with art on their own. Later do a second screening using the eight checklist items to see if more check marks will appear under "Art Skills."

FIGURE 13.1

Screening for art skills

Date: 10 / 22

	Marks	Scribbles	Shapes	Mandalas	Suns	Humans	Animals	Pictures	
Randy	✓	✓							
Ellen	—	—	✓	✓	✓				
Jackie	—	—	✓	—	✓	✓			
Ron	✓								
Billy J.	✓	✓							
Jeff									
Sheila	—	—	—	—	✓	✓	✓	✓	
Josh	✓	✓							
Karyn	✓	✓	✓						
Rebecca	✓	✓	✓						
Lamar	✓								
David	✓	✓							
Michelle	—	—	✓	✓					
Billy S.	✓	✓							
Lionel	✓								

REFERENCES

Haskell, Lendall L. (1979). *Art in the early childhood years.* New York: Merrill/Macmillan.

Kellogg, Rhoda. (1970). *Analyzing children's art.* Palo Alto: National Press Books.

Lasky, Lila, & Rose Mukerji. (1980). *Art: Basic for young children.* Washington, DC: NAEYC.

Smith, Nancy R. (1982). The visual arts in early childhood education: Development and the creation of meaning. In Bernard Spodek (Ed.), *Handbook of research in early childhood education.* New York: Free Press.

OTHER SOURCES

Atack, Sally M. (1982). *Art activities for the handicapped.* Englewood Cliffs, NJ: Prentice-Hall.

Beaty, Janice J. (1992). *Skills for preschool teachers.* New York: Merrill/Macmillan.

Bos, Bev. (1978). *Don't move the muffin tins: A hands-off guide to art for the young child.* Roseville, CA: Turn the Page Press.

Clemens, Sydney Gurewitz. (1991). Art in the classroom: Making every day special. *Young Children, 46*(2), 4–11.

Edwards, Linda Carol. (1990). *Affective development and the creative arts: A process approach to early childhood education.* New York: Merrill/Macmillan.

Jenkins, Peggy Davison. (1980). *Art for the fun of it: A guide for teaching young children.* Englewood Cliffs, NJ: Prentice-Hall.

Thompson, Christine Marme. (1990). "I make a mark": The significance of talk in young children's artistic development. *Early Childhood Research Quarterly, 5,* 215–232.

Warner, Sally. (1989). *Encouraging the artist in your child (even if you can't draw).* New York: St. Martin's Press.

LEARNING ACTIVITIES

1. Use the Child Skills Checklist section "Art Skills" as a screening tool to observe all of the children in your classroom. Compare the children who have checks at the higher levels in the sequence of art skill development with their checks under "Cognitive Development: Classification and Seriation" (Chapter 9), especially in "Recognizes basic geometric shapes," "Recognizes colors," and "Recognizes differences in size." Can you draw any conclusions from this comparison?

2. Based on your screening survey, choose one or two children who have not shown much interest or development in art, and try to involve them in an art activity. Use one of the other Checklist areas in which they have shown interest and skill as the basis for the art activity. Record the result.

3. Set up your art area so that children can use it without adult help or direction. Record by running record what happens in this area on three different days.

4. Carry out one of the suggested art activities from the chapter with a group of children who show interest. Compare their results with their Checklist standing in art skills. What can you conclude from this?

5. Save the art products of one of your children over a 6-month period. Be sure to date them. How do they compare with the sequence of art skill development discussed here?

14 Imagination

Imagination Checklist

❑ Pretends by replaying familiar routines
❑ Needs particular props to do pretend play
❑ Assigns roles or takes assigned roles
❑ May switch roles without warning
❑ Uses language for creating and sustaining plot
❑ Uses exciting, danger-packed themes
❑ Takes on characteristics and actions related to role
❑ Uses elaborate and creative themes, ideas, details

A second important aspect of creativity in young children is their development of imagination. For young children, imagination is the ability to pretend or make believe, to take a role other than their own, to create fanciful situations, or to act out a fantasy of their making. Most children under 7 years old seem to spend a great deal of time engaged in this activity. It is a type of play that many adults fail to see as significant in the development of the child, because they do not understand it. But early childhood specialists have come to recognize imagination as one of the most effective means for promoting the development of the young child's intellectual skills, social skills, language, and most especially, creativity (Smilansky, 1968, p. 12).

One of the basic tools for creating is imagining, the ability to see a picture in our mind's eye. This ability allows us to tap into memories of the past and re-form them as possibilities for the present or future. Children's make-believe relies heavily on this capacity to draw on such internal images and to create new ones. Dorothy and Jerome Singer, who have done extensive research and writing on children's imaginative play, believe that imagining is essential to the development of intellectual and language skills as well. Children remember ideas and words they have actually experienced because the youngsters can associate the ideas with pictures in their minds (Singer & Singer, 1977, p. 6). This association reveals why it is so important for children to have many real experiences. Otherwise, there are few images stored in the youngsters' brains for them to draw on.

A number of adults who have been identified as creative report that they engaged in a great deal of daydreaming and fantasy play as children (Singer, 1973, p. 228). This finding is not surprising when we realize that imaginative play relies heavily on the creative skills of the young child. She must utilize previous experiences in new and different ways. She extracts the essence of a familiar experience such as getting ready for bed, and applies it creatively to a pretend activity such as putting to bed her doll, who doesn't want to go. Or she may take both the role of the doll and of the mother who is losing her patience with the stubborn dolly.

337

The child experiments with the situation, playing it this way one time and that another. If a peer joins in, then there is another point of view to reckon with. If the original player strays too far from her role, she may lose it to a player with more definite ideas on how a mother should act. Or she may switch to a different role herself and try on yet another set of characteristics. She learns to recall fragments of past experiences and combine them in novel ways, adding original dialogue, fresh nuances to her characterizations, and new directions to her plots. No playwright ever had better practice.

In addition to being her own creative playwright, she is also the actor, the director, the audience for other actors, and an interactor with others, whether she plays her role or steps out of it to make "aside" comments on progress of the spontaneous play. Just as with every other aspect of her development, she is creating her own knowledge when she has the freedom to participate in imaginative play.

This time the knowledge is about real life and the other actors in it: how they behave, how they respond to stressful situations, how they carry out their work roles, how they speak, how they interact with one another. Adult observers of imaginative play find that most of the make-believe play of children is centered around "the social problems of adults with whom children have close contacts" (Smilansky, 1968, p. 21). Common themes include the family and home, doctors and hospitals, work and professions, school, and dramatizations of escape, rescue, and superheroes.

Playing at life is not the inconsequential activity many adults seem to think it is. Children who have had extensive practice doing imaginative play are often those who are most successful in life as adults. Many disadvantaged children who have not been allowed or encouraged to engage in such play are also at a disadvantage as adults, for they have missed an important grounding in social, intellectual, and creative skills.

Chapter 5 discusses imaginative play as it applies to the development of children's social skills in solitary, parallel, and group play. This chapter will look at the same phenomenon in relation to the development of creativity in young children. To discover where the children in your classroom stand in the sequence of their development, make an assessment of each child using the eight items of the Imagination Checklist as you observe children pretending in the dramatic play area, at the water table, in the block corner, at the wood bench, with science materials, at the easels, and on the playground.

You will find that young children pretend about everything they do, both alone and with others. Tap into this rich vein of creativity in young children yourself, and you may see life and the world from a completely new and fresh perspective: the *what if* point of view. This "what if" perspective is the true magic of childhood, the belief that children can make life anything they want it to be.

Adults know from the hard facts of reality that life cannot be changed so easily, or can it? What if we also believed we could really make life anything we wanted it to be? Does believing make it so? Children act as if this idea were true. Is there a way we can help them develop into adults who will actually be able to make their adult lives come out the way they want them to be? Is there a way we can preserve the "child" in ourselves so that we can do the same? Take a hard look at the developmental sequence in imaginative play that follows to see what you need to do to keep this spark alive in children and to rekindle its essence in your own life.

❏ PRETENDS BY REPLAYING FAMILIAR ROUTINES

This checklist item describes the earliest of the imaginative play behaviors in young children. Incredibly enough, it appears as early as 1 year (Smilansky, 1968, p. 10). By the age of 18 months, infants may go through the imaginary routine of feeding themselves with an empty spoon and cup, and even saying, "Yummy!" The Singers believe that this tendency to play or replay past events through imagery is one of the basic capacities of the human brain (Singer & Singer, 1977, p. 3).

Two-Year-Olds and Young Three-Year-Olds

By 2 years of age most normal children spend a great deal of time at home or in a toddler program, replaying fragments of everyday experience if given the chance. Pieces of familiar routines are repeated over and over with little change and little effort to expand them into a longer sequence. The toddler will put the baby to bed by putting the doll in the cradle, covering it, and saying, "Nite-nite." Then the toddler will pick up the doll and begin the routine all over again. Once a particular routine is established with a 2-year-old, it seems to become quite rigid, almost like a ritual (Segal & Adcock, 1981, p. 92).

Words are not all that important in the pretending of 2-year-olds, however. The youngsters use them sparingly, mainly to accompany actions or for sound effects. Actions are the main ingredients of the imaginative play of 2-year-olds. Once these youngsters get an idea for pretend play, they try to put it into action immediately. They do not set the stage with words, or search for appropriate props.

Props may be used, though, if they are available. Two-year-olds use props realistically, for the most part. Dishes are used for eating, not usually as a steering wheel or a flying saucer. Because these youngsters are also impulsive in their behavior, props can influence the type of pretend play they engage in. A toy broom can inspire them to sweep, for instance, even though they had no previous plans for cleaning. They do not need props to pretend, however. Some 2-year-olds may even carry on their play with invisible props.

The imaginative play of these youngsters is mainly centered around chores and routines such as eating, going to bed, caring for the baby, getting their hair washed, turning on television, shopping, visiting grandma, driving the car, and getting gas for the car. Two-year-olds are very serious about it, and take offense if adults make fun of their sometimes comical mode of pretending.

Doll play is also a frequent activity for both boys and girls of this age. Dolls are usually undressed, laid in a box or bed, and covered completely over with a piece of cloth in a very ritualized routine (Caplan & Caplan, 1983, p. 143).

The play of 2-year-olds is frequently solitary and rarely occurs with more than one other player. They and their age-mates have not yet developed the social skills for coming together in a common endeavor. When two children this age play together, one usually imitates the other. However, others will join in if they see one child doing something, and sometimes a wild melee ensues. The pretend play of children this young is brief at best, and it suddenly may disintegrate into running and squealing if other children are around.

Young 3-year-olds who have not done much imaginative play may start at this stage of development in your center. Their maturity usually carries them on quickly to a more advanced level.

If You Have Not Checked This Item: Some Helpful Ideas

■ Read a Book

Mashed Potato Mountain by Laurel Dee Gugler (Windsor, Ontario: Black Moss Press, 1988) depicts a little boy, Jamie, pretending with his meal of mashed potatoes, gravy, broccoli, bread, and ice cream. Double-spread pages show tiny Jamie standing amid large white mashed potato mountains with a river of gravy and a forest of broccoli.

■ Provide Appropriate Props

Knowing that the youngest children pretend mainly about familiar household routines, you should have eating, cleaning, and sleeping props available in your dramatic play area. Put out all kinds of baby dolls and their beds as well.

❑ NEEDS PARTICULAR PROPS TO DO PRETEND PLAY

Three-Year-Olds

If 3-year-olds have had a chance to pretend when they were 2, then they gradually develop new skills and interests in their imaginative play. The fragments of familiar routines that occupied the children earlier become more extended and less rigid as the youngsters mature. Three-year-olds begin to think a bit about the pretending they are about to do, rather than acting on a sudden impulse. This forethought leads them to preplanning the play by finding or gathering certain props. In fact, some 3-year-olds cannot proceed with the play until the right prop is found.

The rigidity expressed by many 2-year-olds in their ritualistic manner of pretending is thus carried over by many 3-year-olds in their insistence on particular props in order to play. Three-year-olds may feel they need a particular hat, costume, doll, or steering wheel in order to carry out a role. Many times, in fact, the object is the basis for the play. Three-year-olds very much enjoy dressing up and playing a role, and they have developed a much broader concept of how to do it.

Props very well may serve the children as an instrument for getting out of themselves. Because 3-year-olds are still strongly self-centered, they may need a prop in order to break away from their own point of view. Just as shy children can lose themselves in speaking through a hand puppet or from behind a mask, 3-year-olds may need the extra impetus of an object that is outside of themselves to get them started in pretending to be someone else.

Some 3-year-olds are very involved in imaginary play of a different sort at home. They have an imaginary playmate or invisible friend. This is the most common age for children to invent such a friend. Research finds that first-born children who do not have many playmates may use their imaginations to create such a companion (Segal & Adcock, 1981, p. 10). This research gives additional evidence that pretending is an innate activity with young humans.

Such invisible companions, however, serve a different purpose from the pretend play in nursery school. They are invented companions for children who have none, or loving friends for children who do not receive love from those around them, or protectors for children who need someone to support them. When children come to a preschool program, they usually leave their imaginary friends behind, often permanently. Once the children are occupied with real peers, they have little need for a made-up friend.

Family activities are a large part of 3-year-olds' pretend play in preschool programs. Play researcher Fergus P. Hughes (1991) notes:

> There are clear indications that threes, unlike twos, begin to identify strongly with adults— to become increasingly interested in what adults do and to imagine themselves doing the same things. Perhaps as a result, threes become interested in dramatic play, in which they have an opportunity to act out adult roles for themselves. (p. 74)

Doll play, hospital play, and pretending to be a community helper are also common themes. Three-year-olds also enjoy driving cars and trains, flying jet planes, and being firefighters. These themes are carried out in dramatic play, block building, table block games, clay and paint creations, the water table, the woodworking bench, singing, creative movement, puppet play, and toy telephone activities—anywhere and everywhere children gather.

If You Have Not Checked This Item: Some Helpful Ideas

■ Provide a Variety of Props

In the large motor area, have large wooden riding trucks, wagons, a wheelbarrow, and large hollow blocks and floorboards for building child-size structures. Put out a full-length mirror in the dress-up area. Include costume jewelry, scarves, handbags, wallets, belts, vests, shoes, aprons, all kinds of hats, doctor's equipment, goggles, binoculars, badges, umbrellas, and canes. An assortment of men's and women's clothes in teenage size rather than adult size is often easier for young children to handle.

■ Read a Book

Anna Maria's Blanket by Joanne Barkan (New York: Barron's, 1990) is an imaginary tale in which Anna Maria's pink "security blanket" complains to her about not being carried around anymore. Anna Maria, who is preparing to go to nursery school, is too old for her blanket, but has a hard time convincing the stubborn blanket. The story and double-spread illustrations show all kinds of pretending with stuffed animals and a doll.

❏ ASSIGNS ROLES OR TAKES ASSIGNED ROLES

Three-year-olds usually find it is more fun when several children play together. You will have checked on this behavior previously in your observations concerning social play. This item signals the beginning of peer play for most children. Pretend episodes usually do not last long in the beginning because most children of this age are not yet flexible when it comes to differences of opinions. This inflexibility sometimes shows up when it comes to deciding who will play what role.

Many 3-year-olds try to control imaginative play by assigning the roles. The dominant child takes the role he or she wants and assigns the others, who may or may not agree. Most children this age want their own role. As their creativity blossoms through this type of play, their solutions to role assignment problems are often highly creative and something an adult would not have thought of. Listen to your children to see how they resolve such problems.

The role of mother is a favorite one for girls of this age, so it is a role that is often in contention. What would you do if all four girls who are playing together want to be the mother and no one will give in? Four girls solved the problem among themselves. After a few minutes of discussion—or rather argument—when it became clear that Janie, who spoke up first about being the mother, would not change, nor would the other three, then a different solution needed to be found. The girls accepted the fact that there could be only one mother in the household, but they could not accept that the other girls would be sisters or babies or grandmothers. Suddenly, one of the girls said, "We'll all be other mothers who are visiting Janie this morning," and they were.

Three-year-olds who are playing pretend roles at home often will act the same way in assigning roles, even to adults. "I'll be the mother and you be the baby," is a role reversal commonly proposed by a child to her mother. Go along with the role reversal if you are the adult, and you will enjoy observing how your child plays your role.

Here is a typical role assignment situation played by 3-year-olds and recorded in a running record:

> Sherry is in the play grocery store holding a box of cereal. She hands box to child playing role of cashier. Walks back to grocery shelves. Picks up box and puts it in grocery cart. "Here's our groceries, Mother," she says to Ann who is standing nearby. Picks up bag filled with groceries and carries it to play house. Walks back to grocery store. "I'm gonna be mother," she says loudly to herself. Picks up several boxes off shelf and walks to cashier. Puts groceries in bag. "Mother, it's time to go home," she says to Ann. Ann gives no response but pays for her groceries. "There are no more groceries. We have to leave now," says Sherry. Still gets no

response from Ann. "I'm the mother and you're the grandmother. I'm not a little kid," she says to Ann. No response. They walk to house together. She puts her bag down and helps Ann with hers. "We have to unload everything now." They start to unpack all the groceries. "Oh, no, daughter," she says to Ann, "When it's cleanup time we have to pick all this up." Both girls laugh.

Since Ann was originally the director of this play episode and Sherry had evidently agreed to the role of daughter by taking it, it is interesting to see what strategies Sherry now uses to get out of an unwanted role. First, she states loudly but to herself that she is going to be the mother. She receives no response, so she retains her daughter role at first, but then states outright to Ann that she is the mother and Ann can be the grandmother. Sherry still gets no response. Silence does not signify consent among young children. Silence may only mean that the challenged child does not want to engage in an argument, not that she agrees to give up her role. Sherry tries calling Ann "daughter," but Ann refuses to get involved verbally, so the role problem is still unresolved before cleanup time ends the play.

Another imaginative play episode, previously recorded in Figure 2.2, shows children who are late 3-year-olds and 4-year-olds engaged in the type of role assignment problem being discussed here:

Katy is playing by herself with plastic blocks, making guns; she walks into other room.
K: "Lisa, would you play with me? I'm tired of playing by myself."
They walk into other room to slide and climbing area.
K: "I am Wonder Woman."
L: "So am I."
K: "No, there is only one Wonder Woman. You are Robin."
L: "Robin needs a Batman because Batman and Robin are friends."
All this takes place under slides and climber. Lisa shoots block gun which Katy has given her. Katy falls on floor.
L: (to teacher) "We're playing Superfriends and Wonder Woman keeps falling down."
Katy opens eyes, gets up, and says:
K: "Let's get out our Batmobile and go help the world."
She runs to other room and back, making noises like a car.
L: "Wonder Woman is died. She fell out of the car."
She falls down.
K: "It's only a game, wake up. Lisa, you be Wonder Woman, I'll be ____."
L: "Let's play house now."
Katy begins sliding down the slide.
K: "We have a lot of Superfriends to do." (She says this while sliding.) "Robin is coming after you!" (She shouts to Lisa, running from the slide and into the other room.)
Lisa has gone into the housekeeping area and says to Katy:

L: "Katy, here is your doll's dress." (lost yesterday)
John joins the girls.
L: "I'm Wonder Woman."
K: "I'm Robin."
J: "I'm Batman. Where is the Batmobile?"
K: "It's in here."
They run into the other room and Katy points under the slide, telling John what the Batmobile can do. Then all run to the other room and back again.
K: "John, we are not playing Superfriends any more."

This typical pretending episode illustrates perfectly the kind of role assignment and switching so characteristic of children this age. It is obvious from the children's easy agreement that they have played together before and therefore accept certain conditions. Katy is the director here and assigns the roles. She takes the role of Wonder Woman and assigns Lisa the role of Robin. Lisa really does not agree (we soon see), but she accepts her assignment. She probably has gone through this with Katy before and knows that if she plays along without making a fuss, her turn will come. It comes quite soon, in fact, when she notes that Katy seems to have abandoned the Wonder Woman role by suddenly getting out the Batmobile and "going to help the world."

Here Lisa announces that she is Wonder Woman and has fallen out of the car and died. Katy agrees to Lisa's new role by saying, "It's only a game, wake up. Lisa, you be Wonder Woman." When John joins the game and takes the role of Batman, the girls do not object at first. But obviously they know how to get rid of unwanted players by announcing, "John, we are not playing Superfriends any more."

Observe to discover what other creative ploys your children use to get peers to take role assignments or to get out of assigned roles they don't want and into ones they really want. Other strategies used to resolve play conflicts in a positive manner are discussed on page 130.

If your children are engaged in this kind of dramatic play, you will probably be checking this item. If you leave it blank, it means either that the child is not playing because he has not reached this level of group imaginative play, or that he does not assign roles or accept assignments. If this is the case, he has probably not reached the group play level, because children who play together like this soon come to an understanding about role assignments.

If You Have Not Checked This Item: Some Helpful Ideas

■ Read a Book

A Lion for Lewis by Rosemary Wells (New York: Dial Press, 1982) is the story of dress-up play in the attic by two older children (5-year-olds) and little Lewis (age 3) who always gets assigned to play the inferior roles and never a main character. He is baby to the older children's mother and father, sick child to their doctor and nurse, and maid to their king and princess. Lewis eventually gets his way, however, and much in the manner of real children, by finding something better that the older children really respect: in Lewis's case, a lion suit into which he climbs to turn the play upside down. It is the same kind of creative solution that real children use when they are blocked by their peers.

The development of creativity, as you can see, means much more than becoming an artist or writer. Perhaps the most valuable lesson that children learn from imaginative play, in fact, is how to develop creative solutions to life's sticky interpersonal problems. What an exceptionally strong inducement that is for our promoting of imaginative play in early childhood!

When You Were Little and I Was Big by Priscilla Galloway (Toronto: Annick Press, 1984) is a role-reversal story about a little girl who makes believe she is big and her mother is little. The illustrations show the girl looking like the big mother, only wearing her same red overalls and striped shirt, while the mother appears little. The girl narrates the story and tells her mother what she would do in each one of several everyday situations, just like her mother has already done with her.

❏ MAY SWITCH ROLES WITHOUT WARNING

The pretend play of 3-year-olds is obviously more elaborate than that of 2-year-olds. But because of their free-floating nature, the plots 3-year-olds make up often shift from one event to another without much advance warning. We have witnessed this characteristic before in these children. They write the letters of their names or of words here and there on a sheet of paper, sometimes starting in the middle and working both forward and backward. The teacher also finds that when preschoolers are asked to line up in a straight line, he has 15 different versions of straightness.

Three-year-olds do not seem to be grounded on a common baseline, perhaps because of the right-hemisphere brain dominance at this stage of their life. Its open-endedness seems to be reflected in the free-form thinking of their imaginative play. They may start out playing Superfriends, but soon the activity becomes playing house, with hardly the blink of an eye. Their peers seem to accept these abrupt shifts as a matter of course because it is part of their nature, too.

Adults have more trouble trying to follow such thinking patterns. Our only current experience is with nighttime dreams that may start out with one sequence but evolve into something entirely different when we subconsciously play around with a particular detail.

This type of easy shifting is characteristic of divergent thinking, the process in which individuals generate a variety of novel responses to a situation—in a word, creative thinking. It is the opposite of what usually occurs—convergent thinking, in which individuals move toward a uniform response. Obviously, many more solutions to a problem are generated when we practice divergent thinking. For adults, practicing divergent thinking is not so simple when we have been conditioned for so long to think in a stereotyped format acceptable to all.

The development of creativity calls on us to promote divergent thinking in young children and rekindle its use in our own lives. Divergent thinking is nonconformist in nature and, therefore, somewhat threatening to adults' usual response of going along with the crowd. Most young children have not yet been conditioned to behave in an inhibited manner. Thus they are more open to novel solutions in their imaginative play. If these solutions could be carried over into adult life, what creative possibilities for resolving interpersonal problems might ensue!

Three-year-olds not only move from one episode to another in their pretend play without much concern, but they also switch from one role to another without warning. Although adults are somewhat disconcerted by such illogical moves, peers seem to accept such switches as normal. If you want to be someone else, that's your privilege, seems to be the unspoken rule. However, you must work it out in an appropriate manner if you want others to continue playing with you, seems to be the rest of the agreement.

The previous checklist item discussed the assignment of roles by one child and the acceptance of them by others. Children seem to learn early how to get out of roles they don't want and into roles they do want without disrupting the play.

This behavior may be an illustration of the interesting findings by Gottman and Parkhurst, that the friendships of 3- and 4-year-olds in their study were characterized by the playing of extended fantasy roles and that children this age took particular care to avoid disagreements. When squabbling broke out among them, the children had great difficulty de-escalating it. Therefore, they seemed to create a "climate of agreement" for one another in which they explained or played away disagreements immediately, because of their awareness that disagreements had "unmanageable, adverse consequences for their friendships" (Damon, 1983, p. 141).

If we look back at the pretend play episode with Katy, Lisa, and John, it is evident that all three know who is who and what is going on, even though they are sliding down the slide and running back and forth from one room to the other, and even though the roles have been switched three times. Katy is Wonder Woman, then Robin, then someone unnamed. Lisa is Robin and then Wonder Woman. John is Batman, and then he is excluded from the play.

This format is typical of the play of 3- and 4-year-olds. Their ability to handle such role assignments and switches with a nonchalance or a sensitivity that prevents squabbles is a positive result of imaginative play that has seldom been pointed out. Not all children are able to play this way. Neither are all 3- and 4-year-olds able to participate in group play at this level. But those who have been allowed the freedom and given the support to engage in such play can reach this level. Are they eventually the adults in our society who know "instinctively" how to get along with others? We would like to think so.

If You Have Not Checked This Item: Some Helpful Ideas

■ **Allow Children to Settle Their Own Play Problems**

Unless the players are physically hurting one another, it is better to allow them to settle their own problems. For them to experience a squabble that gets out of hand is important in their learning how to play with one another, as Gottman and Parkhurst discovered.

■ **Read a Book**

Your Turn, Doctor by Carla Perez and Deborah Robison (New York: Dial Books for Young Readers, 1982) is the hilarious story of a role-reversal for the little girl Gloria and her doctor, who is about to give her a physical exam. Gloria refuses, and instead she examines her doctor. Your children who are forever engaged in playing doctor will love the story, but it is also a book every doctor who deals with a young child should know by heart!

❏ USES LANGUAGE FOR CREATING AND SUSTAINING PLOT

Whereas 2-year-olds do most of their pretending without much language, 3-year-olds depend upon language to set the scene and sustain the action. If 3-year-olds are playing by themselves, they often will talk to themselves about what is happening. They also will speak for the characters—all of them. If the youngsters are playing with other children, they often use a great deal of dialogue to carry out their ideas. This behavior promotes their improved use of language and dialogue with others. In addition, it provides yet another opportunity for them to express creativity in the fresh and novel way they use words.

Words direct what the children do, the way they act, who the characters are, the unfolding of the plot, and the way the children resolve conflict. Children involved in pretending who do not have the language skills of the more advanced players are able to listen and eventually to imitate the advanced players' use of language. Everyone involved gets excellent practice in improving speaking skills, trying out new words, and using familiar language in new ways.

One of the new ways for some children to use language is for the expression of feelings. The characters in these spontaneous make-believe situations need to express how they feel about what is happening to them. Many children have trouble putting their feelings into words. Younger children prefer to "act out" rather than to speak out. This type of imaginative play gives them the opportunity to learn how to express feelings.

The youngsters, in fact, are projecting their feelings by expressing what a character feels. Even if the character is a doll, a puppet, or an inanimate figure of a person or an animal, the children have yet another opportunity to speak. Three-year-olds are often more comfortable expressing the feelings of toy people than their own. The youngsters like to take their dolls or stuffed animals to the doctor's office, to listen to these pretend people express their fears, and to comfort them. In doing so, the children sort out their own impressions about the situation and try out their own sometimes novel ideas for resolving problems.

Sara Smilansky (1968) has found three main functions of language in this sort of dramatic play: imitating adult speech, imagining the make-believe situation (mainly dialogue), and managing the play. In this regard, language serves to explain, command, and direct the action (p. 27).

If you listen carefully to the actors in imaginative play, you will note that they carry out all three of these functions. They definitely imitate adult speech. You practically can hear yourself speaking if you are the parent or the teacher of any of these children. Children also bring imagery to life in the characterizations that they express through dialogue. Finally, someone in the group, usually the self-assigned director, is forever stepping outside her role to explain or reaffirm what is going on.

If inner imagery allows the child to pretend in the first place, then talking aloud allows him to expand the meaning of what he visualizes. He not only hears himself speaking, but he also receives feedback from the reactions of others. This feedback helps him to revise and refine ideas and word use. Until he arrives at the point where he can create and sustain the action of pretend situations through language, he will miss the value of using his imagination in this manner. Eventually, he must use mainly language and not just imagining in thinking. Thus imaginative play serves as a sort of transitional activity for the preschool child to learn spoken words for his internal images.

Creative adults, especially writers, need to be able to express their imagery in words like this. Mental pictures are not enough. Many writers admit to experiencing rich fantasy lives as children. Having a variety of opportunities for pretending in the preschool setting may help your children to become such creative adults.

If You Have Not Checked This Item: Some Helpful Ideas

■ Have the Children Read Wordless Picture Books

Most wordless books illustrate their plots in a clear sequence of pictures. Although pictures tell the story, the child needs to express the action and dialogue in words as she reads the book. This gives her excellent practice for doing the same thing in imaginative play. Wordless books are designed for children of various ages and developmental levels. Some are simple, others are extremely complex and sophisticated. Be sure to go through a book ahead of time to see if it is suitable for a particular child.

The Gift by John Prater (New York: Viking Penguin, 1985) is the wordless story of a gift of two little chairs delivered to a boy and girl. They take the chairs out of the cardboard carton, and then use the carton as a takeoff to adventure. The two climb inside and float out the window, through the city, under the ocean, into the jungle, and finally back home again. It is an imaginative story that your "reader" needs to supply the words for.

■ Use Hand Puppets

Have a variety of hand puppets available for the children: animals, characters from books, community helpers, adults, and children figures. A puppet theater made from a cardboard carton can help to motivate the children's use of puppets as play actors. You may need to put on a puppet show yourself to set the stage, so to speak, for your children's dramas. Younger children tend to use puppets as an extension of their arms, using the puppet's mouth for pretend biting rather than for speaking, as mentioned previously. Your modeling behavior can show the children a better way to use puppets.

It is not necessary to have a puppet theater in the beginning, but your more advanced pretenders may expand their repertoire of imaginative play if a puppet theater is available. Make hand puppets or purchase them from toy stores, children's book stores, science museum shops, or store kitchen departments, where they are sold as pot holders.

❑ USES EXCITING, DANGER-PACKED THEMES

Four-Year-Olds

Most 4-year-olds do everything in a more exuberant out-of-bounds manner than 3-year-olds, including pretending. Four-year-olds are more noisy, active, and aware of things outside of themselves. They are fascinated with matters of life and death, and they begin to use such themes more often in their imaginative play. Superheroes and other television characters show up in their pretending. Bad guys are captured. Good guys are rewarded. People get shot and killed.

Adults look askance and blame television. They feel that television watching surely must be bad for young children. By the age of 4, children are viewing an average of 4 hours of television a day. Surely this viewing must affect their pretending and imaginations. Research carried on by children's play specialists Dorothy and Jerome Singer, however, resulted in findings contrary to what they had expected. The Singers found no relationship of statistical significance between watching television and imaginary play. Pretending neither increased nor decreased as a result of watching television.

The strongest correlation the Singers found was between the amount of television watched and overt aggression in the classroom. How true, agree nursery school teachers, without perhaps realizing that 4-year-olds have always exhibited aggression in their play. The real reason for the increased aggression could well be that sitting and watching television for long periods of time does not allow young children to discharge their pent-up energy and aggressive feelings as does normal active play (Segal & Adcock, 1981, p. 138).

Four-year-olds are extremely active, and must have daily opportunities to discharge this pent-up energy. It is only natural for this energy to take the form of powerful superhero character roles from the television programs the children watch. Ask adults who were raised before the days of television what form their wildest pretending took, and you will hear tales of cowboys and Indians, cops and robbers, or American soldiers and Nazis.

The counterargument about superhero play talks about the television cartoons children see that show superheroes controlling others through threat, force, and violence. Many teachers describe superhero play in their classrooms as being characterized by "disjointed bursts of activity which deteriorated rapidly into too-rough, too-loud play" (Pena, French, & Holmes, 1987, p. 11). Some researchers conclude,

Many 4-year-olds use exciting, danger-packed themes in their dramatic play.

"From our observations, it appears that superhero play may not be able to sustain itself and be reasonably free of adult intervention" (Pena et al., 1987, p. 13).

What should a teacher do who has a strong belief in the value of fantasy play, but does not feel that the amount of adult intervention required to keep superhero play from bursting out of bounds is worth the effort? Should superhero play be banned from the classroom entirely? No, say many teachers. There are ways to extract important lessons from this powerful play activity that seems to have so many youngsters in its grip:

> *Star Wars* hero Luke Skywalker learned from his mentor that the Force contained both Good and Evil. Luke had to learn to control the Evil in order to realize the Good. Superhero play is much like the Force; and like Luke Skywalker, we must learn to control the negative aspects of superhero fantasy play in order for children to realize its many benefits. (Johnston, 1987, p. 16)

One of the more creative suggestions is to scale down the most violent play: that is, to turn it into a tabletop activity. Most of the television characters are available in a variety of sizes from dolls to matchbox-scale figures, just right for tabletop play. "By allowing this activity *only* while sitting at a table, running and crashing bodies cease to be a problem. The benefits of superhero play are not diminished simply because children are seated while they play" (Johnston, 1987, p. 17). Pretending, after all, can take place anywhere.

Group play comes into its own when children reach the age of 4. When they first get together, however, it often degenerates like superhero play into a wild sort of activity without plot or dialogue, almost a regression from children's previous role playing (Segal & Adcock, 1981, p. 98). This wildness seems to be a natural progression in their learning to get along with one another. The establishment and recognition of dominance is dealt with in such rough-and-tumble play. Children also develop coping skills as they focus on the sometimes aggressive actions and reactions of peers. Out of these interactions comes a sense of common group purpose that sets the stage for the more organized play to follow.

Teachers can help, not by preventing wild play, but by redirecting its energy into the exciting, danger-packed themes that 4-year-olds favor. Doctor play, always a favorite, can involve taking sick or injured patients to the hospital in an ambulance with a loud siren. One teacher found that her children needed help organizing and elaborating on their ambulance plot. Some of the children were running around the room making loud siren noises. The teacher suggested that they build an ambulance out of large blocks. Now what could they do? This time, the teacher decided to play a role herself. A running record of an observation of 4-year-old Jessica includes the following:

Jessica runs to climber, climbs up and sits on top. Teacher, who is trying to involve children in dramatic play, suggests they use the climber as their hospital. They are building an ambulance out of large blocks. Jessica climbs down and begins stacking blocks one on top of the other. She sits and watches others finish by taping paper plates colored yellow on front to use as headlights. She picks up plate and tapes it to rear of ambulance.

Jessica runs to table to get felt-tip marker. "I want the yellow marker. Lots of yellow." She gets marker. "What am I gonna write on? I want to color something. I'll color the wheels black." Jessica drops yellow marker and picks up black one. She colors in back paper plate wheel with marker. "I want to color something yellow." Teacher suggests steering wheel. She does it.

Jessica runs and climbs into block ambulance. "I'm the driver." She uses her plate as steering wheel. "I wanna be the patient." Jessica gets up and lies down in middle of ambulance. She gets carried to "the hospital" by teacher and other children. She lies by the climber and pretends to be sick, moaning and groaning. Other children leave, but she stays.

Then she gets up and runs to table where teacher is helping children to make doctor bags. Teacher asks her what name she wants on her bag. She answers, "I want to be a nurse, not a doctor." Teacher asks what tools a nurse uses. She answers, "Nurses help, they don't use tools. Doctors use tools." Teacher asks, "What does your mother use when you are sick?" She answers, "I don't know."

Jessica takes bag and runs back to ambulance with bag on arm, smiling. She yells, "Lisa, lay down, you're the patient." Jessica sits in front seat and drives ambulance using paper plate steering wheel. She hops up again and runs to teacher, asking her to be the doctor. She jumps up and down, urging the teacher to hurry. "Hurry, we're ready," she repeats. Teacher comes and helps carry Lisa to hospital.

The teacher noted that more children participated in this particular role play than any others she had witnessed. An ambulance had gone by on the street outside earlier in the morning, siren blaring, and the children who saw it were excited but alarmed. This event prompted their building of the block ambulance. But the teacher's own participation in the play certainly stimulated the extra number of children to become involved. The teacher's idea for extending the play by helping the children make doctor bags added immensely to the drama. The running record, however, caught 4-year-old Jessica just as she normally acted, always on the run.

Jessica's rather stereotyped answers about doctors is also typical of this age. Gender roles seem to become more rigid, with girls insisting on playing the mother, waitress, or teacher, whereas boys often want to play father, driver, policeman, or superhero. Same-gender groups form about this time, with girls' play becoming more relaxed and verbal, and boys' play faster paced and more aggressive (Segal & Adcock, 1981, p. 101).

Block play, for instance, may get out of hand with 4-year-old boys. It sometimes disintegrates into throwing when adults are not around, or even when they are. Try to change the violent direction of the block play by giving players a new task involving excitement or mystery: "Where is the mysterious tunnel I saw on the floor this morning, boys? What, you didn't see it? I'm surprised. I thought you had X-ray vision. I could see it right through the rug. You don't believe me? Well, maybe if you make your own tunnel, you'll be able to see the mystery tunnel, too. Jeff, you and Lennie know how to build tunnels. Maybe you could make a mystery tunnel at one end of the rug, and Rod and Kennie could make a tunnel at the other end. If the tunnels come together in the middle, you'd all be able to run your cars through one long tunnel. What do you think?"

If you observe that individual children who are 4 years old have not started playing with exciting, danger-packed themes, it may be that they are less mature than the others. How do they compare with other 4-year-olds in motor skills, for instance? Obviously, it is not appropriate to push such children into something they are not interested in. Provide them with many opportunities to engage in play themes of their own interests. You will know what some of these are from your observations and conversations with such youngsters.

If You Have Not Checked This Item: Some Helpful Ideas

■ Read a Book

Come Away from the Water, Shirley by John Burningham (New York: Crowell, 1977) is a marvelous example of the imaginative life of a 4- or 5-year-old girl who accompanies her mother and father to the beach. While they sit in their beach chairs and give her directions on the left side of the book's double-spread pages, Shirley and her dog engage in an imaginary pirate ship adventure on all of the right-hand pages. While her mother is telling her not to stroke that dog, "Shirley, you don't know where he's been," the opposite page shows Shirley being forced to walk the plank on the pirate ship as the dog bites the pirate's leg. Shirley's imaginary adventures are wordless, giving children a chance to make up their own dialogue and descriptions.

Before I Go to Sleep by Thomas Hood (New York: Putnam, 1990) is a more sedate story than the first one, about a little boy who lies on his bed pretending on every page to be a different animal, until at last he falls asleep.

■ Provide Big Building Supplies

Children 4 and 5 years old like to build big structures to play in. Have the youngsters use hollow wooden blocks if possible. Or bring in wooden packing crates you get from a wholesaler. Cardboard cartons, plastic milk carton carriers, scrap boards, and lumber can be used for building pretend huts, forts, houses, boats, race cars, and fire engines. Play houses also can be purchased commercially, or made like tents by covering a card table with a blanket or by hanging sheets over lines strung in a corner of the room.

❑ TAKES ON CHARACTERISTICS AND ACTIONS RELATED TO ROLE

Four-year olds have more experience than 3-year-olds when it comes to creating a role in their pretend play. Because they desperately want to participate in the adult world, 4-year-olds try out all sorts of adult roles: mother at work, father at work, doctor, nurse, bus driver, astronaut, waiter, fast-food cook, gas station attendant, mail carrier, firefighter, truck driver, train conductor, or crane operator. In addition, 4-year-olds play their roles with many more realistic details. They select props more carefully, dress up more elaborately, and carry out the role with more appropriate dialogue and actions.

If you listen carefully to 4-year-olds when you are observing them doing imaginative play, you will be able to learn a great deal about their understanding of the people and situations in their world. In addition, you may gain quite a respect for their use of creativity in developing their roles. Even the mundane roles of mother, father, brother, and baby are played with new twists and novel solutions to problems. Dialogue is expanded, and the players even express emotions quite eloquently where appropriate.

Language is used more than ever before to set the scene and create the mood. Because the players are beginning to make greater distinctions between real and pretend, they often make aside-like comments about things that are not real, just pretend, so that you, their peers, and even they themselves understand what is real and what is pretend.

Four-year-olds are also more flexible about taking different roles. Children who would not take a bad guy's role at age 3, may play it to the hilt at age 4.

Observe your children carefully as they pretend in the dramatic play area, in the block corner, at the water table, and on the playground. Are they playing roles with greater realism than before, using expanded dialogue, showing more emotion, and almost becoming the character? If so, you should mark this item on the checklist.

If You Have Not Checked This Item: Some Helpful Ideas

■ Have Many Sets of Feltboard Characters

Children can use cutout characters from their favorite storybooks to play with on a feltboard. Obtain an extra paperback copy of the book, cut out the characters (away from the children), and mount them on cardboard with sandpaper backing. Keep the characters in a manila envelope with a good copy of the book inside. Then children can look at pictures from the story when they play. The youngsters can act out scenes from the book if they want, or they can have the characters participate in brand new adventures. This activity is good practice in role playing with characters the children already know. A child can play by herself or with another child. More than two children at the same feltboard is a bit crowded. Keep more than one feltboard in the book area, if you want this to be a popular activity. Feltboards can be made by mounting felt to a piece of cardboard folded in two and hinged at the top so that it stands easily on a table. Some favorite storybooks in paperback from which you may want to cut out characters are:

> *Will I Have a Friend?* by Miriam Cohen (New York: Collier Books, 1967)
>
> *Corduroy* by Don Freeman (New York: Viking Press, 1968)
>
> *Whistle for Willie* by Ezra Jack Keats (New York: Puffin, 1977)
>
> *Where the Wild Things Are* by Maurice Sendak (New York: Scholastic, 1963)
>
> *Strega Nona* by Tomie de Paola (Englewood Cliffs, NJ: Prentice-Hall, 1975)
>
> *The Three Billy Goats Gruff* by Paul Galdone (New York: Clarion Books, 1973)

■ Read a Book

Reading a book in which the main character is a child who uses his imagination to take on the characteristics and actions of a particular role is another method for motivating children to pretend. In *The Train* by David McPhail (Boston: Little, Brown, 1977), Matthew, who loves trains, dreams that he is involved in fixing a real train, as well as helping the stationmaster, the conductor, and the engineer.

❏ USES ELABORATE AND CREATIVE THEMES, IDEAS, DETAILS

Four-Year-Olds

The themes that 4-year-olds use in their pretending are many of the same ones they used at age 3, only much expanded. The youngsters still enjoy playing house. Both boys and girls play with dolls and take roles in the housekeeping corner. Doll play now includes dressing as well as undressing, but the central action usually involves putting the doll to bed. Many girls of this age prefer playing with little girl dolls rather than baby dolls. Play with dollhouses, however, is still too detailed to hold the interest of most 4-year-olds. They like the dolls more than the houses. Even block structures are not played with as much as they will be played with at age 5. At age 4, the pretending takes place during the process of building, rather than with the finished product afterward.

Doctor play is at its peak at age 4, and it will seldom be as popular again. All kinds of themes involving community helpers are used, especially after a visit by a community helper or a field trip to a work site. Superheroes are popular, as we have seen, especially television characters. Monsters sometimes appear, but they are still a bit too scary for 4-year-olds to handle.

Older Four-Year-Olds and Five-Year-Olds

The pretend play of older 4-year-olds and of 5-year-olds is characterized by the elaborate nature of the drama, no matter whether the theme is a common one or an invented adventure. Five-year-olds add all kinds of details through their dialogue, dressing up, props, and imaginations. Their play gets so involved, in fact, that it even carries over from one day to the next. The players remember where they left off the day before and can start right in again.

There is much more talk during pretend play, as well, because 5-year-olds have a better command of the language. With their improved language usage, they clarify ideas and talk out problems. Concerns about sickness, accidents, and death are dealt with more realistically in the imaginative play of 5-year-olds. Although the youngsters like to use props, those with a high level of fantasy can pretend without props.

Boys and girls begin playing more in groups of the same gender by this time. The structure changes the nature of the play somewhat, with girls' play becoming more calm and boys' play becoming more active. Girls still prefer to play house, but boys more often play superhero or monster. Groups are often larger than before, as friendships expand and children learn how to get along with more than one or two peers.

Five-year-olds like to build big buildings and then play inside the structures. Imaginative play is at its height just before and during this period. After children enter first grade and games-with-rules become the norm, make-believe play begins to wane. It is not at all prevalent among children much after age 7.

By about 7 years of age, a cognitive change that allows more abstract thinking has taken place within the child. What happens to pretending? We speculate that it does not disappear at all but becomes a part of the inner self to be tapped by adults in their daydreaming as well as in their generation of creative ideas. Those adults who experienced a rich fantasy life as children may be the fortunate possessors of the skill to play around with ideas in their heads, just as they did with props and toys as children in the nursery school.

Table 14.1 shows the sequence of children's pretend play development from 1 year through 6 years of age.

As you observe the children in your classroom on the last of the checklist items, you may want to make a list of the themes the children are using in their play. What can you do to help them add more themes to this list? Put out more props? Read more stories? Help the children make more costumes? Take children on more field trips so that the youngsters will have additional real experiences to draw from? All of these activities are good ideas. Try them, and see how your children respond.

If You Have Not Checked This Item: Some Helpful Ideas

■ Read a Book

Children love to hear about *Owliver* by Robert Kraus (New York: Windmill & Dutton, 1974), the little owl who likes to pretend. Owliver first pretends he is an orphan, but when his mother and father object, he pretends to be an actor. This time his father objects and gives him doctor and lawyer toys to encourage more serious interests. His mother, however, gives him acting lessons, including tap dancing. He fools them both, of course, by growing up to become. . .a fireman!

The Trek by Ann Jonas (New York: Mulberry Books, 1985) is the story of a little girl who is big enough to walk to school on her own. As she walks along, she pretends that jungle beasts are everywhere. The illustrations show them hidden in crocodile sidewalks, giraffe trees, zebra hedges, and camel walls.

Amazing Grace by Mary Hoffman, illustrated by Caroline Binch (New York: Dial Books, 1991) is a large-format book with full-page pictures of Grace pretending to be Joan of Arc, Anansi the Spider, a pirate, and Hiawatha from the stories Nana reads to her. But when Grace wants to be Peter Pan in a school play, her peers say she can't because she is a girl and she is black. Nana helps her find a way to be anything she wants to be, including an amazing Peter Pan.

OBSERVING, RECORDING, AND INTERPRETING IMAGINATION

Information from the running record on 3-year-old Sherry found on page 342 has been transferred to the Imagination Checklist in Figure 14.1. This information shows Sherry as a mature player in this imaginative role. Her only blank occurs with "Uses exciting, danger-packed themes," which is more typically observed in a 4-year-old, especially a boy.

Because imaginative play is an area of strength and confidence for Sherry, her teacher should consider using a dramatic play activity to help Sherry in a *Checklist* area that needs strengthening. For example, Sherry has shown little development in the area of written language. Perhaps she could make a sign for the grocery store or pretend to write out a grocery list of things to buy in mock writing. All of a child's development is interrelated. We should thus be sure to use strengths from other areas of a child's development when we design an individual plan to strengthen that child's particular needs.

TABLE 14.1

Development of imagination

Age	Child's Pretend Play Behavior
1–2	Goes through pretend routines of eating or other brief actions, in some cases
2–3	Replays fragments of everyday experience (e.g., putting baby to bed) Repeats routine over and over in ritualistic manner Uses realistic props (if uses props at all)
3–4	Insists often on particular props in order to play May have imaginary playmate at home Uses family, doll play, hospital, cars, trains, planes, and firefighting themes Assigns roles or takes assigned roles May switch roles without warning
4–5	Uses exciting, danger-packed themes (e.g., superheroes, shooting, and running) Is more flexible about taking assigned roles during play Uses more rigid gender roles (e.g., girls as mother, waitress, or teacher; boys as father, doctor, or policeman)
5–6	Plays more with doll house, block structure Includes many more details, much dialogue Carries play over from one day to next sometimes Plays more in groups of same gender

FIGURE 14.1

Imagination observations for Sherry

Child Skills Checklist

Name _Sherry_

Observer _Carolyn_

Program _Arnot Nursery_

Dates _2/17_

Directions:

Put a ✔ for items you see the child perform regularly. Put *N* for items where there is no opportunity to observe. Leave all other items blank.

Item	Evidence	Date
12. Imagination		
_N_ Pretends by replaying familiar routines	She is beyond this level of play	2/17
_✔_ Needs particular props to do pretend play	Uses props such as real boxes & bags in grocery play	2/17
_✔_ Assigns roles or takes assigned roles	Took role as daughter but later tried to assign this role to Ann	2/17
_✔_ May switch roles without warning	Changed role from daughter to mother without warning	2/17
_✔_ Uses language for creating and sustaining plot	Talked constantly during grocery plot	2/17
_____ Uses exciting, danger-packed themes	No	2/17
_✔_ Takes on characteristics and actions related to role	Got groceries off shelf, put them in bag, went to cashier, took them home	2/17
_✔_ Uses elaborate and creative themes, ideas, details	Carried out detailed actions in grocery store plot	2/17

REFERENCES

Caplan, Theresa, & Frank Caplan. (1983). *The early childhood years: The 2 to 6 year old.* New York: Putnam.

Damon, William. (1983). *Social and personality development.* New York: Norton.

Hughes, Fergus P. (1991). *Children, play, and development.* Boston: Allyn & Bacon.

Johnston, John M. (1987). Harnessing the power of superheroes: An alternative view. *Day Care and Early Education, 15*(1), 15–17.

Pena, Sally, Judy French, & Robina Holmes. (1987). A look at superheroes: Some issues and guidelines. *Day Care and Early Education, 15*(1), 10–14.

Segal, Marilyn, & Don Adcock. (1981). *Just pretending: Ways to help children grow through imaginative play.* Englewood Cliffs, NJ: Prentice-Hall.

Singer, Dorothy G., & Jerome L. Singer. (1977). *Partners in play: A step-by-step guide to imaginative play in children.* New York: Harper & Row.

Singer, Jerome L. (1973). *The child's world of make-believe: Experimental studies of imaginative play.* New York: Academic Press.

Smilansky, Sara. (1968). *The effects of sociodramatic play on disadvantaged preschool children.* New York: Wiley.

OTHER SOURCES

Beaty, Janice J. (1992). *Skills for preschool teachers.* New York: Merrill/Macmillan.

Bergen, Doris (Ed.). (1988). *Play as a medium for learning and development.* Portsmouth, NH: Heinemann.

Nourot, Patricia Monighan, & Judith L. Van Hoorn. (1991). Symbolic play in preschool and primary settings. *Young Children, 46*(6), 40–50.

Paley, Vivian Gussin. (1984). *Boys and girls: Superheroes in the doll corner.* Chicago: University of Chicago Press.

LEARNING ACTIVITIES

1. Use the section "Imagination" of the Child Skills Checklist as a screening tool to observe all of the children in your classroom. Compare the children who have checks at the higher levels in the sequence of imagination development with their checks in social play and language development. Can you draw any conclusions from this comparison?

2. Choose a child who has displayed high-level skills in imagination and make a running record of him or her on three different days. What new details did you learn about the child's pretending?

3. Look over the activities suggested, and choose one for use with one of the children whom you have screened as needing help in this area. Carry out the activity you have prescribed for the child. Record the results.

CHAPTER 14

4. Take a field trip with your children to a site of interest where they can see and meet people at work in a special field. Put out appropriate props in your dramatic play area after you return, and record what kinds of pretend play take place. Is the play any different from what went on previously? If so, how do you account for this?

5. Carry out one of the book activities from this chapter with one child or a small group, and see if it stimulates any pretending. How could you extend this pretending?

15 Observing the Whole Child

As you have studied the twelve separate areas of child development included in this observational program, you may have noted that each of the aspects followed a similar pattern in the growth of the child: from the general to the specific. Children learn large muscle control before small motor control. Children recognize overall patterns of cognitive discrimination before the details become clear, speak single words to include whole categories of things before they learn the names for each, draw a circle to represent a person before they learn to add the details, and pretend in stereotyped roles about mothers and fathers before they add the personal touches identifying specific family members.

This book has proceeded in the opposite direction: specific categories of development were detailed first. We have looked in some depth at self-identity, emotional development, social play, prosocial behavior, large motor development, small motor development, cognitive development (classification and seriation as well as number, time, space, and memory), spoken language, prewriting and prereading skills, art skills, and imagination.

Now it is time to look at the whole picture. The child is, of course, a whole being whose development in these areas is proceeding simultaneously. Once you understand the details of this growth, it is possible to make an overall assessment of the developmental skills that each of your children possesses by using the *Child Skills Checklist* as a whole. From such an assessment it is then possible to draw a total picture of the child in order to make individual plans that will promote continued development.

TEACHER OR STUDENT TEACHER AS OBSERVER

In order to draw a total picture of the child, you must step out of your role as caregiver and into the role of objective observer. Do this role changing in your classroom as unobtrusively as possible. Have another staff member take over your duties for a particular period while you observe a single child, making a running record of the child's behaviors, but using the *Checklist* as your guide. Many teachers find that using a clipboard or notebook for backing, with a pencil or pen attached on a string, is a convenient way to record while you sit or stand. Keep away from the activities but as close as possible to the child whom you are observing. Try not to become involved with the children.

If the children ask what you are doing, you can reply that you are busy writing this morning. If they want you to join their activity, you can politely refuse, saying that you have things to write and that you will join them later. If a child wants to use your pencil, you can show him that it is attached to the clipboard and suggest that he use a pencil in the writing area. Children will soon try to imitate you, as you're sure to note. You had better attach a pencil to a notebook in the writing area as well, because children will want theirs to be just like yours.

How long should you spend observing? It is a good idea to observe and record for at least half an hour at a time. If you are doing a running record, this length of time will keep you busy jotting down everything the child does and says, plus his or her interactions with others. If you are recording directly onto the *Checklist*, you should be familiar with the various items by now and not need to spend too much time flipping the pages back and forth to locate an item. You may find, as many observers do, that it is difficult to step back from a busy classroom and keep your concentration on a single child for much longer than half an hour at a time. Yet it is important for you to see as much of the child's involvement in all aspects of the program as possible. The solution is to make a number of observations at different times during the day on different days.

Making a reliable overall assessment of a single child is not possible based on only one observation. You should have as much information as you can gather from as many different days, different activities, and different points of view as possible. The best overall records are a compilation made by all of the classroom staff. Have each person put a date by the items she or he has observed. She may want to indicate her check marks and evidence with a symbol, her initials, or color coding, if you are using the same *Checklist* for all your observations.

Try to avoid making eye contact with the child you are observing. If he or she looks your way, you can look around at the other children. Children are much more observant than we often give them credit for. In spite of your best efforts, the child you are observing will often realize that you are watching him or her, if you keep at it long enough. Most children soon forget about the scrutiny they are undergoing and continue their participation in their activity. If you find, however, that your child seems uncomfortable by your presence and even may try to get away, then you should break off your observation. Try again another day, or let another staff member or another student teacher observe that particular child.

How should you begin? You may want to learn something about a particular child in a certain area of development to start. Perhaps he has difficulty getting involved with the others in the pretend play during free choice period. Plan to begin your observation during this period. You will want to look at the items under "3. Social Play." Other *Checklist* areas that can often be seen at the same time as social play include items under the following sections: "1. Self-Identity," "2. Emotional Development," "4. Prosocial Behavior," "9. Spoken Language," and "12. Imagination." Then either check off the items as you see them, writing in the evidence, or do a running record of everything the child does, and convert it to the *Checklist* afterward.

Circle the *Checklist* area you are observing and then place a check mark for each item you saw the child performing or an *N* for the items you had no opportunity to observe. Leave the item blank if neither of these conditions applies. A blank means that the child had the opportunity to perform the item, but did not do it.

Be sure to make notes after each item, jotting down the evidence that prompted you to check the item (or leave it blank). If you leave the item blank, it is still important to write down your reason—the evidence for leaving the item blank. If you use the same *Checklist* on more than one day in a cumulative manner, be sure to put the date after each item as well.

Making a reliable overall assessment of a single child is not possible based on only one observation.

The time of your next observation may be determined by the areas you have not had the opportunity to observe. For "Self-Identity," for instance, you will want to observe the child when she arrives in the morning, especially at the beginning of the year. "Emotional Development" needs to be observed during lunch or snacktime, toileting, and naptime.

As previously pointed out in Chapter 2, the *Checklist* is not a test. It is a *survey* of an individual child's developmental accomplishments. You should not ask children questions about whether they recognize certain colors, for instance. The youngsters' performance on the items should become evident as you observe the children in their natural play activities. Set up activities that will engage the children in the areas you are interested in observing. Be sure these activities are spontaneous and not forced. If a child does not get involved in "Art Skills" although art activities are available every day, you should leave the items blank. Do not use *N*, no opportunity to observe, when in fact the child has the opportunity to participate in art activities, but chooses not to. You will want to make a note, however, after the items: "Easel painting and table activities of cutting and pasting are available, but Robbie does not get involved in art."

USE OF THE *CHILD SKILLS CHECKLIST*

Sample *Checklist*

The following *Checklist* is an example of its use for 4-year-old Robbie, whom the teacher was concerned about because he seldom joined the others in their play. She observed Robbie on three different days. Note how even short evidence statements add significant information.

Interpretation of *Checklist* Results

When the teacher, Carol J., had finished observing Robbie on three different days for about half an hour each time, she had a much better idea of Robbie's strengths as well as areas needing strengthening. Her observation confirmed for her that Robbie did not usually play with other children, but seemed to prefer to do things on his own. He seemed to be quite independent, making choices on his own, defending his rights, being enthusiastic about the things he chose to do, and smiling much of the time. She chuckled about his characteristic tuneless humming as he busily engaged himself in block building or racing little cars. She always could tell where Robbie was by his humming.

Being happy and smiling were especially important clues to Carol about the overall status of any child in her class. Robbie demonstrated few negative behaviors, in fact, except for his quick temper when other children tried to interfere with his activities. Carol had tried to get him to express his feelings in words, but without success. Now she noted that he really did not speak all that much. Somehow she had missed that important aspect of his behavior because he seemed content, and possibly because he did vocalize—if only to hum.

Now she noted that although she could understand him if she listened closely, his speaking skills were not at the level of the other 4-year-olds. She began to wonder if this might be the reason he did not get involved in playing with the others. Because dialogue and conversation are so much a part of make-believe play, a child without the verbal skills might feel out of place, she reasoned.

She had a strong hunch that Robbie was highly creative. Watching him build elaborate roads for his race car and talk to himself as he played alone or parallel to the others, he seemed to invent all kinds of situations for the miniature people he played with. She noted that creativity certainly did not show up in his arts skills, but she reasoned that his difficulty with small motor skills may have caused him to avoid painting, drawing, and cutting.

In looking for areas of strength, Carol picked out his enthusiasm and good self-concept, his large motor skills, his cognitive skills, and his imaginative play. His special interests seemed to be block building, water play, and all kinds of outdoor play. She felt he was a bright boy who used his cognitive ability in playing by himself, rather than joining others. Areas needing strengthening included language, small motor skills, using writing, drawing, and painting tools, control of his temper, and especially playing with the other children.

Child Skills Checklist

Name _Robbie_   **Observer** _Carol J._

Program _Riverside Head Start_   **Dates** _10/5, 10/7, 10/8_

Directions:
Put a ✔ for items you see the child perform regularly. Put *N* for items where there is no opportunity to observe. Leave all other items blank.

Item	Evidence	Date
1. Self-Identity		
_____ Separates from parents without difficulty	Upset when mother leaves	10/5
___✓___ Does not cling to classroom staff excessively	Plays by himself	10/5
___✓___ Makes eye contact with adults	Looks teacher in the eye when she talks to him	10/5
___✓___ Makes activity choices without teacher's help	Goes directly to activity area of his choice	10/5
_____ Seeks other children to play with	Plays by himself	10/5
_____ Plays roles confidently in dramatic play	Does not do this play	10/5
___✓___ Stands up for own rights	Will not let others take his toys. Pushes. Grabs. Hits	10/7
___✓___ Displays enthusiasm about doing things for self	Hums a tune while he plays	10/5
2. Emotional Development ___✓___ Allows self to be comforted during stressful time	Lets teacher hold him	10/5
___✓___ Eats, sleeps, toilets without fuss away from home	Yes	10/5 10/7 10/8

Item	Evidence	Date
N Handles sudden changes/ startling situations with control		10/5 10/7 10/8
____ Can express anger in words rather than actions	Sometimes hits or pushes when angry. No words	10/5
✓ Allows aggressive behavior to be redirected	Follows teacher's suggestions	10/5
____ Does not withdraw from others excessively	Does not play much with others	10/5 10/7 10/8
✓ Shows interest/attention in classroom activities	Likes blocks, cars, water play especially	10/5 1/8
✓ Smiles, seems happy much of the time	Always smiles & hums	10/5 10/8
3. Social Play N Is unoccupied during free play (or follows teacher)	Is beyond this level	10/5
N Spends time watching others play	Is beyond this level	10/5
✓ Plays by self with own toys/ materials	Pretends with small cars, people	10/8
✓ Plays parallel to others with similar toys/materials	Pretends with car next to other boys with cars	10/8
____ Initiates activity/play with others	No	10/8
____ Gains access to ongoing play in positive manner	Does not try to gain access	10/8
____ Maintains role in ongoing play in positive manner	Does not play much with others	10/8
____ Resolves play conflicts in positive manner	Sometimes hits or pushes	10/5

Item	Evidence	Date
4. Prosocial Behavior		
✓ Shows concern for someone in distress	Comes over to child who is crying	10/5
N Shows delight for someone experiencing pleasure		10/5 10/7 10/8
_____ Shares something with another	Does not seem to know how to share toys. Hits. Pushes	10/5
_____ Gives something of his/her own to another	Did not do this	10/5
_____ Takes turns without a fuss	Has trouble with favorite toys	10/5 10/8
✓ Complies with requests without a fuss	Does what teacher asks	10/5
✓ Helps another to do a task	Helps. Not with building	10/7
N Helps (cares for) another in need		10/5 10/7 10/8
5. Large Motor Development		
✓ Walks down steps alternating feet	Yes	10/5
✓ Runs with control over speed and direction	Does a lot of running	10/5
✓ Jumps over obstacle, landing on two feet	Jumps on playground	10/5
N Hops forward on one foot		10/5
✓ Climbs up and down climbing equipment with ease	Outside. Good control	10/5
N Moves legs/feet in rhythm to beat		10/5

Item	Evidence	Date
_N_ Claps hands in rhythm to beat		10/5
_N_ Beats drum alternating hands in rhythm to beat		10/5
6. Small Motor Development		
_✓_ Shows hand preference (which is _right_)	Eats, picks up things with right	10/5
_✓_ Turns with hand easily (knobs, lids, eggbeaters)	Uses eggbeater in water play easily	10/7
_✓_ Pours liquid into glass without spilling	Fills plastic glasses & bottles at water table	10/7
_____ Unfastens/fastens zippers, buttons, Velcro tabs	Needs help taking off & putting on jacket	10/5
_✓_ Picks up and inserts objects with ease	Puzzles	10/5
_____ Uses drawing/writing tools with control	Does not use these tools	10/5
_____ Uses scissors with control	Does not use scissors	10/5
_N_ Pounds in nails with control	Not available	10/5
7. Cognitive Development: Classification and Seriation		
_N_ Recognizes basic geometric shapes		10/5
_✓_ Recognizes colors	Tells colors of clothes	10/8
_✓_ Recognizes differences in size	Tells sizes of cars	10/5

Item	Evidence	Date
✓ Sorts objects by appearance	Plays table games	10/8
N Recognizes differences in musical tones		10/5
N Reproduces musical tones with voice		10/5
N Arranges events in sequence from first to last		10/5
N Arranges objects in series according to a rule		10/5
8. Cognitive Development: Number, Time, Space, Memory _____ Counts to 20 by rote	Can count to 10	10/8
_____ Counts objects to 20	Counts objects but not to 20	10/8
✓ Knows the daily schedule in sequence	In circle time	10/8
✓ Knows what happened yesterday	circle time	10/8
✓ Can build a block enclosure	Uses blocks with ease	10/8
✓ Can locate an object behind or beside something	With blocks	10/8
N Recalls words to song, chant		
N Can recollect and act on directions of a singing game		

Item	Evidence	Date
9. Spoken Language		
_____ Speaks confidently in the classroom	Speaks very softly	10/5
✓ Speaks clearly enough for adults to understand		10/5
✓ Speaks in expanded sentences	Sometimes	10/5
_____ Takes part in conversations with other children	Not usually	10/5
_____ Asks questions with proper word order	Asks: "When Mama will come?"	10/5
_N__ Makes "No" responses with proper word order		10/5
_____ Uses past tense verbs correctly	Says: "He breaked my road."	10/5
_N__ Plays with rhyming words		
10. Prewriting and Prereading Skills		
_____ Pretends to write by scribbling horizontally	Does not use writing tools	10/5
_____ Includes features of real letters in scribbling	same	10/5
_____ Writes real alphabet letters	same	10/5
_____ Writes words with invented spelling	same	10/5
✓ Retells stories from books with increasing accuracy	Likes hearing stories. Can retell some	10/8

Item	Evidence	Date
_____ Shows awareness that print in books tells story		10/8
_____ Attempts to match telling of story with print in book		10/8
_____ Wants to know what particular print says		10/8
11. Art Skills ✓ Makes random marks or covers paper with color	*Not often. Likes fingerpainting*	10/7
_____ Scribbles on paper	*Does not often use art tools*	10/7
_____ Forms basic shapes	*same*	10/7
_____ Makes mandalas	*same*	10/7
_____ Makes suns	*same*	10/7
_____ Draws human as a circle with arms and legs attached	*same*	10/7
_____ Draws animals, trees, flowers	*same*	10/7
_____ Makes pictorial drawings	*same*	10/7
12. Imagination N Pretends by replaying familiar routines	*He's beyond this level.*	10/5
✓ Needs particular props to do pretend play	*Cars, people*	10/8

Item	Evidence	Date
_____ Assigns roles or takes assigned roles	Doesn't play with others much	10/8
_____ May switch roles without warning	same	10/8
✓ Uses language for creating and sustaining plot	Talks to himself in pretending	10/8
✓ Uses exciting, danger-packed themes	With cars & people	10/8
✓ Takes on characteristics and actions related to role	Motorcycle driver	10/8
✓ Uses elaborate and creative themes, ideas, details	In solitary play	10/8

Sharing *Checklist* Results

In order to confirm her interpretation of the *Child Skills Checklist* observation, Carol shared the results with the two other classroom workers. They were also surprised about how little Robbie verbalized and that they, too, hadn't picked up this fact previously. What had they missed about the other children, they wondered? One of them decided to observe Robbie on her own, using the *Checklist* to see how her results compared with Carol's. The teacher assistants were fascinated by the details Carol had gleaned in a very short time and by the way she had interpreted Robbie's inability to join in group play.

Carol decided to set up a meeting with Robbie's mother to share her findings and talk about how Robbie behaved at home. As always, she featured the positive aspects of Robbie's development and behavior, hoping to use them in helping Robbie improve in the areas where he needed strengthening. Robbie's mother was very interested in Carol's observation. She told Carol that Robbie was the youngest of three brothers, and did not seem to have the language skills at age 4 that his older brothers had shown. She also noted that Robbie preferred to play alone, but she had never considered that his speaking skills might be the cause.

She told how all three boys invented their own games because they had few toys at home. As a single working parent she had all she could do to provide for their food and clothing needs. When Carol suggested that Robbie might like to continue water play at home in the sink with empty containers, his mother thought this was a fine idea and also a way that he might help her with the dishes! She was especially pleased that Carol felt Robbie was bright on the basis of his water play games and block building in the center. She asked Carol for other ideas for making up games with household throwaway items. Carol offered to lend her a booklet full of ideas. When Carol also mentioned that the center liked to send home picture books for parents to read to their children, Robbie's mother said she thought Robbie would like this a lot. She wanted to come back in a few weeks and see how Robbie was doing, to which Carol agreed with pleasure.

Planning for Individuals Based on *Checklist* Results

Once the observation has been completed, the classroom staff can make plans for the individual child by using his areas of strength to help build on his areas needing strengthening. These can be listed on a learning prescription along with particular activities to help the child. Activities to help children improve in each *Checklist* item are described at the end of discussion about the item. The learning prescription that Carol formulated to help Robbie is shown in Figure 15.1. (See Chapter 2 for a reproducible copy of this form.)

After Carol and her staff had agreed upon Robbie's most important strengths and areas needing strengthening, they then discussed what activities they could set up to involve Robbie in helping himself improve in the three areas listed. They decided to ask him to help a new boy, Russ, to learn to use the outside climber because Robbie was so good at it. Talking and helping one other child should not be so difficult for Robbie in the beginning as playing with a larger group.

They looked at the activities listed in Chapter 11, "Spoken Language," and decided to use puppets as a possible way for Robbie to get more involved in speaking with others. Carol would read the book *Louie* to Robbie and a small group of children and then give each of them a puppet that the staff had prepared from paper bags. The staff decided to name Robbie's puppet Ron the Race Car Driver. Carol then would use her own puppet to engage the children in talking through their puppets. Once they got the idea, she would extract herself from the pretending and let them play on their own.

She decided to do this during the activity period every day with small groups of children, always trying to include Robbie. She hoped Robbie and the others would like the activity enough to make other puppets on their own. This would also involve Robbie with small motor and art skills. She also decided to work on Robbie's problem of learning to control his temper through the puppet play—by having her own puppet get angry and hit her, and asking the others to help her puppet express anger differently.

In case Robbie did not get involved in making his own puppet, she thought the medicine dropper activity with colored water in a muffin tin should interest him because of his fascination with water play. The staff decided to try these activities for a week and then discuss the results at their planning session the following week. They also decided to do a similar observation for each of the children as time permitted and to make a similar learning prescription.

FIGURE 15.1

Learning prescription for Robbie

Learning Prescription

Name _Robbie_   **Age** _4_   **Date** _10/12_

Areas of Strength and Confidence

1. _Good self-concept, happy, helpful_
2. _Creative in block building, water play_
3. _Good large motor skills on outside equipment_

Areas Needing Strengthening

1. _Learn to play with others_
2. _Develop better speaking skills_
3. _Improve small motor coordination_

Activities to Help

1. _Ask Robbie to help new boy learn to use climber_

2. _Read Louie and give him puppet to play with_

3. _Do medicine dropper, water & food colors in muffin tins_

Use of the *Checklist* by Preservice Teachers and Student Teachers

Preservice and student teachers can use the *Child Skills Checklist* in a similar manner, making a series of observations of a single child until all of the items have been noted. In order to interpret the checked items or blanks, the observer then should read the particular chapters that discuss these areas.

It is especially helpful for the preservice teacher to make a written report or case study that includes an interpretation of the child's development in each of the 12 principal *Checklist* areas. Such a report should include not only specific information from the observations, but also whatever inferences and conclusions can be drawn from the observational data collected, based on the observer's knowledge of child development.

In Robbie's case, the observer will want to read Chapter 3, "Self-Identity," for example, to find out what it could mean when the child has difficulty separating from the mother, and why the child seems happy but still does not play with other children. Without a great deal of information, an outside observer often is not able to interpret child observations with the confidence of the classroom staff. However, certain inferences and conclusions can be offered based on the data collected, and the outside observer even may make an important contribution to the understanding of a particular child because of a fresh perspective.

In addition to the written interpretation of each of the 12 *Checklist* areas, the observer needs to summarize the overall development of the child in some detail. A learning prescription similar to Carol's learning prescription for Robbie should be done, followed by an explanation for the activities prescribed.

Case studies such as this can be helpful not only to the preservice or student teacher, but also to the supervising classroom teacher and the parent(s) of the child observed. Supervising teachers need to set up case conferences with individual parents (to which student observers are invited) to discuss each student's report.

OBSERVATION OF EACH CHILD

It is important to observe each of your children in this kind of detail during the year. Teachers report that they were able to learn more about each child by stepping back and making a focused observation like this, than simply by having the child in their program for an entire year. It is an eye-opening experience to look at one child in-depth from an observer's point of view, rather than from the perspective of a busy teacher involved with the activities of many other lively youngsters.

College students studying child development report that this type of in-depth look at a real child makes textbooks and courses come alive as well. Parents, too, benefit from the information gained by objective observations. Not only do the parents learn new activities to use with their children at home, but they also often become involved in the fascinating drama of how their own children develop, why their children act the way they do, and how they, as parents, best can help their children to realize their full potentials.

Observing the development of young children is thus a teaching as well as a learning technique that should benefit all of its participants—teachers, students, children, and parents—because it outlines each aspect of child development carefully, objectively, and positively. Promoting development in young children works best when it is focused on an assessment of their strengths. When you know the strengths of each child in every aspect of development, you will be able to design your program to meet an individual's needs as the children in your classroom work and play together creating their own unique selves.

Index of Children's Books

Index

ISBN 0-02-307741-7

90000>

9 780023 077418